THE FABER BOOK OF OPERA

Tom Sutcliffe's musical career started as a boy chorister at Chichester Cathedral. After studying at Oxford University, he was a professional countertenor for six years, making his opera début in *The Coronation of Poppea* at Darmstadt in 1970, having worked as a soloist with Nikolaus Harnoncourt. He then edited the magazine *Music and Musicians* and worked for the *Guardian* for 23 years – most notably as opera critic.

A regular broadcaster on radio and television, he has also written about opera in *Vogue* magazine and was British correspondent of *Opera News*, New York, as well as contributing to *Opera Now* and other specialist music journals. In 1998 he was dramaturg on a new production of *The Turn of the Screw* at the Monnaie in Brussels. He was opera critic of the *London Evening Standard* from 1996–2002. Tom Sutcliffe is the author of *Believing in Opera*, also published by Faber.

James Gillray's caricature 'A bravura air', showing Mrs Billington as Mandane in Thomas *Arne's Artaxerxes* (published 22 Dec 1801)

THE FABER BOOK OF

OPERA

Edited by
Tom Sutcliffe

faber and faber

by the same author
BELIEVING IN OPERA

First published in 2000
This paperback edition first published in 2002
by Faber and Faber Limited
3 Queen Square London WC1N 3AU
Published in the United States by Faber and Faber Inc.
an affiliate of Farrar, Straus and Giroux LLC, New York

Photoset by Wilmaset Ltd
Printed in England by Clays Ltd, St Ives plc

Frontispiece illustration from the collection of Anthony Gasson

A CIP record for this book
is available from the British Library

ISBN 0-571-20684-0

2 4 6 8 10 9 7 5 3 1

TO THE HARD-PRESSED OPERA COMPANIES
OF THE ENGLISH-SPEAKING WORLD
WITHOUT WHOSE GENIUS AND POWER TO THRILL
THE FUTURE WOULD BE BLEAK

Contents

CONTENTS

Putting flesh on ambitious dreams – opera in action

Preface

Opera is the most ephemeral thing in the world to be taken so very seriously. For those who care about it, every single aspect of a performance is vitally significant – and it is in the nature of opera to engage words and music, scene design and clothes, colours, rhythms and movement, including dance, with a sense of people communicating in the most committed vivacious way, to be as complex in elements, yet as simple in essence and effect, as any other conceivable human activity.

That is the challenge and pretension of this most fascinating and rewarding of phenomena. In all its enormous variety of input, opera, while seeming artificial, is actually giving a fuller, more realistic account of the forces of life than any other human art-form. But it is precisely because it so obviously involves conventions, so blatantly demands a leap of faith to function at all as what it claims to be, that opera can simultaneously be a forum for debate and a celebration of that debate's conclusions. What Brecht called '*Verfremdungseffekt*' (usually misleadingly translated into English as 'alienation') is an innate principle of opera. In accordance with this theory, subjective identification with the emotive circumstances of a story obscures the message which the story should convey. How different from so-called 'soap opera', the main supply of popular drama in people's lives, purportedly realistic and unstructured, yet reducing catharsis to an unstoppable series of manipulative, sentimental fixes.

Brecht and Felsenstein, would-be twentieth-century reformers of opera, used the phrase 'realistic music theatre' to define what they wanted opera to be. And their agenda descended directly from Handel, Gluck, Mozart and Wagner – though Handel and Mozart, rather than theorizing, simply practised their own unrepeatable permanent revolutions. Today, the challenge of opera for composers, librettists and interpreters remains extraordinarily unchanged. Indeed, today's new opera composers often seem to be reinventing the wheel, no doubt because they are denied the continuity of lyrical language and repetitive formula on which reliable convention depends. It is crystal clear from these pages what the greatest and most romantic minds expected and demanded of the art-form.

Opera can mobilize a wider variety of elements to move its audience than any other dramatic art-form. But it is not the naturalism or realism of what opera shows which releases that power and brings it to bear. Rather the reverse. One of the mysteries of the theatre (and opera houses are theatres) is just how lifelike what is presented on the stage should be. There is something intrinsically direct and unapologetic about operatic singing with which the subtlety and even delicacy of various operatic characters' inner feelings are very profitably in conflict. Tension between what seems and what is, in opera, is of the essence. Most of what an audience experiences in theatre and opera is taken to be naturalistic. The purpose of the proscenium stage, a room with one wall removed, is to enhance the sense of naturalism. But now that cinema and television can present real life through a candid camera, it has become clear that documentary only acquires significant meaning by being interpretatively edited.

The human mind is a compost heap of memory, fantasy, imagination and conviction, with which the discipline of theatrical realism would be presumed to be at odds. Realism is a slippery word, especially in theatre, where by definition anything goes. Theatre instantly connects with that boundless space in our heads where dreams come true, where profitable debate proceeds over the soul of mankind. Add music to the equation and the game with reality becomes even more poetic, more capable of channelling the power of tragedy, the sentiment of comedy, the softened cruelty of farce. Music, always ambivalent about what it is actually 'saying', invites listeners through its siren allure to identify with the argument.

For those who hate or cannot support opera, the problem is very often the supposed lack of realism. People don't sing what needs to be urgently told, they say. Music may mobilize sentiment very nicely. That, in most people's minds, is what it's for: relaxation and ease, the blissful paralysis of taking a breath when there's time to listen and not rush on. But the fascination of opera is precisely its ability to handle the secret life of everyday, the needs, wishes and ambitions of lovers, the unvoiced doubts of heroes, the distinction between the official account and the interior truth of feeling or intention, while at the same time working music's magic to manhandle the timescale.

Opera is profoundly moving. It knows how to open the tear-duct floodgates. Yet it mostly is too proud and dignified to lower itself to mere momentary catharsis. When we feel in opera, we know why, and we start to formulate our positive response: opera is profound propaganda, and not just in the obvious cases of *Fidelio* and those Verdi masterpieces associated with dangerous Italian nationalism. In such a gradually developing but increasingly inescapable determination about what a piece of theatre with so many elements really means, the objective role of a chorus is crucial, not because of what choruses sing in opera (communal underlining or celebration, rather more often than the critical exegesis they perform in Greek tragedy), but because the act of uttering with one massed voice is itself a reminder of the artificiality of the total presentation.

When Schiller, most operatic of playwrights, decided that Greek theatre offered in the Chorus something that modern theatre needed, which to an extent opera already had, it was precisely because a Chorus could underscore the intended meaning of the play and destroy the illusion of naturalism. The Chorus offered a heightening of poetic diction in the dialogue of individual characters and in the drama generally. Thanks to a Chorus, audiences could know for sure they were being offered illustration rather than 'objective reality'. A Chorus could hold a frame around the central narrative. Brechtian theatre self-consciously continues a theatrical principle enunciated by Schiller in his essay *Über den Gebrauch des Chors in der Tragödie* ('On the Use of the Chorus in Tragedy', quoted here in an unattributed translation from 1847):

The introduction of the Chorus ... if it only served ... to declare open and honourable warfare against naturalism in art ... would be for us a living wall which Tragedy had drawn around herself, to guard her from contact with the world of reality, and maintain her own ideal soil, her poetical freedom ...

This is what the Chorus effects in tragedy. It is, in itself, not an individual but a general conception, yet it is represented by a palpable body which appeals to the senses with an imposing grandeur. It forsakes the contracted sphere of the incidents to dilate itself over the past and the future, over distant times and nations, and general humanity, to deduce the grand results of life, and pronounce the lessons of wisdom. But all this it does with the full power of fancy – with a bold lyrical freedom which ascends, as with godlike step, to the topmost height of worldly things; and it effects it in conjunction with the whole sensible influence of melody and rhythm, in tones and movements.

The Chorus thus exercises a purifying influence on tragic poetry, insomuch as it keeps reflection apart from the incidents, and by this separation arms it with a poetical vigour; as the painter, by means of a rich drapery, changes the ordinary poverty of costume into a charm and an ornament.

But as the painter finds himself obliged to strengthen the tone of colour of the living subject, in order to counterbalance the material influences – so the lyrical effusions of the Chorus impose upon the poet the necessity of a proportionate elevation of his general diction. It is the Chorus alone which entitles the poet to employ this fullness of tone, which at once charms the senses, pervades the spirit and expands the mind. This one giant form on his canvas obliges him to mount all his figures on the cothurnus, and thus impart a tragical grandeur to his picture.

Schiller wanted audiences to identify fully with the picture he painted, but also to apply intelligent moral discernment to the emotional identification his performers would inevitably seek to achieve. The perspective he required is ideally supplied when, walled in by the convention of operatic music, there is no possibility that the naturalism can be misinterpreted as merely 'realistic'. The way music in opera brings the meaning of a drama into sharper focus fulfils what Schiller called 'feeding on dreams'.

To the art of the ideal alone is lent, or rather, absolutely given, the privilege to grasp the spirit of the All, and bind it in a corporeal form. Yet, in truth, even Art cannot present it to the senses, but by means of her creative power to the imaginative faculty alone; and it is thus that she becomes more true than all reality, and more real than all experience. It follows from these premises that the artist can use no single element taken from reality as he finds it – that his work must be ideal in all its parts, if it be designed to have, as it were, an intrinsic reality, and to harmonize with nature.

People are more passionate about opera than about any other live performing art. The subject matter may be light or heavy, profoundly portentous or just plain delightfully silly. But it can operate almost as a liturgy of a profound faith in life. Opera remains, as Nietzsche saw, a neo-classical revival, harking back to the lost formula, the theological alchemy of ancient Greek drama. Those religious festivals for which Euripides, Aeschylus and Sophocles made their plays were not just entertainment like Covent Garden, the Met, Broadway or the West End today. Of course church-going too, even today, can be entertaining as well a 'duty and a service' for the faithful. Clearly, for the ancient Greeks, the stage presented a renewed incarnation of myths at the very heart of the classical imagination – myths that revealed the life of gods in the human world. On the Greek stage, in a form which we would now call opera, and equipped with chorus commentary just like J. S. Bach's great Passions, the truths that were fundamental to one of the profoundest of all human cultures were incarnated and came alive theatrically.

It is no accident that opera as we know it in the Christian world appears to be one of the fruits of the Renaissance and Reformation. The rituals of Christianity can be very operatic – indeed the grand Requiem by that great humanist Giuseppe Verdi is regarded by many as one of his greatest operas. On the opera stage an incarnational trade between individuals and ideas is dramatically represented, and that – even more than the involvement of music with dramatic poetry – may well be the aspect of opera that most closely resembles the ancient Greek theatre where the faithful and religiously committed were served a vital part of their religious and cultural nourishment in the most potently imaginative way possible.

Perhaps it is easier for the theatre to be a forum for religious ideas when the culture officially 'believes in' a lengthy cast list of gods and heroes than when it is dominated by the less discursive, more static model of a Trinity of divine persons. The Christian myths have not yet become standard material for opera, though Bach's Passions and Handel's oratorios have always counted on their stageability within the theatre of the mind. But a glance at what belief means in many of the religions of the world suggests that an understanding of theology as a form of imaginative theatre is closer to truth than an aggressive jumble of warring fundamentalisms. For many modern opera-goers who are humanist unbelievers, it may make very appealing sense to think of the world of religion as a kind of conceptual theatre where systems of virtue and morality are dramatized and where the idea of God is incarnated in performance. Opera early on in Rome caught the attention of princes of the Church. How the imagination operates in the development of theology is very similar to how it operates in the theatre. As Dryden put it, 'Humane Impossibilities are to be received, as they are in Faith.' Opera could make accessible to a world of increasingly complex faith and doubt much of the expressive realism and fantasy within the Christian tradition. The only genuine difference between opera and oratorio lies in the conventions governing dialogue and physical context.

Count Francesco Algarotti defined with great precision exactly what the ambition of opera should be in 1755 (this anonymous English translation having been published in Glasgow in 1768).

There yet remain several articles that might be added to a subject of this nature, which is the result of so many different arts, each in itself important, copious and not ignoble. Let it however suffice, for me to have pointed out the way thus far, having proposed to myself no other view, than to shew the intimate connection that ought to be kept up among the several constituent parts of the musical drama or opera; by which means the effect will be one regular and harmonious *whole*. The doctrine here laid down will be found sufficient, whenever it shall be so lucky as to be honoured by the countenance of a sovereign, blessed with a refined understanding and delicacy of taste: because, through such a wished-for promotion, may be restored to its ancient rank in the public's esteem, a species of scenical exhibition, to whose accomplishment and final embellishing, all the polite arts emulously concur. Therefore, for many other reasons that might be assigned, it is an object not unworthy of a place in the attention even of those who govern kingdoms. At so happy an epoch as that hinted here, we should behold the theatre no longer as a place destined for the reception of a tumultuous assembly, but as the meeting of a solemn audience ... Then would the Opera be no longer called an irrational, monstrous, and grotesque composition: on the contrary, it would display a lively image of the Grecian tragedy, in which architecture, poetry, music, dancing and every kind of theatrical apparatus united their efforts to create an illusion of such resistless power over the human mind, that from the combination of a thousand pleasures, formed so extraordinary a one, as in our world has nothing to equal it.

The challenge continues, easy to ridicule, wondrous to attain.

After fully four hundred years of operatic history, there is a marvellous treasury of writing about the art – buoyantly loaded with the thoughts, ambitions, hopes, memories and perceptive conclusions of an extraordinary range of literary, theatrical and musical genius. Eighty-six authors, many of them practitioners rather than historians, musicologists or critics, are brought together in this anthology. Its first aim is to provide substantial nourishment, not just provocative samples or diverting hints that whet the appetite.

Opera is not an obvious combination of elements. Its recipes have been controversial throughout its history, and it has attracted the serious as well as the flippant attention of profound and talented thinkers and literary virtuosi in various European languages. A good number of items appear here in English for the first time. Many other extracts have not been readily available outside the great academic libraries for a very long time.

The credentials of opera had to be established before it could play a full part in the growing body of literary fiction from which the first segment of my anthology is drawn. There are a number of gems by great or by popular names, the earliest a delightfully satirical sketch

from Thackeray's *Vanity Fair*. The pretensions of opera as a performing art and the social and cultural aspirations of its most usual
audience both suffer, unquestionably, from vanity. But the life of
opera in fiction is not mere incidental decoration. When Forster's
visitors to Italy in *Where Angels Fear to Tread* take in a local *Lucia di
Lammermoor*, the untidy, vivacious attitude of the locals to their
entertainment contrasts very significantly, as does so much other
incident in the book, with the buttoned-up character of its Anglo-
Saxon protagonists. In *War and Peace*, Natasha's experience at the
opera is enough to drive her completely out of character. She dreams
(not being able to concentrate very seriously on the performance,
though she does describe what happens on stage quite fully) of
standing on the velvet-covered edge of her box and singing along with
the soprano. Opera, from Tolstoy's essentially unsympathetic view-
point, which is well illustrated in his amusingly detailed and extended
reaction to Wagner's *Ring* in an essay in *What is Art?*, is just the sort
of treacherous, dishonest environment where Anatol can lead Natasha
astray and make her prey to his impassioned seduction. The work
described by Natasha sounds very Russian, if unhistorical – no doubt
one of those popular peasanty Singspiels that preceded Glinka's *A Life
for the Tsar*. In 1812, the Bolshoi in Moscow lay some years in the
future.

Warm-blooded Italians have done far less theorizing about opera,
once the initial burst of aristocratic prologues and prefaces was over,
than those for whom opera was a foreign import whose naturalization
required justifying. Italians simply got on with writing the operas, and
polishing the form to the pinnacle of Abbé Metastasio's poetic
challenge and beyond. The course of operatic development in Italy
was bumpier once *opera seria* was overtaken by other fashions.
Romanticism, represented first and most notably by Mozart and Da
Ponte's Italian comedies, gave a radical jolt to the form that
dominated European culture for two centuries. When the expressive
range and melodic detail of Wagner's musical language came to be
digested by Puccini and his 'verismo' colleagues, the fertility of the
Italian tradition produced wonderful flowers that still command
universal popularity. In the course of the twentieth century, the Italian
operatic voice seems to have fallen silent in the making of new
masterpieces.

The response of French, German and English writers and thinkers to the Italian hegemony – despite Lully's adoption of the French language in his acquired empire – sustained a debate about the art-form for more than a century: about what subjects it should deal with, what skills it should contain and how it should be taken by its audience. The Italians, of course, sustained a virtual monopoly of the castrated male star opera-singers who dominated the art for more than one hundred and fifty years until 1830. But they were culturally isolated by the very ease and discretion with which musical eunuchs were procured in the fragmented political condition of a land divided by the Papal States.

There is such a quantity of good writing on opera that the selection must inevitably be partial. This path has been beaten before – notably in Ulrich Weisstein's *Essence of Opera*, published thirty years ago in the USA. I could have filled many pages with the vicissitudes of impresarios and the comic fallacy that unites many volumes of singers' reminiscence – that, because life on stage all too often resembles the Marx Brothers' *A Night at the Opera* or Mae West's memorable excursion into *Samson and Dalila* in her delightful *Goin' to Town*, the answer to directorial ambitions and artistic seriousness is to repeat the mantra 'it's a joke' – that defining phrase of English ambiguity and English humour. Of that whole genre I have been able to include some delicious *soupçons*, but not great drafts, which I much regret. Memoirs about opera and the performing arts generally go out of print all too quickly. I should love to have given new circulation to Ida Cook's *We Followed Our Stars* with its breathless descriptions of how a pair of sensible English ladies who happened to be opera fans obtained the cooperation of Clemens Krauss – even getting the schedule of the National Theater in Munich changed in order to rescue refugees and their effects from Nazi Germany.

It is evident that as live theatre disappears, the enthusiasm of being there, and for performers the difficulties of touring, will increasingly be a thing of the past. There will be television and film memoirs, of course. But art-forms where error can be edited out will no longer need the heroic collaboration of performers and audiences in pretending that all is really well. The motto of live performances was given to us by Shakespeare in *A Midsummer Night's Dream*: 'The best in this kind are but shadows, and the worst are no worse if imagination amend them.' The culture of amendment and with it a whole universe of individual fantasy and imagination looks as if it may be coming to an end.

Do not look here for representative samples of many professional critics. Shaw is readily available elsewhere. I wish there had been room for more Hanslick. There is criticism by Debussy, Berlioz, Tchaikovsky, Virgil Thomson, composers all. The writing of Thomas Love Peacock and Leigh Hunt on music should be better known. I have preferred Richard Wagner the critic in Paris to Wagner the prolix theorist, so much less crisp than Nietzsche. Names that have not frequented operatic anthologies before include Grillparzer, Hazlitt, Beerbohm, Heine, Hegel and Schiller. Pieces that give me special pleasure are E. T. A. Hoffmann's wonderful short story, *The Poet and the Composer*, Walter Legge's anatomy of Callas, Heinrich Mann's comic description of a *Lohengrin* performance, generous chunks of Thomas Bernhard's *Wittgenstein's Nephew*, a very detailed account of Wieland Wagner's Bayreuth by Claude Lust, and a substantial extract from Diderot's *Rameau's Nephew*.

This book owes a considerable debt to my collaborator Matthew Scott's enthusiasm for – and knowledge of – criticism at the dawn of the Romantic age in German and French as well as in English literature, and to his excellent translations. Various enthusiasts and experts have helped me with suggestions and in other ways: Patrick O'Connor, Stephen Mead, Ivan Hewitt, David Brown, Pamela Rosenberg, Jacques and Nelly Lasserre, Anthony Gasson, Bayan Northcott, David Cairns, Denis Stevens, Andrew Porter, John Burgess, Max Loppert, Tim Coleman and not least my wife, Meredith Oakes.

Tom Sutcliffe
Streatham
March 2000

Occasion for Romance

Opera in Fiction

'His Transparency of Pumpernickel's court theatre'
WILLIAM MAKEPEACE THACKERAY

Wherever the party stopped, and an opportunity was offered, Mr Jos left his own card and the Major's upon 'Our Minister'. It was with great difficulty that he could be restrained from putting on his cocked hat and tights to wait upon the English consul at the Free City of Judenstadt, when that hospitable functionary asked our travellers to dinner. He kept a journal of his voyage, and noted elaborately the defects or excellences of the various inns at which he put up, and of the wines and dishes of which he partook.

As for Emmy, she was very happy and pleased. Dobbin used to carry about for her her stool and sketch-book, and admired the drawings of the good-natured little artist, as they never had been admired before. She sate upon steamers' decks and drew crags and castles, or she mounted upon donkeys and ascended to ancient robber-towers, attended by her two aides-de-camp, Georgy and Dobbin. She laughed, and the Major did too, at his droll figure on donkey-back, with his long legs touching the ground. He was the interpreter for the party, having a good military knowledge of the German language; and he and the delighted George fought the campaigns of the Rhine and the Palatinate. In the course of a few weeks, and by assiduously conversing with Herr Kirsch on the box of the carriage, Georgy made prodigious advance in the knowledge of High Dutch, and could talk to hotel waiters and postilions in a way that charmed his mother, and amused his guardian.

Mr Jos did not much engage in the afternoon excursions of his fellow-travellers. He slept a good deal after dinner, or basked in the arbours of the pleasant inn-gardens. Pleasant Rhine gardens! Fair scenes of peace and sunshine – noble purple mountains, whose crests are reflected in the magnificent stream – who has ever seen you, that has not a grateful memory of those scenes of friendly repose and beauty? To lay down the pen, and even to think of that beautiful Rhineland makes one happy. At this time of summer evening, the cows are trooping down from the hills, lowing and with their bells tinkling, to the old town, with its old moats, and gates, and spires, and chestnut-trees, with long blue shadows stretching over the grass; the sky and the river below flame in crimson and gold; and the moon

3

is already out, looking pale towards the sunset. The sun sinks behind the great castle-crested mountains, the night falls suddenly, the river grows darker and darker, lights quiver in it from the windows in the old ramparts, and twinkle peacefully in the villages under the hills on the opposite shore.

So Jos used to go to sleep a good deal with his bandanna over his face and be very comfortable, and read all the English news, and every word of Galignani's admirable newspaper (may the blessings of all Englishmen who have ever been abroad rest on the founders and proprietors of that piratical print!), and whether he woke or slept his friends did not very much miss him. Yes, they were very happy. They went to the Opera often of evenings – to those snug, unassuming dear old operas in the German towns, where the noblesse sits and cries and knits stockings on the one side, over against the bourgeoisie on the other; and His Transparency the Duke and his Transparent family, all very fat and good-natured, come and occupy the great box in the middle; and the pit is full of the most elegant slim-waisted officers with straw-coloured mustachios, and twopence a-day on full pay. Here it was that Emmy found her delight, and was introduced for the first time to the wonders of Mozart and Cimarosa. The Major's musical taste has been before alluded to, and his performances on the flute commended. But perhaps the chief pleasure he had in these operas was in watching Emmy's rapture while listening to them. A new world of love and beauty broke upon her when she was introduced to those divine compositions: this lady had the keenest and finest sensibility, and how could she be indifferent when she heard Mozart? The tender parts of 'Don Juan' awakened in her raptures so exquisite that she would ask herself when she went to say her prayers of a night, whether it was not wicked to feel so much delight as that with which 'Vedrai Carino' and 'Batti Batti' filled her gentle little bosom? But the Major, whom she consulted upon this head, as her theological adviser (and who himself had a pious and reverent soul), said that, for his part, every beauty of art or nature made him thankful as well as happy; and that the pleasure to be had in listening to fine music, as in looking at the stars in the sky, or at a beautiful landscape or picture, was a benefit for which we might thank heaven as sincerely as for any other worldly blessing. And in reply to some faint objections of Mrs Amelia's (taken from certain theological works like the 'Washerwoman of Finchley Common' and others of that school, with which Mrs Osborne had been furnished during her life at Brompton), he told her an Eastern fable of the Owl who thought that the sunshine was unbearable for the eyes, and that the Nightingale was a most overrated bird. 'It is one's nature to sing and the other's to hoot,' he said, laughing, 'and with such a sweet voice as you have yourself, you must belong to the Bulbul faction.'

I like to dwell upon this period of her life, and to think that she was cheerful and happy. You see she has not had too much of that sort of existence as yet, and has not fallen in the way of means to educate her tastes or her intelligence. She has been domineered over hitherto by vulgar intellects. It is the lot of many a woman. And as every one of the dear sex is the rival of the rest of her kind, timidity passes for folly in their charitable judgments; and gentleness for dulness; and silence – which is but timid denial of the unwelcome assertion of ruling folks, and tacit protestantism – above all, finds no mercy at the hands of the female Inquisition. Thus, my dear and civilized reader, if you and I were to find ourselves this evening in a society of greengrocers, let us say; it is probable that our conversation would not be brilliant; if, on the other hand, a greengrocer should find himself at your refined and polite tea-table, where everybody was saying witty things, and everybody of fashion and repute tearing her friends to pieces in the most delightful manner, it is possible that the stranger would not be very talkative, and by no means interesting or interested.

And it must be remembered, that this poor lady had never met a gentleman in her life until this present moment. Perhaps these are rarer personages than some of us think for. Which of us can point out many such in his circle – men whose aims are generous, whose truth is constant, and not only constant in its kind but elevated in its degree; whose want of meanness makes them simple: who can look the world honestly in the face with an equal manly sympathy for the great and the small? We all know a hundred whose coats are very well made, and a score who have excellent manners, and one or two happy beings who are what they call in the inner circles, and have shot into the very centre and bull's eye of the fashion; but of gentlemen how many? Let us take a little scrap of paper and each make out his list.

My friend the Major I write, without any doubt, in mine. He had very long legs, a yellow face, and a slight lisp, which at first was rather ridiculous. But his thoughts were just, his brains were fairly good, his life was honest and pure, and his heart warm and humble. He certainly had very large hands and feet, which the two George Osbornes used to caricature and laugh at; and their jeers and laughter perhaps led poor little Emmy astray as to his worth. But have we not all been misled about our heroes, and changed our opinions a hundred times? Emmy, in this happy time, found that hers underwent a very great change in respect of the merits of the Major.

Perhaps it was the happiest time of both their lives, indeed, if they did but know it – and who does? Which of us can point out and say that was the culmination – that was the summit of human joy? But at all events, this couple were very decently contented, and enjoyed as pleasant a summer tour as any pair that left England that year. Georgy was always present at the play, but it was the Major who put Emmy's shawl on after the entertainment; and in the walks and excursions the young lad would be on a-head, and up a tower-stair or a tree, whilst the soberer couple were below, the Major smoking his cigar with great placidity and constancy, whilst Emmy sketched the site or the ruin. It was on this very tour that I, the present writer of a history of which every word is true, had the pleasure to see them first, and to make their acquaintance.

It was at the little comfortable Ducal town of Pumpernickel (that very place where Sir Pitt Crawley had been so distinguished as an *attaché*; but that was in early early days, and before the news of the battle of Austerlitz sent all the English diplomatists in Germany to the right about) that I first saw Colonel Dobbin and his party. They had arrived with the carriage and courier at the Erbprinz Hotel, the best of the town, and the whole party dined at the *table-d'hôte*. Everybody remarked the majesty of Jos, and the knowing way in which he sipped, or rather sucked, the Johannisberger, which he ordered for dinner. The little boy, too, we observed, had a famous appetite, and consumed schinken, and braten, and kartoffeln, and cranberry jam, and salad, and pudding, and roast-fowls, and sweet-meats, with a gallantry that did honour to his nation. After about fifteen dishes, he concluded the repast with dessert, some of which he even carried out of doors; for some young gentlemen at table, amused with his coolness and gallant free and easy manner, induced him to pocket a handful of macaroons, which he discussed on his way to the theatre, whither everybody went in the cheery social little German place. The lady in black, the boy's mamma, laughed and blushed, and looked exceedingly pleased and shy as the dinner went on, and at the various feats and instances of *espièglerie* on the part of her son. The Colonel – for so he became very soon afterwards – I remember joked the boy with a great deal of grave fun, pointing out dishes which he *hadn't* tried, and entreating him not to baulk his appetite, but to have a second supply of this or that.

It was what they call a *gast-rolle* night at the Royal Grand Ducal Pumpernickelisch Hof, – or Court theatre; and Madame Schroeder Devrient, then in the bloom of her beauty and genius, performed the part of the heroine in the wonderful opera of 'Fidelio'. From our places in the stalls we could see our four friends of the *table-d'hôte* in the loge which Schwendler of the Erbprinz kept for his best guests: and I could not help remarking the effect which the magnificent actress and music produced upon Mrs Osborne, for so we had heard the stout gentleman in the mustachios call her. During the astonishing Chorus of the Prisoners, over which the delightful voice of the actress rose and soared in the most ravishing harmony, the English lady's face wore such an expression of wonder and delight that it struck even little Fipps, the *blasé* attaché, who drawled out, as he fixed his glass upon her, 'Gayd, it really does one good to see a woman caypable of that stayte of excaytement.' And in the Prison Scene where Fidelio, rushing to her husband, cries, 'Nichts nichts mein Florestan,' she fairly lost herself and covered her face with her handkerchief. Every woman in the house was snivelling at the time: but I suppose it was because it was predestined that I was to write this particular lady's memoirs that I remarked her.

The next day they gave another piece of Beethoven: 'Die Schlacht bei Vittoria'. Malbrook is introduced at the beginning of the per-formance, as indicative of the brisk advance of the French Army. Then come drums, trumpets, thunder of artillery, and groans of the dying, and at last in a grand triumphant swell, 'God save the King' is performed.

There may have been a score of Englishmen in the house, but at the burst of that beloved and well-known music, every one of them – we young fellows in the stalls, Sir John and Lady Bullminster (who had taken a house at Pumpernickel for the education of their nine children), the fat gentleman with the mustachios, the long Major in white duck trowsers, and the lady with the little boy upon whom he was so sweet: even Kirsch, the courier in the gallery – stood bolt upright in their places, and proclaimed themselves to be members of the dear old British nation. As for Tapeworm, the Chargé d'Affaires, he rose up in his box and bowed and simpered, as if he would represent the whole empire. Tapeworm was nephew and heir of old Marshal Tiptoff, who has been introduced in this story as General Tiptoff, just before Waterloo, who was Colonel of the —th regiment, in which Major Dobbin served, and who died in this year full of honours, and of an aspic of plovers' eggs; when the regiment was graciously given by his Majesty to Colonel Sir Michael O'Dowd, KCB, who had commanded it in many glorious fields.

Tapeworm must have met with Colonel Dobbin at the house of the Colonel's Colonel, the Marshal, for he recognised him on this night at the theatre; and with the utmost condescension, his Majesty's minister came over from his own box, and publicly shook hands with his new-found friend.

'Look at that infernal sly-boots of a Tapeworm,' Fipps whispered, examining his chief from the stalls. 'Wherever there's a pretty woman he always twists himself in.' And I wonder what were diplomatists made for but for that?

'Have I the honour of addressing myself to Mrs Dobbin?' asked the Secretary, with a most insinuating grin.

Georgy burst out laughing, and said, 'By Jove, that *is* a good 'un.' – Emmy and the Major blushed; we saw them from the stalls.

'The lady is Mrs George Osborne,' said the Major, 'and this is her brother, Mr Sedley, a distinguished officer of the Bengal Civil Service: permit me to introduce him to your lordship.'

My lord nearly sent Jos off his legs, with the most fascinating smile. 'Are you going to stop in Pumpernickel?' he said. 'It is a dull place: but we want some nice people, and we would try and make it *so* agreeable to you. Mr – Ahum – Mrs Oho – I shall do myself the honour of calling upon you to-morrow at your inn.' – And he went away with a Parthian grin and glance, which he thought must finish Mrs Osborne completely.

The performance over, the young fellows lounged about the lobbies, and we saw the society take its departure. The Duchess Dowager went off in her jingling old coach, attended by two faithful and withered old maids of honour, and a little snuffy spindle-shanked gentleman in waiting, in a brown jasey and a green coat covered with orders – of which the star and the grand yellow cordon of the order of

St Michael of Pumpernickel were most conspicuous. The drums rolled, the guards saluted, and the old carriage drove away.

Then came His Transparency the Duke and Transparent family, with his great officers of state and household. He bowed serenely to everybody. And amid the saluting of the guards, and the flaring of the torches of the running footmen, clad in scarlet, the Transparent carriages drove away to the old Ducal Schloss, with its towers and pinnacles standing on the Schlossberg. Everybody in Pumpernickel knew everybody. No sooner was a foreigner seen there, than the Minister of Foreign Affairs, or some other great or small officer of state, went round to the Erbprinz, and found out the name of the new arrivals.

We watched them, too, out of the theatre. Tapeworm had just walked off, enveloped in his cloak, with which his gigantic chasseur was always in attendance, and looking as much as possible like Don Juan. The Prime Minister's lady had just squeezed herself into her sedan, and her daughter, the charming Ida, had put on her calash and clogs, when the English party came out, the boy yawning drearily, the Major taking great pains in keeping the shawl over Mrs Osborne's head, and Mr Sedley looking grand, with a crush opera-hat on one side of his head, and his hand in the stomach of a voluminous white waistcoat. We took off our hats to our acquaintance of the *table-d'hôte*, and the lady, in return, presented us with a little smile and a curtsey, for which everybody might be thankful.

The carriage from the inn, under the superintendence of the bustling Mr Kirsch, was in waiting to convey the party; but the fat man said he would walk, and smoke his cigar on his way homewards; so the other three, with nods and smiles to us, went without Mr Sedley; Kirsch, with the cigar-case, following in his master's wake.

We all walked together, and talked to the stout gentleman about the *agrémens* of the place. It was very agreeable for the English. There were shooting-parties and battues; there was a plenty of balls and entertainments at the hospitable Court; the society was generally good; the theatre excellent, and the living cheap.

'And our Minister seems a most delightful and affable person,' our new friend said. 'With such a representative, and – and a good medical man, I can fancy the place to be most eligible. Good-night, gentlemen.' And Jos creaked up the stairs to bedward, followed by

Kirsch with a flambeau. We rather hoped that nice-looking woman would be induced to stay some time in the town.

Vanity Fair, 1847–8

'The Prima-donna as an echo of conscience'
GUSTAVE FLAUBERT

The idea of the theatre quickly germinated in Bovary's head, for he at once communicated it to his wife, who at first refused, alleging the fatigue, the worry, the expense; but, for a wonder, Charles did not give in, so sure was he that this recreation would be good for her. He saw nothing to prevent it: his mother had sent them three hundred francs which he had no longer expected; the current debts were not very large, and the falling in of Lheureux's bills was still so far off that there was no need to think about them. Besides, imagining that she was refusing from delicacy, he insisted the more; so that by dint of worrying her she at last made up her mind, and the next day at eight o'clock they set out in the 'Hirondelle'.

The druggist, whom nothing whatever kept at Yonville, but who thought himself bound not to budge from it, sighed as he saw them go.

'Well, a pleasant journey!' he said to them; 'happy mortals that you are!'

Then addressing himself to Emma, who was wearing a blue silk gown with four flounces:

'You are as lovely as a Venus. You'll cut a figure at Rouen.'

The diligence stopped at the 'Croix Rouge' in the Place Beauvoisine. It was the inn that is in every provincial faubourg, with large stables and small bedrooms, where one sees in the middle of the court chickens pilfering the oats under the muddy gigs of the commercial travellers – a good old house, with worm-eaten balconies that creak in the wind on winter nights, always full of people, noise, and feeding, whose black tables are sticky with coffee and brandy, the thick windows made yellow by the flies, the damp napkins stained with cheap wine, and that always smells of the village, like plough-boys dressed in Sunday-clothes, has a café on the street, and towards the countryside a kitchen-garden. Charles at once set out. He muddled up the stage-boxes with the gallery, the pit with the boxes; asked for explanations, did not understand them; was sent from the box-office to the acting-manager; came back to the inn, returned to the theatre, and thus several times traversed the whole length of the town from the theatre to the boulevard.

Madame Bovary bought a bonnet, gloves, and a bouquet. The doctor was much afraid of missing the beginning, and, without having had time to swallow a plate of soup, they presented themselves at the doors of the theatre, which were still closed.

The crowd was waiting against the wall, symmetrically enclosed between the balustrades. At the corner of the neighbouring streets huge bills repeated in quaint letters '*Lucie de Lammermoor* – Lagardy – Opera – etc.' The weather was fine, the people were hot, perspiration trickled amid the curls, and handkerchiefs taken from pockets were mopping red foreheads; and now and again a warm wind that blew from the river gently stirred the border of the tick awnings hanging from the doors of the public-houses. A little lower down, however, one was refreshed by a current of icy air that smelt of tallow, leather, and oil. This was an exhalation from the Rue des Charrettes, full of large dingy warehouses where casks are always being rolled about.

For fear of seeming ridiculous, Emma before going in wished to have a little stroll in the harbour, and Bovary prudently kept his tickets in his hand, in the pocket of his trousers, which he pressed against his stomach.

Her heart began to beat as soon as she reached the vestibule. She involuntarily smiled with vanity on seeing the crowd rushing to the right by the other corridor while she went up the staircase to the reserved seats. She was as pleased as a child to push open with her finger the wide tapestried doors. She breathed in with all her might the dusty smell of the lobbies, and when she was seated in her box she bent forward with the air of a duchess.

The theatre was beginning to fill; opera-glasses were taken from their cases, and the subscribers, catching sight of one another, were bowing. They came to seek relaxation in the fine arts after the anxieties of business; but 'business' was not forgotten; they still talked cottons, spirits of wine, or indigo. The heads of old men were to be seen, inexpressive and peaceful, with their hair and complexions looking like silver medals tarnished by steam of lead. The young beaux were strutting about in the pit, showing in the opening of their waistcoats their pink or apple-green cravats, and Madame Bovary from above admired them leaning on their canes with golden knobs in the open palm of their yellow gloves.

Now the lights of the orchestra were lit, the lustre, let down from the ceiling, throwing with the glitter of its facets a sudden gaiety over the theatre; then the musicians came in one after the other; and first there was the protracted hubbub of the basses grumbling, violins squeaking, cornets trumpeting, flutes and flageolets whining. But three knocks were heard on the stage, a rolling of drums began, the brass instruments played some chords, and the curtain, rising, discovered a country scene.

It was the cross-roads of a wood, with a fountain shaded by an oak to the left. Peasants and lords with plaids on their shoulders were singing a hunting-song together; then a captain suddenly came on, who evoked the spirit of evil by lifting both his arms to heaven. Another appeared; they went away, and the hunters started afresh.

She felt herself transported to the reading of her youth, into the midst of Walter Scott. She seemed to hear through the mist the sound of the Scotch bagpipes re-echoing over the heather. Then her remembrance of the novel helping her to understand the libretto, she followed the story phrase by phrase, while vague thoughts that came back to her dispersed again at once with the bursts of music. She gave herself up to the lullaby of the melodies, and felt all her being vibrate as if the violin bows were drawn over her nerves. She had not eyes enough to look at the costumes, the scenery, the actors, the painted trees that shook when anyone walked, and the velvet caps, cloaks, swords — all those imaginary things that floated amid the harmony as in the atmosphere of another world. But a young woman stepped forward, throwing a purse to a squire in green. She was left alone, and the flute was heard like the murmur of a fountain or the warbling of birds. Lucie attacked her cavatina in G-major bravely. She plained of love; she longed for wings. Emma too, fleeing from life, would have liked to fly away in an embrace. Suddenly Edgar-Lagardy appeared.

He had that splendid pallor that gives something of the majesty of marble to the ardent races of the South. His vigorous form was tightly clad in a brown-coloured doublet; a small chiselled poniard hung against his left thigh, and he distributed languishing glances, showing his white teeth. They said that a Polish princess having heard him sing one night on the beach at Biarritz, where he mended boats, had fallen in love with him. She had ruined herself for him. He had deserted her for other women, and this sentimental celebrity did not fail to enhance his artistic reputation. The diplomatic mummer took care always to slip into his advertisements some poetic phrase about the fascination of his person and the susceptibility of his soul. A fine organ, imperturbable coolness, more temperament than intelligence, more power of emphasis than of real singing, helped to make up the charm of this admirable charlatan nature, in which there was something of the hairdresser and the toreador.

From the first scene he evoked enthusiasm. He pressed Lucie in his arms, he left her, he came back, he seemed desperate; he had outbursts of rage, then elegiac gurglings of infinite sweetness, and the notes escaped from his bare neck full of sobs and kisses. Emma leant forward to see him, clutching the velvet of the box with her nails. She was filling her heart with these melodious lamentations that were drawn out to the accompaniment of the double-basses, like the cries of the drowning in the tumult of a tempest. She recognised all the intoxication and the anguish that had almost killed her. The voice of the *prima donna* seemed to her to be but an echo of her conscience, and this illusion that charmed her appeared an actual part of her own life. But no one on earth had loved her with such love. He had not wept like Edgar that last moonlit night when they said, 'To-morrow! tomorrow!' The theatre rang with cheers; they recommenced the entire movement; the lovers spoke of the flowers on their tomb, of vows, exile, fate, hopes; and when they uttered the final adieu, Emma gave a sharp cry that mingled with the vibrations of the last chords.

'But why,' asked Bovary, 'does that gentleman persecute her?'

'No, no!' she answered; 'he is her lover!'

'Yet he vows vengeance on her family, while the other one who came on before said, "I love Lucie and she loves me!" Besides, he went off with her father arm in arm. For he certainly is her father, isn't he – the ugly little man with a cock's feather in his hat?'

Despite Emma's explanations, as soon as the recitative duet began in which Gilbert lays bare his abominable machinations to his master Ashton, Charles, seeing the false troth-ring that is to deceive Lucie, thought it was a love-gift sent by Edgar. He confessed, moreover, that he did not understand the story because of the music, which interfered very much with the words.

'What does it matter?' said Emma. 'Do be quiet!'

'Yes, but you know,' he went on, leaning against her shoulder, 'I like to understand things.'

'Be quiet! be quiet!' she cried impatiently.

Lucie advanced, half supported by her women, a wreath of orange-blossoms in her hair, and paler than the white satin of her gown. Emma dreamed of her marriage-day; she saw herself at home again amid the corn in the little path as they walked to the church. Oh, why had not she, like this woman, resisted, implored? She, on the contrary, had been joyous, without seeing the abyss into which she was throwing herself. Ah! if in the freshness of her beauty, before the soilure of marriage and the disillusions of adultery, she could have anchored her life upon some great, strong heart, then virtue, tenderness, voluptuousness, and duty blending, she would never have fallen from so high a happiness. But that happiness, no doubt, was a lie invented for the despair of all desire. She now knew the smallness of the passions that art exaggerated. So, striving to divert her thoughts, Emma determined now to see in this reproduction of her sorrows only a plastic fantasy, well enough to please the eye, and she even smiled internally with disdainful pity when at the back of the stage under the velvet hangings a man appeared in a black cloak.

His large Spanish hat fell at a gesture he made, and immediately the instruments and the singers began the sextet. Edgar, flashing with fury, dominated all the others with his clearer voice; Ashton hurled homicidal provocations at him in deep notes; Lucie uttered her shrill plaint, Arthur, aside modulated his tones in the middle register, and the bass of the minister pealed forth like an organ, while the voices of the women repeating his words took them up in chorus delightfully. They were all in a row gesticulating, and anger, vengeance, jealousy, terror, and stupefaction breathed forth at once from their half-opened mouths. The outraged lover brandished his naked sword; his guipure ruffle rose with jerks to the movements of his chest, and he walked from right to left with long strides, clanking against the boards the silver-gilt spurs of his soft boots, widening out at the ankles. He, she thought, must have an inexhaustible love to lavish it upon the crowd with such effusion. All her small fault-findings faded before the poetry of the part that absorbed her; and, drawn towards this man by the illusion of the character, she tried to imagine to herself his life – that resonant, extraordinary, splendid life, which might have been hers if fate had willed it. They would have known one another, loved one another. With him, through all the kingdoms of Europe, she would have travelled from capital to capital, sharing his fatigues and his pride, picking up the flowers thrown to him, herself embroidering his costumes. Then each evening, at the back of a box, behind the golden trellis-work, she would have drunk in eagerly the expansions of this soul that would have sung for her alone; from the stage, even as he acted, he would have looked at her. But the mad idea seized her that he was looking at her; it was certain. She longed to run to his arms, to take refuge in his strength, as in the incarnation of love itself, and to say to him, to cry out, 'Take me away! carry me with you! let us go! Thine, thine! all my ardour and all my dreams!'

The curtain fell.

The smell of the gas mingled with the breathing; the waving of the fans made the air more suffocating. Emma wanted to go out; the crowd filled the corridors, and she fell back in her fauteuil, with palpitations that choked her. Charles, fearing that she would faint, ran to the refreshment-room to get a glass of barley-water.

He had great difficulty in getting back to his seat, for his elbows were jerked at every step because of the glass he held in his hands, and he even spilt three-fourths on the shoulders of a Rouen lady in short sleeves, who, feeling the cold liquid running down to her loins, uttered cries like a peacock, as if she were being assassinated. Her husband, who was a mill-owner, railed at the clumsy fellow, and while with her handkerchief she was wiping up the stains from her handsome cherry-coloured taffeta gown, he angrily muttered about indemnity, costs, reimbursement. At last Charles reached his wife, saying to her, quite out of breath:

'*Ma foi!* I thought I should have had to stay there. There is such a crowd – *such* a crowd!'

He added:

'Just guess whom I met up there! Monsieur Léon!'

'Léon?'

'Himself! He's coming along to pay his respects.' And as he finished these words the ex-clerk of Yonville entered the box.

He held out his hand with the ease of a gentleman; and Madame Bovary extended hers, without doubt obeying the attraction of a stronger will. She had not felt it since that spring evening when the rain fell upon the green leaves, and they had said good-bye standing at the window. But soon recalling herself to the necessities of the situation, with an effort she shook off the torpor of her memories, and began stammering a few hurried words.

'Ah, good day! What! you here?'

'Silence!' cried a voice from the pit, for the third act was beginning.

'So you are at Rouen?'

'Yes.'

'And since when?'

'Turn them out! turn them out!' People were looking at them. They were silent.

But from that moment she listened no more; and the chorus of the guests, the scene between Ashton and his servant, the grand duet in D-major, all were for her as far off as if the instruments had grown less sonorous and the characters more remote. She remembered the games at cards at the druggist's, and the walk to the nurse's, the reading in the arbour, the *tête-à-tête* by the fireside – all that poor love, so calm and so protracted, so discreet, so tender, and that she had nevertheless forgotten. And why had he come back? What combination of circumstances had brought him back into her life? He was standing behind her, leaning with his shoulder against the wall of the box; now and again she felt herself shuddering beneath the hot breath from his nostrils falling upon her hair.

'Does this amuse you?' he said, bending over her so closely that the end of his moustache brushed her cheek. She replied carelessly:

'Oh, dear me, no, not much.'

Then he proposed that they should leave the theatre and go and take an ice somewhere.

'Oh, not yet; let us stay,' said Bovary. 'Her hair's undone; this is going to be tragic.'

But the mad scene did not at all interest Emma, and the acting of the singer seemed to her exaggerated.

'She screams too loud,' said she, turning to Charles, who was listening.

'Yes – perhaps – a little,' he replied, undecided between the frankness of his pleasure and his respect for his wife's opinion.

Then with a sigh Léon said:

'The heat is –'

'Unbearable! Yes!'

'Do you feel unwell?' asked Bovary.

'Yes, I am stifling; let us go.'

Monsieur Léon put her long lace shawl carefully about her shoulders, and all three went off to sit down in the harbour, in the open air, outside the windows of a café.

First they spoke of her illness, although Emma interrupted Charles from time to time, for fear, she said, of boring Monsieur Léon; and the latter told them that he had come to spend two years at Rouen in a large office, in order to get practice in his profession, which was different in Normandy and Paris. Then he inquired after Berthe, the Homais, Mère Lefrançois, and as they had, in the husband's presence, nothing more to say to one another, the conversation soon came to an end.

People coming out of the theatre passed along the pavement, humming or shouting at the top of their voices, 'O bel ange, ma Lucie!' Then Léon, playing the dilettante, began to talk music. He had seen Tamburini, Rubini, Persiani, Grisi, and, compared with them, Lagardy, despite his grand outbursts, was nowhere.

'Yet,' interrupted Charles, who was slowly sipping his rum-sherbet, 'they say that he is quite admirable in the last act. I regret leaving before the end, because it was beginning to amuse me.'

'Why,' said the clerk, 'he will soon give another performance.'

But Charles replied that they were going back next day. 'Unless,' he added, turning to his wife, 'you would like to stay alone, pussy?'

And changing his tactics at this unexpected opportunity that presented itself to his hopes, the young man sang the praises of Lagardy in the last number. It was really superb, sublime. Then Charles insisted:

'You would get back on Sunday. Come, make up your mind. You are wrong if you feel that this is doing you the least good.'

The tables round them, however, were emptying; a waiter came and stood discreetly near them. Charles, who understood, took out his purse; the clerk held back his arm, and did not forget to leave two more pieces of silver that he chinked on the marble.

'I am really sorry,' said Bovary, 'about the money which you are –'

The other made a careless gesture full of cordiality, and taking his hat said:

'It is settled, isn't it? To-morrow at six o'clock?'

Charles explained once more that he could not absent himself longer, but that nothing prevented Emma –

'But,' she stammered, with a strange smile, 'I am not sure –'

'Well, you must think it over. We'll see. Night brings counsel.' Then to Léon, who was walking along with them, 'Now that you are in our part of the world, I hope you'll come and ask us for some dinner now and then.'

The clerk declared he would not fail to do so, being obliged, moreover, to go to Yonville on some business for his office. And they parted before the Saint-Herbland Passage just as the cathedral clock struck half-past eleven.

Madame Bovary, 1857
tr. E. Marx-Aveling, 1886

'Natasha's fantasy should be warning of danger'
LEO TOLSTOY

Chapter VIII

That evening the Rostofs went to the opera, Marya Dmitrievna having secured them tickets. Natasha felt no desire to go, but it was impossible for her to refuse her hostess's kindness, which had been designed expressly for her pleasure. When, after she was already dressed, and had gone into the parlor to wait for her father, she surveyed herself in the great pier-glass, and saw how pretty, how very pretty, she was, she felt even more melancholy than before, but her melancholy was mingled with a feeling of sweet and passionate love.

'*Bozhe moi!* if he were only here I should not be so stupidly shy before him as I was before. I would throw my arms around him and cling close to him, and make him look at me with those deep, penetrating eyes of his, with which he has so often looked at me; and then I would make him laugh, as he laughed then, and his eyes – how plainly I can see his eyes even now,' said Natasha to herself. 'And what do I care for his father and his sister? I love him. I love him, him alone, with his dear face and eyes, with his smile, like that of a man and like that of a child too. – No, it is better not to think about it, to forget him, and to forget that time, too, absolutely. I cannot endure this suspense. I shall be crying again,' – and she turned away from the mirror, exercising all her self-control not to burst into tears. 'And how can Sonya be so calm and unconcerned in her love for Nikolenka, and wait so long and patiently?' she wondered, as she saw her cousin coming toward her, also in full dress, and with her fan in her hand. 'No, she is entirely different from me. I cannot.'

Natasha at that moment felt herself so full of passion and tenderness that it was not enough to love, and to know that she was loved. What she wanted now, at this instant, was to throw her arms around her lover's neck, and speak to him, and hear him speak those words of love of which her heart was full.

As she rode along in the carriage, sitting next to her father, and dreamily looking at the lamp-lights that flashed through the frost-covered windows, she felt still deeper in love, and still more melancholy than ever, and she quite forgot with whom and where she was going.

Their carriage fell into the long line, and the wheels slowly creaked over the snow as they drew up to the steps of the theatre. The two girls gathered up their skirts and quickly jumped out; the count clambered down, supported by the footmen, and, making their way through the throng of ladies and gentlemen and programme-venders, the three went into the corridor that led to their box. Already the sounds of music were heard through the closed doors.

'Nathalie, your hair,' whispered Sonya in French. The *kapelldiener*, hastening past the ladies, politely opened their box door. The music sounded louder, the brightly lighted rows of boxes occupied by ladies with bared shoulders and arms, and the parterre filled with brilliant uniforms, dazzled their eyes. A lady who entered the adjoining box shot a glance of feminine envy at Natasha. The curtain was still down, and the orchestra was playing the overture.

Natasha, shaking out her train, went forward with Sonya and took her seat, glancing at the brightly lighted boxes on the opposite side of the house. The sensation, which she had not experienced for a long time, of having hundreds of eyes staring at her bare arms and neck, affected her all at once with mixed pleasure and discomfort, and called up a whole swarm of recollections, desires, and emotions associated with that sensation.

Natasha and Sonya, both remarkably pretty girls, and Count Ilya Andreyitch, who had not been seen for a long time in Moscow, naturally attracted general attention. Moreover, every one had a general notion that Natasha was engaged to marry Prince Andrei, and everybody knew that ever since the engagement the Rostofs had been residing at their country estate; therefore they looked with much curiosity at the 'bride' of one of the most desirable men in Russia.

Natasha's beauty, as everybody told her, had improved during their stay in the country, and that evening, owing to her excited state of mind, she was extraordinarily beautiful. No one could have failed to be struck by her exuberance of life and beauty, and her complete indifference to everything going on around her. Her dark eyes wandered over the throng, not seeking for any one in particular, and her slender arm, bare above the elbow, leaned on the velvet rim of the box, while, with evident unconsciousness of what she was doing, she crumpled her programme, folding and unfolding it in time with the orchestra.

'Look, there's Alenina,' said Sonya, 'with her mother, I think.'

'Saints! Mikhail Kiriluitch has grown fat, though,' exclaimed the old count.

'See, there's our Anna Mikhailovna. What kind of a head-dress has she on?'

'There are the Karagins, and Boris with them. Evidently enough, an engaged couple. – Drubetskoi must have proposed.'

'What! didn't you know it? 'Twas announced to-day,' said Shinshin, coming into their box.

Natasha looked in the same direction that her father was looking, and saw Julie, who, with a string of pearls around her fat red neck, – covered with powder, as Natasha knew well, – was sitting next her mother with a radiantly happy face. Behind them could be seen Boris's handsome head, with sleekly brushed hair. He was leaning over so that his ear was close to Julie's mouth, and as he looked askance at the Rostofs he was saying something to his 'bride'.

'They are talking about us, – about me,' thought Natasha, 'and she's probably jealous of me, and he is trying to calm her. They need not worry about it. If they only knew how little I cared about them!'

Behind them sat Anna Mikhailovna, festive and blissful, and wearing her habitual expression of utter resignation to God's will. Their box was redolent of that atmosphere characteristic of a newly engaged couple, which Natasha knew and loved so well. She turned away, and suddenly all the humiliating circumstances of her morning visit recurred to her memory.

'What right has he not to be willing to receive me as a relation? Akh! I'd best not think about this, at least not till *he* comes back,' said she to herself, and she began to scan the faces of strangers or acquaintances in the parterre.

In the front row, in the very middle of the house, leaning his back against the railing, stood Dolokhof in Persian costume, with his curly hair combed back into a strange and enormous ridge. He was standing in full view of the whole theatre, knowing that he was attracting the attention of everybody in the house, yet looking as unconcerned as though he were in the privacy of his own room. Around him were gathered a throng of the gilded youth of Moscow, and it was evident that he was their leader.

Count Ilya Andreyitch, with a smile, nudged the blushing Sonya, and called her attention to her former suitor.

'Did you recognize him? and where did he turn up from?' asked the count of Shinshin. 'He had disappeared entirely, had he not?'

'Yes, completely,' replied Shinshin. 'While he was in the Caucasus he deserted, and they say he became minister to some reigning prince in Persia. After that he killed the Shah's brother, and now all the young ladies of Moscow have lost their wits over him. *Dolohoff le Persan*, and that's the end of it. Here with us there's nothing to be done without Dolokhof. They swear by him. He is made a subject of invitation, as though he were a sterlet,' said Shinshin. 'Dolokhof and Anatol Kuragin have turned the heads of all our young ladies.'

Just then into the next box came a tall, handsome lady with a tremendous plait of hair, and a great display of plump white shoulders and neck, around which she wore a double string of large pearls. She was a long time in settling herself, with a great rustling of her stiff silk dress.

Natasha found herself involuntarily gazing at that neck, those shoulders and pearls, and that head-dress, and she was amazed at their beauty. Just as Natasha was taking a second look at her, the lady glanced round, and, fixing her eyes on Count Ilya Andreyitch, nodded her head and smiled.

It was the Countess Bezukhaya, Pierre's wife.

Ilya Andreyitch, who knew every one in society, leaned over and spoke with her. 'Have you been here long, countess?' he inquired. 'I'm coming in, I'm coming in soon to kiss your hand. I'm in town on business, and have got my girls with me. They say Semyonova plays her part superbly,' said Ilya Andreyitch. 'I hope Count Piotr Kirillovitch has not entirely forgotten us. Is he here?'

'Yes, he was intending to come,' said Ellen, and she gave Natasha a scrutinizing look.

Count Ilya Andreyitch again sat back in his place. 'Isn't she pretty, though?' asked he of Natasha.

'A perfect marvel,' replied the latter. 'I could understand falling in love with her.'

By this time the last notes of the overture were heard, and the baton of the kapellmeister rapped upon the stand. Those gentlemen who were in late slipped down to their places, and the curtain rose.

As soon as the curtain went up silence reigned in the parterre and the boxes, and all the gentlemen, young and old, whether in uniforms or in civilian's dress, and all the ladies, with precious stones glittering on their bare bosoms, with eager expectation turned their attention to the stage.

Natasha also tried to look.

Chapter IX

Smooth boards formed the centre of the stage, on the sides stood painted canvases representing trees, in the background a cloth was stretched out on boards, in the foreground girls in red bodices and white petticoats were sitting around. One, who was exceedingly stout, wore a white silk dress. She sat by herself on a low footstool, to the back of which was glued green cardboard. They were all singing something. After they had finished their chorus the girl in white advanced towards the prompter's box, and a man in silk tights on his stout legs, and with a feather and a dagger, joined her, and began to sing and wave his arms.

The man in the tights sang alone, then she sang, then they were both silent. The orchestra played, and the man began to turn down the fingers on the girl's hand, evidently waiting for the beat when they should begin to sing their parts together. They sang a duet, and then all in the audience began to clap and to shout, and the man and woman on the stage, who had been representing lovers, got up, smiling and letting go of hands, and bowed in all directions.

After her country life, and the serious frame of mind into which Natasha had lately fallen, all this seemed to her wild and strange. She was unable to follow the thread of the opera, and it was as much as she could do to listen to the music. She saw only painted canvas and oddly dressed men and women going through strange motions, talking and singing in a blaze of light. She knew what all this was meant to represent, but it all struck her as so affected, unnatural and absurd that some of the time she felt ashamed for the actors, and again she felt like laughing at them.

She looked around at the faces of the spectators, to see if she could detect in them any of this feeling of ridicule and perplexity which she felt; but all these faces were absorbed in what was taking place on the stage, or, as it seemed to Natasha, expressed a hypocritical enthusiasm.

'This must be, I suppose, very life-like,' said Natasha. She kept gazing now at those rows of pomaded heads in the parterre, then at the half-naked women in the boxes, and most of all at her neighbor Ellen, who, as undressed as she could well be, gazed with a faint smile of satisfaction at the stage, not dropping her eyes, conscious of the brilliant light that overflowed the auditorium, and the warm atmosphere, heated by the throng.

Natasha gradually began to enter into a state of intoxication which she had not experienced for a long time. She had no idea who she was, or where she was, or of what was going on before her. She gazed, and let her thoughts wander at will, and the strangest, most disconnected ideas flashed unexpectedly through her mind. Now she felt inclined to leap upon the edge of the box and sing the aria which the actress had just been singing, then she felt an impulse to tap with her fan a little old man who was sitting not far off, then again to lean over to Ellen and tickle her.

At one time, when there was perfect silence on the stage just before the beginning of an aria, the door that led into the parterre near where the Rostofs were seated creaked on its hinges, and a man who came in late was heard passing down to his seat.

'There goes Kuragin,' whispered Shinshin.

The Countess Bezukhaya turned her head and smiled at the new-comer. Natasha followed the direction of the Countess Bezukhaya's eyes, and saw an extraordinarily handsome adjutant, who, with an air of extreme self-confidence, but at the same time of good breeding, was just passing by their box.

This was Anatol Kuragin, whom she had seen and noticed some time before at a ball in Petersburg. He now wore his adjutant's uniform, with epaulet and shoulder-knot. He advanced with a supreme air of youthful gallantry, which would have been ludicrous had he not been so handsome, and had his handsome face not worn such an expression of cordial good humor and merriment.

Although it was during the act, he sauntered along the carpeted corridor, slightly jingling his spurs, and holding his perfumed, graceful head on high with easy grace. Glancing at Natasha, he joined his sister, laid his exquisitely gloved hand on the edge of her box, nodded to her, and bent over to ask some question in reference to Natasha.

'Mais charmante,' said he, evidently referring to her. She understood less from hearing his words than from the motion of his lips.

Then he went forward to the front row and took his seat near Dolokhof, giving him a friendly, careless nudge with his elbow, though the others treated him with such worshipful consideration. The other, with a merry lifting of the eyebrows, gave him a smile, and put up his foot against the railing.

'How like brother and sister are!' said the count; 'and how handsome they both are!'

Shinshin, in an undertone, began to tell the count some story about Kuragin's intrigues in Moscow, to which Natasha listened simply because he had spoken of her as charmante.

The first act was over. All in the parterre got up, mingled together, and began to go and come. Boris came to the Rostofs' box, received their congratulations very simply, and, smiling abstractedly and raising his brows, invited Natasha and Sonya, on behalf of his betrothed, to be present at their wedding, and then left them. Natasha, with a bright, coquettish smile, had talked with him and congratulated him on his engagement, although it was the same Boris with whom she had been in love only a short time before. This, in her intoxicated, excited state, seemed to her perfectly simple and natural.

The bare-bosomed Ellen sat near her, and showered her smiles indiscriminately on all, and in exactly the same way Natasha smiled on Boris.

Ellen's box was crowded by the most influential and witty men of the city, who also gathered around the front of it, on the parterre side vying with each other, apparently, in their desire to let it be known that they were acquainted with her.

Kuragin, throughout that entr'acte, stood with Lopukhof, with his back to the stage, in the very front row, and kept his eyes fixed on the

Rostofs' box. Natasha felt certain that he was talking about her, and it afforded her gratification. She even turned her head slightly, in a way which, in her opinion, best showed off the beauty of her profile.

Before the beginning of the second act, Pierre, whom the Rostofs had not seen since their arrival, made his appearance. His face wore an expression of sadness, and he was stouter than when Natasha had last seen him. Without recognizing any one, he passed down to the front row. Anatol joined him, and began to make some remark, looking and pointing to the Rostofs' box. A flash of animation passed over Pierre's face as he caught sight of Natasha, and he hastily made his way across through the seats to where she was. Then, leaning his elbows on the edge of her box, he had a long conversation with her.

While she was talking with Pierre she heard a man's voice in the Countess Bezukhaya's box, and something told her that it was Anatol Kuragin. She glanced round, and their eyes met. She almost smiled, and he looked straight into her eyes with such an admiring, tender gaze that it seemed to her strange to be so near him, to see him, to be so sure that she pleased him, and yet not to be acquainted with him!

In the second act the stage represented a cemetery, and there was a hole in the canvas, which represented the moon, and the footlights were turned down, and the horns and contrabasses began to play in very deep tones, and the stage was invaded from both sides by a throng of men in black mantles. These men began to wave their arms, brandishing what seemed to be daggers. Then some other men rushed forward, and proceeded to drag away by main force that damsel who, in the previous act, had been dressed in white, but was now in a blue dress. But before they dragged her away they sang with her for a long time, and at the sound of three thumps on something metallic behind the scenes all fell on their knees and began to sing a prayer. A number of times all these actions were interrupted by the enthusiastic plaudits of the spectators. Every time during this act that Natasha looked down into the parterre she saw Anatol Kuragin, with his arm carelessly thrown across the back of his seat, and gazing at her. It was pleasant for her to feel that she had so captivated him, and it never entered her head that in all this there was anything improper.

When the second act was over, the Countess Bezukhaya stood up, leaned over to the Rostofs' box, – thereby exposing her whole bosom, – beckoned the old count to come to her, and then, paying no heed to those who came to her box to pay her their homage, she began a smiling, confidential conversation with him.

'You must certainly make me acquainted with your charming girls,' said she; 'the whole city are talking about them, and I don't know them.'

Natasha got up and made a courtesy to this magnificent countess. The flattery of this brilliant beauty was so intoxicating to her that she blushed with pleasure and gratification.

'I mean to be a Muscovite also,' said Ellen. 'And aren't you ashamed of yourself, to hide such pearls in the country?'

The Countess Bezukhaya, by good rights, had the reputation of being a fascinating woman. She could say the opposite of what she thought, and could flatter in the most simple and natural manner.

'Now, my dear count, you must allow me to see something of your daughter. Though I don't expect to be here very long, – you don't either, I believe, – I shall try to make them have a good time. – I heard a good deal about you in Petersburg, and I wanted to make your acquaintance,' said she, turning to Natasha with her stereotyped, bewitching smile. 'I heard about you from my "page", Drubetskoi. – Have you heard, by the way, that he was engaged? – and from my husband's friend Bolkonsky, Prince Andrei Bolkonsky,' said she, with special emphasis, signifying thereby that she knew of his relations toward Natasha. Then she proposed that, in order to become better acquainted, one of the young ladies should come over into her box for the rest of the performance, and Natasha went.

During the third act the scene represented a palace, wherein many candles were blazing, while on the walls hung paintings representing full-bearded knights. In the centre stood, apparently, a tsar and tsaritsa. The tsar was gesticulating with his right hand, and, after singing something with evident timidity, and certainly very wretch-edly, he took his seat on a crimson throne.

The damsel, who at first had been dressed in white and then in blue, was now in nothing but a shift, with dishevelled hair, and stood near the throne. She was warbling some doleful ditty addressed to the tsaritsa, but the tsar peremptorily waved his hand, and from the side scenes came a number of bare-legged men and bare-legged women, and began to dance all together.

Then the fiddles played a very dainty and merry tune. One girl, with big bare legs and thin arms, coming out from among the others, went behind the scenes, and, having adjusted her corsage, came into the centre of the stage, and began to caper about and knock her feet together.

The whole parterre clapped their hands and shouted, 'Bravo!'

Then a man took his stand in one corner. The orchestra played louder than ever, with a clanging of cymbals and blare of horns, and this bare-legged man, alone by himself, began to make very high jumps and kick his feet together. This man was Duport, who earned sixty thousand rubles a year by his art. All in the parterre, in the boxes, and in the 'upper paradise' began to thump and shout with all their might, and the man paused and smiled, and bowed to all sides. Then some others danced, – bare-legged men and women; then one of the royal personages shouted something with musical accompaniment, and all began to sing. But suddenly a storm arose. Chromatic scales and diminished sevenths were heard in the orchestra, and all scattered behind the scenes, carrying off with them again one of those who was present, and the curtain fell.

Once more among the audience arose a terrible roar and tumult, and all, with enthusiastic faces, shouted at once, 'Duport! Duport! Duport!'

Natasha no longer looked upon this as strange or unusual. With a sense of satisfaction she looked around her, smiling joyously.

'*N'est-ce pas qu'il est admirable*, – Duport?' asked Ellen, turning to her.

'*Oh, oui!*' replied Natasha.

Chapter X

During the *entr'acte* a draught of cold air made its way into Ellen's box, as the door was opened and Anatol came in, bowing and trying not to disturb any one.

'Allow me to present my brother,' said Ellen, uneasily glancing from Natasha to Anatol.

Natasha turned her pretty, graceful head toward the handsome young man, and smiled at him over her shoulder. Anatol, who was as fine-looking near at hand as he was at a distance, sat down by her and said that he had been long wishing for the pleasure of her acquaintance, – ever since the Naruishkins' ball, where he had seen her, and never forgotten her.

Kuragin was far cleverer and less affected with women than he was in the society of men. He spoke fluently and simply, and Natasha had a strange and agreeable feeling of ease in the company of this man, about whom so many rumors were current. He was not only not terrible, but his face even wore a naïve, jolly, and good-natured smile.

Kuragin asked her how she enjoyed the play, and told her how Semyonova, at the last performance, had gotten a fall while on the stage.

'Do you know, countess,' said he, suddenly addressing her as though she were an old acquaintance, 'we have been arranging a fancy-dress party. You ought to take part in it. It will be very jolly. We shall all rendezvous at the Karagins'. Please come, won't you?' he insisted.

In saying this he did not once take his smiling eyes from her face, her neck, her naked arms. Natasha was not left in doubt of the fact that he admired her. This was agreeable, but somehow she felt constrained and troubled by his presence. When she was not looking at him she was conscious that he was staring at her shoulders, and she involuntarily tried to catch his eyes, so that he might rather fix them on her face. But while she thus looked him in the eyes she had a terrified consciousness that that barrier of modesty, which, she had always felt before, kept other men at a distance, was down between him and her. Without being in the least able to explain it, she was conscious within five minutes that she was on a dangerously intimate footing with this man. She nervously turned a little, for fear he might put his hand on her bare arm, or kiss her on the neck. They talked about the simplest matters, and yet she felt that they were more intimate than she had ever been with any other man. She looked at Ellen and at her father, as though asking them what this all meant; but Ellen was busily engaged in conversation with some general, and paid no heed to her imploring look, and her father's said nothing more to her than what it always said: 'Happy? Well, I am glad of it.'

During one of those moments of constraint, while Anatol's prominent eyes were calmly and boldly surveying her, Natasha, in order to break the silence, asked him how he liked Moscow. Natasha asked the question and blushed. It seemed to her all the time that she was doing something unbecoming in talking with him. Anatol smiled, as though to encourage her.

'At first I was not particularly charmed with Moscow, because what a city ought to have, to be agreeable, is pretty women; isn't that so?

Well, now I like it very much,' said he, giving her a significant look. 'Will you come to our party, countess? Please do,' said he; and, stretching out his hand toward her bouquet, and lowering his voice, he added in French, 'You will be the prettiest. Come, my dear countess, and, as a pledge, give me that flower.'

Natasha did not realize what he was saying any more than he did, but she had a consciousness that in his incomprehensible words there was an improper meaning. She knew not what reply to make, and turned away, pretending not to have heard him. But the instant that she turned away the thought came to her that he was there behind her, and so near.

'What is he doing now? Is he ashamed of himself? Is he angry? Is it my business to make amends?' she asked herself. She could not refrain from glancing round.

She looked straight into his eyes, and his nearness and self-possession, and the good-natured warmth of his smile, overcame her.

She gave him an answering smile, and gazed straight into his eyes, and once more she realized, with the feeling of horror, that there was no barrier between them.

The curtain again went up. Anatol left the box, calm and serene. Natasha rejoined her father in her own box, but already she was under the dominion of this world into which she had entered. Everything that passed before her eyes now seemed to her perfectly natural, while all her former thoughts concerning her lover, and the Princess Mariya, and her life in the country, vanished from her mind as though all that had taken place long, long ago.

In the fourth act there was a strange kind of devil, who sang and gesticulated until a trap beneath him was opened, and he disappeared. This was all that Natasha noticed during the fourth act. Something agitated and disturbed her, and the cause of this annoyance was Kuragin, at whom she could not help looking.

When they left the theatre Anatol joined them, summoned their carriage, and helped them to get seated. As he was assisting Natasha he squeezed her arm above the elbow. Startled and blushing she looked at him. His brilliant eyes returned her gaze, and he gave her a tender smile.

Not until she reached home was Natasha able clearly to realize all that had taken place, and when she suddenly remembered Prince Andrei she was horror-struck; and as they all sat drinking tea she groaned aloud, and, flushing scarlet, ran from the room.

'My God! I am lost,' she said to herself. 'How could I have let it go so far?' she wondered. Long she sat hiding her flushed face in her hands, striving to give herself a clear account of what had happened to her, and she could not do so, nor could she explain her feelings. Everything seemed to her dark, obscure, and terrible.

Then, in that huge, brilliant auditorium, where Duport, with his bare legs and his spangled jacket, capered about on the dampened stage to the sounds of music, and the girls and the old men and Ellen much *decolletée*, with her calm and haughty smile, were all applauding and enthusiastically shouting bravo, – there, under the protection of this same Ellen, everything was perfectly clear and simple; but now, alone by herself, it became incomprehensible.

'What does it mean? What means this fear that I experience in his presence? What mean these stings of conscience which I experience now?' she asked herself.

If only her mother had been there Natasha would have made confession of all her thoughts, before going to bed that night. She knew that Sonya, with her strict and wholesome views, would either entirely fail to understand, or would be horrified by, her confession. Natasha accordingly tried, by her own unaided efforts, to settle the question that tormented her.

'Have I really forfeited Prince Andrei's love, or not?' she asked herself, and then, with a re-assuring smile, she replied to her own question: 'What a fool I am to ask this! What is the sense of it? None! I have done nothing. I was not to blame for this. No one will know about it, and I shall not see him any more,' said she to herself. 'Of course it is evident no harm has been done; there's nothing to repent of, and no reason why Prince Andrei should not love me *just as I am*. But what do I mean by just as I am? O my God! my God! why is he not here?'

Natasha grew calm for an instant, but then some instinct told her that, even though nothing had happened and no harm had been done, still the first purity of her love for Prince Andrei was destroyed.

And once more she let her imagination bring up her whole conversation with Kuragin, and she recalled his face and his motions, and the tender smile that this handsome, impudent man had given her after he had squeezed her arm.

War and Peace, 1863–9
tr. Nathan Haskell Dole

'Glib divisions, French spies, and figure dancers'
RICHARD BRINSLEY SHERIDAN

Mrs Dangle. Yes; but wasn't the farce damned, Mr Dangle? And to be sure it is extremely pleasant to have one's house made the motley rendezvous of all the lackeys of literature; the very high 'Change of trading authors and jobbing critics! – Yes, my drawing-room is an absolute register-office for candidate actors, and poets without character. – Then to be continually alarmed with misses and ma'ams piping hysteric changes on Juliets and Dorindas, Pollys and Ophelias; and the very furniture trembling at the probationary starts and unprovoked rants of would-be Richards and Hamlets! – And what is worse than all, now that the manager has monopolized the Opera House, haven't we the signors and signoras calling here, sliding their smooth semibreves, and gargling glib divisions in their outlandish throats – with foreign emissaries and French spies, for aught I know, disguised like fiddlers and figure dancers?

The Critic, 1779

'Jacinta, broody at the Royal Theatre, Madrid'
BENITO PÉREZ GALDÓS

Their season ticket for an orchestra box at the Royal Theater was Don Baldomero's idea; he couldn't have cared less about going to the opera, but he wanted Barbarita to go to them so that when they were retiring, or after they were already in bed, she could relate to him what she had seen at that 'fabulous coliseum.' It just so happened that she didn't find the Royal particularly exciting either, but she gladly accepted so that Jacinta could go. Jacinta, in turn, wasn't much of a theater-goer, but she was delighted to be able to take her unmarried sisters to the Royal; if it weren't for her, she knew they'd never get a glimpse of a stage. Juan, who was very fond of music, had reserved a box higher up and close to the stage where he sat with six friends at all performances.

The Santa Cruz women didn't dress conspicuously for the theater. Any looks in their direction were intended for the younger chicks, symmetrically arranged in the most noticeable seats. Barbarita usually sat in the front row so that she could aim her opera glasses squarely at the audience and be able to tell Baldomero something more than the details of the opera's plot and the stage effects. The two married sisters, Candelaria and Benigna, went from time to time. Jacinta went almost always, but it wasn't much fun for her. Pampered by our good Lord, who had surrounded her with tenderness and well-being and ensconced her in a most healthy, appealing, and serene environment (unusual in this valley of tears), she nevertheless used to say in a plaintive tone that she 'didn't enjoy anything.' She, who was envied by everyone, envied any poor barefoot beggarwoman she saw go by with a bundle, a little suckling wrapped in rags. Her eyes followed children in whatever shape or form they took, whether they were rich ones dressed in sailor suits and led along by an English nanny, or runny-nosed poor ones wrapped in yellow flannel, dirty, with dandruff in their hair and a crust of drooly bread in their hand. She didn't yearn for just one; she wanted to be surrounded by a whole mob, from the talkative and mischievous five-year-old scamp down to the babe in arms who spends the day laughing like a fool, guzzling milk, and making a fist.

Fortunata y Jacinta, 1886–7
tr. Agnes Moncy Gullón

'Playing Marguerite to a real-life Faust'
OUIDA

'Can you not sleep? do not stare so with your great eyes!' said Prince Zouroff angrily to his wife, as the night train rushed through the heart of France, and Vere gazed out over the snow-whitened moonlit country, as the land and the sky seemed to fly past her.

In another carriage behind her was her great jewel box, set between two servants, whose whole duty was to guard it.

But she never thought of her jewels; she was thinking of the moth and the star; she was thinking of the summer morning on the white cliff of the sea. For she knew that Corrèze was in Paris.

It was not any sort of love that moved her, beyond such lingering charmed fancy as remained from those few hours' fascination. But a great reluctance to see him, a great fear of seeing him, was in her. What could he think of her marriage! And she could never tell him why she had married thus. He would think her sold like the rest, and he must be left to think so.

The express train rushed on through the cold calm night. With every moment she drew nearer to him – the man who had bidden her keep herself 'unspotted from the world'.

'And what is my life,' she thought, 'except one long pollution!'

She leaned her white cheek and her fair head against the window, and gazed out at the dark flying masses of the clouds; her eyes were full of pain, wide opened, lustrous; and, waking suddenly and seeing her thus opposite him, her husband called to her roughly and irritably with an oath: 'Can you not sleep?'

It seemed to her as if she never slept now. What served her as sleep seemed but a troubled, feverish dull trance, disturbed by hateful dreams.

It was seven o'clock on the following evening when they arrived in Paris. Their carriage was waiting, and she and Madame Nélaguine drove homeward together, leaving Zouroff to follow them. There was a faint light of an aurora borealis in the sky, and the lamps of the streets were sparkling in millions; the weather was very cold. Their coachman took his way past the opera-house. There were immense crowds and long lines of equipages.

In large letters in the strong gaslight it was easy to read upon the placards.

'*Faust* . . . Corrèze.'

The opera was about to commence.

Vere shrank back into the depths of the carriage. Her companion leaned forward and looked out into the night.

'Paris is so fickle; but there is one sovereign she never tires of – it is Corrèze,' said Madame Nélaguine, with a little laugh, and wondered to see the colourless cheek of her young sister-in-law flush suddenly and then grow white again.

33

'Have you ever heard Corrèze sing?' she asked quickly. Vere hesitated.

'Never in the opera. No.'

'Ah! to be sure, he left Russia suddenly last winter; left as you entered it,' said Madame Nélaguine, musing, and with a quick side-glance.

Vere was silent.

The carriage rolled on, and passed into the courtyard of the Hotel Zouroff between the gilded iron gates, at the instant when the applause of Paris welcomed upon the stage of its opera its public favourite.

The house was grand, gorgeous, brilliant; adorned in the taste of the Second Empire, to which it belonged; glittering and overladen, superb yet meretricious. The lines of servants were bowing low; the gilded gasaliers were glowing with light, there were masses of camellias and azaleas, beautiful and scentless, and heavy odours of burnt pastilles on the heated air.

Vere passed up the wide staircase slowly, and the hues of its scarlet carpeting seemed like fire to her tired eyes.

She changed her prison-house often, and each one had been made more splendid than the last, but each in its turn was no less a prison; and its gilding made it but the more dreary and the more oppressive to her.

'You will excuse me, I am tired,' she murmured to her sister-in-law, who was to be her guest, and she went into her own bed-chamber and shut herself in, shutting out even her maid from her solitude.

Through the curtained windows there came a low muffled sound; the sound of the great night-world of that Paris to which she had come, heralded for her beauty by a thousand tongues.

Why could she not be happy?

She dropped on her knees by her bed of white satin, embroidered with garlanded roses, and let her head fall on her arms, and wept bitterly.

In the opera-house the curtain had risen, and the realisation of all he had lost was dawning upon the vision of Faust.

The voice of her husband came to her through the door.

'Make your toilette rapidly,' he said; 'we will dine quickly; there will be time to show yourself at the opera.'

Vere started and rose to her feet.

'I am very tired; the journey was long.'

'We will not stay,' answered Prince Zouroff. 'But you will show yourself. Dress quickly.'

'Would not another night —'

'*Ma chère*, do not dispute. I am not used to it.'

The words were slight, but the accent gave them a cold and hard command, to which she had grown accustomed.

She said nothing more, but let her maid enter by an inner door.

The tears were wet on her lashes, and her mouth still quivered. The woman saw and pitied her, but with some contempt.

'Why do you lament like that?' the woman thought; 'why not amuse yourself?'

Her maids were used to the caprices of Prince Zouroff, which made his wife's toilette a thing which must be accomplished to perfection in almost a moment of time. A very young and lovely woman, also, can be more easily adorned than one who needs a thousand artificial aids. They dressed her very rapidly in white velvet, setting some sapphires and diamonds in her bright hair.

'Give me that necklace,' she said, pointing to one of the partitions in one of the open jewel cases; it was the necklace of the moth and the star.

In ten minutes she descended to dinner. She and her husband were alone. Madame Nélaguine had gone to bed fatigued.

He ate little, but drank much, though one of the finest artists of the Paris kitchens had done his best to tempt his taste with the rarest and most delicate combination.

'You do not seem to have much appetite,' he said, after a little while. 'We may as well go. You look very well now.'

He looked at her narrowly.

Fatigue conquered, and emotion subdued, had given an unusual brilliancy to her eyes, an unusual flush to her cheeks. The white velvet was scarcely whiter than her skin; about her beautiful throat the moth trembled between the flame and the star.

'Have you followed my advice and put some rouge?' he asked suddenly.

Vere answered simply, 'No.'

'Paris will say that you are handsomer than any of the others,' he said carelessly. 'Let us go.'

Vere's cheeks flushed more deeply as she rose in obedience. She knew that he was thinking of all the other women whom Paris had associated with his name.

She drew about her a cloak of white feathers, and went to her carriage. Her heart was sick, yet it beat fast. She had learned to be quite still, and to show nothing that she felt under all pain; and this emotion was scarcely pain, this sense that so soon the voice of Corrèze would reach her ear.

She was very tired; all the night before she had not slept: the fatigue and feverishness of the long unbroken journey were upon her, making her temples throb, her head swim, her limbs feel light as air. But the excitement of one idea sustained her, and made her pulses quicken with fictitious strength: so soon she would hear the voice of Corrèze.

A vague dread, a sense of apprehension that she could not have explained, were upon her; yet a delighted expectation came over her also, and was sweeter than any feeling that had ever been possible to her since her marriage.

As their carriage passed through the streets, her husband smoked a cigarette, and did not speak at all. She was thankful for the silence, though she fancied in it he must hear the loud fast beating of her heart.

It was ten o'clock when they reached the opera-house. Her husband gave her his arm, and they passed through the vestibule and passage, and up the staircase to that door which at the commencement of the season had been allotted to the name of Prince Zouroff.

The house was hushed; the music, which has all the ecstasy and the mystery of human passion in it, thrilled through the stillness. Her husband took her through the corridor into their box, which was next that which had once been the empress's. The vast circle of light seemed to whirl before her eyes.

Vere entered as though she were walking in her sleep, and sat down.

On the stage there were standing alone Margherita and Faust.

The lights fell full upon the classic profile of Corrèze, and his eyelids were drooped, as he stood gazing on the maiden who knelt at his feet. The costume he wore showed his graceful form to its greatest advantage, and the melancholy of wistful passion that was expressed on his face at that moment made his beauty of feature more impressive. His voice was silent at that moment when she saw him thus once more, but his attitude was a poem, his face was the face that she had seen by sunlight where the sweetbriar sheltered the thrush.

Not for her was he Faust, not for her was he the public idol of Paris. He was the Saint Raphael of the Norman seashore. She sat like one spellbound gazing at the stage.

Then Corrèze raised his head, his lips parted, and uttered the

> Tu vuoi, ahime!
> Che t' abbandoni.

It thrilled through the house, that exquisite and mysterious music of the human voice, seeming to bring with it the echo of a heaven for ever lost.

Women, indifferent to all else, would weep when they heard the voice of Corrèze.

Vere's heart stood still; then seemed to leap in her breast as with a throb of new warm life. Unforgotten, unchanged, unlike any other ever heard on earth, this perfect voice fell on her ear again, and held her entranced with its harmony. The ear has its ecstasy as have other senses, and this ecstasy for the moment held in suspense all other emotion, all other memory.

She sat quite motionless, leaning her cheek upon her hand. When he sang, she only then seemed herself to live; when his voice ceased, she seemed to lose hold upon existence, and the great world of light around her seemed empty and mute.

Many eyes were turning on her, many tongues were whispering of her, but she was unconscious of them. Her husband, glancing at her, thought that no other woman would have been so indifferent to the stare of Paris as she was; he did not know that she was insensible of it; he only saw that she had grown very pale again, and was annoyed, fearing that her entry would not be the brilliant success that he desired it to be.

'Perhaps she was too tired to come here,' he thought with some impatience.

But Paris was looking at her in her white velvet, which was like the snows she had quitted, and was finding her lovely beyond compare, and worthy of the wild rumours of adoration that had come before her from the north.

The opera, meanwhile, went on its course; the scenes changed, the third act ended, the curtain fell, the theatre resounded with the polite applause of a cultured city.

She seemed to awake as from a dream. The door had opened, and her husband was presenting some great persons to her.

'You have eclipsed even Corrèze, Princess,' said one of these. 'In looking at you, Paris forgot for once to listen to its nightingale; it was fortunate for him, since he sung half a note false.'

'Since you are so tired we will go,' said her husband, when the fourth act was over; when a score of great men had bowed themselves in and out of her box, and the glasses of the whole house had been levelled at the Russian beauty, as they termed her.

'I am not so very tired now!' she said wistfully.

She longed to hear that voice of Faust as she had never longed for anything.

'If you are not tired you are capricious, *ma chère*,' said her husband, with a laugh. 'I brought you here that they might see you; they have seen you; now I am going to the club. Come.'

He wrapped her white feathery mantle round her, as though it were snow that covered her, and took her away from the theatre as the curtain rose.

He left her to go homeward alone, and went himself to the Rue Scribe.

She was thankful.

'You sang false, Corrèze!' said mocking voices of women gaily round him in the *foyer*. He was so eminent, so perfect, so felicitously at the apex of his triumph and of art, that a momentary failure could be made a jest of without fear.

'Pardieu!' said Corrèze, with a shrug of his shoulders. 'Pardieu! do you suppose I did not know it? A fly flew in my throat. I suppose it will be in all the papers to-morrow. That is the sweet side of fame.'

He shook himself free of his tormentors, and went to his brougham as soon as his dress was changed. It was only one o'clock, and he had all Paris ready to amuse him.

But he felt out of tone and out of temper with all Paris; another half-note false and Paris would hiss him – even him.

He went home to his house in the Avenue Marigny, and sent his coachman away.

'The beast!' he said to himself, as he entered his chamber; he was thinking of Sergius Zouroff. He threw himself down in an easy chair, and sat alone lost in thought; whilst a score of supper-tables were the duller for his absence, and more than one woman's heart ached, or passion fretted, at it.

'Who would have thought the sight of her would have moved me so!' he said to himself in self-scorn. 'A false note! – I!'

Moths, 1880

'The public viewed as gargoyles and waxworks'
LORD BERNERS

He went outside and stood on the theatre steps near the entrance. He felt himself once more a mere cipher in his own glory.

It was the close of a fine summer day and the sky was still bright. Sunlight shone into the portico and lit up the faces of the people. Made up for artificial light most of the women resembled garish waxworks and the men in their evening dress had an unnatural, self-conscious air like guests at a foreign wedding.

Crowds, especially when struggling to get somewhere, never give a very flattering impression of humanity, and every face seemed to bear the stamp of folly or unpleasantness. Presumably most of them were cultured people, many of them ornaments of society, members of the élite. And these were the people, Emanuel reflected, on whose verdict the life of a work of art depended. Immortal fame seemed hardly worth striving for. Better to live for a few years obscurely in the heart of a friend than for ever in the memories of such people as these. The type, he feared, would persist until the final cataclysm came to sweep away humanity itself and all the fruits of human endeavour. He felt a sudden desire to fly from the town and bury himself far off in the country.

Count Omega, 1941

'Gino and Lucia disturb memories of Charlie's Aunt'
E. M. FORSTER

Philip found a certain grace and lightness in his companion which he had never noticed in England. She was appallingly narrow, but her consciousness of wider things gave to her narrowness a pathetic charm. He did not suspect that he was more graceful too. For our vanity is such that we hold our own characters immutable, and we are slow to acknowledge that they have changed, even for the better.

Citizens came out for a little stroll before dinner. Some of them stood and gazed at the advertisements on the tower.

'Surely that isn't an opera-bill?' said Miss Abbott.

Philip put on his pince-nez. ' "*Lucia di Lammermoor*. By the Master Donizetti. Unique representation. This evening." '

'But is there an opera? Right up here?'

'Why, yes. These people know how to live. They would sooner have a thing bad than not have it at all. That is why they have got to have so much that is good. However bad the performance is tonight, it will be alive. Italians don't love music silently, like the beastly Germans. The audience takes its share – sometimes more.'

'Can't we go?'

He turned on her, but not unkindly. 'But we're here to rescue a child!'

He cursed himself for the remark. All the pleasure and the light went out of her face, and she became again Miss Abbott of Sawston – good, oh, most undoubtedly good, but most appallingly dull. Dull and remorseful: it is a deadly combination, and he strove against it in vain, till he was interrupted by the opening of the dining-room door.

They started as guiltily as if they had been flirting. Their interview had taken such an unexpected course. Anger, cynicism, stubborn morality – all had ended in a feeling of goodwill towards each other and towards the city which had received them. And now Harriet was here – acrid, indissoluble, large; the same in Italy as in England – changing her disposition never, and her atmosphere under protest.

Yet even Harriet was human, and the better for a little tea. She did not scold Philip for finding Gino out, as she might reasonably have done. She showered civilities on Miss Abbott, exclaiming again and again that Caroline's visit was one of the most fortunate coincidences in the world. Caroline did not contradict her.

'You see him tomorrow at ten, Philip. Well, don't forget the blank cheque. Say an hour for the business. No, Italians are so slow; say two. Twelve o'clock. Lunch. Well – then it's no good going till the evening train. I can manage the baby as far as Florence –'

'My dear sister, you can't run on like that. You don't buy a pair of gloves in two hours, much less a baby.'

'Three hours, then, or four; or make him learn English ways. At Florence we get a nurse –'

'But, Harriet,' said Miss Abbott, 'what if at first he was to refuse?'

'I don't know the meaning of the word,' said Harriet impressively. 'I've told the landlady that Philip and I only want our rooms one night, and we shall keep to it.'

'I dare say it will be all right. But, as I told you, I thought the man I met on the Rocca a strange, difficult man.'

'He's insolent to ladies, we know. But my brother can be trusted to bring him to his senses. That woman, Philip, whom you saw will carry the baby to the hotel. Of course you must tip her for it. And try, if you can, to get poor Lilia's silver bangles. They were nice quiet things, and will do for Irma. And there is an inlaid box I lent her – lent, not gave – to keep her handkerchiefs in. It's of no real value; but this is our only chance. Don't ask for it; but if you see it lying about, just say –'

'No, Harriet; I'll try for the baby, but for nothing else. I promise to do that tomorrow, and to do it in the way you wish. But tonight, as we're all tired, we want a change of topic. We want relaxation. We want to go to the theatre.'

'Theatre? Here? And at such a moment?'

'We should hardly enjoy it, with the great interview impending,' said Miss Abbott, with an anxious glance at Philip.

He did not betray her, but said, 'Don't you think it's better than sitting in all the evening and getting nervous?'

His sister shook her head. 'Mother wouldn't like it. It would be most unsuitable – almost irreverent. Besides all that, foreign theatres are notorious. Don't you remember those letters in the *Church Family Newspaper*?'

'But this is an opera – *Lucia di Lammermoor* – Sir Walter Scott – classical, you know.'

Harriet's face grew resigned. 'Certainly one has so few opportunities of hearing music. It is sure to be very bad. But it might be better than sitting idle all the evening. We have no books, and I lost my crochet at Florence.'

'Good. Miss Abbott, you are coming too?'

'It is very kind of you, Mr Herriton. In some ways I should enjoy it; but – excuse the suggestion – I don't think we ought to go to cheap seats.'

'Good gracious me!' cried Harriet, 'I should never have thought of that. As likely as not, we should have tried to save money and sat among the most awful people. One keeps on forgetting this is Italy.'

'Unfortunately I have no evening dress; and if the seats –'

'Oh, that'll be all right,' said Philip, smiling at his timorous, scrupulous womenkind. 'We'll go as we are, and buy the best we can get. Monteriano is not formal.'

So this strenuous day of resolutions, plans, alarms, battles, victories, defeats, truces, ended at the opera. Miss Abbott and Harriet were both a little shamefaced. They thought of their friends at Sawston, who were supposing them to be now tilting against the powers of evil. What would Mrs Herriton, or Irma, or the curates at the Back Kitchen say if they could see the rescue-party at a place of amusement on the very first day of its mission? Philip, too, marvelled at his wish to go. He began to see that he was enjoying his time in Monteriano, in spite of the tiresomeness of his companions and the occasional contrariness of himself.

He had been to this theatre many years before, on the occasion of a performance of *La Zia di Carlo* (*Charley's Aunt*, 1892) a popular farce by Brandon Thomas. Since then it had been thoroughly done up, in the tints of the beetroot and the tomato, and was in many other ways a credit to the little town. The orchestra had been enlarged, some of the boxes had terracotta draperies, and over each box was now suspended an enormous tablet, neatly framed, bearing upon it the number of that box. There was also a drop-scene, representing a pink and purple landscape, wherein sported many a lady lightly clad, and two more ladies lay along the top of the proscenium to steady a large and pallid clock. So rich and so appalling was the effect that Philip could scarcely suppress a cry. There is something majestic in the bad taste of Italy; it is not the bad taste of a country which knows no better; it has not the nervous vulgarity of England, or the blinded vulgarity of Germany. It observes beauty, and chooses to pass it by. But it attains to beauty's confidence. This tiny theatre of Monteriano spraddled and swaggered with the best of them, and these ladies with their clock would have nodded to the young men on the ceiling of the Sistine.

Philip had tried for a box, but all the best were taken; it was rather a grand performance, and he had to be content with stalls. Harriet was fretful and insular. Miss Abbott was pleasant, and insisted on praising everything; her only regret was that she had no pretty clothes with her.

'We do all right,' said Philip, amused at her unwonted vanity.

'Yes, I know; but pretty things pack as easily as ugly ones. We had no need to come to Italy like guys.'

This time he did not reply, 'But we're here to rescue a baby.' For he saw a charming picture, as charming a picture as he had seen for years – the hot red theatre; outside the theatre, towers and dark gates and medieval walls; beyond the walls, olive-trees in the starlight and white winding roads and fireflies and untroubled dust; and here in the middle of it all Miss Abbott, wishing she had not come looking like a guy. She had made the right remark. Most undoubtedly she had made the right remark. This stiff surburban woman was unbending before the shrine.

'Don't you like it all?' he asked her.

'Most awfully.' And by this bald interchange they convinced each other that Romance was here.

Harriet, meanwhile, had been coughing ominously at the drop-scene, which presently rose on the grounds of Ravenswood, and the chorus of Scotch retainers burst into cry. The audience accompanied with tappings and drummings, swaying in the melody like corn in the wind. Harriet, though she did not care for music, knew how to listen to it. She uttered an acid 'Shish!'

'Shut it,' whispered her brother.

'We must make a stand from the beginning. They're talking.'

'It is tiresome,' murmured Miss Abbott; 'but perhaps it isn't for us to interfere.'

Harriet shook her head and shished again. The people were quiet, not because it is wrong to talk during a chorus, but because it is natural to be civil to a visitor. For a little time she kept the whole house in order, and could smile at her brother complacently.

Her success annoyed him. He had grasped the principle of opera in Italy – it aims not at illusion but at entertainment – and he did not want this great evening party to turn into a prayer-meeting. But soon the boxes began to fill, and Harriet's power was over. Families greeted each other across the auditorium. People in the pit hailed their brothers and sons in the chorus, and told them how well they were singing. When Lucia appeared by the fountain there was loud applause, and cries of 'Welcome to Monteriano!'

'Ridiculous babies!' said Harriet, settling down in her stall.

'Why, it is the famous hot lady of the Apennines,' cried Philip; 'the one who had never, never before –'

'Ugh! Don't. She will be very vulgar. And I'm sure it's even worse here than in the tunnel. I wish we'd never –'

Lucia began to sing, and there was a moment's silence. She was stout and ugly; but her voice was still beautiful, and as she sang the theatre murmured like a hive of happy bees. All through the coloratura she was accompanied by sighs, and its top note was drowned in a shout of universal joy.

So the opera proceeded. The singers drew inspiration from the audience, and the two great sextets were rendered not unworthily. Miss Abbott fell into the spirit of the thing. She, too, chatted and laughed and applauded and encored, and rejoiced in the existence of beauty. As for Philip, he forgot himself as well as his mission. He was not even an enthusiastic visitor. For he had been in this place always. It was his home.

Harriet, like M. Bovary on a more famous occasion, was trying to follow the plot. Occasionally she nudged her companions, and asked them what had become of Walter Scott. She looked round grimly. The audience sounded drunk, and even Caroline, who never took a drop, was swaying oddly. Violent waves of excitement, all arising from very little, went sweeping round the theatre. The climax was reached in the mad scene. Lucia, clad in white, as befitted her malady, suddenly gathered up her streaming hair and bowed her acknowledgements to the audience. Then from the back of the stage – she feigned not to see it – there advanced a kind of bamboo clothes-horse, stuck all over with bouquets. It was very ugly, and most of the flowers in it were false. Lucia knew this, and so did the audience; and they all knew that the clothes-horse was a piece of stage property, brought in to make the performance go year after year. None the less did it unloose the great deeps. With a scream of amazement and joy she embraced the animal, pulled out one or two practicable blossoms, pressed them to her lips, and flung them into her admirers. They flung them back, with loud melodious cries, and a little boy in one of the stage-boxes snatched up his sister's carnations and offered them. 'Che carino!' exclaimed the singer. She darted at the little boy and kissed him. Now the noise became tremendous. 'Silence! Silence!' shouted many old gentlemen behind. 'Let the divine creature continue!' But the young men in the adjacent box were imploring Lucia to extend her civility to them. She refused, with a humorous expressive gesture. One of them hurled a bouquet at her. She spurned it with her foot. Then,

44

encouraged by the roars of the audience, she picked it up and tossed it to them. Harriet was always unfortunate. The bouquet struck her full in the chest, and a little *billet-doux* fell out of it into her lap.

'Call this classical?' she cried, rising from her seat. 'It's not even respectable! Philip! Take me out at once.'

'Whose is it?' shouted her brother, holding up the bouquet in one hand and the *billet-doux* in the other. 'Whose is it?'

The house exploded, and one of the boxes was violently agitated, as if someone was being hauled to the front. Harriet moved down the gangway, and compelled Miss Abbott to follow her. Philip, still laughing and calling 'Whose is it?' brought up the rear. He was drunk with excitement. The heat, the fatigue and the enjoyment had mounted into his head.

'To the left!' the people cried. 'The innamorato is to the left.'

He deserted his ladies and plunged towards the box. A young man was flung stomach downwards across the balustrade. Philip handed him up the bouquet and the note. Then his own hands were seized affectionately. It all seemed quite natural.

'Why have you not written?' cried the young man. 'Why do you take me by surprise?'

'Oh, I've written,' said Philip hilariously. 'I left a note this afternoon.'

'Silence! Silence!' cried the audience, who were beginning to have enough. 'Let the divine creature continue.' Miss Abbott and Harriet had disappeared.

'No! No!' cried the young man. 'You don't escape me now.' For Philip was trying feebly to disengage his hands. Amiable youths bent out of the box and invited him to enter it.

'Gino's friends are ours –'

'Friends?' cried Gino. 'A relative! A brother! Fra Filippo, who has come all the way from England and never written.'

'I left a message.'

The audience began to hiss.

'Come in to us.'

'Thank you – ladies – there is not time –'

The next moment he was swinging by his arms. The moment after he shot over the balustrade into the box. Then the conductor, seeing that the incident was over, raised his baton. The house was hushed, and Lucia di Lammermoor resumed her song of madness and death.

Philip had whispered introductions to the pleasant people who had pulled him in – tradesmen's sons perhaps they were, or medical students, or solicitors' clerks, or sons of other dentists. There is no knowing who is who in Italy. The guest of the evening was a private soldier. He shared the honour now with Philip. The two had to stand side by side in the front, and exchange compliments, whilst Gino presided, courteous, but delightfully familiar. Philip would have a spasm of horror at the muddle he had made. But the spasm would pass, and again he would be enchanted by the kind, cheerful voices, the laughter that was never vapid, and the light caress of the arm across his back.

He could not get away till the play was nearly finished, and Edgardo was singing amongst the tombs of his ancestors. His new friends hoped to see him at the Garibaldi tomorrow evening. He promised; then he remembered that if they kept to Harriet's plan he would have left Monteriano. 'At ten o'clock, then,' he said to Gino. 'I want to speak to you alone. At ten.'

'Certainly!' laughed the other.

Miss Abbott was sitting up for him when he got back. Harriet, it seemed, had gone straight to bed.

'That was he, wasn't it?' she asked.

'Yes, rather.'

'I suppose you didn't settle anything?'

'Why, no; how could I? The fact is – well, I got taken by surprise, but after all, what does it matter? There's no earthly reason why we shouldn't do the business pleasantly. He's a perfectly charming person, and so are his friends. I'm his friend now – his long-lost brother. What's the harm? I tell you, Miss Abbott, it's one thing for England and another for Italy. There we plan and get on high moral horses. Here we find what asses we are, for things go off quite easily, all by themselves. My hat, what a night! Did you ever see a really purple sky and really silver stars before? Well, as I was saying, it's absurd to worry; he's not a pawky father. He wants that baby as little as I do. He's been ragging my dear mother – just as he ragged me eighteen months ago, and I've forgiven him. Oh, but he has a sense of humour!'

Where Angels Fear to Tread, 1905

'Ortrud's dressing-gown, corset and "Jewish impudence"'
HEINRICH MANN

Lady Fortune, who had of late been toying capriciously with their existence, led them one evening to a production of *Lohengrin*. Both of their mothers had to agree to stay home; the engaged couple had made up their minds to disregard propriety and sit alone in a proscenium box. The wide, red plush sofa against the wall, where one could sit and not be seen, was caved-in and spotted, which lent it a charmingly dubious air. Guste claimed to know that this box actually belonged to the officers, who received visits here from actresses!

'We've put the actresses safely behind us,' Diederich declared, and he hinted that until recently, with a certain lady from the theater, whose name of course he could not mention, he had—. Guste's feverish questions were interrupted in time by the conductor's tapping. They took their seats.

'Hänisch has become even flabbier,' Guste remarked at once, nodding down towards the conductor. Upon Diederich he made a highly artistic yet unhealthy impression. He kept time with all his limbs, with straggly locks of black hair flying about his large gray face, upon which pendulous sacks of fat jiggled in unison, while rhythmic undulations could be seen under his coat and trousers. The orchestra was in full swing, but Diederich nevertheless made it clear that he set no store by overtures. Guste remarked that this was nothing compared to the productions of *Lohengrin* put on in Berlin! The curtain rose, and already she was giggling disparagingly. 'Heavens, look at Ortrud! She's wearing a dressing gown and a corset!' Diederich was paying more attention to the King under the oak tree, by all appearances the most prominent personality. His bearing did not give a particularly dashing impression; Wulckow made decidedly better use of his bass voice and beard. His words, however, were perfectly sound from a national point of view. 'To defend the Empire's honor, in the East and in the West.' Bravo! Every time he sang the word 'German' he thrust his hand upward, and the music, for its part, substantiated the sentiment. In other respects as well the music underscored vigorously what one was supposed to hear. Vigorous, that was the word. Diederich wished he had had such music when he gave his speech in the sewer debate. The sight of the herald, on the other hand, put him in a melancholy mood, for he bore an uncanny resemblance to Fatty Delitzsch in all his bygone beery guilelessness. This discovery prompted Diederich to take a closer look at the faces of the other vassals, and he found Neo-Teutons everywhere. Their paunches and beards had grown considerably, and they had clad themselves against the tough times in plate armor. It also seemed that not all of them had attained favorable positions in life; the noblemen looked like mid-level public servants of the middle ages, with leathery faces and knock-knees, and those of lesser birth looked even less dashing, but relations with them would most certainly have been carried out in the most impeccable form. Indeed, Diederich noticed from the very beginning that he felt quite at home in this opera. Shields and swords, lots of clanking armor, patriotic sentiments, 'Ha!' and 'Hail!' and upraised banners and the German Oak Tree. It nearly made one want to play along.

The feminine half of Brabant society, however, left much to be desired. Guste posed derisive questions: now which is the one with whom he—? 'Maybe that nanny goat there in the off-the-shoulder dress? Or the fat cow with the gold hoops between her horns?' And Diederich was on the verge of deciding that the black-haired lady with the corset was the one for him when he noticed in time that she was the very one who did not appear in an irreproachable light in the whole affair. Her husband Telramund seemed at first to have a passable sense of form, but a highly unsavory bit of gossip entered the picture here as well. Alas! German loyalty was threatened even here, where it appeared in all its glory, by the Jewish machinations of the dark-haired race. Elsa's appearance removed all doubt as to which side could truly be characterized by the notion of class. The worthy King need not have handled the matter with such objectivity; Elsa's decidedly Germanic cast, her flowing blond hair, the deportment so becoming of her race offered from the beginning certain guarantees. Diederich caught her eye, she looked up, she smiled sweetly. At this point he reached for the opera glass, but Guste snatched it away. 'So it's Merée, isn't it?' she hissed, and as he smiled suggestively: 'You certainly have fine tastes, I can consider myself flattered. That scrawny little Jew!' – 'Jew?' – 'Merée, of course, everyone knows her name is Meseritz, and she's forty years old.' – He sheepishly took the glass that Guste offered him with a smirk, and saw for himself. Oh well, the world of appearances. Disappointed, Diederich settled back in his seat. Nevertheless, he could not prevent Elsa's chaste presentiment of feminine sensuality from touching him every bit as deeply as it did the King and the noblemen. He, too, deemed the ordeal a superbly practical solution; it insured that no one would be compromised. That the noblemen would never agree to take part in such shady business was of course quite predictable. One had to expect something extraordinary. The music did its part; it prepared one, so to speak, for whatever might come. Diederich's mouth hung open and his eyes shone with such vacuous rapture that Guste had to suppress convulsions of laughter. Now he was ready, everyone was ready, and Lohengrin could make his appearance. He came, he sparkled, he sent away the enchanted swan, he sparkled even more entrancingly. Vassals, noblemen, and King all succumbed to the same astonishment that befell Diederich. Higher powers did not exist for nothing ... Indeed, the highest power of all was embodied here, glaring enchantingly. Be it the helmet of the swan or that of the eagle: Elsa knew very well why she fell plump upon her knees before him. Diederich, for his part, glared at Guste, who immediately swallowed her laughter. She too had learned what it was like to be the subject of everyone's gossip and to be rid of the first one and not to be able to show one's face anywhere and to really have no choice but to leave town: but then the hero and savior appeared and ignored all the gossip and offered his hand in spite of it all! 'So shall it be!' said Diederich and nodded down toward the kneeling Elsa – while Guste, with downcast eyes, sank against his shoulder in contrite submission.

The subsequent events could be counted on one's fingers.

Telramund brought himself into sheer disgrace. No one undertook the slightest action against the powers-that-be. Toward their representative, Lohengrin, even the King behaved at best like one of the more prominent territorial sovereigns. He joined in the chorus of voices singing the hymn of victory to his superior. The stronghold of sound opinions was extolled with fervor, and the revolutionaries were admonished to shake the German dust from their slippers.

The second act – Guste, in quiet devotion, was still eating one praline after another – illustrated in an edifying manner the contrast between the splendid festivities being celebrated without a trace of discord by those of sound opinion in the elegantly illuminated halls of the palace, and the two dark insurgents reclining in abject squalor on the cobblestones. 'Arouse thyself, o comrade in disgrace!' Diederich was certain he himself had uttered this at some fitting opportunity. He associated Ortrud with certain personal memories: a vulgar little tramp, what more could one say? But something moved in him when she beguiled her man and wrapped him around her finger. He dreamed ... Ortrud had a definite edge on Elsa, the silly goose, with whom she did what she pleased; she had that certain something possessed by all assertive and severe women. Elsa, to be sure, was a woman one could marry. He stole a glance at Guste. 'There can be joy without regret,' remarked Elsa, and Diederich to Guste: 'I should certainly hope so.'

The well-rested noblemen and vassals were then informed by Fatty Delitzsch that, by the grace of God, they now had a new sovereign. Only yesterday they had stood by Telramund, loyal and true; today they were true and loyal subjects of Lohengrin. They allowed themselves no opinion and swallowed everything placed before them. 'We'll bring the *Reichstag* around to that point before long,' Diederich vowed.

When Ortrud wanted to enter the cathedral ahead of Elsa, however, Guste was incensed. 'That really isn't necessary, I hate it when she does that. Especially since she hasn't anything left, and just on general principle.' – 'Jewish impudence,' Diederich muttered. Furthermore, he could not help but find it imprudent, to put it mildly, of Lohengrin to place it so clearly within Elsa's power to determine whether or not he should divulge his name and thereby place the whole deal at risk. One ought never to give women such power. Why would one want to? The last thing he needed to do was to prove to the vassals that he, in spite of the grumbler Telramund, had clean hands and a clean scutcheon: their patriotic opinions were marred not by the least bit of wariness.

Guste promised him that in the third act would come the loveliest part, but she would simply have to have more pralines. When these had been duly procured, the strains of the Wedding March began to swell, and Diederich sang along. The vassals in the wedding pro-cession suffered a considerable loss of dash appearing without their armor and banners; Lohengrin, too, would have been better off not showing up in a doublet. At the sight of him Diederich was inspired anew with a sense for the value of a uniform. Happily, the ladies had made their exit, with their voices like sour milk. But the King! He simply could not tear himself away from the presence of the newlywed couple; he tried to ingratiate himself with them and seemed to have no greater wish than to stay on as a spectator. Diederich, who had found the King far too conciliatory all along, now simply called him a nincompoop.

Finally he found the door, and Lohengrin and Elsa on the sofa busied themselves with 'the bliss that only God bestows'. At first, their embraces involved only the upper body; the lower parts sat as far from one another as possible. The more they sang, however, the closer they sidled up to each other – whereby their faces turned frequently toward Hähnisch. Hähnisch and his orchestra seemed to fan the flame of their passion: it was understandable, for Diederich and Guste as well in their quiet box panted softly and cast each other burning glances. Their feelings were swept along in the wake of the enchanting tones that Hähnisch teased forth with flailing limbs, and their hands followed in turn. Diederich let his slide down between Guste's seat and her back, he encircled her below and murmured in rapture: 'The first time I saw that, I said to myself, she's the one!'

But just then they were wrenched from this magical spell by an incident which seemed destined to occupy Netzig's art lovers for quite some time hence. Lohengrin showed his undershirt! He was just striking up 'Do you not breathe the same sweet scents as I,' when there it came, out of the back of his doublet, which had popped open. Until a visibly perturbed Elsa managed to button him up again, the audience stirred with restless agitation, only to succumb once more to the magical spell. Guste, to be sure, who had choked on a praline, was struck with a thought. 'How long has he been wearing that undershirt? And anyway, he hasn't got anything with him, the swan swam off with all his luggage!' Diederich reprimanded her sternly for having dared to think. 'You're every bit the silly goose that Elsa is,' he declared. For Elsa was on the verge of spoiling everything because she could not keep herself from asking Lohengrin about his political secrets. The revolution was utterly crushed, for Telramund's cowardly assassination attempt failed by the grace of God; but the women, as Diederich had to admit to himself, had an even greater subversive potential when one did not keep a tight rein on them.

After the transfiguration scene, this became clear beyond all doubt. Oak tree, banners, all the patriotic accoutrements were there again, and 'For German soil the German sword, thus is the Empire's power restored:' bravo! But Lohengrin really did seem determined to withdraw from public life. 'Doubt was cast upon me from all sides,' he too could rightfully say. He raised his voice in accusation against the dead Telramund and the unconscious Elsa. Since neither of them contradicted him, he would most certainly have been vindicated in the end, but what was more, he did indeed stand at the top of the ranking. For now he revealed himself. The very mention of his name threw the assembly, who had never heard of him before, into riotous commotion. The vassals were beside themselves with excitement; they seemed to have been prepared for anything but the fact that his name was Lohengrin. With all the more fervor they entreated their beloved sovereign to refrain just this once from the fateful step of abdication. But Lohengrin remained hoarse and unapproachable. Besides, the swan was waiting. One last bit of impudence on the part of Ortrud turned out to be her undoing, to the general satisfaction of all present. Unfortunately, Elsa herself sank to the battlefield immediately thereafter. Upon all of this Lohengrin turned his back and departed, drawn not by the disenchanted swan, but by a muscular dove. His place was taken by the young, newly arrived Gottfried, who became the third sovereign in so many days to whom the nobles and vassals, loyal and worthy as ever, knelt down and paid homage.

'That's what comes of it all,' remarked Diederich, helping Guste into her coat. All of these catastrophes, which were the fundamental emanations of Power itself, had left him feeling edified and deeply satisfied. 'That's what comes of what?' Guste demanded to know, feeling contentious. 'Just because she wants to know who he is? She has every right to ask that, it's a matter of common decency.' – 'There is a higher meaning to it all,' Diederich explained to her with severity. 'The business with the Grail, that's supposed to mean that the highest sovereign is responsible, after God, only to his own conscience. And we in turn are responsible to him. When the interest of His Majesty is at stake, I don't care what the circumstances are; I'm not saying anything, but if it comes down to it,—' He indicated with a gesture that he too, if he were to find himself in such a predicament, would sacrifice Guste without a second thought. This incensed Guste. 'Why that's murder! Why should I have to pay with my life just because Lohengrin is an apathetic old sheep? Elsa couldn't even get a rise out of him on their wedding night!' And with that, Guste turned up her nose, just as she had done when she walked out of the Cabinet of Love, where nothing had happened either.

The couple made up on the way home. 'This is the art we need!'

cried Diederich. 'This is German art!' For here, he felt, all patriotic demands were fulfilled, in the words as well as in the music. Rebellion was tantamount to crime in this world. The existing, the legitimate were celebrated with splendor; the highest value was placed on nobility and on the grace of God; and the masses, a chorus perpetually surprised by the events which transpired, surged willingly into battle against the enemies of their lords. The warlike underpinnings and the mystical spires, both of these were thus maintained. Furthermore, it struck a familiar and reassuring chord that in this world the man was the one more richly endowed with beauty and favor. 'I feel my heart begin to melt, when I behold this delightful man,' as the men sang together with the King. Thus was the music, for its part, full of manly bliss, heroic in its luxuriance and patriotic even in its ardor. Who could resist? A thousand performances of such an opera, and there would be no one left who was not nationally disposed! Diederich pronounced: 'The theater is one of my weapons as well!' A lèse-majesté trial would be hard put to rouse the citizens so thoroughly from their slumber. 'I may have sent Lauer to prison, but I take my hat off to the man who wrote *Lohengrin*.' He proposed a telegram of approval to Wagner. Guste had to explain to him that this was no longer possible. Having once embarked on such a lofty flight of thought, Diederich began to expound upon art in general. There existed among the various arts an order of precedence. 'The highest is music, and for this reason it is the German art. And then comes drama.'

'Why?' asked Guste.

'Because it can be set to music sometimes, and because you don't have to read it, and, well,—'

'And what comes after that?'

'Portraiture, of course, because of the portraits of the Emperors. The rest isn't so important.'

'And the novel?'

'That's no art. At least not a German art, thank God. The name alone tells you that.'

The Loyal Subject, 1919
tr. Ernest Boyd and Daniel Theisen

'Family trees and female form in the Academy boxes'
EDITH WHARTON

On a January evening of the early seventies, Christine Nilsson was singing in *Faust* at the Academy of Music in New York.

Though there was already talk of the erection, in remote metropolitan distances 'above the Forties,' of a new Opera House which should compete in costliness and splendor with those of the great European capitals, the world of fashion was still content to reassemble every winter in the shabby red and gold boxes of the sociable old Academy. Conservatives cherished it for being small and inconvenient, and thus keeping out the 'new people' whom New York was beginning to dread and yet be drawn to; and the sentimental clung to it for its historic associations, and the musical for its excellent acoustics, always so problematic a quality in halls built for the hearing of music.

It was Madame Nilsson's first appearance that winter, and what the daily press had already learned to describe as 'an exceptionally brilliant audience' had gathered to hear her, transported through the slippery, snowy streets in private broughams, in the spacious family landau, or in the humbler but more convenient 'Brown *coupé*.' To come to the Opera in a Brown *coupé* was almost as honorable a way of arriving as in one's own carriage; and departure by the same means had the immense advantage of enabling one (with a playful allusion to democratic principles) to scramble into the first Brown conveyance in the line, instead of waiting till the cold-and-gin congested nose of one's own coachman gleamed under the portico of the Academy. It was one of the great livery-stableman's most masterly intuitions to have discovered that Americans want to get away from amusement even more quickly than they want to get to it.

When Newland Archer opened the door at the back of the club box the curtain had just gone up on the garden scene. There was no reason why the young man should not have come earlier, for he had dined at seven, alone with his mother and sister, and had lingered afterward over a cigar in the Gothic library with glazed black-walnut bookcases and finial-topped chairs which was the only room in the house where Mrs Archer allowed smoking. But, in the first place, New York was a metropolis, and perfectly aware that in metropolises it was 'not the thing' to arrive early at the Opera; and what was or was not 'the thing' played a part as important in Newland Archer's New York as the inscrutable totem terrors that had ruled the destinies of his forefathers thousands of years ago.

The second reason for his delay was a personal one. He had dawdled over his cigar because he was at heart a dilettante, and thinking over a pleasure to come often gave him a subtler satisfaction than its realization. This was especially the case when the pleasure was a delicate one, as his pleasures mostly were; and on this occasion the moment he looked forward to was so rare and exquisite in quality that – well, if he had timed his arrival in accord with the prima donna's stage-manager he could not have entered the Academy at a more significant moment than just as she was singing: 'He loves me – he loves me not – *he loves me!*' and sprinkling the falling daisy petals with notes as clear as dew.

She sang, of course, '*M'ama!*' and not 'He loves me,' since an unalterable and unquestioned law of the musical world required that the German text of French operas sung by Swedish artists should be translated into Italian for the clearer understanding of English-speaking audiences. This seemed as natural to Newland Archer as all the other conventions on which his life was moulded: such as the duty of using two silver-backed brushes with his monogram in blue enamel to part his hair, and of never appearing in society without a flower (preferably a gardenia) in his buttonhole.

'*M'ama ... non m'ama ...*,' the prima donna sang, and '*M'ama!*,' with a final burst of love triumphant, as she pressed the dishevelled daisy to her lips and lifted her large eyes to the sophisticated countenance of the little brown Faust-Capoul, who was vainly trying, in a tight purple velvet doublet and plumed cap, to look as pure and true as his artless victim.

Newland Archer, leaning against the wall at the back of the club box, turned his eyes from the stage and scanned the opposite side of the house. Directly facing him was the box of old Mrs Manson Mingott, whose monstrous obesity had long since made it impossible for her to attend the Opera, but who was always represented on fashionable nights by some of the younger members of the family. On this occasion, the front of the box was filled by her daughter-in-law, Mrs Lovell Mingott, and her daughter, Mrs Welland; and slightly withdrawn behind these brocaded matrons sat a young girl in white with eyes ecstatically fixed on the stage-lovers. As Madame Nilsson's '*M'ama!*' thrilled out above the silent house (the boxes always stopped talking during the Daisy Song) a warm pink mounted to the girl's cheek, mantled her brow to the roots of her fair braids, and suffused the young slope of her breast to the line where it met a modest tulle tucker fastened with a single gardenia. She dropped her eyes to the immense bouquet of lilies-of-the-valley on her knee, and Newland Archer saw her white-gloved finger tips touch the flowers softly. He drew a breath of satisfied vanity and his eyes returned to the stage.

No expense had been spared on the setting, which was acknowledged to be very beautiful even by people who shared his acquaintance with the Opera houses of Paris and Vienna. The foreground, to the footlights, was covered with emerald green cloth. In the middle distance symmetrical mounds of woolly green moss bounded by croquet hoops formed the base of shrubs shaped like orange-trees but studded with large pink and red roses. Gigantic pansies, considerably larger than the roses, and closely resembling the floral penwipers made by female parishioners for fashionable clergymen, sprang from the moss beneath the rose-trees; and here and there a daisy grafted on a rose-branch flowered with a luxuriance prophetic of Mr Luther Burbank's far-off prodigies.

In the center of this enchanted garden Madame Nilsson, in white cashmere slashed with pale blue satin, a reticule dangling from a blue girdle, and large yellow braids carefully disposed on each side of her muslin chemisette, listened with downcast eyes to M. Capoul's impassioned wooing, and affected a guileless incomprehension of his designs whenever, by word or glance, he persuasively indicated the ground floor window of the neat brick villa projecting obliquely from the right wing.

'The darling!' thought Newland Archer, his glance flirting back to the young girl with the lilies-of-the-valley. 'She doesn't even guess what it's all about.' And he contemplated her absorbed young face with a thrill of possessorship in which pride in his own masculine initiation was mingled with a tender reverence for her abysmal purity. 'We'll read *Faust* together ... by the Italian lakes...' he thought, somewhat hazily confusing the scene of his projected honeymoon with the masterpieces of literature which it would be his manly privilege to reveal to his bride. It was only that afternoon that May Welland had let him guess that she 'cared' (New York's consecrated phrase of maiden avowal), and already his imagination, leaping ahead of the engagement ring, the betrothal kiss and the march from *Lohengrin*, pictured her at his side in some scene of old European witchery.

He did not in the least wish the future Mrs Newland Archer to be a simpleton. He meant her (thanks to his enlightening companionship) to develop a social tact and readiness of wit enabling her to hold her own with the most popular married women of the 'younger set,' in which it was the recognized custom to attract masculine homage while playfully discouraging it. If he had probed to the bottom of his vanity (as he sometimes nearly did) he would have found there the wish that his wife should be as worldly-wise and as eager to please as the married lady whose charms had held his fancy through two mildly agitated years; without, of course, any hint of the frailty which had so nearly marred that unhappy being's life, and had disarranged his own plans for a whole winter.

How this miracle of fire and ice was to be created, and to sustain itself in a harsh world, he had never taken the time to think out; but he was content to hold his view without analyzing it, since he knew it was that of all the carefully-brushed, white-waistcoated, buttonhole-flowered gentlemen who succeeded each other in the club box, exchanged friendly greetings with him, and turned their opera glasses critically on the circle of ladies who were the product of the system. In matters intellectual and artistic Newland Archer felt himself distinctly the superior of these chosen specimens of old New York gentility; he had probably read more, thought more, and even seen a good deal more of the world, than any other man of the number. Singly they betrayed their inferiority; but grouped together they represented 'New York,' and the habit of masculine solidarity made him accept their doctrine on all the issues called moral. He instinctively felt that in this respect it would be troublesome – and also rather bad form – to strike out for himself.

'Well – upon my soul!' exclaimed Lawrence Lefferts, turning his opera glass abruptly away from the stage. Lawrence Lefferts was, on the whole, the foremost authority on 'form' in New York. He had probably devoted more time than anyone else to the study of this intricate and fascinating question; but study alone could not account for his complete and easy competence. One had only to look at him, from the slant of his bald forehead and the curve of his beautiful fair moustache to the long patent-leather feet at the other end of his lean and elegant person, to feel that the knowledge of 'form' must be congenital in anyone who knew how to wear such good clothes so carelessly and carry such height with so much lounging grace. As a young admirer had once said of him: 'If anybody can tell a fellow just when to wear a black tie with evening clothes and when not to, it's Larry Lefferts.' And on the question of pumps versus patent-leather 'Oxfords' his authority had never been disputed.

'My God!' he said; and silently handed his glass to old Sillerton Jackson.

Newland Archer, following Lefferts's glance, saw with surprise that his exclamation had been occasioned by the entry of a new figure into old Mrs Mingott's box. It was that of a slim young woman, a little less tall than May Welland, with brown hair growing in close curls about her temples and held in place by a narrow band of diamonds. The suggestion of this headdress, which gave her what was then called a 'Josephine look,' was carried out in the cut of the dark blue velvet gown rather theatrically caught up under her bosom by a girdle with a large old-fashioned clasp. The wearer of this unusual dress, who seemed quite unconscious of the attention it was attracting, stood a moment in the center of the box, discussing with Mrs Welland the propriety of taking the latter's place in the front right-hand corner; then she yielded with a slight smile, and seated herself in line with Mrs Welland's sister-in-law, Mrs Lovell Mingott, who was installed in the opposite corner.

Mr Sillerton Jackson had returned the opera glass to Lawrence Lefferts. The whole of the club turned instinctively, waiting to hear what the old man had to say; for old Mr Jackson was as great an authority on 'family' as Lawrence Lefferts was on 'form.' He knew all the ramifications of New York's cousinships; and could not only elucidate such complicated questions as that of the connection between the Mingotts (through the Thorleys) with the Dallases of South Carolina, and that of the relationship of the elder branch of Philadelphia Thorleys to the Albany Chiverses (on no account to be confused with the Manson Chiverses of University Place), but could also enumerate the leading characteristics of each family: as, for instance, the fabulous stinginess of the younger lines of Leffertses (the Long Island ones); or the fatal tendency of the Rushworths to make foolish matches; or the insanity recurring in every second generation of the Albany Chiverses, with whom their New York cousins had always refused to intermarry – with the disastrous exception of poor Medora Mason, who, as everybody knew ... but then her mother was a Rushworth.

In addition to this forest of family trees, Mr Sillerton Jackson carried between his narrow hollow temples, and under his soft thatch of silver hair, a register of most of the scandals and mysteries that had smouldered under the unruffled surface of New York society within the last fifty years. So far indeed did his information extend, and so acutely retentive was his memory, that he was supposed to be the only man who could have told you who Julius Beaufort, the banker, really was, and what had become of handsome Bob Spicer, old Mrs Manson Mingott's father, who had disappeared so mysteriously (with a large sum of trust money) less than a year after his marriage, on the very day that a beautiful Spanish dancer who had been delighting thronged audiences in the old Opera-house on the Battery had taken ship for Cuba. But these mysteries, and many others, were closely locked in Mr Jackson's breast; for not only did his keen sense of honor forbid his repeating anything privately imparted, but he was fully aware that his reputation for discretion increased his opportunities of finding out what he wanted to know.

The club box, therefore, waited in visible suspense while Mr Sillerton Jackson handed back Lawrence Lefferts's opera glass. For a moment he silently scrutinized the attentive group out of his filmy blue eyes overhung by old veined lids; then he gave his moustache a thoughtful twist, and said simply: 'I didn't think the Mingotts would have tried it on.'

The Age of Innocence, 1920

'Tristan and Albertine make an ulterior unity'
MARCEL PROUST

Taking advantage of the fact that I still was alone, and drawing the curtains together so that the sun should not prevent me from reading the notes, I sat down at the piano, opened at random Vinteuil's sonata which happened to be lying there, and began to play; seeing that Albertine's arrival was still a matter of some time but was on the other hand certain, I had at once time to spare and peace of mind. Lulled by the confident expectation of her return escorted by Françoise and by the assurance of her docility as by the blessedness of an inner light as warming as the light of the sun, I could dispose of my thoughts, detach them for a moment from Albertine, apply them to the sonata. I did not even go out of my way to notice how, in the latter, the combination of the sensual and the anxious motifs corresponded more closely now to my love for Albertine, from which jealousy had been for so long absent that I had been able to confess to Swann my ignorance of that sentiment. No, approaching the sonata from another point of view, regarding it in itself as the work of a great artist, I was carried back upon the tide of sound to the days at Combray – I do not mean Montjouvain and the Méséglise way, but to my walks along the Guermantes way – when I myself had longed to become an artist. In abandoning that ambition *de facto*, had I forfeited something real? Could life console me for the loss of art? Was there in art a more profound reality, in which our true personality finds an expression that is not afforded it by the activities of life? For every great artist seems so different from all the rest, and gives us so strongly that sensation of individuality for which we seek in vain in our everyday existence! Just as I was thinking thus, I was struck by a passage in the sonata. It was a passage with which I was quite familiar, but sometimes our attention throws a different light upon things which we have known for a long time and we remark in them what we have never seen before. As I played the passage, and although Vinteuil had been trying to express in it a fancy which would have been wholly foreign to Wagner, I could not help murmuring 'Tristan,' with the smile of an old family friend discovering a trace of the grandfather in an intonation, a gesture of the grandson who has never set eyes on him. And as the friend then examines a photograph which enables him to specify the likeness, so, on top of Vinteuil's sonata, I set up on the music-rest the score of *Tristan*, a selection from which was being given that afternoon, as it happened, at a Lamoureux concert. In admiring the Bayreuth master, I had none of the scruples of those who, like Nietzsche, are bidden by a sense of duty to shun in art as in life the beauty that tempts them, and who, tearing themselves from *Tristan* as they renounce *Parsifal*, and, in their spiritual asceticism, progressing from one mortification to another, succeed, by following the most bloody of the stations of the cross, in exalting themselves to the pure cognition and perfect adoration of *Le Postillon de*

Longjumeau. I was struck by how much reality there is in the work of Wagner as I contemplated once more those insistent, fleeting themes which visit an act, recede only to return again and again, and, sometimes distant, dormant, almost detached, are at other moments, while remaining vague, so pressing and so close, so internal, so organic, so visceral, that they seem like the reprise not so much of a musical motif as of an attack of neuralgia.

Music, very different in this respect from Albertine's society, helped me to descend into myself, to discover new things: the variety that I had sought in vain in life, in travel, but a longing for which was none the less renewed in me by this sonorous tide whose sunlit waves now came to expire at my feet. A twofold diversity. As the spectrum makes visible to us the composition of light, so the harmony of a Wagner, the colour of an Elstir, enable us to know that essential quality of another person's sensations into which love for another person does not allow us to penetrate. Then a diversity inside the work itself, by the sole means that exist of being effectively diverse: to wit, combining diverse individualities. Where a minor composer would claim to be portraying a squire, or a knight, while making them both sing the same music, Wagner on the contrary allots to each separate appellation a different reality, and whenever a squire appears, it is an individual figure, at once complicated and simplified, that, with a joyous, feudal clash of warring sound, inscribes itself in the vast tonal mass. Whence the plenitude of a music that is indeed filled with so many different strains, each of which is a person. A person or the impression that is given us by a momentary aspect of nature. Even that which, in this music, is most independent of the emotion that it arouses in us preserves its outward and absolutely precise reality; the song of a bird, the call of a hunter's horn, the air that a shepherd plays upon his pipe, each carves its silhouette of sound against the horizon. True, Wagner would bring them forward, appropriate them, introduce them into an orchestral whole, make them subservient to the highest musical concepts, but always respecting their original nature, as a carpenter respects the grain, the peculiar essence of the wood that he is carving.

But notwithstanding the richness of these works in which the contemplation of nature has its place alongside the action, alongside the individuals who are not merely the names of characters, I thought how markedly, all the same, these works partake of that quality of being – albeit marvellously – always incomplete, which is the characteristic of all the great works of the nineteenth century, that century whose greatest writers somehow botched their books, but, watching themselves work as though they were at once workman and judge, derived from this self-contemplation a new form of beauty, exterior and superior to the work itself, imposing on it a retroactive unity, a grandeur which it does not possess. Without pausing to consider the man who belatedly saw in his novels a *Human Comedy*, or those who entitled heterogeneous poems or essays *The Legend of the Centuries* or *The Bible of Humanity*, can we not say none the less of the last of these that he so admirably personifies the nineteenth century that the greatest beauties in Michelet are to be sought not so much in his work itself as in the attitudes that he adopts towards his work, not in his *History of France* nor in his *History of the Revolution*, but in his prefaces to those books? Prefaces, that is to say pages written after the books themselves, in which he considers the books, and with which we must include here and there certain sentences beginning as a rule with a: 'Dare I say?' which is not a scholar's precaution but a musician's cadence. The other musician, he who was delighting me at this moment, Wagner, retrieving some exquisite fragment from a drawer of his writing-table to introduce it, as a retrospectively necessary theme, into a work he had not even thought of at the time he composed it, then having composed a first mythological opera, and a second, and afterwards others still, and perceiving all of a sudden that he had written a tetralogy, must have felt something of the same exhilaration as Balzac when the latter, casting over his books the eye at once of a stranger and of a father, finding in one the purity of Raphael, in another the simplicity of the Gospel, suddenly decided, shedding a retrospective illumination upon them, that they would be better brought together in a cycle in which the same characters would reappear, and touched up his work with a swift brush-stroke, the last and the most sublime. An ulterior unity, but not a factitious one, otherwise it would have crumbled into dust like all the other systematisations of mediocre writers who with copious titles and sub-titles give themselves the appearance of having pursued a single and transcendent design. Not factitious, perhaps indeed all the more real for being ulterior, for being born of a moment of enthusiasm when it is discovered to exist among fragments which need only to be joined together; a unity that was unaware of itself, hence vital and not logical, that did not prohibit variety, dampen invention. It emerges (but applied this time to the work as a whole) like such and such a fragment composed separately, born of an inspiration, not required by the artificial development of a thesis, which comes to be integrated with the rest. Before the great orchestral movement that precedes the return of Isolde, it is the work itself that has attracted towards itself the half-forgotten air of a shepherd's pipe. And, no doubt, just as the orchestra swells and surges at the approach of the ship, when it takes hold of these notes of the pipe, transforms them, imbues them with its own intoxication, breaks their rhythm, clarifies their tonality, accelerates their movement, expands their instrumentation, so no doubt Wagner himself was filled with joy when he discovered in his memory the shepherd's tune, incorporated it in his work, gave it its full wealth of meaning. This joy moreover never forsakes him. In him, however great the melancholy of the poet, it is consoled, transcended – that is to say, alas, to some extent destroyed – by the exhilaration of the fabricator. But then, no less than by the similarity I had remarked just now between Vinteuil's phrase and Wagner's, I was troubled by the thought of this Vulcan-like skill. Could it be this that gave to great artists the illusory aspect of a fundamental, irreducible originality, apparently the reflexion of a more than human reality, actually the result of industrious toil? If art is no more than that, it is no more real than life and I had less cause for regret. I went on playing *Tristan*. Separated from Wagner by the wall of sound, I could hear him exult, invite me to share his joy, I could hear the immortally youthful laughter and the hammer-blows of Siegfried ring out with redoubled vigour; but the more marvellously those phrases were struck, the technical skill of the craftsman served merely to make it easier for them to leave the earth, birds akin not to Lohengrin's swan but to that aeroplane which I had seen at Balbec convert its energy into vertical motion, glide over the sea and vanish in the sky. Perhaps, as the birds that soar highest and fly most swiftly have more powerful wings, one of these frankly material vehicles was needed to explore the infinite, one of these 120 horse-power machines – the Mystère model – in which nevertheless, however high one flies, one is prevented to some extent from enjoying the silence of space by the overpowering roar of the engine!

A la recherche du temps perdu: La Prisonnière, 1924
tr. Scott Moncrieff and Kilmartin, revised D. J. Enright

'A friendship based on disagreeing about Karajan'
THOMAS BERNHARD

Whenever my musical thought was nearly dead inside me I merely had to visit Paul for it to revive. The poor chap, I thought, is locked up in the Ludwig Pavilion, maybe even in a straitjacket, and he would so much like to be at the opera. He was the most enthusiastic opera-goer Vienna had ever had, that is well known to the initiates. He was the opera buff who, even after his total impoverishment and finally also embitterment, which was inevitable, treated himself to a daily visit to the opera, day after day, at least with a standing-room ticket, terminally sick he stood through six hours of *Tristan* and at the end still had the strength to burst into shouts of Bravo or whistles like no one else before or after him at the House on the Ringstrasse. He was feared as a first-nighter. With his enthusiasm, because he came out with it a few seconds ahead of the rest, he would sweep the whole opera house along. On the other hand his first whistles would scuttle the greatest and most expensive productions because *he* so wished it, because *he* happened to be in that mood. I can make a success when I want to and when the conditions for it are ripe and these are always ripe, he would say, and I can equally make a total flop when the conditions for it are ripe and these are always ripe: when I am the first to shout Bravo or the first to whistle. For decades the Viennese failed to notice that the author of their operatic triumphs had ultimately been Paul, just as he was the author of the flops at the House on the Ringstrasse, flops which, if *he* wanted it to be so, could not have been more radical or more disastrous. But his pro or contra at the opera house had nothing to do with objectivity, only with his capriciousness, with his fickleness, with his madness. Many conductors whom he could not stand had fallen into his trap in Vienna and he had whistled and booed them out, actually foaming at the mouth. Only with Karajan, whom he hated, did he fail. Karajan's genius was too great to be even irritated by Paul. I have watched and studied Karajan for decades and to me he is the most important conductor of the century, along with Schuricht whom I *loved*; Karajan I have *admired*, I have to admit, ever since childhood, and always ranked him at least as high as any musician with whom Karajan ever worked. Paul hated Karajan with all the means at his disposal and out of accustomed hatred called him nothing but a charlatan, myself from my own experience over decades saw him as the first among all musical workers in the whole world, and the more famous Karajan became the better he became, which my friend, like the rest of the world of music, would not admit. From childhood I have watched Karajan's genius develop and become more perfect, I witnessed nearly all the rehearsals of concerts and operas he conducted in Salzburg and Vienna. The first concerts I heard in my life were conducted by Karajan, the first operas I heard likewise by Karajan. Thus, I am bound to say, I had a good basis from the beginning for my musical progress. Karajan's name ensured, from the outset, a furious argument between myself and Paul, and so long as Paul was alive we argued about Karajan again and again. But neither did I succeed in convincing Paul of Karajan's genius with my arguments concerning Karajan, nor did Paul convince me with his arguments against Karajan, that is about his being a charlatan. To Paul – and this did not upset his philosophical system – opera was, as it were, the summit of the world, right to his death, whereas to me it was, even then, a very early passion which had become somewhat eclipsed, an art form I continued to love but which, for a good many years now, I could do without. For many years Paul, when he still had money, used to travel the whole globe from one opera house to another, only to proclaim the Vienna Opera the greatest of all in the end. *The Met is nothing. Covent Garden is nothing. The Scala is nothing.* They were all nothing compared with Vienna. *But of course*, he would say, *the Vienna Opera also is really good only once a year.* Only once a year, but, nevertheless. He had been able to afford, in the course of a *crazy* three years' trip, to visit all the so-called world opera houses in turn. As a result he came to know practically all the major and great and truly important conductors and the men and women courted or chastized by them. His head, basically, was an opera head, and his own life, which increasingly, and in his final years with the greatest rapidity, had become a terrible existence, became an opera, naturally a grand opera, and accordingly one with a thoroughly tragic ending. At the moment this opera of his was once more being enacted at the Steinhof and in the Ludwig Pavilion which, as I was soon to discover, was one of the most neglected in the whole of the Steinhof. The *Herr Baron*, as my friend was styled by everybody, had once again seen his white tail-coat, which, as I know, had been tailored for him by Knize and which, even in the final years of his life, he very often, behind my back as it were, wore at night, predominantly in the so-called *Eden Bar*, exchanged for a straitjacket. [...]

In the Hermann Pavilion and finally in death agony I clearly realized what my relationship with my friend Paul really meant to me, that in truth it was the most valuable of all my relationships with men, the only one I have endured for more than a very short period and one which I would not wish to do without under any circumstances. Now, suddenly, I was afraid for that person who had suddenly become the closest one to me, that I might lose him, and actually in two respects: *through my death* as well as *through his*, because just as near to death as I had myself been in the Hermann Pavilion these past few weeks and months, as indeed I had distinctly felt, so near was he to his in the Ludwig Pavilion. Suddenly I longed for that person who had truly been the only male one with whom I was able to converse in a way that suited me, to have a subject and to develop it, no matter of what kind and be it the most difficult. How long had I been deprived of these conversations, this ability to listen, to enlighten, simultaneously to *receive*, I reflected, how far back were those conversations of ours about Webern, about Schönberg, about Satie, about *Tristan* and *Die Zauberflöte*, about *Don Giovanni* and *Entführung*? How long was it since together with me, in the courtyard at Nathal, he had listened to the *Rhenish Symphony* under Schuricht? Only now, in the Hermann Pavilion, did I realize what I was missing, what I had been deprived of by my renewed illness and what, basically, I could not do without if I wished to exist. Of course I had friends, the very best of friends, but none whose prodigal inventiveness or whose sensibility could compare with Paul's, [...]

To have to work in order to earn money, his livelihood so to speak, had been something entirely new to him and everybody had expected him to fail. But they had been wrong, because Paul, until shortly before his end, when he was simply no longer able to walk to the insurance institution on the Schottenring, had gone to the office, arriving punctually and leaving punctually, all quite properly. *I am an absolutely exemplary employee*, he often said and I never doubted his statement. He had, I believe, met his wife Edith, his second wife, in Berlin – either, as I assume, before or after or during a visit to the opera. She was a niece of the composer Giordano, the composer of

Andrea Chenier, and her relations were mainly in Italy, which she visited every year with or without Paul, but mostly without Paul, her third husband, in order to regenerate. I was decidedly fond of her and was pleased whenever I saw her sitting at the *Bräunerhof* over a cup of coffee. I had the pleasantest conversations with her and, apart from coming from *a very good family*, she was of well above average intelligence and charming to boot. That she was also very elegant was a matter of course for a wife of Paul Wittgenstein. During the no doubt bitterest years, when her husband's illness was rapidly and irresistibly progressing towards an expected death, when his attacks occurred at ever shorter intervals and he was spending more time at Steinhof and at the Wagner-Jauregg hospital in Linz than he did in Vienna or by the Traunsee, she never complained, although I knew very well under what difficult circumstances she had to live. She loved Paul and she had never left him to feel alone for a minute even though she had been parted from him most of the time, because she was always at Stallburggasse, in that small turn-of-the-century flat, while her husband was more or less vegetating at Steinhof or at the Wagner-Jauregg hospital in Linz, formerly known only as *Niedernhart*, in his straitjacket in some appalling ward alongside others like him. His attacks did not come out of the blue, they always heralded their arrival weeks before when his hands would suddenly begin to shake, when he could not finish a sentence but would talk ceaselessly, for hours on end, when it was impossible to stop his flow of words, when he suddenly had a totally irregular gait in that, walking alongside you, he would suddenly walk very fast for ten or eleven steps and then exceptionally slowly for three, four or five paces, when he would address strangers in the street and for no obvious reason, or when, for instance, he would order a bottle of champagne at Sacher's at ten in the morning but instead of drinking it let it get warm and leave it standing there. But these are harmless trifles. What was worse was that he would snatch up the complete breakfast tray ordered by him and brought to his table by the waiter and fling it at the silk-tapestry-covered wall. At the Petersplatz, the square by St Peter's Cathedral, he once, to my knowledge, got into a taxi and uttered only the word *Paris*, whereupon the driver, who knew him, actually drove him to Paris, where a Wittgenstein aunt residing there then had to pay the taxi bill. He also came to me to Nathal by taxi several times, only for half an hour, *just to see you*, as he said, only to be driven back to

Vienna straight away, after all a distance of two hundred and ten kilometres each way, that is four hundred and twenty in all. He was unable, when he was, as he himself put it, *ripe* again, to hold a glass and every other moment he would lose control and burst into tears. He would always meet one in supremely elegant clothes, bequeathed to him by dead friends or given him as presents by others still living, and he would, for instance, sit at Sacher's in a white suit at ten in the morning, in the *Bräunerhof* in a grey pinstripe at half-past eleven, in the Ambassador in a black one at half-past one and back at Sacher's in a corn-yellow one at half-past three in the afternoon. Wherever he walked or stood he would intone not only complete Wagnerian arias but very often half of *Siegfried* or half of the *Walküre* in his brittle voice, unconcerned by his surroundings. In the street he not only addressed total strangers, asking them if they did not share his opinion that after Klemperer it had become unbearable to listen to any music (most of those he thus addressed had never heard of Klemperer and had no idea of music, but that did not worry him): when he felt like it he would give a lecture on *Stravinsky* or *Die Frau ohne Schatten* right in the street and announce that he would *shortly* produce *Die Frau ohne Schatten* on the Traunsee, on the lake, with the best musicians in the world. *Die Frau ohne Schatten* was his favourite opera, leaving aside Wagner's operas. In actual fact he had time and again inquired of the most famous male and female singers what kind of fees they would demand for a guest performance in *Die Frau ohne Schatten* on the Traunsee. *I am building a floating stage*, he often said, *and the Philharmonic will play on a second floating stage at the foot of the Traunstein*. Die Frau ohne Schatten *belongs on the Traunsee, it must be performed between Traunkirchen and the Traunstein*, that is what he said. *Klemperer's death has foiled my plan*, he said, *with Böhm* Die Frau ohne Schatten *will feel like a hangover to me*. On one occasion he had got Knize, the best and most expensive tailor in Vienna, to measure him for two white tail-coats at a time. When the suits were ready he had sent word to the firm of Knize that surely it was actually absurd to deliver two white tail-coats to him when he had not had *one black one* made for him by the firm of Knize; perhaps the firm of Knize thought he was crazy? The fact is that for weeks on end he had gone to the firm of Knize for the sole purpose of having continual alterations made to the two tail-coats ordered by him. Not just for weeks but for months on end was the firm of Knize tormented by him with requests for alterations and at the moment when the two white tail-coats were ready Paul totally denied that he had ever ordered two tail-coats from the firm of Knize, *white tail-coats, where do they get this idea, I am not crazy am I, having two white tail-coats tailor-made for me, and of all places by the firm of Knize*. The firm of Knize, furnished with a bundle of evidence, demanded that Paul should pay the *bill*, which of course, since Paul had no money, had to be paid by the Wittgenstein family.

Wittgenstein's Nephew, 1982
tr. Ewald Osers, 1986

'Unflattering memories of the diva assoluta'
ETHAN MORDDEN

'Tell me about your first meeting with Adriana. How did she strike you?'

'Oh, *never!* I thought. So fat and shy, always the eyes on the ground so she shall not see the rough laughter of boys. She was hurt, she was feelings, when she came to me. Well, poor thing, she was not what they wanted. But she was clever. I saw it at once. An excellent pianist. And *devoted!* She used to arrive hours early and sit outside listening to the other students' lessons. I thought to myself, She hasn't much to work with – the figure of a cow, the many fears, the strange timbre. Maestro Sesto Contramin, her mentor in Italy – he called it "una grande vociaccia."' A big, ugly noise. 'Nothing to work with, but ferocious determination. What are you doing, please?'

This was addressed to the maid, who had taken out a white lace handkerchief and was twirling it about. By way of reply, the maid stared keenly at the diva's bodice, dabbed at her right breast with the lace, then examined something she had picked up. 'A bit of halvah,' she confided to me.

'She was *destined* for opera,' the diva went on, 'and I was destined to bring her into the world of song. Scales! Technique! Placement! The thrill! The portamento! So many students become impatient. They want to sing arias the first day. Not Adriana. *Foundation!* That's what she wanted. She had to build a voice out of nothing, and she knew it. She had no love, but she had her work.'

'No love at all? She didn't go out with—'

'Who would have her? Besides, as I often told her, sex and music don't go together.'

'Too bad,' said the maid. 'If they did, you'd have been an international sensation.'

'I *was!*'

The Venice Adriana, 1998

'The boys' brigade out in force for *Billy Budd*'
ALAN HOLLINGHURST

I found James leaning in a corner of the foyer, lips pursed over the score.

'Taking it a bit seriously, aren't you darling?' I said.

'Darling.' We kissed drily, rapidly. 'No, it's frightfully good, actually.'

'Well, I'm glad you're going to enjoy it.' I gazed around despairingly at the white tuxedos and bare shoulders. It was far too hot to be in an opera-house, and I had come along in what was virtually a pair of pyjamas – a super-light African cotton outfit, the queenery of which was chastened by a hint of martial arts.

'Everybody's looking at you,' said James, who, adorably, was wearing a suit and tie. 'God knows what Lord B. will think.' He had a pleasantly snobbish respect for our family; my grandfather was very fond of James, whom he saw as a humane and practical person, with charming manners and a keen interest in the arts.

'I despise them all,' I protested, turning away from a macabre trio of queens, very got-up with gloves and velvet bow-ties. 'The way some of these creatures look at you, you feel as though you're being violated – ocularly.'

James was a little embarrassed, had not yet slipped out of the responsibilities of the day, was to be on his best behaviour, and yet also, I knew, longed to side with extravagance. I was in a mood of atrocious egotism, brought on by what had turned out to be absolute adoration from Phil, but I seemed to sense, as I looked across the hall and up the long mirrored stairway, a further perspective, in which James and I were together as we had been in the past.

'They might pay less attention to you,' he said, 'if you didn't look like something out of the *Arabian Nights*. You appear to have an erection, as well.'

'Of course I've got an erection. I'm in love.'

James gave me a comically shrewd look. 'Oh God. And who's the victim this time?'

'What a horrid thing to say!' I swept the audience with another glare. 'He's a boy from the Corry, actually – a body-builder – short – dark hair – called Phil.' Just saying that made me wish I were with him even more. I glanced at James and saw a look of terrible anxiety pass over his face.

'I wonder if it's anyone I've seen there,' he said. Then: 'Ah – here's Lord B.'

My grandfather, looking very fine with sleek, grey hair and sun-browned face, was making his way courteously through the crowd. 'James. Very good to see you.' They shook hands and grinned. 'Turning in, old boy?' he said to me. 'I could have a bed made up in the box.' At the same time he shook me by the scruff of the neck, insisting on his joke even as he showed he did not mean it. The glow of mutual appreciation permeated my mood. We started upstairs.

'Did you have a sleep after lunch?' I enquired.

'I think I probably did drop off – how about you?'

'Mm – I spent all afternoon in bed,' I replied truthfully.

'Frightfully good lunch, though. Do you know this restaurant, James?'

'Where did you go?'

'The Crépuscule des Dieux.' He chuckled. 'It ought to be just up your street...' He meant, because of Wagner, though he can't have been unaware of the discreetly homosexual style of the whole place, the waiters in tails with long white aprons, the rich older men treating their bored and flirtatious young dolly-boys. 'Not the food for you, though, perhaps – all swimming in blood!' James loathed jokes of this kind but he managed a disgusted smile. He'd passed a demanding New Year at Marden once, subsisting entirely on roast potatoes and Stilton, and pretending indifference as chargers of pheasant, goose and almost raw beef were borne in by the staff.

Upstairs, my grandfather remembered the name of the doorman who walked along the corridor with us, saying, just at the last moment,

'And how's your wife, Roy?' (Roy being the man's surname rather than his Christian name).

'I'm afraid she died, my lord,' Roy said in a well-seasoned way. Here was a test for my grandfather, for a merely courtesy concern had turned on him and presented him with a real little tragedy. I stood and watched him pat the man on the back in a brotherly way, and nod his head impressively.

'They're pretty terrible, these bereavements,' he said. 'And it doesn't get any better, I'm afraid.' As Roy said, 'No, my lord,' he was already leaving him, having done the convincingly human thing and yet not involved himself in the least. He pulled the door to and placed us, him in the middle, and James nearer the stage.

My grandfather was a Director of Covent Garden, and I had seen many operas with him from this same box. Yet I never felt it was a good point to watch the performance from: for the privacy and elevation of the box we paid the cost of seeing the orchestra, a view into the wings and an imperfect vantage on the upper stage. The privacy, anyway, was an ambiguous thing, since the eyes of the stalls dwelt on the boxes as though on the balconies of a royal residence. I was aware of the bad effect this had on me – an affected unawareness of the rest of the house, exaggerated laughter and enthralment in the remarks of my companions. I did not like myself much for this – indeed the box represented to me in some ways the penalties of exposure, discomfort and pitilessness which were paid for privilege. Tonight I sprawled over the red plush sill and let James and my grandfather talk until the lights went down.

It was *Billy Budd*, an opera I recalled as a gauche, almost amateur affair, and I had not in the least expected to enjoy it; and yet, when Captain Vere's monologue ended and the scene on board the *Indomitable* opened up, with the men holy-stoning the deck and singing their oppressed, surging chorus, I was covered in goose-flesh. When Billy, press-ganged from his old ship, sang his farewell to his former life and comrades – 'Farewell, old *Rights o' Man*, farewell' – the tears streamed down my face. The young baritone, singing with the greatest beauty and freshness, brought an extraordinary quality of resisted pathos to Billy; in the stammering music his physiognomy, handsome and forthright and yet with a curious fleshy debility about the mouth, made me believe it as his own tragedy.

None of this should have surprised me. I had not heard any music

72

for a few days, and I was all charged up, glowing and gratified, so that my sense of everything was heightened. I felt every phrase of the music in a physical way, as if I had turned into a little orchestra myself.

In the interval we had champagne, though James would only take a drop, saying it would give him a headache. He was prone to bad headaches, often of a nervous kind (for instance, when he had a clear weekend after being on call for two or three weeks he would spend it supine in a darkened room, a hand pressed to his brow). The heat and intensity of a theatre always brought on a bit of a head for him too. I think he concentrated exceptionally hard – at a concert he would either follow the score or his knuckles would be white with tension – whereas I, though I was gripped and appalled by the opera, blubbing again at the despair of the poor little Novice, his body and spirit broken by his flogging, had also had periods of several minutes' duration when I had paid no attention at all, thinking about Phil, and sex, and what I was going to do later.

My grandfather looked at me apprehensively. 'Are you enjoying it, darling?' he asked.

'I think it's wonderful,' I said. 'It's a funny old production, but there's something quite touching about that.'

'Mm – I agree. Quite unchanged since the very first performance, of course. It's a museum piece, still being used after thirty years. We had a lot of talk about a new production, but we felt the loot could be better spent on something else.'

'Yes.' I was on for more champagne already.

'What do you think, James?'

'Oh, I'm enjoying it,' James said, with an emphasis that suggested reservations. His eyes were darkly rimmed, he looked sallow with lack of sleep, and I wondered what it would be like to come to the crowded unreality of a theatre after a day's long concentration on illness and misery.

'I don't know if it's a piece you especially care for.'

'It's always more moving and impressive than you expect,' James said, as so often echoing my own feelings; but our solidarity brought us to the edge of difficult terrain. What he would want to talk about would be the suppressed or (in his usual term) deflected sexuality of the opera. We must all have recognised it, though it would have had an importance, even an eloquence, to James and me that would have been quite lost on my grandfather. He had spent all his adult life in circles where good manners, lofty savoir-faire and plain callousness conspired to avoid any recognition that homosexuality even existed. The three of us in our hot little box were trapped with this intensely British problem: the opera that was, but wasn't, gay, the two young gay friends on good behaviour, the mandarin patriarch giving nothing of his feelings away.

I decided to brave it, and said: 'It's an odd piece, though, partly the sex thing, of course. Claggart's bit about beauty and handsomeness could win a prize for general ghastly creepiness. He's sort of coming out with it and not coming out with it at the same time.'

My grandfather hesitated diplomatically before saying: 'That was very much Forster's line actually. Though I don't think it's generally known.'

'Did you meet Forster?' James blurted in reverence and surprise.

'Oh, only occasionally, you know. But I do clearly recall the first night of *Billy Budd*. Britten himself was in the pit, of course. It made a fairly big impression, though I remember opinion was very divided about it. Many people understandably didn't altogether care for the Britten–Pears thing.' James looked blank and I frowned, but my grandfather went on. 'There was a party afterwards that Laura and I went to and I had quite a long chat with old Forster about the libretto.'

'What was he like?' asked James. My grandfather smiled wearily – he did not care to be interrupted. Then James looked mortified.

'He seemed satisfied with it, but there was something distinctly contrary about him. I was quite surprised when he openly criticised some of the music. Claggart's monologue in particular he thought was wrong. He wanted it to be much more ... open, and sexy, as Willy puts it. I think *soggy* was the word he used to describe Britten's music for it.'

I thought this was extremely interesting, and my grandfather looked pleased, as if he had belatedly discovered the use of something he had dutifully been carrying about for years. I felt matters had subtly changed, an admission been made. But then that 'understandable' dislike of Britten and Pears – there was a little phrase I might myself take on through life, wanting to forget it or to disprove the unpleasant truth it hinted at. I tilted out the last of the champagne and watched James talking to his host. I seemed to see him as a boy, a shy but exemplary sixth-former reporting to a master. The open score on the sill of the box was like a book in a portrait codifying some special accomplishment, the entry to a world of sensibility where he had found himself when young, and to which, hard-working and solitary, he must still have access.

I was smiling reflectively, perhaps irritatingly, at him as we were joined by Barton Maggs, one of the most assiduous and proprietary opera-goers in London and abroad, on his interval tour of the nobs.

'Oh dear, oh dear – Denis, Will...' he nodded upswept, sandy eyebrows at us.

'Do you know James Brooke? Professor Maggs...' He discharged a further nod at James. He seemed to be out of breath, getting round everybody in time, and his weight was emphasised by a too tight and youthful seersucker suit and white moccasins on small womanly feet.

'Fair to middling, I'd say, wouldn't you?' he proposed.

'We were just saying how good we thought it was.' Maggs had no sense of humour and no awareness either that we would instinctively treat him with irony.

'Oh dear – it's funny, isn't it, I always think how funny, there not being any women in it. Some people claim not to notice.' He looked around as if *anything* might happen.

'You couldn't have *women* in it, though, could you. I mean, it takes place on a *ship*.' I felt that just about summed it up.

My grandfather engaged with it drolly. 'Still, I think you want a sort of Buttercup figure, don't you, Barty – selling tobacco and peppermints to the crew...'

'Perhaps Captain Vere's sisters and his cousins and his aunts could be brought in,' I said. 'I'm sure they'd quell any mutiny.'

'Oh yes, h'm. I do miss hearing a good soprano though,' he said, and looked almost bereft, as if Britten had let him down in not providing the display of palpitating femininity that so many homosexuals crave. The warning bell was already ringing and he busily took his leave.

My grandfather was reminiscing about Forster again (matter which was all new to me as well, so that I asked myself why I had never as it were interviewed him about his past) when James broke in a second time. 'I say, isn't that Pears down there?' We all turned to look.

Pears was shuffling very slowly along the aisle towards the front of the stalls, supported by a man on either side. Most of the bland audience showed no recognition of who he was, though occasionally someone would stare, or look away hurriedly from the singer's stroke-slackened but beautiful white-crested head. Then there was the protracted and awkward process of getting him along his already repopulated row. James and I were mesmerised, and seeing him in the flesh I felt the whole occasion subtly transform, and the opera whose ambiguity we had carped at take on a kind of heroic or historic character under the witness of one of its creators. Even though I felt he would be enjoying it, I believed in its poignancy for him, seeing other singers performing it on the same stage in the same sets as he had done decades before, under the direction of the man he loved. It had become an episode in his past, just as the blessing of Billy Budd was in the memory of the elderly Captain Vere. Indeed, gazing at Pears,who was doubtless embarrassed and uncomfortable as he finally regained his seat, I reacted to him as if he were himself an operatic character – just as I had entered with spurious, or purely aesthetic emotion into Charles Nantwich's war-time adolescence, and the loss of his shell-damaged idol in a Hertfordshire mental hospital. It was an irresistible elegiac need for the tendernesses of an England long past.

Then the lights went down, my grandfather said curtly, 'I don't give him long,' and we all applauded the orchestra.

The Swimming-pool Library, 1988

Stage for a different reality

Opera in discussion

'The new technique for marrying words and music'
CHARLES BURNEY

Persons of taste and letters in Tuscany, being discontented with every former attempt at perfecting dramatic poetry and exhibitions, determined to unite the best lyric poet, with the best musician of their time; three Florentine noblemen, therefore, Giovanni Bardi count of Vernio, Pietro Strozzi, and Jacopo Corsi, all learned and enlightened lovers of the fine arts, chose Ottavio *Rinuccini*, and Jacopo *Peri*, their countrymen, to write and set to Music the drama of *Dafne*, which was performed in the house of Signor Corsi, in 1597, with great applause, and this seems the true æra whence the *opera*, or drama, *wholly set to Music*, and in which the dialogue was neither sung in measure, nor declaimed without Music, but *recited* in simple musical tones, which amounted not to singing, and yet was different from speech, should be dated. After this successful experiment, Rinuccini wrote *Euridice* and *Arianna*, two other dramas for the same kind of Music.

In the same year, however, that Ariadne, set to Music by Jacobo [*sic*] Peri, was performed at Florence, there was a sacred drama, *oratorio*, morality, or mystery in Music, of the same kind, by Emilio del Cavaliere, performed at Rome; which makes it difficult to determine who was the original inventor of that peculiar species of melody, or chant, which is called *recitative*, and which has ever since been the true characteristic of the opera and oratorio. To the printed copies of Peri's *opera*, and Cavaliere's *oratorio*, both published in 1600, there is a long preface, in which the origin of the invention is claimed by each of these composers: Peri, however, modestly says, 'though Signor del Cavaliere, with wonderful invention, brought our kind of Music on the public stage before any other that I know of; yet Signor Jacopo Corsi, and Ottavio Rinuccini, were pleased, so early as the year 1594, to wish that I would *adopt it*, in a different way, and set the fable of Daphne, written by Ottavio Rinuccini, to Music, in order to try the power of this species of melody, which they imagined to be such as was used by the ancient Greeks and Romans throughout their dramas.'

However, in the dedication of the oratorio, *dell' Anima, e del Corpo*, to Cardinal Aldovrandini, it is said by the editor, Guidotti, that the work consists of 'Singular and new musical compositions, made in imitation of that style with which the ancient Greeks and Romans are supposed to have produced such great effects by their dramatic representations.' He adds, that 'seeing the great applause which was universally given to the productions of Signor Emilio del Cavaliere (a Roman gentleman) who had been able by his own industry and abilities so happily to revive the melody of the ancient declamation; particularly in three pastorals which were repeatedly recited in the presence of his serene highness the duke of Tuscany: during the year 1590, was composed *il Satiro*, as was *la Disperatione di Fileno*, and both were privately performed in the same year: and in 1595 *il Giuoco della Cieca* was exhibited in the presence of Cardinal Monte, and Mont' Alto, as well as the archduke Ferdinand, with great admiration, *as nothing like it had ever been seen or heard before.*' And farther, fixing the precise time when this oratorio was performed at Rome, he says, 'nothing could prove more indisputably what power this style of singing had in exciting devotion, and affecting the heart, than the prodigious applause of the concourse of people assembled together at the performance of this sacred drama in the oratorio of Vallicella in Rome, last February.'

Emilio del Cavaliere, the composer, in his own advertisement to the reader, speaks of his Music as that of the ancients, recovered, or revived, and as having such powers over the affections as could excite grief, pity, joy, and pleasure, as was effectually shewn in a scene of his *Disperatione di Fileno*, which, when *recited* by Signora Archilei, whose excellence in Music is universally known, drew tears from the audience, while the character of Fileno made them laugh.*

There are such instructions given in this preface for the performance of his simple and infant drama, as would now suit the best productions of Metastasio, set by the best composers, for the best singers of modern times.

Giovanni Batista Doni, a learned and elegant writer on Music,

---

* Though the performers are never mentioned in the *Dramatis Personæ* to the first musical dramas, yet it appears that Italy has never been without singers of great abilities, and powers to captivate and enchant an audience. Gagliano, in his preface to the Daphne of Rinuccini, which he set to Music a second time, allows that a great deal of its success was owing to the singers; and mentions the great taste and feeling with which Jacopo Peri sung his own Music, of which there was no forming an adequate idea by those who had never heard him. But long before this period, *Castiglione*, in his *Cortegiano*, describes the different abilities of the two singers *Bidon* and *Marchetto Cara*.

though extremely warped in his judgment by a predilection for antiquity, in a dissertation on the Origin of Stage-singing, during his own time, gives so curious and instructive an account of the first operas which were performed at Florence, that I shall translate the chief part of it.

'Some kind of *Cantilena*, or melody, has been introduced in dramatic representations, at all times, either in the form of intermezzi (interludes), between the acts; or, occasionally, in the body and business of the piece. But it is still fresh in the memory of every one, when the WHOLE DRAMA was first set to Music, and sung from the beginning to the end; because, anterior to the attempt of *Emilio del Cavaliere*, a Roman gentleman, extremely well versed in Music, there seems to have been nothing of that kind undertaken that is worth mentioning. This composer published a drama at Rome in 1600, called *dell' Animo, e del Corpo*; in the preface to which, mention is made of a piece represented at Florence in 1588, at the nuptials of the grand duchess, in which were many fragments of his Music; and where, likewise, two years after, was represented another drama set by him, called *Il Satiro*.

'It is necessary, however, to declare here, that those melodies are very different from such as are at present composed in what is commonly called *recitative*; being no other than *ariets*, full of contrivance, repetitions, echoes, &c. which are totally different from the true and genuine theatrical Music, of which Signor Emilio could know nothing, for want of being acquainted with ancient authors, and the usages of antiquity. It may therefore be said, that the first attempt at reviving theatrical Music, after being lost for so many ages, was made at Florence, where so many noble arts have been recovered. This extraordinary event was brought about by the invention of *recitative*, which is now universally received, practised, and preferred to the madrigal style, in which the words are so utterly unintelligible.

'The beginning of this century (1600), was the æra of musical recitation on the public stage at Florence, though it had been used there in several private exhibitions before. There resided in that city, during these times, Signor Gio. Bardi de' Conti di Vernio, who was afterwards called to the service of Pope Clement VIII, by whom he was tenderly beloved, and made his Maestro di Camera. This most accomplished nobleman, was particularly attached to the study of antiquity, and to the theory and practice of Music, to which he had applied himself for many years so closely, that he became, for the time in which he lived, a correct and good composer. His house was the constant rendezvous of all persons of genius, and a kind of flourishing academy where the young nobility often assembled to pass their leisure hours in laudable exercises and learned discourse: but particularly on musical subjects, when it was the wish of all the company to recover that art of which the ancients related such wonders, as well as other noble inventions which had been ruined by the eruptions of barbarians.

'During these discussions, it was universally allowed that as modern Music was extremely deficient in grace, and the expression of words, it became necessary in order to obviate these objections, that some other species of Cantilena, or melody, should be tried by which the words should not be rendered unintelligible, nor the verse destroyed.

'Vincenzio Galilei was at this time in some credit among musicians; and, flattered with his reputation, pursued his musical studies with such diligence that, either by the help he received from others, or by the force of his own genius, he composed his work upon the Abuse of modern Music, which has since gone through two impressions. Animated by success, Galilei attempted new things, and assisted by Signor Giovanni, was the first who composed melodies for a single voice, having modulated that pathetic scene of Count Ugolino, written by Dante, which he sung himself very sweetly, to the accompaniment of a viol. This essay certainly pleased very much in general; however, there were some individuals who laughed at the attempt; notwithstanding which, he set in the same style, parts of the Lamentations of Jeremiah, which were performed to a devout assembly.

'At this time, Giulio Caccini Romano, a young, elegant, and spirited singer, used to attend these meetings at the house of the Count di Vernio; and being seized with a strong passion for this kind of Music, he studied it with great diligence; composing and singing to a single instrument, which was generally the theorbo, or large lute, played by *Bardilla*, who happened then to be at Florence.

'Caccini, therefore, in imitation of Galilei, but in a more beautiful and pleasing style, set many canzonets and sonnets written by excellent poets, and not by such wretched scribblers as were usually employed before, and are still very frequently the favourites of musicians; so that he may be said to have been the first to see this error, and to discover that the art of counterpoint will not alone complete the education of a musician, as is generally imagined; and he afterwards confessed, in a discourse prefixed to one of his works, that the conversations held at the Count del Vernio's were of more use to him than thirty years study and exercise of his art. Here he likewise claims the merit of having first published songs for a single voice, which, indeed, had the greatest success. And it must be confessed, that we owe to him, in a great measure, the new and graceful manner of singing, which at that time spread itself all over Italy; for he composed a great number of airs which he taught to innumerable scholars, and among the rest to his daughter, who became a famous singer, and still continues very excellent in that faculty.

'But not to defraud any one of his just praise, it is necessary to acknowledge in this place, that Luca Marenzio, who flourished now at Rome, had brought the madrigal style to the highest degree of perfection, by the beautiful manner in which he made all the several parts of his compositions sing; for before his time, if the harmony was full and masterly, nothing else was required.

'In the recitative style, however, Caccini had a formidable rival in Jacopo Peri, a Florentine, who was not only a good composer, but a famous singer, and performer on keyed instruments, having been taught by Christopher Malvezzi; and applying with great diligence and enthusiasm to this kind of singing, succeeded wonderfully, and met with universal applause.

'After the departure of Signor Bardi from Florence, Signor Jacopo Corsi became the patron of Music and its professors, as well as of every other art and science; so that his house, during the remainder of his life, continued to be the retreat of the Muses and their votaries, of every country, as well as of Tuscany. Ottavio Rinuccini was at this time united with him in the strictest bands of friendship, which seldom is durable, unless cemented by sympathetic affections; and being, as is well known, an excellent poet, whose works are, to the last degree, natural, pathetic, full of grace, and, in a particular manner, calculated for Music; as poetry and Music are sister arts, he had an opportunity of cultivating both together, with equal success, and of communicating his discoveries and refinements to this illustrious assembly.

'The first poem, set in this new way, and performed at the house of Signor Corsi, was *Dafne*, a pastoral written by Rinuccini, and set by Jacopo Peri and Caccini in a manner which charmed the whole city. Afterwards, other little fables and entire dramas were thus recited;

but, above all, the *Euridice* of Rinuccini, written and set to Music for the royal nuptials of Mary of Medicis with the most Christian King Henry IV. The Music of this drama, which was publicly exhibited at Florence, in the most splendid manner, was chiefly composed by Jacopo Peri, who performed a part in it himself, as in his *Dafne* he had represented Apollo; the rest of the Music was composed by Caccini, and the whole was exhibited in 1600; in which year, and on the same occasion, was also performed the *Rape of Cephalus*, in which the chief part was set by Caccini.

'Great applause was likewise bestowed on *Ariadne*, another dramatic production of Rinuccini, and cloathed in suitable melody by Claudio Monteverde, at present Maestro di Capella to the republic of Venice. He afterwards published the principal part of this production, which is the *Lamentation of Ariadne*, and perhaps the most beautiful composition of this kind which our times have produced. Thus the original and true architects of this species of scenical Music were Jacopo Corsi, and Ottavio Rinuccini, assisted by the three eminent artists above-mentioned, who had conferred great honour upon our city, as well as on the profession of Music.'

It is not difficult to discover from this account, that all the patrons and artists of this new species of Music, except Monteverde, were *Dilettanti*, and *shallow contrapuntists*, who, as is usual, condemned and affected to despise that which they could not understand, and in which they were unable to excel. The learned contrapuntists, on the contrary, had abused their art, to the ruin of lyric poetry, and confined it in such narrow limits, that even instrumental Music made no advances in their hands; for all they produced, that was not in canon and fugue, was utterly dry, fanciless, and despicable. These early attempts, however, at clearness, grace, and facility, though they now appear but mean and feeble, had a happy effect upon the art. In process of time they approximated parties, (for when was Music any more than politics, without its cabals and factions!) and in appealing to the public ear, by bringing Music on the stage, drove pedantry to lament the degeneracy of the age in holes and corners; and encouraged zeal and unprejudiced musical learning to unite with taste in simplifying the art, and calling upon the graces for assistance.

As EURIDICE was the first musical drama, after the invention of recitative, that was publicly represented, I shall endeavour to give my readers all the information concerning it that I have been able to collect.

This drama, written by OTTAVIO RINUCCINI, and set by JACOPO PERI, was performed at Florence in 1600, on occasion of the marriage of Mary of Medicis, to Henry IV. of France. The poem, and the Music, were published separately, the same year. The poet, in his dedication to the Queen of France, says, 'It is generally imagined that the tragedies of the ancient Greeks and Romans were entirely sung; but this noble kind of singing had not till now been revived, or even attempted, to my knowledge, by any one; and I used to think, that the inferiority of our Music, to that of the ancient, was the cause; till hearing the compositions of Jacopo Peri to the fable of *Daphne*, I wholly changed my opinion. This drama, written merely as an experiment, pleased so much, that I was encouraged to produce *Euridice*, which was honoured with still more applause, when sung to the Music of the same composer Jacopo Peri, who with wonderful art, unknown before, having merited the favour and protection of the Grand Duke our sovereign, it was exhibited in a most magnificent manner at the nuptials of your majesty in the presence of the Cardinal Legate, and innumerable princes and nobles of Italy and France,' &c. The only copy of the Music that I have been able to find was in the library of the Marchese Rinuccini, a descendant of the author, at Florence; in examining and making extracts from which, I observed that it was printed in score and barred, two very uncommon circumstances at the time of its publication; that the recitative seemed to have been not only the model of subsequent composers of early Italian operas, but of the French operas of Lulli; that figures were often placed over the base to indicate the harmony, as a ♭ for a minor third, a ♯ for a major third, and a 10 and 11 for the octaves of the third and fourth; that the time is changed as frequently as in the old French serious operas, and though the word *aria* sometimes occurs, it is as difficult to distinguish air from recitative, in this drama, by any superiority of melody, as in those of Lulli; except in the choruses which were sung and danced at the same time, like those on the French stage.

Peri, in his preface, after enumerating the great personages who were present at the representation, and the eminent musicians to whom his Music had been shewn, tells us, that it was sung by the most excellent performers of the time; among whom were Signor Francesco Rasi, a nobleman of Arezzo, who represented the part of Aminto; Signor Brandi, Arcetro; and Signor Melchior Palantrotto, Pluto. He then tells us, that 'behind the scenes, Signor Jacopo Corsi played the

85

harpsichord; Don Garzia Montalvo the *chitarone*, or large *guitar*; Messer Giovambatista dal Violino the *lira grande*, or *voil da gamba*; and Messer Giovanni Lapi a *large lute*.'

These four seem to have composed the whole band. For though he celebrates the performance of Giovambatista Jacomelli on the violin, neither he, nor any one else, played on that instrument at the exhibition. He concludes his account of this drama by owning that some parts of it were composed by Giulio Caccini, detto Romano, 'whose great merit was known to the whole world,' because it was to be sung by persons dependent on him; by which he probably means to say, that they were his scholars. He boasts of having *opened the road* for others, by his essays at dramatic Music.

The only arrangement of sounds, however, resembling an air in Euridice, is a short *Zinfonia*, which the reader will find on the next plates.

GIULIO CACCINI, *detto Romano*, set this entire drama likewise to Music, *in stilo rappresentativo*, and published it in 1600, at Florence. There is still another resemblance in Lulli's operas to these first attempts at the musical drama in Italy, which is, that every one that I have seen has a *prologue*, set to what is called an air, such as the reader will likewise see on the next plates; where will be inserted a scene of recitative, spoken by Dafne *nuncia*, who relates the melancholy event that had befallen Euridice.

MONTEVERDE, one of the principal legislators of the musical drama, set the opera of *Orfeo*, for the court of Mantua, in 1607, which was printed at Venice 1615. And in examining this Drama, it is as difficult to distingish airs from recitative, as in the operas of Peri and Caccini, except where there are more than two parts employed, which happens but seldom.

It has been said that recitative had great obligations to Monteverde; for though Emilio del Cavaliere, Jacopo Peri, and Caccini, had attempted that style before him, yet he had so much improved it, that he might almost be called its inventor. But being in possession of most of the works of these early dramatic composers, I am unable to discover Monteverde's superiority. More forms of phrases of musical recitation still in use, may be found in Peri and Caccini, than in Monteverde. But what surprised me still more, was that his counterpoint in two parts is more frequently deficient than in the other two composers, who had never, like him, distinguished themselves in the learned style of masses, motets, and madrigals. His controversy with Artusi, early in life, for breach of rule, has been already mentioned; but though, in the new *musica rappresentativa*, he was to emancipate himself from the trammels of canon, fugue, and other restraints which had been thought necessary in composing *à capella*, and was now to have a poetical and picturesque Music, more varied and impassioned than that of the church or chamber; yet there were certain fundamental rules and prohibitions, totally independent of taste, which to violate, would offend cultivated ears.

A General History of Music, 1804

'Talking winds are rather hard to credit'
CLAUDIO MONTEVERDI

In addition, I have noticed that the interlocutors are winds, Cupids, little Zephyrs and Sirens: consequently many sopranos will be needed, and it can also be stated that the winds have to sing – that is, the Zephyrs and the Boreals. How, dear Sir, can I imitate the speech of the winds, if they do not speak? And how can I, by such means, move the passions? Ariadne moved us because she was a woman, and similarly Orpheus because he was a man, not a wind. Music can suggest, without any words, the noise of winds and the bleating of sheep, the neighing of horses and so on and so forth; but it cannot imitate the speech of winds because no such thing exists.

Next, the dances which are scattered throughout the fable do not have dance measures. And as to the story as a whole – as far as my no little ignorance is concerned – I do not feel that it moves me at all (moreover I find it hard to understand), nor do I feel that it carries me in a natural manner to an end that moves me. *Arianna* led me to a just lament, and *Orfeo* to a righteous prayer, but this fable leads me I don't know to what end. So what does Your Lordship want the music to be able to do? Nevertheless I shall always accept everything with due reverence and honour if by chance His Highness should so command and desire it, since he is my master without question.

Letters of Monteverdi, 1616
tr. Denis Stevens, 1980

'A French view of operatic principles'
CHARLES DE SAINT ÉVREMOND

I have long had a desire to tell your Grace my thoughts of Operas, and to acquaint you with the difference I have observ'd betwixt the Italian and French way of singing. The occasion I had of speaking of it, at the Duchesse *Mazarin's*, has rather increased than satisfied that desire; therefore I will gratify it in the Discourse I now send to your Grace.

I shall begin with great freedom, and tell your Grace, that I am no great admirer of Comedies in musick, such as now a-days are in request. I confess I am not displeased with their magnificence; the Machines have something that is surprizing; the Musick, in some places, is charming; the whole together seems wonderful: but it must be granted me also, that this wonderful is very tedious; for where the Mind has so little to do, there the Senses must of necessity languish. After the first pleasure that surprize gives us, the eyes are taken up, and at length grow weary of being continually fix'd upon the same object. In the beginning of the Concerts, we observe the justness of the Concords; and amidst all the Varieties that unite to make the sweetness of the harmony, nothing escapes us. But 'tis not long before the Instruments stun us; and the Musick is nothing else to our ears but a confused sound that suffers nothing to be distinguish'd. Now how is it possible to avoid being tir'd with the *Recitativo*, which has neither the charm of singing, nor the agreeable energy of speech? The Soul fatigued by a long attention, wherein it finds nothing to affect it, seeks some relief within it self; and the Mind, which in vain expected to be entertained with the show, either gives way to idle musing, or is dissatisfied that it has nothing to employ it. In a word, the fatigue is so universal, that every one wishes himself out of the house; and the only comfort that is left to the poor spectators, is the hopes that the Show will soon be over.

The reason why, commonly, I soon grow weary at Operas, is, that I never yet saw any which appear'd not to me despicable, both as to the Contrivance of the subject, and the Poetry. Now it is in vain to charm the Ears, or gratify the Eyes, if the Mind be not satisfied; for my Soul being in better intelligence with my mind than with my senses, struggles against the impressions which it may receive, or at least does not give an agreeable consent to them, without which, even the most delightful Objects can never afford me any great pleasure. An extravagance set off with Musick, Dances, Machines, and fine Scenes, is a pompous piece of folly, but 'tis still a folly. Tho' the embroidery is rich, yet the ground it is wrought upon is such wretched stuff that it offends the sight.

There is another thing in Operas so contrary to Nature, that I cannot be reconciled to it; and that is the singing of the whole Piece, from beginning to end, as if the Persons represented were ridiculously match'd, and had agreed to treat in musick both the most common, and most important affairs of Life. Is it to be imagin'd that a master calls his servant, or sends him on an errand, singing; that one friend imparts a secret to another, singing; that men deliberate in council, singing; that orders in time of battle are given, singing; and that men are melodiously killed with swords and darts? This is the downright way to lose the life of Representation, which without doubt is preferable to that of Harmony: for, Harmony ought to be no more than a bare attendant, and the great masters of the Stage have introduc'd it as pleasing, not as necessary, after they have perform'd all that relates to the Subject and Discourse. Nevertheless, our thoughts run more upon the Musician than the Hero in the Opera: *Luigi*, *Cavalli*, and *Cesti*, are still present to our imagination. The mind not being able to conceive a Hero that sings, thinks of the Composer that set the song; and I don't question but that in the Operas at the Palace-Royal, *Lulli* is an hundred times more thought of than *Theseus* or *Cadmus*.

I pretend not, however, to banish all manner of singing from the Stage: there are some things which ought to be sung, and others that may be sung without trespassing against reason or decency: Vows, Prayers, Praises, Sacrifices, and generally all that relates to the service of the Gods, have been sung in all Nations, and in all times; tender and mournful Passions express themselves naturally in a sort of querulous tone; the expressions of Love in its birth; the irresolution of a soul toss'd by different motions, are proper matters for Stanzas, as Stanzas are for Musick. Every one knows that the Chorus was introduc'd upon the Grecian Theatre, and it is not to be denied, but that with equal reason it might be brought upon ours. So far, in my opinion, Musick may be allow'd: all that belongs to Conversation, all that relates to Intrigues and Affairs, all that belongs to Council and Action, is proper for Actors to rehearse, but ridiculous in the mouth of

Musicians to sing. The Grecians made admirable Tragedies where they had some singing; the Italians and the French make bad ones, where they sing all.

Would you know what an Opera is? I'll tell you, that it is an *odd medley of Poetry and Musick, wherein the Poet and Musician, equally confined one by the other, take a world of pains to compose a wretched performance*. Not but that you may find agreeable Words and very fine Airs in our Operas; but you will more certainly find, at length, a dislike of the Verses, where the genius of the Poet is so crampt; and be cloy'd with the singing, where the Musician is spent by too long a service.

If I thought my self capable of giving counsel to Persons of Quality, who delight in the Theatre, I would advise them to take up their old relish for good Comedies, where Dances and Musick might be introduced. That would not, in the least, hurt the Representation. The *Prologue* might be sung with an agreeable Accompaniement. In the *Intermedes* [Musick and Dancing between the Acts] singing might animate words, that should be as the life of what had been represented. After the end of the Play the *Epilogue* might be sung, or some Reflections upon the finest things in the Play; which would fortify the idea, and rivet the impressions they had made upon the Spectators. Thus you might find enough to satisfy both the Senses and the Mind; wanting neither the charms of singing in a bare Representation, nor the beauty of acting in a long continued course of Musick.

It remains that I give you my advice in general for all Comedies, where any singing is used; and that is, to leave to the Poet's discretion the whole management of the Piece. The Musick must be made for the words, rather than the Words for the musick. The Musician is to follow the Poet's directions; only, in my opinion, *Lulli* is to be exempted, who knows the Passions better, and enters farther into the heart of man, than the Authors themselves. *Cambert*, without doubt, hath an excellent genius, proper for an hundred different sorts of Musick, and all well managed with a just symphony of Voices and Instruments: no *Recitativo* is better understood, nor better diversified than his; but as to the nature of the Passions, and the quality of the Sentiments that are to be expressed, he ought to receive from the Authors those lights which *Lulli* can give them; and submit to be directed, when *Lulli*, thro' the strength of his Genius, may justly be allowed to be the director.

Before I put an end to my Discourse, I will tell your Grace what a small esteem the Italians have for our Operas, and how great a dislike those of Italy give us. The Italians, who apply themselves wholly to the Representation, and take a particular care in expressing things, cannot endure that we should give the name of Opera to a mixture of Dances and Musick, which have not a natural relation, or exact connexion with the Subject. The French, on the other hand, accustom'd to the beauty of their Entries, the delightfulness of their Airs, and charms of their Symphony, cannot endure the ignorance, or ill use of the Instruments in the Operas of Venice, and are weary of a long *Recitativo*, which becomes tedious for want of variety. I cannot properly tell you what this *Recitativo* of theirs is; but I know very well that it is neither singing nor reciting; it is somewhat unknown to the Antients, which may be defined, *an awkward use of Musick and Speech*. I confess, I have found things inimitable in the Opera of *Luigi*, both for the expression of the Thoughts, and the charms of the Musick; but the common *Recitativo* was very tiresome, insomuch that the Italians themselves impatiently expected those fine places, which in their opinion came too seldom. I shall in a few words sum up the greatest defects of our Operas: one thinks he is going to a Representation, where nothing will be represented; and expects to see a Comedy, but finds nothing of the spirit of Comedy.

So much I thought I might say concerning the different constitution of Operas. As for the manner of singing, which we in France call *Execution*, I think, without partiality, that no Nation can justly vie with us. The Spaniards have admirable pipes; but with their warblings and shakings, they seem to mind nothing in their singing, but to out-rival the Nightingales. The Italian singing is either feign'd, or at least forc'd: for want of knowing exactly the nature or degree of the Passions, they burst out into laughter, rather than sing, when they would express any Joy; if they sigh, you shall hear violent sobs form'd in the throat, and not Sighs which unawares escape from the passion of an amorous heart; instead of a doleful tone, they fall into the loudest Exclamations; the Tears of absence, are with them the downright weeping at a funeral; sadness becomes so sorrowful in their mouths, that they roar rather than complain; and sometimes they express a languishing passion, as a natural fainting. Perhaps there may be at present some alteration in their way of singing; and by conversing with us, they may be improved as to the justness of a neat

Execution, as we are improved by them, as to the beauties of a stronger and bolder Composition.

I have seen Plays in England, wherein there is a great deal of musick; but to speak my thoughts with discretion, I could not accustom my self to the English singing. I came too late to find a relish in that which is so different from all others. There is no Nation that affords greater Courage in the men, more Beauty in the women, nor more Wit in both sexes. 'Tis impossible to have every thing; and where so many good qualities are so common, 'tis no misfortune that a good Taste is a rarity there. 'Tis certain that 'tis very rarely to be found: but those persons that have it, possess it in as eminent a degree of niceness and perfection, as any in the world; being distinguish'd from the rest of their Nation, either by an exquisite Art, or by a most happy Genius.

Solus Gallus cantat; none but the Frenchman sings. I will not be so injurious to all other Nations, as to maintain what an Author has publish'd, *Hispanus flet, dolet Italus, Germanus boat, Flander ululat, & solus Gallus cantat*: I shall leave these pretty distinctions with the Author, and only beg leave to back my opinion by the authority of *Luigi*, who would not endure that the Italians should pretend to sing his Airs, after he had heard them sung by *Nyert*, *IIilaire*, and the little *Varenne*. On his return to Italy, he made all the Musicians of that Nation his Enemies, by saying openly at Rome, as he had said at Paris, that to make fine Musick, Italian Airs must come out of a French mouth. He made little account of our Songs, except those of *Boisset*, which he admired, as well as the consort of our Violins, our Lutes, Harpsichords, and Organs: and how would he have been charmed with our Flutes, if they had been then in use? It is most certain, that he was much disgusted with the harshness of the greatest Masters of Italy, when he had once heard the sweet touch, and agreeable manner of the French.

I should be too partial, if I insisted only upon our advantages: therefore I must own, that no people have a slower apprehension both for the true sense of Words, and for humouring the thought of the Composer, than the French. There are but few who less understand the quantity, and who with greater difficulty find out the pronunciation; but when, by long study, they have surmounted all these difficulties, and are Masters of what they sing, nothing comes near them. The same thing happens to us in our instrumental Musick, and particularly in Concerts, where we can pretend to nothing very sure or just, till after an infinite number of Rehearsals; but when once we are perfect in them, nothing can be so just and fine. The Italians, for all their profound skill in Musick, bring their Art to our ears without any sweetness. The French, not satisfied to take away from the skill the first harshness that shews the labour of the Composition, find in the beauty of their Performance, as it were a charm for our Souls, and I know not what that touches; which they carry home to the very Heart.

I forgot to speak to your Grace about *Machines*, so easy it is for man to forget that which he would have laid aside. Machines may satisfy the curiosity of ingenious Men, who love Mathematical Inventions, but they'll hardly please persons of good judgment in the Theatre: the more they surprize, the more they divert the mind from attending to the Discourse; and the more admirable they are, the less Tenderness and exquisite Sense they leave in us, to be touch'd and charm'd with the Musick. The Antients made no use of Machines, but when there was a necessity of bringing in some God; nay, the Poets themselves were generally laughed at for suffering themselves to be reduc'd to that necessity. If men love to be at expences, let them lay out their Money upon fine Scenes, the use whereof is more natural and more agreeable than that of Machines. Antiquity, which expos'd their Gods, even at the gates, and chimney-corners; Antiquity, I say, as vain and credulous as it was, exposed them, nevertheless, but very rarely upon the Stage. Now the belief of them is gone, the Italians, in their Operas, have brought the Pagan Gods again into the world; and have not scrupled to amuse men with these ridiculous vanities, only to make their Pieces look great, by the introduction of that dazzling and surprizing Wonderful. These Stage Deities have long enough abused Italy: but the People there being happily undeceived at last, are digusted with those very Gods they were so fond of before, and have return'd to Plays, which, in truth, cannot pretend to the same exactness, but are not so fabulous, and which with a little indulgence, may pass well enough with men of sense.

It hath happen'd with us as to our Gods and Machines, what happens with the Germans as to our Modes and Fashions: we now take up what the Italians have laid aside; and as if we would atone for the fault of being prevented in the invention, we run extravagantly into a Custom which they brought up preposterously. In truth, we cover the Earth with Deities, and make them dance in troops, whereas they made them descend with discretion, and on the most important occasions. As *Ariosto* carried too far the Wonderful of Poetry, by a vain profusion of Fables, so we strain even Fable it self by a confused assembly of Gods, Shepherds, Heroes, Enchanters, Apparitions, Furies, and Devils. I admire *Lulli*, as well for the diversion of Dances, as for what concerns the Voices and Instruments; but the constitution of our Operas must appear very extravagant to those who are true Judges of the Probable and the Wonderful.

Nevertheless, a man runs a risk of having his Judgment call'd in question, if he dares declare his good taste; and I advise others, when they hear any discourse of Operas, to keep their knowledge a secret to themselves. For my own part, who am past the age and time of signalizing my self in the world by the invention of Modes, and the merit of new Fancies, I am resolv'd to strike in with good Sense, and to follow Reason tho' in disgrace, with as much zeal, as if it were still in as great vogue as formerly. That which vexes me most at this our fondness for Operas, is that they tend directly to ruin the finest thing we have, I mean *Tragedy*, than which nothing is more proper to elevate the Soul, or more capable to form the Mind.

After this long Discourse, let us conclude, that the constitution of our Operas cannot be more faulty than it is. But it is to be acknowledg'd at the same time, that no man can perform better than *Lulli*, upon an ill-conceiv'd Subject; and that it is not easy to out-do *Quinault* in what belongs to his part.

Letter to the Duke of Buckingham, 1678
tr. Des Maizeaux, 1728

'How to convert an Italian form to English purposes'
JOHN DRYDEN

If Wit has truly been defin'd a Propriety of Thoughts and Words, then that Definition will extend to all Sorts of Poetry; and amongst the rest, to this present Entertainment of an *Opera*. Propriety of Thought is that Fancy which arises naturally from the Subject, or which the Poet adapts to it. Propriety of Words, is the cloathing of those Thoughts with such Expressions as are naturally proper to them: And from both these, if they are judiciously perform'd, the Delight of Poetry results. An *Opera* is a Poetical Tale, or Fiction, represented by Vocal and Instrumental Musick, adorn'd with Scenes, Machines, and Dancing. The suppos'd Persons of this Musical *Drama* are generally supernatural, as Gods, and Goddesses, and Heroes, which at least are descended from them, and are in due time to be adopted into their Number. The Subject therefore being extended beyond the Limits of Humane Nature, admits of that sort of marvellous and surprizing Conduct, which is rejected in other Plays. Humane Impossibilities are to be receiv'd, as they are in Faith; because where Gods are introduc'd, a Supreme Power is to be understood, and second Causes are out of doors: Yet Propriety is to be observ'd even here. The Gods are all to manage their peculiar Provinces; and what was attributed by the Heathens to one Power, ought not to be perform'd by any other. *Phœbus* must foretel, *Mercury* must charm with his *Caduceus*, and *Juno* must reconcile the Quarrels of the Marriage-Bed. To conclude, they must all act according to their distinct and peculiar Characters. If the Persons represented were to speak upon the Stage, it wou'd follow of necessity, That the Expressions should be Lofty, Figurative, and Majestical: But the Nature of an *Opera* denies the frequent use of those Poetical Ornaments: For Vocal Musick, though it often admits a Loftiness of Sound; yet always exacts an harmonious Sweetness: or to distinguish yet more justly, the Recitative Part of the *Opera* requires a more Masculine Beauty of Expression and Sound: The other, which (for want of a proper *English* Word) I must call *The Songish Part*, must abound in the Softness and Variety of Numbers; its principal Intention being to please the Hearing, rather than to gratify the Understanding. It appears indeed preposterous at first sight. That Rhyme, on any consideration, should take place of Reason. But in order to resolve the Problem, this fundamental Proposition must be settled, That the first Inventors of any Art or Science, provided they have brought it to Perfection, are, in reason, to give Laws to it; and according to their Model, all After-Undertakers are to build. Thus in Epique Poetry, no Man ought to dispute the Authority of *Homer*, who gave the first Being to that Master-piece of Art, and endued it with that Form of Perfection in all its Parts, that nothing was wanting to its Excellency. *Virgil* therefore, and those very few who have succeeded him, endeavour'd not to introduce or innovate any thing in a Design already perfected, but imitated the Plan of the Inventor; and are only so far true Heroick Poets, as they have built on the Foundations of *Homer*. Thus *Pindar*, the Author of those Odes, (which are so admirably restor'd by Mr *Cowley* in our Language,) ought for ever to be the Standard of them; and we are bound, according to the practice of *Horace* and Mr *Cowley*, to copy him. Now, to apply this Axiom to our present Purpose, whosoever undertakes the writing of an *Opera*, (which is a Modern Invention though built indeed on the Foundations of Ethnick Worship,) is oblig'd to imitate the Design of the *Italians*, who have not only invented, but brought to Perfection, this sort of Dramatick Musical Entertainment. I have not been able by any search, to get any light either of the Time when it began, or of the first Author. But I have probable Reasons which induce me to believe, that some *Italians* having curiously observ'd the Gallantries of the *Spanish Moors* at their *Zambra's* or Royal Feasts, where Musick, Songs, and Dancing were in Perfection; together with their Machines, which are usual at their *Sortiia's*, or running at the Ring, and other Solemnities, may possibly have refin'd upon those Moresque Divertisements, and produc'd this delightful Entertainment, by leaving out the warlike part of the Carousels, and forming a Poetical Design for the use of the Machines, the Songs, and Dances. But however it began, (for this is only conjectural,) we know that for some Centuries, the Knowledge of Musick has flourish'd principally in *Italy*, the Mother of Learning and of Arts; that Poetry and Painting have been there restor'd, and so cultivated by *Italian* Masters, that all *Europe* has been enrich'd out of their Treasury, and the other Parts of it in relation to those delightful Arts, are still as much Provincial to *Italy*, as they were in the time of the *Roman* Empire. Their first *Opera*'s seem to have been intended for the Celebration of the Marriages of their Princes, or for the Magnificence of some general time of Joy. Accordingly the Expences of them were from the Purse of the Sovereign, or of the Republick, as they are still practis'd at *Venice*, *Rome*, and at other Places at their Carnivals. *Savoy* and *Florence* have often us'd them in their Courts, at the Weddings of their Dukes. And at *Turin* particularly, was perform'd the *Pastor Fido*, written by the famous *Guarini*, which is a Pastoral *Opera* made to solemnize the Marriage of a Duke of *Savoy*. The Prologue of it has given the Design to all the *French*; which is, a Compliment to the Sovereign Power by some God or Goddess; so that it looks no less than a kind of Embassy from Heaven to Earth. I said in the beginning of this Preface, that the Persons represented in *Opera*'s are generally Gods, Goddesses, and Heroes descended from them, who are suppos'd to be their peculiar Care; which hinders not, but that meaner Persons may sometimes gracefully be introduc'd, especially if they have relation to those first Times, which Poets call the *Golden Age*: wherein by reason of their Innocence, those happy Mortals were suppos'd to have had a more familiar Intercourse with Superior Beings; and therefore Shepherds might reasonably be admitted, as of all Callings the most innocent, the most happy, and who by reason of the spare Time they had, in their almost idle Employment, had most Leisure to make Verses, and to be in Love; without somewhat of which Passion, no *Opera* can possibly subsist.

'Tis almost needless to speak any thing of that noble Language, in which this Musical *Drama* was first invented and perform'd. All, who are conversant in the *Italian*, cannot but observe, that it is the softest, the sweetest, the most harmonious, not only of any Modern Tongue, but even beyond any of the Learned. It seems indeed to have been invented for the sake of Poetry and Musick; the Vowels are so abounding in all Words, especially in Terminations of them, that excepting some few Monosyllables, the whole Language ends in them. Then the Pronunciation is so Manly, and so Sonorous, that their very Speaking has more of Musick in it than *Dutch Poetry* and *Song*. It has withal deriv'd so much Copiousness and Eloquence from the *Greek* and *Latin*, in the Composition of Words, and the Formation of them, that (if after all we must call it Barbarous) 'tis the most Beautiful and most Learned of any Barbarism in Modern Tongues. And we may, at least, as justly praise it, as *Pyrrhus* did the *Roman* Discipline and Martial Order, that it was of *Barbarians*, (for so the *Greeks* call'd all other Nations) but had nothing in of Barbarity. This Language has in a manner been refin'd and purify'd from the *Gothick*, ever since the time of *Dante*; which is above Four Hundred Years ago; and the *French*, who now cast a longing Eye to their Country, are not less ambitious to possess their Elegance in Poetry and Musick; in both which they labour at Impossibilities. 'Tis true indeed, they have reform'd their Tongue, and brought both their Prose and Poetry to a Standard; the Sweetness as well as the Purity is much improv'd by throwing off the unnecessary Consonants, which made their Spelling tedious, and their Pronunciation harsh: But after all, as nothing can be improv'd beyond its own *Species*, or farther than its original Nature will allow; as an ill Voice, though never so thoroughly instructed in the Rules of Musick, can never be brought to sing harmoniously, nor many an honest Critick ever arrive to be a good Poet, so neither can the natural Harshness of the *French*, or their perpetual ill Accent be ever refin'd into perfect Harmony like the *Italian*. The *English* has yet more natural Disadvantages than the *French*; our original *Teutonick* consisting most in Monosyllables, and those incumbred with Consonants, cannot possibly be freed from those Inconveniencies. The rest of our Words, which are deriv'd from the *Latin* chiefly, and the *French*, with some small Sprinklings of *Greek*, *Italian*, and *Spanish*, are some Relief in Poetry, and help us to soften our uncouth Numbers; which together with our *English Genius*, incomparably beyond the Trifling of the *French*, in all the nobler Parts of Verse, will justly give us the Preheminence. But, on the other hand, the Effeminacy of our Pronunciation (a Defect common to us and to the *Danes*,) and our Scarcity of Female Rhymes have left the Advantage of Musical Composition for Songs, tho' not for Recitative, to our Neighbours.

Through these Difficulties, I have made a shift to struggle in my Part of the Performance of this *Opera*; which, as mean as it is, deserves at least a Pardon, because it has attempted a Discovery beyond any former Undertaker of our Nation; only remember, that if there be no North-East Passage to be found, the Fault is in Nature, and not in me. Or, as *Ben Johnson* tells us in the *Alchymist*, when Projection had fail'd, and the Glasses were all broken, there was enough however in the Bottoms of them to cure the Itch; so I may thus be positive, That if I have not succeeded, as I desire, yet there is somewhat still remaining, to satisfy the Curiosity or Itch of Sight and Hearing. Yet I have no great Reason to despair; for I may, without Vanity, own some Advantages, which are not common to every Writer; such as are the Knowledge of the *Italian* and *French* Language, and the being conversant with some of their best Performances in this Kind; which have furnish'd me with such Variety of Measures, as have given the Composer Monsieur *Grabut* what Occasions he cou'd wish, to shew his extraordinary Talent, in diversifying the Recitative, the Lyrical Part, and the Chorus: In all which, (not to attribute any Thing to my own Opinion,) the best Judges, and those too of the best Quality, who have honour'd his Rehearsals with their Presence, have no less commended the Happiness of his Genius than his Skill. And let me have the Liberty to add one Thing; that he has so exactly express'd my Sense, in all Places, where I intended to move the Passions, that he seems to have enter'd into my Thoughts, and to have been the Poet as well as the Composer. [...]

'Tis no easy Matter in our Language to make Words so smooth, and Numbers so harmonious, that they shall almost set themselves. And yet there are Rules for this in Nature: And as great a Certainty of Quantity in our Syllables, as either in the *Greek* or *Latin:* But let Poets and Judges understand those first, and then let them begin to study *English.* When they have chaw'd awhile upon these Preliminaries, it may be they will scarce adventure to tax me with want of Thought and Elevation of Fancy in this Work; for they will soon be satisfied, that those are not of the Nature of this Sort of Writing: The Necessity of double Rhimes, and ordering of the Words and Numbers for the Sweetness of the Voice, are the main Hinges on which an *Opera* must move; and both of these are without the Compass of any Art to teach another to perform; unless Nature in the first Place has done her Part, by enduing the Poet with that Nicety of Hearing, that the Discord of Sounds in Words shall as much offend him, as a Seventh in Musick wou'd a good Composer. I have therefore no Need to make Excuses for Meanness of Thought in many Places: The *Italians*, with all the Advantages of their Language, are continually forc'd upon it; or rather they affect it. The chief Secret is in the Choice of Words; and by this Choice I do not here mean Elegancy of Expression, but Propriety of Sound, to be varied according to the Nature of the Subject. [...]

The same Reasons which depress Thought in an *Opera*, have a stronger Effect upon the Words; especially in our Language: For there is no maintaining the Purity of *English* in short Measures, where the Rhime returns so quick, and is so often Female, or double Rhime, which is not natural to our Tongue, because it consists too much of Monosyllables, and those too, most commonly clogg'd with Consonants; for which Reason I am often forc'd to coin new Words, revive some that are antiquated, and botch others; as if I had not serv'd out my Time in Poetry, but was bound 'Prentice to some Doggrel Rhimer, who makes Songs to Tunes, and sings them for a Livelihood. 'Tis true, I have not been often put to this Drudgery; but where I have, the Words will sufficiently shew, that I was then a Slave to the Composition, which I will never be again: 'Tis my Part to invent, and the Musician's to humour that Invention. I may be counsell'd, and will always follow my Friend's Advice, where I find it reasonable; but will never part with the Power of the *Militia*.

I am now to acquaint my Reader with somewhat more particular concerning this *Opera*, after having begg'd his Pardon for so long a Preface to so short a Work. It was originally intended only for a Prologue to a Play, of the Nature of the *Tempest*; which is a Tragedy mix'd with *Opera*; or a *Drama* written in Blank Verse, adorn'd with Scenes, Machines, Songs and Dances: So that the Fable of it is all spoken and Acted by the best of the Comedians; the other Part of the Entertainment to be perform'd by the same Singers and Dancers who are introduc'd in this present *Opera*. It cannot properly be call'd a Play, because the Action of it is suppos'd to be conducted sometimes by supernatural Means, or Magick; nor an *Opera*, because the Story of it is not sung. But more of this at its proper Time: But some intervening Accidents having hitherto deferr'd the Performance of the main Design, I propos'd to the Actors, to turn the intended Prologue into an Entertainment by it self, as you now see it, by adding two Acts more to what I had already written. The Subject of it is wholly Allegorical; and the Allegory it self so very obvious, that it will no sooner be read than understood. 'Tis divided according to the plain and natural Method of every Action, into three Parts. For even *Aristotle* himself is contented to say simply, That in all Actions there is a Beginning, a Middle, and an End; after which Model, all the *Spanish* Plays are built.

The Descriptions of the Scenes, and other Decorations of the Stage, I had from Mr *Betterton*, who has spar'd neither for Industry, nor Cost, to make this Entertainment perfect, nor for Invention of the Ornaments to beautify it.

To conclude, though the Enemies of the Composer are not few, and that there is a Party form'd against him of his own Profession, I hope, and am perswaded, that this Prejudice will turn in the End to his Advantage. For the greatest Part of an Audience is always uninteress'd, though seldom knowing; and if the Musick be well compos'd, and well perform'd, they who find themselves pleas'd, will be so wise as not to be impos'd upon, and fool'd out of their Satisfaction. The Newness of the Undertaking is all the Hazard: When *Opera's* were first set up in *France*, they were not follow'd over eagerly; but they gain'd daily upon their Hearers, 'till they grew to that Height of Reputation, which they now enjoy. The *English*, I confess, are not altogether so Musical as the *French*; and yet they have been pleas'd already with the *Tempest*, and some Pieces that follow'd, which were neither much better written, nor so well compos'd as this. If it finds Encouragement, I dare promise my self to mend my Hand, by making a more pleasing Fable: In the mean Time, every loyal *English man* cannot but be satisfy'd with the Moral of this, which so plainly represents the Double Restoration of his Sacred Majesty.

Preface to *Albion and Albanius*, 1735

'A double career as singer and courtesan'
JOHN ROSSELLI

She was the daughter of a cook and a washerwoman; at fourteen she married the assistant to a dentist who worked in the crowded open space outside the viceregal castle at the heart of Naples. Her job was to draw the customers to the dentist's booth by singing in both Neapolitan and Italian; with her fine voice and looks she soon was being kept by members of the nobility, and her husband was paid off and dispatched to Rome, though she seems not to have broken off all relations with him.

Ciulla then took singing lessons (whether for the first time or not is unclear) and made her opera debut in the Naples public theatre, where through the next four years she sang parts requiring technical competence. Because of her continuing sexual adventures she was several times threatened with expulsion from Naples and at least once expelled. In 1675 she went on what seems to have been a tour of several leading Italian towns, accompanied by a large train including a castrato (who may have been her singing partner) and a bravo. She returned a widow; rumour – unsubstantiated – said she had had her husband killed. She sang again, this time at the Viceroy's, but soon afterwards, whether owing to the rumour or to a scurrilous pamphlet naming her lovers, she was arrested and put into a conventual home for fallen women. She was got out eighteen days later by a young man from a rich family, who presently married her even though he too had to undergo two months' imprisonment.

Ciulla, it seems, had made a vow to the Madonna that if she could marry she would be faithful to her new husband; she gave the Madonna all her jewels, lived with her Carluccio in quiet suburban ease, and gave birth to her only child, a daughter, when she was thirty-eight.

Singers of Italian Opera, 1992

'Theatrical illusions that can't be serious'
JOSEPH ADDISON

No. 5   Tuesday, March 6, 1711

Spectatum admissi risum teneatis? . . .
Hor.*

An Opera may be allowed to be extravagantly lavish in its Decorations, as its only Design is to gratify the Senses, and keep up an indolent Attention in the Audience. Common Sense however requires, that there should be nothing in the Scenes and Machines which may appear Childish and Absurd. How would the Wits of King *Charles*'s Time have laughed to have seen *Nicolini* exposed to a Tempest in Robes of Ermin, and sailing in an open Boat upon a Sea of Paste-Board? What a Field of Raillery would they have been let into, had they been entertain'd with painted Dragons spitting Wild-fire, enchanted Chariots drawn by *Flanders* Mares, and real Cascades in artificial Land-skips? A little Skill in Criticism would inform us that Shadows and Realities ought not to be mix'd together in the same Piece; and that Scenes, which are designed as the Representations of Nature, should be filled with Resemblances, and not with the Things themselves. If one would represent a wide Champion Country filled with Herds and Flocks, it would be ridiculous to draw the Country only upon the Scenes, and to crowd several Parts of the Stage with Sheep and Oxen. This is joining together Inconsistencies, and making the Decoration partly Real and partly Imaginary. I would recommend what I have here said, to the Directors, as well as to the Admirers, of our Modern Opera.

As I was walking in the Streets about a Fortnight ago, I saw an ordinary Fellow carrying a Cage full of little Birds upon his Shoulder; and, as I was wondering with my self what Use he would put them to, he was met very luckily by an Acquaintance, who had the same

* *Motto.* Horace, *Ars Poetica*, 5: Admitted to the sight, would you not laugh?

Curiosity. Upon his asking him what he had upon his Shoulder, he told him, that he had been buying Sparrows for the Opera. Sparrows for the Opera, says his Friend, licking his Lips, what are they to be roasted? No, no, says the other, they are to enter towards the end of the first Act, and to fly about the Stage.

This strange Dialogue awakened my Curiosity so far that I immediately bought the Opera, by which means I perceived that the Sparrows were to act the part of Singing Birds in a delightful Grove: though upon a nearer Enquiry I found the Sparrows put the same Trick upon the Audience, that Sir *Martin Mar-all* practised upon his Mistress; for, though they flew in Sight, the Musick proceeded from a Consort of Flagellets and Bird-calls which was planted behind the Scenes. At the same time I made this Discovery, I found by the Discourse of the Actors, that there were great Designs on foot for the Improvement of the Opera; that it had been proposed to break down a part of the Wall, and to surprize the Audience with a Party of an hundred Horse, and that there was actually a Project of bringing the *New-River* into the House, to be employed in Jetteaus and Water-works. This Project, as I have since heard, is post-poned 'till the Summer-Season; when it is thought the Coolness that proceeds from Fountains and Cascades will be more acceptable and refreshing to People of Quality. In the mean time, to find out a more agreeable Entertainment of the Winter-Season, the Opera of *Rinaldo* is filled with Thunder and Lightning, Illuminations, and Fireworks; which the Audience may look upon without catching Cold, and indeed without much Danger of being burnt; for there are several Engines filled with Water, and ready to play at a Minute's Warning, in case any such Accident should happen. However, as I have a very great Friendship for the Owner of this Theater, I hope that he has been wise enough to *insure* his House before he would let this Opera be acted in it.

It is no wonder, that those Scenes should be very surprizing, which were contrived by two Poets of different Nations, and raised by two Magicians of different Sexes. *Armida* (as we are told in the Argument) was an *Amazonian* Enchantress, and poor Seignior *Cassani* (as we learn from the *Persons represented*) a Christian Conjurer (*Mago Christiano*). I must confess I am very much puzzled to find how an *Amazon* should be versed in the Black Art, or how a good Christian, for such is the Part of the Magician, should deal with the Devil.

[. . .]

But to return to the Sparrows; there have been so many Flights of them let loose in this Opera, that it is feared the House will never get rid of them; and that in other Plays, they may make their Entrance in very wrong and improper Scenes, so as to be seen flying in a Lady's Bed-Chamber, or pearching upon a King's Throne; besides the Inconveniences which the Heads of the Audience may sometimes suffer from them. [...]

No. 13   Thursday, March 15, 1711

Dic mihi si fueras tu Leo qualis eris?
                Mart.*

There is nothing that of late Years has afforded Matter of greater Amusement to the Town than Signior *Nicolini*'s Combat with a Lion in the *Hay-Market*, which has been very often exhibited to the general Satisfaction of most of the Nobility and Gentry in the Kingdom of *Great Britain*. Upon the first Rumour of this intended Combat, it was confidently affirmed, and is still believed by many in both Galleries, that there would be a tame Lion sent from the *Tower* every Opera Night, in order to be killed by *Hydaspes*; this Report, tho' altogether groundless, so universally prevailed in the upper Regions of the Play-House that some of the most refined Politicians in those Parts of the Audience gave it out in Whisper, that the Lion was a Cousin-German of the Tyger who made his Appearance in King *William*'s Days, and that the Stage would be supplied with Lions at the publick Expence, during the whole Session. Many likewise were the Conjectures of the Treatment which this Lion was to meet with from the hands of Signior *Nicolini*; some suppos'd that he was to Subdue him in *Recitatevo*, as *Orpheus* used to serve the wild Beasts in his time, and afterwards to knock him on the head; some fancied that the Lion would not pretend to lay his Paws upon the Hero, by Reason of the received Opinion, that a Lion will not hurt a Virgin. Several, who pretended to have seen the Opera in *Italy*, had inform'd their Friends, that the Lion was to act a Part in *High-Dutch*, and roar twice or thrice to a thorough Base, before he fell at the Feet of *Hydaspes*. To clear up a Matter that was so variously reported, I have made it my Business to

---

* *Motto*. Martial, *Epigrams*, 12. 92. 4: Tell me, if you were a lion what kind would you be?

examine whether this pretended Lion is really the Savage he appears to be, or only a Counterfeit.

But before I communicate my Discoveries, I must acquaint the Reader, that upon my walking behind the Scenes last Winter, as I was thinking on something else, I accidentally justled against a monstrous Animal that extreamly startled me, and upon my nearer Survey of it, appeared to be a Lion-Rampant. The Lion, seeing me very much surprized, told me, in a gentle Voice, that I might come by him if I pleased: *For* (says he) *I do not intend to hurt any body*. I thanked him very kindly, and passed by him. And in a little time after saw him leap upon the Stage, and act his Part with very great Applause. It has been observ'd by several, that the Lion has changed his manner of Acting twice or thrice since his first Appearance; which will not seem strange, when I acquaint my Reader that the Lion has been changed upon the Audience three several times. The first Lion was a Candle-snuffer, who being a Fellow of a testy, cholerick Temper over-did his Part, and would not suffer himself to be killed so easily as he ought to have done; besides, it was observ'd of him, that he grew more surly every time he came out of the Lion; and having dropt some Words in ordinary Conversation, as if he had not fought his best, and that he suffered himself to be thrown upon his Back in the Scuffle, and that he would wrestle with Mr *Nicolini* for what he pleased, out of his Lion's Skin, it was thought proper to discard him: And it is verily believed to this Day, that had he been brought upon the Stage another time, he would certainly have done Mischief. Besides, it was objected against the first Lion, that he reared himself so high upon his hinder Paws, and walked in so erect a Posture, that he looked more like an old Man than a Lion.

[...]

The Acting Lion at present is, as I am informed, a Country Gentleman, who does it for his Diversion, but desires his Name may be concealed. He says very handsomely in his own Excuse, that he does not Act for Gain, that he indulges an innocent Pleasure in it, and that it is better to pass away an Evening in this manner, than in Gaming and Drinking: But at the same time says, with a very agreeable Raillery upon himself, that if his Name should be known, the ill-natured World might call him, *The Ass in the Lion's Skin* [...]

I must not conclude my Narrative, without taking Notice of a groundless Report that has been raised, to a Gentleman's Disadvantage, of whom I must declare my self an Admirer; namely, that Signior *Nicolini* and the Lion have been seen sitting peaceably by one another, and smoking a Pipe together, behind the Scenes; by which their common Enemies would insinuate, that it is but a sham Combat which they represent upon the Stage: But upon Enquiry I find, that if any such Correspondence has passed between them, it was not till the Combat was over, when the Lion was to be looked upon as dead, according to the received Rules of the *Drama*. Besides, this is what is practised every day in *Westminster-Hall*, where nothing is more usual than to see a Couple of Lawyers, who have been tearing each other to pieces in the Court, embracing one another as soon as they are out of it.

[. . .]

No. 18   Wednesday, March 21, 1711

. . . Equitis quoque jam migravit ab aure voluptas
Omnis ad incertos oculos & gaudia vana.

Hor.*

It is my Design in this Paper to deliver down to Posterity a faithful Account of the *Italian* Opera, and of the gradual Progress which it has made upon the *English* Stage: For there is no Question but our great Grand-children will be very curious to know the Reason why their Forefathers used to sit together like an Audience of Foreigners in their own Country, and to hear whole Plays acted before them in a Tongue which they did not understand.

Arsinoe was the first Opera that gave us a Taste of *Italian* Musick. The great Success this Opera met with, produced some Attempts of forming Pieces upon *Italian* Plans, which should give a more natural and reasonable Entertainment than what can be met with in the elaborate Trifles of that Nation. This alarm'd the Poetasters and Fidlers of the Town, who were used to deal in a more ordinary Kind of Ware; and therefore laid down an establish'd Rule, which is receiv'd as such to this Day, *That nothing is capable of being well set to Musick, that is not Nonsense.*

This Maxim was no sooner receiv'd, but we immediately fell to translating the *Italian* Operas; and as there was no great Danger of

---

* *Motto.* Horace, *Epistles*, 12. 1. 187–8:
  But now our *Nobles* too are Fops and Vain,
  Neglect the Sense, but love the Painted Scene. CREECH.

hurting the Sense of those extraordinary Pieces, our Authors would often make Words of their own which were entirely foreign to the Meaning of the Passages they pretended to translate; their chief Care being to make the Numbers of the *English* Verse answer to those of the *Italian*, that both of them might go to the same Tune. Thus the famous Song in *Camilla*,

> *Barbara si t'intendo, &c.*
> *Barbarous Woman, yes, I know your Meaning,*

which expresses the Resentments of an angry Lover, was translated into the *English* Lamentation

> *Frail are a Lover's Hopes, &c.*

And it was pleasant enough to see the most refined Persons of the *British* Nation dying away and languishing to Notes that were filled with a Spirit of Rage and indignation. It happen'd also very frequently, where the Sense was rightly translated, the necessary Transposition of Words which were drawn out of the Phrase of one Tongue into that of another, made the Musick appear very absurd in one Tongue that was very natural in the other. I remember an *Italian* Verse that ran thus Word for Word,

> *And turn'd my Rage into Pity;*

which the *English* for Rhime sake translated,

> *And into Pity turn'd my Rage.*

By this Means the soft Notes that were adapted to *Pity* in the *Italian*, fell upon the Word *Rage* in the *English*; and the angry Sounds that were tuned to *Rage* in the Original, were made to express *Pity* in the Translation. It oftentimes happen'd likewise, that the finest Notes in the Air fell upon the most insignificant Words in the Sentence. I have known the Word *And* pursu'd through the whole Gamut, have been entertain'd with many a melodious *The*, and have heard the most beautiful Graces, Quavers and Divisions bestow'd upon *Then*, *For*, and *From*; to the eternal Honour of our *English* Particles.

The next Step to our Refinement, was the introducing of *Italian* Actors into our Opera; who sung their Parts in their own Language, at the same Time that our Countrymen perform'd theirs in our native Tongue. The King or Hero of the Play generally spoke in *Italian*, and his Slaves answer'd him in *English*: The Lover frequently made his Court, and gain'd the Heart of his Princess in a Language which she did not understand. One would have thought it very difficult to have carry'd on Dialogues after this Manner, without an Interpreter between the Persons that convers'd together; but this was the State of the *English* Stage for about three Years.

At length the Audience grew tir'd of understanding Half the Opera, and therefore to ease themselves intirely of the Fatigue of Thinking, have so order'd it at Present that the whole Opera is perform'd in an unknown Tongue. We no longer understand the Language of our own Stage; insomuch that I have often been afraid, when I have seen our *Italian* Performers chattering in the Vehemence of Action, that they have been calling us Names, and abusing us among themselves; but I hope, since we do put such an entire Confidence in them, they will not talk against us before our Faces, though they may do it with the same Safety as if it were behind our Backs. In the mean Time I cannot forbear thinking how naturally an Historian, who writes Two or Three Hundred Years hence, and does not know the Taste of his wise Fore-fathers, will make the following Reflection, *In the Beginning of the Eighteenth Century the* Italian *Tongue was so well understood in* England, *that Opera's were acted on the publick Stage in that Language.*

One scarce knows how to be serious in the Confutation of an Absurdity that shews itself at the first Sight. It does not want any great Measure of Sense to see the Ridicule of this monstrous Practice; but what makes it the more astonishing, it is not the Taste of the Rabble, but of Persons of the greatest Politeness, which has establish'd it.

If the *Italians* have a Genius for Musick above the *English*, the *English* have a Genius for other Performances of a much higher Nature, and capable of giving the Mind a much nobler Entertainment. Would one think it was possible (at a Time when an Author lived that was able to write the *Phaedra* and *Hippolitus*) for a People to be so stupidly fond of the *Italian* Opera, as scarce to give a Third Days Hearing to that admirable Tragedy? Musick is certainly a very agreeable Entertainment, but if it would take the entire Possession of our Ears, if it would make us incapable of hearing Sense, if it would exclude Arts that have a much greater Tendency to the Refinement of humane Nature: I must confess I would allow it no better Quarter than *Plato* has done, who banishes it out of his Commonwealth.

At present, our Notions of Musick are so very uncertain, that we do not know what it is we like; only, in general, we are transported with any thing that is not *English*: So it be of a foreign Growth, let it be *Italian*, *French*, or *High-Dutch*, it is the same thing. In short, our *English* Musick is quite rooted out, and nothing yet planted in its stead.

When a Royal Palace is burnt to the Ground, every Man is at Liberty to present his Plan for a new one; and tho' it be but indifferently put together, it may furnish several Hints that may be of Use to a good Architect. I shall take the same Liberty in a following Paper, of giving my Opinion upon the Subject of Musick, which I shall lay down only in a problematical Manner to be considered by those who are Masters in the Art.

No. 29   Tuesday, April 3, 1711

... Sermo linguâ concinnus utrâque
Suavior: ut Chio nota si commista Falerni est.
                        Hor.*

There is nothing that has more startled our *English* Audience, than the *Italian Recitativo* at its first Entrance upon the Stage. People were wonderfully surprized to hear Generals singing the Word of Command, and Ladies delivering Messages in Musick. Our Country-men could not forbear laughing when they heard a Lover chanting out a Billet-doux, and even the Superscription of a Letter set to a Tune. The Famous Blunder in an old Play of *Enter a King and two Fidlers Solus*, was now no longer an Absurdity, when it was impossible for a Hero in a Desart, or a Princess in her Closet, to speak any thing unaccompanied with Musical Instruments.

But however this *Italian* Method of acting in *Recitativo* might appear at first hearing, I cannot but think it much more just than that which prevailed in our *English* Opera before this Innovation: The Transition from an Air to Recitative Musick being more natural than the passing from a Song to plain and ordinary Speaking, which was the common Method in *Purcell*'s Opera's.

The only Fault I find in our present Practice is the making use of *Italian Recitativo* with *English* Words.

---

* *Motto*. Horace, *Satires*, I. 10. 23–24: A style, where both tongues make a happy blend, has more charm, as when the Falernian wine is mixed with Chian.

To go to the Bottom of this Matter, I must observe, that the Tone, or (as the *French* call it) the Accent of every Nation in their ordinary Speech is altogether different from that of every other People, as we may see even in the *Welsh* and *Scotch*, who border so near upon us. By the Tone or Accent, I do not mean the Pronunciation of each particular Word, but the Sound of the whole Sentence. Thus it is very common for an *English* Gentleman, when he hears a *French* Tragedy, to complain that the Actors all of them speak in a Tone; and therefore he very wisely prefers his own Country-men, not considering that a Foreigner complains of the same Tone in an *English* Actor.

For this Reason, the Recitative Musick in every Language should be as different as the Tone or Accent of each Language, for otherwise what may properly express a Passion in one Language, will not do it in another. Every one who has been long in *Italy* knows very well, that the Cadences in the *Recitativo* bear a remote Affinity to the Tone of their Voices in ordinary Conversation, or to speak more properly, are only the Accents of their Language made more Musical and Tuneful.

Thus the Notes of Interrogation, or Admiration, in the *Italian* Musick (if one may so call them) which resemble their Accents in Discourse on such Occasions, are not unlike the ordinary Tones of an *English* Voice when we are angry; insomuch that I have often seen our Audiences extreamly mistaken as to what has been doing upon the Stage, and expecting to see the Hero knock down his Messenger, when he has been asking him a Question; or fancying that he quarrels with his Friend, when he only bids him Good-morrow.

For this Reason the *Italian* artists cannot agree with our *English* Musicians, in admiring *Purcell*'s Compositions, and thinking his Tunes so wonderfully adapted to his Words, because both Nations do not always express the same Passions by the same Sounds.

I am therefore humbly of Opinion, that an *English* Composer should not follow the *Italian* Recitative too servilely, but make use of many gentle Deviations from it, in Compliance with his own Native Language. He may Copy out of it all the lulling Softness and *Dying Falls* (as *Shakespear* calls them,) but should still remember that he ought to accommodate himself to an *English* Audience, and by humouring the Tone of our Voices in ordinary Conversation, have the same Regard to the Accent of his own Language, as those Persons had to theirs whom he professes to imitate. It is observed, that several of the singing Birds of our own Country learn to sweeten their Voices, and mellow the Harshness of their natural Notes, by practising under those that come from warmer Climates. In the same manner I would allow the *Italian* Opera to lend our *English* Musick as much as may grace and soften it, but never entirely to annihilate and destroy it. Let the Infusion be as strong as you please, but still let the Subject Matter of it be *English*.

A Composer should fit his Musick to the Genius of the People, and consider that the Delicacy of Hearing, and Taste of Harmony, has been formed upon those Sounds which every Country abounds with: In short, that Musick is of a Relative Nature, and what is Harmony to one Ear, may be Dissonance to another.

The same Observations which I have made upon the recitative part of Musick, may be applied to all our Songs and Airs in general.

Signior *Baptist Lully* acted like a Man of Sense in this Particular. He found the *French* Musick extreamly defective, and very often barbarous: However, knowing the Genius of the People, the Humour of their Language, and the prejudiced Ears he had to deal with, he did not pretend to extirpate the *French* Musick, and plant the *Italian* in its stead; but only to Cultivate and Civilize it with innumerable Graces and Modulations which he borrow'd from the *Italian*. By this means the *French* Musick is now perfect in its kind; and when you say it is not so good as the *Italian*, you only mean that it does not please you so well, for there is scarce a *Frenchman* who would not wonder to hear you give the *Italian* such a Preference. The Musick of the *French* is indeed very properly adapted to their Pronunciation and Accent, as their whole Opera wonderfully favours the Genius of such a gay airy People. The Chorus in which that Opera abounds, gives the Parterre frequent Opportunities of joining in Consort with the Stage. This Inclination of the Audience to Sing along with the Actors, so prevails with them, that I have sometimes known the Performer on the Stage do no more in a Celebrated Song, than the Clerk of a Parish Church, who serves only to raise the Psalm, and is afterwards drown'd in the Musick of the Congregation. Every Actor that comes on the Stage is a Beau. The Queens and Heroines are so Painted, that they appear as Ruddy and Cherry-cheek'd as Milk-maids. The Shepherds are all Embroider'd, and acquit themselves in a Ball better than our *English* Dancing-Masters. I have seen a couple of Rivers appear in red Stockings; and *Alpheus*, instead of having his Head cover'd with Sedge and Bull-Rushes, making Love in a fair full-bottom'd Perriwig, and a Plume of Feathers, but with a Voice so full of Shakes and Quavers that I should have thought the Murmurs of a Country Brook the much more agreeable Musick.

I remember the last Opera I saw in that Merry Nation, was the Rape of *Proserpine*, where *Pluto*, to make the more tempting Figure, puts himself in a *French* Equipage, and brings *Ascalaphus* along with him as his *Valet de Chambre*. This is what we call Folly and impertinence; but what the *French* look upon as Gay and Polite.

I shall add no more to what I have here offer'd than that Musick, Architecture and Painting, as well as Poetry and Oratory, are to deduce their Laws and Rules from the general Sense and Taste of Mankind, and not from the Principles of those Arts themselves; or in other Words, the Taste is not to conform to the Art, but the Art to the Taste. Musick is not design'd to please only Chromatick Ears, but all that are capable of distinguishing harsh from disagreeable Notes. A Man of an ordinary Ear is a Judge whether a Passion is express'd in proper Sounds, and whether the Melody of those Sounds be more or less pleasing.

The Spectator, 1711

'The fundamental principles of the art-form'
FRANCESCO ALGAROTTI

As soon as the desired regulation shall have been introduced on the theatre, it will then be incumbent to proceed to the various constituent parts of an Opera, in order that those amendments should be made in each, whereof they severally now appear the most deficient. The leading object to be maturely considered is the nature of the subject to be chosen; an article of much more consequence, than is commonly imagined; for the success or failure of the drama depends, in a great measure, on a good or bad choice of the subject. It is here of no less consequence, than, in architecture, the plan is to an edifice; or the canvas, in painting, is to a picture; because, thereon the poet draws the outlines of his intended representation, and its colouring is the task of the musical composer. It is therefore the poet's duty, as chief engineer of the undertaking, to give directions to the dancers, the machinists, the painters; nay, down even to those who are entrusted with the care of the wardrobe, and dressing the performers. The poet is to carry in his mind a comprehensive view of the *whole* of the drama; because those parts, which are not the productions of his pen, ought to flow from the dictates of his actuating judgment which is to give being and movement to the whole.

At the first institution of Operas, the poets imagined the heathen mythology to be the best source from which they could derive subjects for their dramas. Hence Daphne, Euridice, Ariana, were made choice of by Octavius Rinuccini, and are looked upon as the eldest musical dramas; having been exhibited about the beginning of the last century. There was besides Poliziano's Orpheus, which also had been represented with instrumental accompaniments; as well as another performance that was no more than a medley of dancing and music, contrived by Bergonzo Rolla, for the entertainment of a duke of Milan, in the city of Tortona. A particular species of drama was exhibited at Venice for the amusement of Henry the Third; it had been set to music by the famous Zarlino. – Add to these, some other performances, which ought only to be considered, as so many rough sketches and preludes to a complete Opera.

The intent of our poets, was to revive the Greek tragedy in all its lustre, and to introduce Melpomene on our stage, attended by music, dancing, and all that imperial pomp, with which, at the brilliant periods of a Sophocles and Euripides, she was wont to be escorted. And that such splendid pageantry might appear to be the genuine right of tragedy, the poets had recourse for their subjects to the heroic ages, and heathen mythology. From that fountain, the bard, according to his inventive pleasure, introduced on the theatre all the deities of paganism; now shifting his scene to Olympus, now fixing it in the Elysian shades, now plunging it down to Tartarus, with as much ease as if to Argos or to Thebes. And thus by the invention of superiour beings, he gave an air of probability to most surprizing and wonderful events. Every circumstance being thus elevated above the sphere of mortal existence, it necessarily followed, that the singing of actors in an Opera, appeared a true imitation of the language made use of by the deities they represented.

This then was the original cause, why in the first dramas that had been exhibited in the courts of sovereigns, or the palaces of princes, in order to celebrate their nuptials, such expensive machinery was employed; not an article was omitted that could excite an idea of whatever is most wonderful to be seen either on earth, or in the heavens. – To superadd a greater diversity, and thereby give a new animation to the whole, a crowded chorus of singers were admitted, as well as dances of various contrivance, with a special attention that the execution of the ballet should coincide, and be combined with the choral song: all which pleasing effects were made to spring naturally from the subject of the drama.

No doubt then can remain of the exquisite delight that such magic representations must have given to an enraptured assembly; for although it consisted but of a single subject, it nevertheless displayed an almost infinite variety of entertainment. There is even now frequent opportunity of seeing on the French musical theatre, a spirited likeness to what is here advanced; because the Opera was first introduced in Paris by Cardinal Mazarine, whither it carried the same magnificent apparatus with which it had made its appearance at his time in Italy.

These representations must, however, have afterwards suffered not a little by the intermixture of buffoon characters, which are such ill-suited companions to the dignity of heroes and of Gods; for by making the spectators laugh out of season, they disconcert the solemnity of the piece. Some traces of this theatric impropriety, are even now observable in the eldest of the French musical dramas.

The Opera did not long remain confined in the courts of sovereigns, and palaces of princes, but emancipating itself from such thraldom, display'd its charms on public theatres, to which the curious of all ranks were admitted, for pay. But in this situation, as must obviously occur to whoever reflects, it was impossible that the pomp and splendour which was attendant on this entertainment from its origin, could be continued. The falling off in that article, was occasioned principally by the exorbitant salaries the singers insisted on, which had been but inconsiderable at the first outset of the musical drama; as for instance, a certain female singer was called *La Centoventi*, *The Hundred-and-Twenty*, for having received so many crowns, for her performance during a single carnival. A sum which hath been amazingly exceeded since, almost beyond all bounds.

Hence arose the necessity for opera-directors to change their measures, and to be as frugally economical on one hand, as they found themselves unavoidably profuse on the other. Through such saving, the Opera may be said to have fallen from heaven upon the earth, and being divorced from an intercourse with gods, to have humbly resigned itself to that of mortals.

Thence forward prevailed a general renunciation of all subjects to be found in the fabulous accounts of the heathen deities, and none were made choice of, but those derived from the histories of humble mankind, because less magnificent in their nature, and therefore less liable to large disbursements for their exhibition.

The directors, obliged to circumspection, for their own safety, were induced to imagine they might supply the place of all that costly pomp and splendid variety of decoration, to which the dazzled spectators had been accustomed so long, by introducing a chaster regularity into their drama, seconded by the auxiliary charms of a more poetical diction, as well as by the concurring powers of a more exquisite musical composition. This project gained ground the faster from the public's observing, that one of these arts was entirely employed in modelling itself on our ancient authors; and the other, solely intent on enriching itself with new ornaments; which made Operas to be looked upon by many, as having nearly reached the pinnacle of perfection. However, that these representations might not appear too naked and uniform, interludes and ballets, to amuse the audience, were introduced between the acts; and thus, by degrees, the opera took that form, which is now practised on our theatres.

It is an uncontrovertible fact, that subjects for an operatical drama, whether taken from pagan mythology or historians, have inevitable inconveniencies annexed to them. The famous subjects, on account of the great number of machines, and magnificent apparatus, which they require, often distress the poet into limits too narrow for him, to carry on and unravel his plot with propriety; because he is not allowed either sufficient time or space to display the passions of each character, so absolutely necessary to the compleating of an opera, which, in the main, is nothing more than a tragic-poem recited to musical sounds; and from the inconvenience alluded to here, it has happened that a great number of the French Operas, as well as the first of the Italian are nothing better than entertainments for the eye; having more the appearance of a masquerade than of a regular dramatic performance: because therein the principal action is whelmed, as it were, under a heap of accessaries; and the poetical part being so flimsy and wretched, it was, with just reason, called a string of madrigals.

On the other hand, the subjects taken from history, are liable to the objection of their not being so well adapted to music, which seems to exclude them from all plea of probability. This impleaded error may be observed every day upon the Italian stage. For who can be brought to think, that the trillings of an air flow so justifiably from the mouth of a Julius Caesar or a Cato, as from the lips of Venus or Apollo? Moreover, historical subjects do not furnish so striking a variety, as those that are fabulous; they are apt to be too austere and monotonous. The stage, in such representations, would for ever exhibit an almost solitary scene, unless we are willing to number among the ranks of actors, the mob of attendants that crowd after sovereigns, even into their closets. Besides, it is no easy matter to contrive ballets or interludes suitable to subjects taken from history; because all such entertainments ought to form a kind of social union, and become, as it were, constituent parts of the whole. Such, for example, on the French stage, is 'The Ballet of the Shepherds', that celebrates the marriage of Medoro with Angelica, and makes Orlando acquainted with this accumulated wretchedness. But this is far from being the effect of entertainments obtruded into the Italian Operas; in which, although the subject be Roman, and the ballet consist of dancers dressed like Roman soldiers, yet so unconnected is it with the business of the drama, that the scozzese or furlana might as well be danced. And this is the reason why subjects chosen from history, are for the most part necessitated to appear naked, or to make use of such alien accoutrements as neither belong, nor are by any means suitable to them.

In order to obviate such inconveniencies, the only means left to the poet is, to exert all his judgment and taste in chusing the subject of his drama, that thereby he may attain his end, which is to delight the eyes and the ears, to rouze up, and to affect the hearts of an audience, without the risk of sinning against reason or common sense: wherefore, the most prudent method he can adopt, will be to make choice of an event that has happened either in very remote times, or in countries very distant from us, and quite estranged from our usages, which may afford various incidents of the marvellous, notwithstanding that the subject, at the same time, be extremely simple and not unknown: two desirable requisites.

The great distance of place where the action is fixed, will prevent the recital of it to musical sounds, from appearing quite so improbable to us. The marvellousness of the theme will furnish the author with an opportunity of interweaving therewith dances, chorusses, and a variety of scenical decorations. The simplicity and notoriety of it will exempt his muse from the perplexing trouble and tedious preparations necessary to make the personages of a drama known, that, suitable to his notification, may be displayed their passions, the main spring and actuating spirit of the stage.

The two operas of Dido, and of Achilles in Sciros, written by the celebrated Metastasio, come very near to the mark proposed here. The subjects of these dramatic poems are simple, and taken from very remote antiquity, but without being too far fetched. In the midst of their most impassioned scenes, there is an opportunity of introducing splendid banquets, magnificent embassies, embarkations, chorusses, battles, conflagrations, etc. so as to give a farther extension to the sovereignty of the musical drama, and make its rightfulness be more ascertained than has been hitherto allowed.

The same doctrine may be advanced in regard to an Opera on the subject of Montezuma, as much on account of the greatness, as of the novelty of such an action, as that emperor's catastrophe must afford. A display of the Mexican and Spanish customs, seen for a first time together, must form a most beautiful contrast; and the barbaric magnificence of America, would receive various heightenings by being opposed in different views to that of Europe.

Several subjects may likewise be taken from Ariosto and Tasso, equally fitting as Montezuma, for the opera-theatre; for, besides these being so universally known, they would furnish not only a fine field for exercising the passions, but also for introducing all the surprizing illusions of the magic art.

An Opera of Aeneas in Troy, or of Iphigenia in Aulis, would answer the same purpose; and to the great variety for scenes and machinery, still greater heightenings might be derived from the enchanting *poetry* of Virgil and Euripides.

There are many other subjects to the full as applicable to the stage, and that may be found equally fraught with marvellous incidents. Let then a poet, who is judicious enough, make a prudent collection of the subjects truly dramatic, that are to be found in tracing the fabulous accounts of the heathen gods, and do the same also in regard to more modern times. Such a proceeding relative to the Opera, would not be unlike to what is oft-times found necessary in states, which it is impossible to preserve from decay, and in the unimpaired enjoyment of constitutional vigour, without making them revert from time to time to their original principles.

'An Essay on Operas', tr. anon, 1768

'Some pluses and minuses of tragedy as opera'
VOLTAIRE

Since you intend to frequent our productions during your stay in Paris, I will tell you something about the opera, although I do not deal expressly with tragedy and comedy in this work. My reason is that there have been excellent treatises written on tragic and comic theatre, especially in the prefaces to our best plays; but almost nothing has been said about opera.

Saint-Evremond has worn himself out railing coldly against this sort of work. He finds it ridiculous to put passions and dialogues into song. He did not know that the Greek and Roman tragedies were sung, or that their stage had a melody comparable to our recitative, which was composed by a musician, and that the choruses were done like ours. Who doesn't know that music is an expression of the passions? Saint-Evremond, in praising *Sophonisbe* and in condemning the opera, shows that he has little taste and no ear.

The great fault of our opera is that a tragedy cannot be all passion. It needs motive, detail, and events drawn out over time, and music cannot adequately render that which is not heart-felt. [. . .] In opera, one is therefore reduced to removing all those details that are not innately interesting but which contribute to making a play interesting over all. One mentions love, and yet, in these works, even this passion never has the right connotations to touch us and render its full effect.

The declarations of Phèdre and Orosmane cannot be suffered in operatic theatre. Our recitative exerts a brevity and limpness, which leads almost of necessity to mediocrity. *Atys* and *Armide* are hardly to be elevated above this level. The scenes between Orestes and Iphigenia are very beautiful, but this very superiority leaves the rest of the opera behind. [. . .] Theseus, in the opera of that name, says to his mistress without preparation: 'I am the son of the King.' She replies to him: 'You, sire?' The secret of his birth is not otherwise explained. This is a serious failing. And if this recognition had been well prepared and handled, if all the details necessary to make it seem both realistic and surprising had been employed, the failing would have been even greater, because the music would have made these details tedious.

Here then is an intrinsically defective text. Add to all these imperfections that of being subservient to the sterility of the musicians, who cannot express all the words of our language as well as the Italians can theirs. They have to compose little airs on to which the poet is forced to add a number of trivial and dull words, which often bear no relation to the play. [...] This puerile constraint is further augmented by the paucity of expressions in our language suitable for musicians. [...] This is why there has not been a decent musical tragedy since Quinault. The authors have realized the extreme difficulties in mixing a grand and pathetic theme incorporating action with social scenes, in omitting the necessary details, and yet being interesting. They are almost always thrown into an even more mediocre genre, namely the ballet. [...]

A single love scene, well set to music and sung by a fêted actor, draws all of Paris and renders true beauties insipid. The court cannot stand *Polyeucte* once they have been to the ballet where they have heard a few easily memorable couplets. Thus is bad taste re-enforced, and one insensibly forgets that which made the nation great. I repeat once again that the opera must be set on a different footing if it is not to merit the spite that it has won in all of the nations of Europe.

The Knowledge of the beauties and defects of poetry and rhetoric in the French language [*Connaissance des Beautés et des Défauts de la Poésie et de l'Eloquence dans la langue française* 1749], tr. Matthew Scott

One of your nation's celebrated authors has said that tragedy, wandering and abandoned since the fine days of Athens, has searched country after country for someone who can help to restore its former glory, without being able to find him.

If he means that no nation has theatres in which the chorus is always present, singing strophes, epodes and antistrophes to the accompaniment of a solemn dance; that no nation makes their actors appear on a raised stage, their faces covered with a mask that shows sadness on one side and joy on the other; and that declamation in our tragedies is not set to the music of flutes, then he is undoubtedly right. I am not sure if this is our loss. I do not know whether the form of our tragedies, more closely linked to nature, is not of equal value to the Greek, which had a more imposing apparatus.

If the author wants to say that in general this great genre has not been esteemed as it was since the Renaissance; that there are nations in Europe who have treated the successors of Sophocles and Euripides with ingratitude; that our theatres are not the superb structures that the Athenians gloried in; and that we do not take the same pains with these spectacles that have become so necessary in our huge towns, then one should be entirely of his opinion.

Where can one find a sight that will lend us an impression of the Greek stage? Perhaps its legacy lies in your tragedies called operas. 'What!' they will tell you, 'could Italian opera bear any resemblance to the theatre of Athens?' Yes. The recitative is precisely the chant of the ancients. It is declamation in notes and accompanied by musical instrumentation. This chanting, which is only boring in your worst tragic operas, is to be admired in your fine plays. The choruses that you have added in recent years, and which are intimately linked to the plot, resemble the choruses of the ancients all the more since they are expressed in music quite different from the recitative. Equally, the strophe, epode and antistrophe of the Greeks were sung quite differently from the chant. Add to these the fact that in several of the tragic operas of the celebrated Metastasio, the unities of place, action and time are observed, and that these plays are full of the poetry of expression and the continual refinement which embellishes nature without changing it. Since the Greeks, this is a talent that only Racine here and Addison in England have possessed.

I am aware that these tragedies, so imposing in the charm of their music and the magnificence of their spectacle, have a flaw that the Greeks always avoided; I also know that this flaw has made monsters of the most beautiful, and moreover the most structured plays. It consists of the addition to all the scenes of short, cropped arias or detached ariettas that interrupt the action and stress the trills of an effeminate, if brilliant, voice at the expense of interest and good sense. The grand author, whom I have referred to, and who has taken many of his plays from our tragic theatre, remedied this now universal flaw by virtue of his genius. The lyrics of his arias often add to the plot and are passionate. They are sometimes comparable to the most beautiful parts of Horace's odes. [...] Still, it has to be admitted that opera, in seducing the Italians by virtue of its music, has destroyed one aspect of Greek tragedy while reviving another.

Our French opera should cause us even more trouble. Our chants are far less reminiscent of normal declamation than yours. They are more languid and never allow the scenes their proper length. They demand short dialogues in cropped aphorisms, each developing into a kind of song. [...] Among our many flaws, we share with you an infinite number of detached arias in our most tragic operas, but ours are even more flawed than yours because they are less fitted to the plot. The lyrics are almost always written to serve the composer, who, being unable to express the virile and energetic aspects of our language in his little songs, requires lyrics that are effeminate, limp, vague, foreign to the plot and suited as much as possible to short arias, which are similar to those known in Venice as 'barcarolles'. [...]

Despite these flaws, I still deign to think that our fine tragic operas, such as *Atys*, *Armide* and *Thésée*, are those that can give us some idea of the theatre of Athens. For, like those of the Greeks, these tragedies are sung and the chorus, however perverted we have made it and however insipidly panegyrical it has become with its romantic morals, still resembles that of the Greeks in being often on stage.

Ultimately, one must admit that the form of our tragic operas returns us to the form of Greek tragedy in some respects. In general it seems to me, from consulting the men of letters who know antiquity, that these tragic operas are both the copy and the ruin of the Attic tragedy. They are copies inasmuch as they admit the chant, the choruses, machines and gods. They are destructive because they accustom young people to know themselves through sound rather than spirit; to prefer the ear to the soul and trills to sublime thoughts; and to value the most insipid and worst written works when they are sustained by a few arias that please them. But in spite of all these flaws, the delight that results from this happy mix of scenes, choruses, dance, symphonies and the variety of settings, undercuts even the critic; and the best comedy or tragedy is never as assiduously attended as a mediocre opera by the same people. Regular, noble and severe beauties are not the most sought after by the mass: if *Cinna* is performed once or twice, *Les Fêtes vénitiennes* plays for three months; an epic poem is read less than licentious epigrams; a little novel is more debated than the life of a president. Scarcely anyone commissions great painters, but people fight over distorted figures from China, and fragile ornaments. People love and treasure cabinets, but neglect noble architecture; in short, in all genres the little charms soar above the true merits.

Essay on ancient and modern tragedy, addressed to His Eminence Monseigneur Cardinal Quirini, Noble Venetian, Bishop of Brescia, the Vatican Librarian [*Dissertation sur la tragédie ancienne modeme*, 1748], tr. Matthew Scott

'Helpful hints for composers of *opera seria*'
PIETRO METASTASIO

My dear Monsieur Hasse has never been absent from my heart since I quitted Vienna; but, hitherto, I have not been able to devote myself to your service, because in this most idle bustle I am hardly my own master [except] when I sleep. So fully am I engaged in walking, shooting, music, cards, and conversation, that not a moment remains for private meditation, without defrauding society. Yet, in spite of all these impediments, I am penetrated with such remorse for having so long neglected you, that I am now determined to obey your commands. But what can I possibly suggest to you which has not already occurred to your own mind? After so many illustrious proofs of knowledge, judgment, grace, expression, invention, and ingenuity, with which you only have been able to dispute the palm of harmonic primacy with our nation: after having breathed with your seducing notes into so many poetical compositions that life and soul which the authors themselves were unable to furnish or imagine, what light, advertisement, or instruction, can you expect me to furnish? If I were only to mention things with which you are *not* acquainted, my letter would already be finished; but if you wish me to converse with you, God knows when I should have done.

And now, as *Attilio Regolo* is to be the subject of my letter, I shall begin by developing the characters, which, perhaps, are not expressed in so lively a manner in the piece, as I had conceived them in my mind.

In *Regolo*, it has been my intention to delineate the character of a Roman hero of consummate virtue, according to the pagan idea, not only in principle, but practice; whose fortitude has been long tried, and is proof against every caprice of fortune. A rigid and scrupulous observer, as well of justice and probity, as of the laws and customs which time and the great authority of his ancestors have rendered sacred to his country. Sensible to all the gentler passions of humanity, but superior to each. A great commander, good citizen, and an affectionate father; but never considering these characters as distinct from his country, or otherwise among the blessings or evils of life, than as they eventually contribute to the welfare or injury to that whole of which he considered himself as a part. A great friend to glory, but regarding it merely as a reward to which individuals should aspire, by sacrificing their own interest and happiness to public utility.

With these internal qualities, I attribute to my prototype a magnetic exterior, without pomp; reflecting, but serene; authoritative, but humane; equal, considerate, and composed. I should not like that his voice or gestures should be violent, except in two or three situations of the opera, in which a sensible deviation from the constant tenor of his subsequent conduct would exalt his ruling passions, which are patriotism and glory. You must not be alarmed, my dear Sir, I shall be much shorter in the description of the other characters.

In the personage of the Consul, *Manlio*, I have tried to represent one of those great men, who, in the midst of every civil and military virtue, suffer themselves to be carried away by the rage of emulation, beyond all warrantable bounds. I wish this rivalry to be strongly marked, as well as his hostile disposition of mind towards Regolo. These will appear in the first scene with Attilia, as well as in the beginning of the next, in which the Senate hears Regolo, and the Carthaginian Ambassadors. His subsequent change of sentiment, into respect and tenderness for Regolo, will render his character more admirable, and more pleasing; it will exalt the virtue of Regolo, by demonstrating its efficacy in producing such stupendous effects, and will add to the second scene of the second act, which is that for which I feel the greatest partiality. The characteristic of Manlio is a natural propensity to emulation, which when he discovers, he corrects, but does not relinquish.

Publio is the young lion that promises all the force of the sire, but is not yet furnished with tusks and claws; and it may easily be conjectured through his impetuosity, passion, and the inexperience of youth, what he will be, when arrived at maturity.

Licinio is a pleasing young man, valiant and resolute, but extremely impassioned. Hence it is very difficult to convince him of the necessity of sacrificing the genius of his wife, and even the life of his benefactor to glory, and the service of his country.

Amilcare is an African, not accustomed to the maxims of probity and justice, which the Romans, at this time, professed, and much less [accustomed] to their practice: hence, from the beginning, he remains in astonishment, being unable to comprehend a way of thinking so diametrically opposite to that of his country. He is, however, ambitious of imitating what he sees; but, for want of moderation, goes awkwardly to work. However, during his short residence at Rome, if he did not acquire the Roman virtue, he at least learned to envy those who possessed it.

The ruling passion of *Attilia* is tenderness and veneration for her father, whom she not only prefers to Rome itself, but to her lover. Convinced by authority and example, she, at length, adopts her father's sentiments, but in the trial of that fortitude, which she wished to imitate, she manifestly sinks under the weakness of her sex. In *Barce*, I figured to myself a pleasing, beautiful and lively African. Her temperament, like that of her nation, is amorous, and her tenderness for Amilcare extreme. In him, all her hopes, her fears, thoughts and cares, are centred. She is even more attached to her lover than the manners of her country; and is not only more indifferent than him about the Roman passion for glory, but thanks the Gods for having preserved her from its contagion.

These are the general outlines of the portraits I meant to draw; but you know that the pencil is not always faithful to the traces of the mind. It therefore depends upon you, who are not only an excellent artist, but a perfect friend to clothe my personages in so masterly a manner, that if their features should not strike, they may be recognized, at least, by their dress and ornaments.

And now, to come to particulars, according to your desire, I shall speak of the recitatives, some of which I should wish to be animated by instruments; but in pointing them out I do not pretend to limit your ideas: where mine meet with your wishes, adopt them; but where we disagree, I beg of you not to change your opinion, in mere complacency.

In the first act, I find two situations in which instruments may assist me. The first is the whole harangue of Attilio to Manlio, in the second scene, beginning: 'A che vengo! Ah! sino a quando'. After the words *A che vengo*, the instruments should begin to be heard; and, afterwards, sometimes silent, sometimes accompanying the voice, and sometimes by reinforcing, to give energy and fire to an oration in itself violent;

and I should like this accompaniment to continue to the end of the verse: '*La barbara or qual è? Cartago o Roma?*'

But I believe that it will be necessary, particularly in this scene, to avoid the inconvenience of making the singer wait for the chord; otherwise all the heat and energy of the speech would be chilled, and the instruments, instead of animating, would enervate the recitative, and render the picture disjointed, obscure, and suffocated in the frame. So that it seems here, as if all *ritornelli*, or interstitial symphonies, should be avoided.

The other situation is in the seventh scene of the same act; and is precisely one of those little places in which I should wish Regolo to quit his moderation, and think more of himself than usual. There are only twelve verses that I should wish to have accompanied; which begin at: '*Io venissi a tradirvi –*' and end with: '*Come al nome di Roma Africa tremi*'.

If you should think accompaniment necessary here, I recommend the same economy of time as before; that the actor may not be embarrassed or obliged to wait, by which that fire would be diminished, which I wish to have increased.

And now we are speaking of the seventh scene of the first act, if you have no objection, I should wish to have a very short symphony after this verse of Manlio: '*T'acheta: ei viene*', to give time for the Consul and the Senators to take their places, and to allow Regolo leisure for advancing slowly, and in a pensive manner. The character of the symphony should be majestic, slow, and sometimes interrupted; expressing as it were the state of Regolo's mind, in reflecting upon his now entering that place as a slave, in which he formerly presided as consul. I should like, that during one of these breaks in the symphony, Amilcare should come in to speak; when, during the silence of the instruments, he should pronounce these verses: '*Regolo, a che t'arresti? è forse nuovo/per te questo soggiorno?*' And the symphony should not be concluded, till after Regolo's answer: '*Penso qual ne partii, qual vi ritorno*'. But after these words, I should not wish the instruments to perform any thing more than a mere close.

In the second act, there seems to me no other recitative which requires accompaniment, than the soliloquy of Regolo, which begins thus: '*Tu palpiti, o mio cor!*' This ought to be recited sitting, till after the following words: '*... Ah! no. De' vili/questo è il linguaggio...*' The rest to be performed standing; for as the exit of Regolo happens at the change of scene, it would be difficult if he were sitting. But in order that he may have time and space to move about slowly, stopping from time to time, and manifesting himself to be immersed in thought, it is necessary that the instruments should introduce, assist, and second, his reflections. While the actor is sitting, as his reflections consist of doubts and suspensions, they will afford an opportunity for extraneous modulation, and short *ritornelli* for the instruments; but the instant he rises, the rest of the scene requires resolution and energy: so that I recur to my former wish, for economy of time.

And now we are speaking of this scene, I must beg of you to correct the original, which I transmitted in the following manner. There is a meaning implied, which upon reflection seems to want clearness in the expression. '... *Ah! no. De' vili/questo è il linguaggio. Inutilmente nacque/chi sol vive a se stesso; è sol da questo/nobile affetto ad obliar s'impara/se per altrui. Quando ha di ben la terra/alla gloria si dee ...*'

Though there are places in the third act, as well as in the other two, which I may have neglected to mention, where violins may be opportunely employed; yet I must observe, that this ornament should not be rendered too familiar; and I should be glad, if in this third act, particularly, no accompanied recitative occurred, till the *last scene*. This is prevented by the noise and tumult of the people, who cry out, '*Regolo resti.*' The noise of these cries ought to be great, to imitate reality, and to manifest what a respectful silence the mere presence of Regolo could obtain, from a whole tumultuous people. The instruments should be silent when the other personages speak; and, if you approve of it, may be employed whenever the protagonist speaks in the last scene; varying, however, the movement and modulation, not merely to express and enforce the words or sentiments, as is thought a great merit by other composers, but to paint also the situation of mind of him who pronounces these words and sentiments, at which such masters as you always aspire. For you know, as well as I, that the same words and sentiments may be uttered, according to the diversity of situation, in such a manner as to express either joy, sorrow, anger or pity. I should hope from such hands as yours, that a recitative always accompanied by instruments, would not be such a tiresome thing as it usually is, from others. In the first place, because you will preserve that economy of time which I have so much recommended; particularly, as you likewise so well know how to perfect the art, by the judicious and alternate use of *pianos* and *fortes*, by *rinforzandos*, by *staccatos*, slurs, accelerating and retarding the measure, *arpeggios*, shakes, *sostenutos*, and above all, by new modulation, of which you alone seem to know the whole arcana. But if, in spite of so many subsidiaries, you should be of a different opinion, I shall readily give way to your experience, and be perfectly contented, if the following verses are accompanied by violins; that is, the first ten, from: '*Regolo resti! ed io l'ascolto! ed io...*' to the verse: '*Meritai l'odio vostro?*' Then from the verse: '*No, possibil non è: de' miei Romani...*' to '*Esorto cittadin, padre comando,*' and lastly from '*Romani, addio: siano i congedi estremi...*' to the end.

You imagine now, I suppose, that this tiresome discussion is over. No, Sir, we have still a short addendum to tack to it. I should wish that the last chorus were one of that kind, with which you have excited in the audience a desire of hearing it, unknown before; and that there should be such a stamp set on the *addio*, with which the Romans take a final leave of Regolo, as shall demonstrate, that this chorus is not like most others, a superfluity, but a most essential part of the catastrophe.

I here quit the subject, not indeed, for want of materials, or will to converse with you longer; but because I am really tired myself, and fearful of tiring you.

Signor Annibali is desirous that I should write something to him, concerning his part. But I must entreat you to read to him such passages of this letter, as you may think likely to afford him any satisfaction. I have not time to peruse what I have written; think then, whether it is possible for me to transcribe any part of it.

Present a thousand affectionate compliments in my name, to the incomparable Signora Faustina, and believe me, upon all occasions, yours most truly.

Letter to Johann Adolf Hasse, 20 October, 1749

'The invisible trade in gelding choirboys'
CHARLES BURNEY

I enquired throughout Italy at what place boys were chiefly qualified for singing by castration, but could get no certain intelligence. I was told at Milan that it was at Venice; at Venice that it was at Bologna;

but at Bologna the fact was denied, and I was referred to Forence; from Florence to Rome, and from Rome I was sent to Naples. The operation most certainly is against law in all these places, as well as against nature; and all the Italians are so much ashamed of it, that in every province they transfer it to some other. However, with respect to the Conservatorios at Naples, Mr Jemineau, the British consul, who has so long resided there, and who has made very particular enquiries, assured me, and this account was confirmed by Dr Cirillo, an eminent and learned Neapolitan physician, that this practice is absolutely forbidden in the Conservatorios, and that the young Castrati come from Leccia in Puglia; but, before the operation is performed, they are brought to a Conservatorio to be tried as to the probability of voice, and then are taken home by their parents for this barbarous purpose. It is said, however, to be death by the laws to all those who perform the operation, and excommunication to every one concerned in it, unless it is done, as is often presented, upon account of some disorders which may be supposed to require it, and with the consent of the boy. And there are instances of its being done even at the request of the boy himself, as was the case of the Grassetto at Rome...M. de la Lande...ascertained that there are shops in Naples with this inscription: '*Qui si castrono ragazzi*'; but I was utterly unable to see or hear of any such shops during my residence in that city. [...]

Quoted in Heriot, *Life and Times of the Castrati*, 1956

'Different ways with a tragic text'
DENIS DIDEROT

I: Which sort of tragedy would you like to see established in the lyric theatre?

DORVAL: The ancient.

I: Why not domestic tragedy?

DORVAL: Because tragedy, and indeed all work destined for the lyric theatre, needs to be measured; and domestic tragedy seems to me to preclude versification.

I: But do you believe that this genre will supply the musician with all the resources appropriate to his art? Every art has its needs. It seems to be a question of them, as in the senses. The senses are not only those of touch: nor the arts only of imitation. But each sense touches and each art imitates in a manner that is appropriate.

DORVAL: In music there are two styles, the one simple, the other mannered. What would you have to say, if I were to show you, without leaving my dramatic poets, sections from them in which the composer can use the energy of one or the richness of another at will? When I say composer, I mean a man of genius: quite a different thing from those who know only how to weave in modulations and combine notes.

I: Please, Dorval, one of these pieces.

DORVAL: Very gladly. It is said that Lully himself had noticed the one I am going to cite. Perhaps it shows that this artist's oeuvre only needed poems of a different genre, and that he felt himself a genius capable of greater things.

Clytemnestra, from whom they are about to snatch her daughter for sacrifice, sees with a trembling heart the sacrificial knife raised over her breast, her blood flowing, and a priest consulting the gods. Troubled by these images, she cries out:

> ... O mère infortunée!
> De festons odieux ma fille couronnée
> Tend la gorge aux couteaux par son père apprêtés.
> Calchas va dans son sang ... Barbares, arrêtez;
> C'est le pur sang du dieu qui lance le tonnerre.
> J'entends gronder la foundre et sens trembler la terre.
> Un dieu vengeur, un dieu fait retentir ces coups.

[Racine, *Iphigénie*, V. iv]*

I know more lyrical verses in neither Quinault nor any other poet, nor of a situation more fitting to imitation in music. The state of Clytemnestra must draw a cry of nature from her bowels, and the musician will carry this to my ear with all its nuances.

* O mother of misfortune!
  My daughter garlanded with horrid crown
  Brings her breast to a blade made sharp by her sire!
  In her blood Calchas is going to ... Barbarians, stop!
  'Tis the pure blood of the god of thunderbolts.
  I hear lightning strike. I feel the earth quake.
  A god, a vengeful god, makes such shocks resound.

If he composes the piece in a simple style, he will meet the sadness and despair of Clytemnestra: he will not begin to work until he is himself oppressed by the terrible images that obsess her. The perfect subject for an obligatory recitative is in the first lines. How well one can divide them into the different phrases of a ritual lament! First section: 'O ciel! . . . O mère infortunée! . . .' Second: 'De festons odieux ma fille couronnée . . .' Third: 'Tend la gorge aux couteaux par son père apprêtés . . .' Fourth: 'Par son père! . . .' Fifth: 'Calchas va dans son sang . . .' What qualities could one not deliver in such a symphony? I seem to hear lamentation, sadness, horror, dismay and fury.

The aria begins at 'Barbares, arrêtez'. Let the composer deliver these words in as many ways as he likes; he would be a model of extreme sterility if these words were not an inexhaustible source of melodies to him.

Lively thus: 'Barbares, Barbares, arrêtez, arrêtez . . . C'est le pur sang du dieu qui lance le tonnerre . . . C'est le sang . . . C'est le pur sang du dieu qui lance le tonnerre . . . Ce dieu vous voit . . . vous entend . . . vous menace, barbares . . . arrêtez! . . . J'entends gronder la foudre . . . je sens trembler la terre . . . arrêtez . . . Un dieu, un dieu vengeur fait retentir ces coups . . . arrêtez, barbares . . . Mais ne rien les arrête . . . Ah ma fille! . . . ah mère infortunée! . . . Je la vois . . . je vois couler son sang . . . elle meurt . . . ah, barbares! Ô ciel! . . .' What a variety of sentiments and images!

Suppose we leave these lines to Mlle Dumesnil. Unless I am much mistaken, she will render this chaos, these feelings that succeed one another in her soul. Her genius will provide the lead, and it will be with her performance in mind that the composer should imagine and write. Let us try the experience and you will see nature furnish singer and musician with the same ideas.

But say the musician prefers a pictorial style. Different declamation, different ideas, a different melody will follow. He will use the voice where the other composer has relied upon the instruments. He will make a storm brew up. He will have lightning strike. He will have it fall in thunder. He will show me Clytemnestra frightening the murderers of her daughter with the image of the god whose blood they are going to shed. With all possible truth and force, he will transport this image to my imagination, already rattled by the pathos of the poetry and the situation. If the first composer was entirely occupied with Clytemnestra's different tones, then this one is somewhat concerned with her mode of expression. It is no longer the mother of Iphigenia that I hear. It is the thunder growling, the earth quaking, the air resounding with appalling noise.

A third composer unites the best of both styles. He will seize upon the cry of nature at its most violent and inarticulate, and will use it as a basis for melody. It is on the strings of this melody that he will make thunder growl and lightning strike. Perhaps he will undertake to show a vengeful god, but he will make sure that the other qualities of this painting come out, like the cries of a weeping mother.

However prodigious the genius of this artist, he will not achieve either one of his goals without taking something away from the other. All that he accords to the production of tableaux will detract from the pathos. The whole will produce more of an effect on the ears, but less on the soul. This composer will be more admired by other artists, than by men of taste.

Dorval and I [*Dorval et Moi*, 1757], tr. Matthew Scott

'Back to melodic basics with Rameau's crazy nephew'
DENIS DIDEROT

HE: I have been to hear this music by Duni and our other youngsters, and that has finished me off.

I: So you approve of this style of music?

HE: Of course.

I: And you find beauty in these modern tunes?

HE: Do I find beauty? Good Lord, you bet I do! How well it is suited to the words! what realism! what expressiveness!

I: Every imitative art has its model in nature. What is the musician's model when he writes a tune?

HE: Why not go back to the beginning? What is a tune?

I: I confess the question is beyond me. That's what we are all like: in our memories we have nothing but words, and we think we understand them through the frequent use and even correct application we make of them, but in our minds we have only vague notions. When I pronounce the word 'tune' I have no clearer idea than you and most of your kind when you say 'reputation, blame, honour, vice, virtue, modesty, decency, shame, ridicule'.

HE: A tune is an imitation, by means of the sounds of a scale (invented by art or inspired by nature, as you please), either by the voice or by an instrument, of the physical sounds or accents of passion. And you see that by changing the variables the same definition would apply exactly to painting, eloquence, sculpture or poetry. Now to come to your question: what is the model for a musician or a tune? Speech, if the model is alive and thinking; noise, if the model is inanimate. Speech should be thought of as a line, and the tune as another line winding in and out of the first. The more vigorous and true the speech, which is the basis of the tune, and the more closely the tune fits it and the more points of contact it has with it, the truer that tune will be and the more beautiful. And that is what our younger musicians have seen so clearly. When you hear *Je suis un pauvre diable* you think you can tell it is a miser's plaint, for even if he didn't sing he would address the earth in the same tone when hiding his gold therein: *O terre, reçois mon trésor.* And that young girl, for example, who feels her heart beating, who blushes and in confusion begs his lordship to let her go – how else could she express herself? There are all kinds of characters in these works, and an infinite variety of modes of speech. Sublime, I tell you! Go and listen to the piece when the young man, feeling himself on the point of death, cries: *Mon cœur s'en va.* Listen to the air, listen to the instrumental setting, and then try and tell me the difference there is between the real behaviour of a dying man and the turn of this air. You will see whether the line of the melody doesn't coincide exactly with that of speech. I am not going into time, which is another condition of song; I am sticking to expression, and nothing is more obvious than the following passage which I have read somewhere: *Musices seminarium accentus.* Accent is the nursery-bed of melody. Hence you can tell how difficult the technique of recitative is, and how important. There is no good tune from which you cannot make a fine recitative, and no recitative from which a skilled person cannot make a fine tune. I would not like to guarantee that a good speaker will sing well, but I should be surprised if a good singer could not speak well. Believe all I say on this score, for it is the truth.

I: I should be only too willing to believe you if I were not prevented by one little difficulty.

HE: What difficulty?

I: Just this: if this kind of music is sublime, then that of the divine Lully, Campra, Destouches and Mouret, and even, between ourselves, of your dear uncle, must be a bit dull.

HE (whispering into my ear): I don't want to be overheard, and there are lots of people here who know me, but it *is* dull. It's not that I care twopence about dear uncle, if 'dear' he be. He is made of stone. He would see my tongue hanging out a foot and never so much as give me a glass of water, but for all his making the hell of a hullaballoo at the octave or the seventh – la-la-la, dee-dee-dee, tum-te-tum – people who are beginning to get the hang of things and no longer take a din for music will never be content with that. There should be a police order forbidding all and sundry to have the *Stabat* of Pergolesi sung. That *Stabat* ought to have been burned by the public hangman. Lord! these confounded Bouffons, with their *Serva Padrone*, their *Tracallo*, have given us a real kick in the backside. In the old days a thing like *Tancrède*, *Issé*, *L'Europe galante*, *Les Indes* and *Castor*, *Les Talents lyriques* ran for four, five or six months. The performances of *Armide* went on for ever. But nowadays they all fall down one after the other, like houses of cards. And Rebel and Francoeur breathe fire and slaughter and declare that all is lost and they are ruined, and that, if these circus performers are going to be put up with much longer, national music will go to the devil and the Royal Academy in the cul-de-sac will have to shut up shop. And there is some truth in it, too. The old wigs who have been going there every Friday for the past thirty or forty years are getting bored and beginning to yawn, for some reason or other, instead of having a good time as they used to. And they wonder why, and can't find the answer. Why don't they ask me? Duni's prophecy will come true, and the way things are going I'll be damned if, four or five years after *Le Peintre amoureux de son modèle*, there will be as much as a cat left to skin in the celebrated Impasse. The good people have given up their own symphonies to play Italian ones, thinking they would accustom their ears to these without detriment to their vocal music, just as though orchestral music did not bear the same relationship to singing (allowances being made for the greater freedom due to range of instrument and nimbleness of finger) as

singing to normal speech. As though the violin were not the
mimic of the singer who in his turn will become the mimic of the
violin one of these days, when technical difficulty replaces beauty.
The first person to play Locatelli was the apostle of modern
music. What nonsense! We shall become inured to the imitation
of the accents of passion and of the phenomena of nature by
melody or voice or instrument, for that is the whole extent and
object of music; and shall we keep our taste for rapine, lances,
glories, triumphs and victories? *Va-t-en voir s'ils viennent, Jean.*
They supposed they could weep or laugh at scenes from tragedy
or comedy set to music, that the tones of madness, hatred,
jealousy, the genuine pathos of love, the ironies and jokes of the
Italian or French stage could be presented to their ears and that
nevertheless they could still admire *Ragonde* and *Platée*. You can
bet your boots that even if they saw over and over again with
what ease, flexibility and gentleness the harmony, prosody,
ellipses and inversions of the Italian language suited the art,
movement, expressiveness and turns of music and relative length
of sounds, they would still fail to realize how stiff, dead, heavy,
clumsy, pedantic and monotonous their own language is. Well,
there it is. They have persuaded themselves that after having
mingled their tears with those of a mother mourning the death of
her son, or trembled at the decree of a tyrant ordering a murder,
they won't get bored with their fairy-tales, their insipid
mythology, their sugary little madrigals which show up the bad
taste of the poet as clearly as they do the poverty of the art
which uses them. Simple souls! It is not so, and cannot be. Truth,
goodness and beauty have their claims. You may contest them,
but in the end you will admire. Anything not bearing their stamp
is admired for a time, but in the end you yawn. Yawn, then,
gentlemen, yawn your fill, don't you worry! The reign of nature
is quietly coming in, and that of my trinity, against which the
gates of hell shall not prevail: truth, which is the father, begets
goodness, which is the son, whence proceeds the beautiful, which
is the holy ghost. The foreign god takes his place unobtrusively
beside the idol of the country, but little by little he strengthens
his position, and one fine day he gives his comrade a shove with
his elbow and wallop! down goes the idol. That, they say, is how
the Jesuits planted Christianity in China and the Indies. And the

Jansenists can say what they like, this kind of politics which moves noiselessly, bloodlessly towards its goal, with no martyrs and not a single tuft of hair pulled out, seems the best to me.

I: There is a certain amount of sense in everything you have been saying.

HE: Sense! It's as well, for devil take me if I have been trying. It just comes, easy as wink. I am like those musicians in the Impasse, when my uncle arrived; if I hit the mark, well and good. A coal-heaver will always talk better about his own job than a whole Academy and all the Duhamels in the world...

(And off he went, walking up and down and humming some of the tunes from *L'Ile des Fous*, *Le Peintre amoureux de son modèle*, *Le Maréchal ferrant* and *La Plaideuse*, and now and again he raised his hands and eyes to heaven and exclaimed: 'Isn't that beautiful! God, isn't it beautiful! How can anyone wear a pair of ears on his head and question it?' He began to warm up and sang, at first softly, then, as he grew more impassioned, he raised his voice and there followed gestures, grimaces and bodily contortions, and I said: 'Here we go, he's getting carried away and some new scene is working up.' And indeed off he went with a shout: *Je suis un pauvre misérable ... Monseigneur, Monseigneur, laissez-moi partir ... O terre, reçois mon or, conserve bien mon trésor ... Mon âme, mon âme, ma vie! O terre! ... Le voilà le petit ami, le voilà le petit ami! Aspettare e non venire. ... A Zerbina penserete ... Sempre in contrasti con te si sta ...* He sang thirty tunes on top of each other and all mixed up: Italian, French, tragic, comic, of all sorts and descriptions, sometimes in a bass voice going down to the infernal regions, and sometimes bursting himself in a falsetto voice he would split the heavens asunder, taking off the walk, deportment and gestures of the different singing parts: in turn raging, pacified, imperious, scornful. Here we have a young girl weeping, and he mimes all her simpering ways, there a priest, king, tyrant, threatening, commanding, flying into a rage, or a slave obeying. He relents, wails, complains, laughs, never losing sight of tone, proportion, meaning of words and character of music. All the chess-players had left their boards and gathered round him. Outside, the café windows were thronged with passers-by who had stopped because of the noise. There were bursts of laughter fit to split the ceiling open. He noticed nothing, but went on, possessed by such a frenzy, an enthusiasm so near to madness that it was uncertain whether he would ever get over it, whether he should not be packed off in a cab straight to Bedlam. Singing a part of the Jomelli *Lamentations* he rendered the finest bits of each piece with incredible accuracy, truth and emotion, and the fine accompanied recitative in which the prophet depicts the desolation of Jerusalem was mingled with a flood of tears which forced all eyes to weep. Everything was there: the delicacy of the air and expressive power as well as grief. He laid stress upon the places where the composer had specially shown his great mastery, sometimes leaving the vocal line to take up the instrumental parts which he would suddenly abandon to return to the voice part, intertwining them so as to preserve the connecting links and the unity of the whole, captivating our souls and holding them in the most singular state of suspense I have ever experienced. Did I admire? Yes, I did. Was I touched with pity? Yes, I was. But a tinge of ridicule ran through these sentiments and discoloured them.

But you would have gone off into roars of laughter at the way he mimicked the various instruments. With cheeks puffed out and a hoarse, dark tone he did the horns and bassoons, a bright, nasal tone for the oboes, quickening his voice with incredible agility for the stringed instruments to which he tried to get the closest approximation; he whistled the recorders and cooed the flutes, shouting, singing and throwing himself about like a mad thing: a one-man show featuring dancers, male and female, singers of both sexes, a whole orchestra, a complete opera-house, dividing himself into twenty different stage parts, tearing up and down, stopping, like one possessed, with flashing eyes and foaming mouth. The weather was terribly hot, and the sweat running down the furrows of his brow and cheeks mingled with the powder from his hair and ran in streaks down the top of his coat. What didn't he do? He wept, laughed, sighed, his gaze was tender, soft or furious: a woman swooning with grief, a poor wretch abandoned in the depth of his despair, a temple rising into view, birds falling silent at eventide, waters murmuring in a cool, solitary place or tumbling in torrents down the mountain side, a thunderstorm, a hurricane, the shrieks of the dying mingled with the howling of the tempest and the crash of thunder; night with its shadows, darkness and silence, for even silence itself can be depicted in sound. By now he was quite beside himself. Knocked up with fatigue, like a man coming out of a deep sleep or long trance, he stood there motionless, dazed, astonished, looking about him and trying to recognize his surroundings. Waiting for his strength and memory to come back, he mechanically wiped his face. Like a person waking up to see a large number of people gathered round his bed and totally oblivious or profoundly ignorant of what he had been doing, his first impulse was to cry out 'Well, gentlemen, what's up? What are you laughing at? Why are you so surprised? What's up?' Then he went on: 'Now that's what you call music and a musician. And yet, gentlemen, you mustn't look down on some of the things in Lully. I defy anyone to better the scene *Ah, j'attendrai*, without altering the words. You mustn't look down on some parts of Campra, or my uncle's violin airs and his gavottes, his entries for soldiers, priests, sacrificers ... *Pâles flambeaux, nuit plus affreuse que les ténèbres ... Dieu du Tartare, Dieu de l'oubli ...*' At this point he raised his voice, held on to the notes, and neighbours came to their windows while we stuck our fingers in our ears. 'This,' he went on, 'is where you need lung-power, a powerful organ, plenty of wind. But soon it will be good-bye to Assumption, Lent and Epiphany have already come and gone. They don't yet know what to set to music, nor, therefore, what a musician wants. Lyric poetry has yet to be born. But they will come to it through hearing Pergolesi, the Saxon, Terradoglias, Trasetta and the rest; through reading Metastasio they will have to come to it.')

I: You mean to say that Quinault, La Motte, Fontenelle didn't know anything about it?

HE: Not for the modern style. There aren't six lines together in all their charming poems that you can set to music. Ingenious aphorisms, light, tender, delicate madrigals, but if you want to see how lacking all that is in material for our art, the most exacting of all, not even excepting that of Demosthenes, get someone to recite these pieces, and how cold, tired and monotonous they will sound! There is nothing in them that can serve as a basis for song. I would just as soon have to set the *Maximes* of La Rochefoucauld or the *Pensées* of Pascal to music. It is the animal cry of passion that should dictate the melodic line, and these moments should tumble out quickly one after the other, phrases must be short and the meaning self-contained, so that the musician can utilize the whole and each part, omitting one word or repeating it, adding a missing word, turning it all ways like a polyp, without destroying it. All this makes lyric poetry in French a much more difficult problem than in languages with inversions which have these natural advantages ... *Barbare, cruel, plonge ton poignard dans mon sein. Me voilà prête à recevoir le coup fatal. Frappe. Ose.* ... *Ah! je languis, je meurs.* ... *Un feu secret s'allume dans mes sens.* ... *Cruel amour, que veux-tu de moi?* ... *Laisse-moi la douce paix dont j'ai joui.* ... *Rends-moi la raison.* ... The passions must be strong and the sensibility of composer and poet must be very great. The aria is almost always the peroration of a scene. What we want is exclamations, interjections, suspensions, interruptions, affirmations, negations; we call out, invoke, shout, groan, weep or have a good laugh. No witticisms, epigrams, none of your well-turned thoughts – all that is far too removed from nature. And don't imagine that the technique of stage actors and their declamation can serve as a model. Pooh! we want something more energetic, less stilted, truer to life. The simple language and normal expression of emotion are all the more essential because our language is more monotonous and less highly stressed. The cry of animal instinct or that of a man under stress of emotion will supply them.

(While he was saying all this the crowds round us had melted away, either because they understood nothing he was saying or found it uninteresting, for generally speaking a child like a man and a man like a child would rather be amused than instructed; everybody was back at his game and we were left alone in our corner. Slumped on a seat with his head against the wall, arms hanging limp and eyes half shut, he said: 'I don't know what's the matter with me; when I came here I was fresh and full of life and now I am knocked up and exhausted, as though I had walked thirty miles. It has come over me all of a sudden.')

I: Would you like a drink?

HE: I don't mind if I do. I feel hoarse. I've no go left in me and I've a bit of a pain in my chest. I get it like this nearly every day, I don't know why.

I: What will you have?

HE: Whatever you like. I'm not fussy. Poverty has taught me to make do with anything.

(Beer and lemonade are brought. He fills and empties a big glass two or three times straight off. Then, like a man restored, he coughs hard, has a good stretch and goes on:)

But don't you think, my lord Philosopher, that it is a very odd thing that a foreigner, an Italian, a Duni should come and teach us how to put the stress into our own music, and adapt our vocal music to every speed, time, interval and kind of speech without upsetting prosody? And yet it wouldn't have taken all that doing. Anyone who had ever heard a beggar asking for alms in the street, a man in a towering rage, a woman mad with jealousy, a despairing lover, a flatterer – yes, a flatterer lowering his voice and dwelling on each syllable in honeyed tones – in short a passion, any passion, so long as it was strong enough to act as a model for a musician, should have noticed two things: one, that syllables, whether long or short, have no fixed duration nor even a settled connexion between their durations, and the other, that passion does almost what it likes with prosody; it jumps over the widest intervals, so that a man crying out from the depths of his grief: '*Ah, malheureux que je suis!*' goes up in pitch on the exclamatory syllable to his highest and shrillest tone, and down on the others to his deepest and most solemn, spreading over an octave or even greater interval and giving each sound the quantity required by the turn of the melody without offending the ear, although the long and short syllables are not kept to the length or brevity of normal speech. What a way we have come since we used to cite the parenthesis in *Armide: Le vainqueur de Renaud (si quelqu'un le peut être)*, or: *Obéissons sans balancer* from *Les Indes galantes* as miracles of musical declamation! Now these miracles make me shrug my shoulders with pity. The way art is advancing I don't know where it will end! Meanwhile let's have a drink.

Ramean's Nephew, 1761, tr. L. W. Tancock, 1966

'This is what opera is – in my book'
JEAN-JACQUES ROUSSEAU

Opera: Dramatic and lyric spectacle wherein one does one's best to unite all the charms of the fine arts through the representation of impassioned action, in order to excite interest and illusion by virtue of pleasurable feelings.

The constituent parts of an opera are the poem, the music and the decorative production. Through poetry one speaks to the mind, through music to the ear, through painting to the eyes; and the whole unites at once to move the heart and to produce the same impression through these various organs. Of these three, my subject permits consideration of the first and last only as they relate to the second; and I will therefore turn immediately to this.

The art of agreeably combining sounds can be understood in two very different ways. Considered as a phenomenon of nature, music restricts its effect to feeling and to the physical pleasure that results from melody, harmony and rhythm: such is generally the effect of the music of the church, of dance music and of songs. But as an essential ingredient in lyrical theatre, whose main aim is imitative, music becomes one of the fine arts. It is able to paint a whole picture, to excite the emotions and to struggle with poetry, lending the latter a new power, embellishing it with fresh charms, and triumphing over it by crowning it.

The sounds of the speaking voice, being neither sustained nor harmonious, are ineffable and cannot consequently ally themselves agreeably with those of the singing voice and with instruments – at least not in our languages, which are so far from being musical. Since we would not be able to comprehend those passages from the Greeks or the manner of recitation, without supposing their language to have been so accented that the inflection during sustained declamation formed appreciable musical intervals in itself, we can say that their plays were types of opera. And it is because of this that it was not possible for there to have been true opera among them.

From the difficulty of uniting song and speech in our languages, it is easy to sense that the addition of music as an essential part of lyric drama must give it a different character from tragedy or comedy, and make of it a third type with rules of its own. But these differences cannot be determined without a perfect understanding of that added element, of the means of uniting it with speech and of its natural relation to the human heart. These are details that belong more to the philosopher than to the artist and it must be left up to a pen capable of elucidating all the arts to explain both the rules to those who profess the principles, and the source of their pleasure to men of taste.

Limiting myself to a few historical rather than critical observations on this subject, I will first remark that the Greeks had no theatrical genre like our lyric drama and that what they called lyric drama did not resemble ours at all. As they had plenty of accentuation in their language and little sound in their concerts, all their poetry was musical and all their music declamatory. So much so in fact that their song was little more than sustained discourse, and they actually sang their verse, just as they announce at the start of their plays. By imitation, this has passed into Latin and on to us as the crass use of 'I sing' when one doesn't sing at all. As for their 'lyric mode', it was a heroic poetry in which the style was pompous and figurative, and which was preferably accompanied by the lyre or zither. It is certain that Greek tragedies were recited in a style very similar to song, and that they were accompanied by instruments that introduced the choruses.

But if one is therefore inclined to think that there were operas comparable to ours, then one must imagine operas without arias. For it seems to be proven to me that, with the exception of pure instrumentation, Greek music was merely recitative. It is true that this recitative, which united the charm of musical sound with all the harmony of poetry and all the force of declamation, must have had much more energy than modern recitative in which it is hardly possible to use one of these except at the expense of the others. In our current languages, which in the main reflect the rudeness of the climate in which they originated, the application of music to speech is far less natural. An uncertain prosody is ill suited to meter. Silent syllables, harsh stresses, and sounds that are neither varied nor striking do not easily lend themselves to melody. And poetry uniquely scanned by the number of syllables delivers a harmony that little agrees with musical rhythm and that will continually obstruct the diversity of values and movements. These are the difficulties to be overcome or avoided in the invention of a lyrical drama. However, they have attempted to produce a suitable language by choosing the appropriate words, phrases and verses, and this, called lyrical, was rich or poor in proportion to the sweetness or rudeness of him who uttered it.

Having, in some sense, shaped speech for music, there was then the question of setting music to it, and of rendering it fit for the lyric theatre so that the whole could be taken for a single idiom. This produced the need for constant singing to imitate constant speech: a need that increases because the language itself is unmusical. For the less the language has a softness of accent, the more the passage from speech to song or vice versa appears harsh and shocking to the ear. Hence the need to substitute a spoken discourse for a sung discourse, which could so imitate it that it would only be the supreme justice who would distinguish it from speech.

This manner of uniting music and poetry in the theatre was sufficient stimulus for interest and illusion among the Greeks because it was natural. For the opposite reason, it would not suffice with us. In listening to a hypothetical and constrained language, we have difficulty conceiving of its intent. Considerable noise provokes little emotion for us; this gives rise to the need to bring physical pleasure to the aid of the moral and to supply energy to expression through the attraction of harmony. The less one knows how to touch the heart, the more one needs to discover the ear, and we are forced to search the sensation for the pleasure that feeling refuses to give us. Thus the origin of arias; choruses; the symphony, and that enchanting melody, which modern music elaborates at the expense of poetry but which the connoisseur rebukes at the theatre when it flatters rather than moves him.

At the birth of the opera its inventors, wanting to avoid the unnatural union of music and speech in the imitation of human life, advised its transportation to heaven and hell. And failing to know how to speak for men, they preferred to make gods and devils sing than heroes and shepherds. Soon magic and the marvellous became the preserve of the lyric stage, and happy to enrich a new genre they didn't bother to check whether they had made a good choice. In order to sustain such a tough illusion, it needed all the seductive force of human imagination among a people whose love of pleasure, especially in the fine arts, reigned supreme. That famous nation, whose ancient grandeur resides only in artistic theory, squandered its taste and leading lights in order to give this new spectacle all the éclat it needed.

All over Italy, we saw the erection of theatres equal in size to royal palaces and equal in elegance to the monuments they were to replace. To adorn them, they devised the arts of perspective and decoration. Artists of all kinds went there with the hope of displaying their talents. The most ingenious machines, the most daring wire-flights, storms, lightning, thunder, and all the tricks of the ring were employed to amaze the eyes. And at the same time, a multitude of instruments and voices stunned the ears.

Despite all this, the action always remained cold and all the plots lacked interest. As there was no mystery that could not be easily solved by a *deus ex machina*, the audience, who all knew the power of the poet, idly relied upon him to rescue their heroes from the gravest of dangers. Thus the stage machinery was vast without producing much effect because the imitation was so imperfect and crude. The action held no interest for us being so far removed from nature, and the senses take badly to illusion when the heart is not in it. Reckoned all in all, it would have been difficult to bore an audience at greater cost.

This spectacle, as imperfect as it was, gained the long-term admiration of its contemporaries, who knew nothing better. They even congratulated themselves at the discovery of such a beautiful genre: they said, 'Here is a new principle to add to those of Aristotle; here wonder is added to terror and pity.' They did not see that this apparent richness was really a sign of sterility like the flowers that cover fields before they are mown. Through not knowing how to touch the audience, composers wanted to overcome them, and this so-called wonder was in fact only a puerile astonishment of which they should have been ashamed. A false air of magnificence, fairy tale, and enchantment impressed the audience to such a point that they would speak only with enthusiasm and respect of a theatre that in fact deserved nothing but boos. In all good faith, they revered both the production and the fanciful objects presented: it was as if it were better to make the King of the Gods speak flatly than the last man, and as if Molière's servants were not preferable to Pradon's heroes.

Although the authors of these first operas had scarcely any goal beyond dazzling the eyes and stunning the ears, it was hard for the composers to avoid attempting to draw an expression of the feelings scattered in the libretto from their art. The songs of nymphs, the hymns of priests, and the cries of warriors did not so fill these crude dramas that they were left without moments of interest or situations in which the spectator asked to be moved. Independent of a musical declamation that was often ill suited to the language, one soon had the feeling that the choice of movement, harmony and song was not indifferent to what was being said. By consequence, the effect of the music, hitherto intended simply for the senses, could be extended to the heart. The melody, which was originally only separated from the poetry by necessity, took advantage of this independence to provide absolute, and purely musical, beauties. The discovery and perfection of harmony offered them new routes to please and move the audience, and rhythm, free of the discomfort of poetic scansion, also acquired a form of separate and independent cadence.

Music, thereby becoming a third art of imitation, soon had its own language, expression and space, entirely independent of poetry. [...] Until then, opera had existed only as it was able to, for what better use could one make of a musical theatre that did not know how to portray anything, than to use it to represent non-existent things and those whose images no one could compare with objects? It is impossible to know whether one is affected by the portrayal of the marvellous as one would be by presence but everyone can judge for himself or herself whether the artist was able to speak to the passions in a true language or whether natural objects have been well represented. Also, once music had learned to paint and to speak, the charms of feeling caused those of the magic wand to be neglected. The theatre was purged of mythological jargon, interest was substituted for the marvellous, the machinery of poets and carpenters was destroyed and the lyric drama took on a form more noble and less expansive. [...]

These observations gave rise to a second reform no less important than the first. One sensed that opera required nothing cold and rational, nothing that the spectator could hear so calmly as to reflect upon its absurdity. And in this inheres the essential difference between lyric drama and pure tragedy. All political deliberation, all conspiracies, expositions, narratives, sententious maxims, in a word, everything that speaks only to reason was to be banished from the language of the heart, along with *jeux d'esprit*, madrigals and anything concerned with thought. Even the tone of simple gallantry, which ill suits grand passions, was to be scarcely admitted to fill out tragic scenarios, because its effect almost always spoils them – as one is never more aware of an actor singing than when he sings a mere song. The passion of feelings, the violence of emotions are therefore the principal object of lyric drama, and the illusion which constitutes the charm is destroyed as soon as the author and actor leave the spectator to himself for a moment. These are the principles upon which modern opera is based. [...]

From what I have said, one can see that there is more of a bridge than it seems between visual machinery, or production, and music, or aural machinery, given two senses that appear to have nothing in common. And in certain regards, constituted as it is, opera is not the complete monstrosity that it seemed to be. Wanting to lend the interest and movement that was lacking in music, we have seen the introduction of the vulgar tricks of machines and of flights on wires, and until composers knew how to move us emotionally, they were content to overwhelm us. Having become pathetic and impassioned, it is therefore natural that music should have returned these awful, unnecessary supplements to the world of the fairground. Thus the opera, purged of all these degrading wonders, has become an equally touching and majestic spectacle, worthy of the pleasure of men of taste, and of interest to sensitive souls.

The Dictionary of Music [*Dictionnaire de la Musique*, 1764], tr. Matthew Scott

'Too much singing can lead to puberty'
JOHANN WILHELM VON ARCHENHOLZ

A very particular accident happened a few years ago to a singer of the name of Balani. This man was born without any visible signs of those parts which are taken out in castration, he was, therefore, looked upon as a true-born castrato; an opinion, which was even confirmed by his voice. He learned music, and sung for several years upon the theatre with great applause. One day, he exerted himself so uncommonly in singing an arietta, that all of a sudden those parts, which had so long been concealed by nature, dropped into their proper place. The singer from this very instant lost his voice, which became even perceptible in the same performance, and with it he lost every prospect of a future subsistence.

Quoted in Heriot, *Life and Times of the Castrati*, 1956

'A revolutionary plan for operatic reform'
CHRISTOPH WILLIBALD GLUCK

To Grand Duke Leopold of Toscana
[before 16th December 1767]*

Royal Highness!

When I began to write the music for *Alceste*, I resolved to free it from all the abuses which have crept in either through ill-advised vanity on the part of singers or through excessive complaisance on the part of composers, with the results that for some time Italian opera has been disfigured and from being the most splendid and most beautiful of all stage performances has been made the most ridiculous and the most wearisome. I sought to restrict the music to its true purpose of serving to give expression to the poetry and to strengthen the dramatic situations, without interrupting the action or hampering it with unnecessary and superfluous ornamentations. I believed that it should achieve the same effect as lively colours and a well-balanced contrast of light and shade on a very correct and well-disposed painting, so animating the figures without altering their contours. So I have tried to avoid interrupting an actor in the warmth of dialogue with a boring intermezzo or stopping him in the midst of his discourse, merely so that the flexibility of his voice might show to advantage in a long passage, or that the orchestra might give him time to collect his breath for a cadenza. I did not think I should hurry quickly through the second part of an air, which is perhaps the most passionate and most important, in order to have room to repeat the words of the first part regularly four times or to end the aria quite regardless of its meaning, in order to give the singer an opportunity of showing how he can render a passage with so-and-so many variations at will; in short, I have sought to eliminate all the abuses, against which sound common sense and reason have so long protested in vain.

I imagined that the overture should prepare the spectators for the action, which is to be presented, and give an indication of its subject; that the instrumental music should vary according to the interest and

---

* Grand Duke Leopold of Toscana, who later became Emperor Leopold II (born 5th May 1747, died 1st March 1792), was a particularly gifted patron of music, whom Cherubini, amongst others, had to thank for his training.

passion aroused, and that between the aria and the recitative there should not be too great a disparity, lest the flow of the period be spoiled and rendered meaningless, the movement be interrupted inopportunely, or the warmth of the action be dissipated. I believed further that I should devote my greatest effort to seeking to achieve a noble simplicity; and I have avoided parading difficulties at the expense of clarity. I have not placed any value on novelty, if it did not emerge naturally from the situation and the expression; and there is no rule I would not have felt in duty bound to break in order to achieve the desired effect.

These are my principles. Happily all my intentions fitted admirably with the libretto, in which the famous author [Calzabigi],* having devised a new plan for the lyrical drama, had replaced florid descriptions, superfluous comparisons, sententious and frigid moralisation with the language of the heart, with strong passion, interesting situations and an ever-varied spectacle. My maxims have been vindicated by success, and the universal approval expressed in such an enlightened city [Vienna] has convinced me that simplicity, truth and lack of affectation are the sole principles of beauty in all artistic creations. None the less, in spite of repeated demands by the most respectable persons that I should decide to publish this opera of mine in print, I have realized how much danger lies in fighting against such widespread and deep-rooted prejudices, and I have found it necessary to avail myself in advance of the powerful protection of Your Royal Highness by imploring the favour of prefixing my opera with His August Name, which so justly carries with it the approval of all enlightened Europe. The great protector of the fine arts, who rules over a nation which is famed for having freed them from universal oppression and for having set in each of them the finest examples, in a city which has always been the first to break the yoke of vulgar prejudice and pave the way to perfection, can alone undertake the reform of this noble spectacle, in which all the fine arts play such a large part. When this has been accomplished, I shall have the glory of having moved the first stone, and this public testimony of Your Highness's protection, for which I have the honour to declare myself

---

* The famous author was Ranieri Simone Francesco Maria Calzabigi, born at Leghorn on 23rd December 1714.

with the most humble respect Your Royal Highness's Most humble, most devoted, most dutiful servant Christoph Gluck.

Preface to Alceste, The Collected Correspondence and Papers of Christoph Willibald Gluck, ed. H. Muller von Asow and E. H. Muller von Asow, tr. S. Thomson, 1962

To Duke Giovanni of Braganza
[30th October 1700]

Your Highness,

In dedicating to Your Highness this my newest work, I seek less a protector than a judge. A mind fortified against the prejudices of convention, with sufficient knowledge of the great principles of art, and taste formed not so much on great models as on the unvarying fundamentals of beauty and truth – these are the qualities I seek in my Maecenas, and which I find united in Your Highness. The only reason that induced me to issue my music for *Alceste* in print was the hope of finding successors, who would take the path already opened, and, urged on by the full support of an enlightened public, would be encouraged to eliminate the abuses introduced into Italian opera and bring it as close to perfection as possible. I regret that I have so far attempted this in vain. Countless arbiters of taste and pedants, who form the greatest barrier to progress in the fine arts, have pronounced against a method which, were it to gain a footing, would destroy at a stroke all their pretensions in the direction of criticism and all their capacity to achieve anything themselves. These people believed they could make an assessment of *Alceste* on the basis of informal rehearsals, badly directed and worse executed; they calculated what the effect might be in a theatre on the basis of what took place in a room – with the same cunning means as those employed in olden days in a town in Greece, where statues which were designed to stand on very high columns were judged from a distance of a few feet. Perhaps one sensitive ear found a vocal line too harsh, or a transition too violent, or badly prepared, without realizing that in its proper place it might perhaps sound greatly expressive or make the most beautiful juxtaposition. A single pedant seized upon an intentional licence, or perhaps condemned a printing error, as an unforgivable sin against the mysteries of harmony, and then voices were raised in unison against this barbaric and eccentric music. It is true that other scores are assessed by the same criterion, and that they are judged with the same confidence which admits no possibility of error, but Your Highness can at once see the reason for this. The more that truth and perfection are sought, the more necessary are precision and exactness. The differences which distinguish Raphael from a host of ordinary painters are imperceptible, and any change of contour which would not damage the likeness of a caricature would completely disfigure the portrait of a fine lady. Nothing but a change in the mode of expression is needed to turn my aria from *Orfeo*, 'Che farò senza Euridice', into a dance for marionettes. One note held or shortened, a neglected increase in speed, a misplaced appoggiatura in the voice, or a trill, passage-work, or roulade can ruin a whole scene in such an opera, though it does nothing to, or does nothing but improve, an opera of the common sort. The presence of the composer is therefore as important to the performance of this kind of music as, so to say, the presence of the sun to the works of nature. [The sun] is absolutely the spirit and the life, and without it everything remains in chaos and darkness.

But we have to be prepared to meet such obstacles as long as we live in the world of people who believe themselves empowered to judge the fine arts because they have the advantage of possessing a pair of eyes and a pair of ears, no matter of what sort. A passion for wanting to talk of that of which they understand least is a defect unhappily all too common among men, and I have recently seen one of the greatest philosophers of the century struggle to write about music, and pronounce, like oracles, 'Dreams of the blind and follies of romance'.* Your Highness will have already read the text of *Paride*, and will have noticed that it did not provide the composer's imagination with those strong passions, those noble portraits, and those tragic situations which moved the spectators in *Alceste*, and which give so much opportunity for grand musical effects; you will therefore surely not expect the same force and energy in the music; just as one does not demand in a painting in full light the same degree of chiaroscuro and the same strong contrasts that the painter can employ in a subject which allows the choice of subdued light. Here we are not dealing

---

* The philosopher referred to is presumably Rousseau, whose dictionary articles were cited by Forkel in his attack on *Alceste*.

with a wife on the point of losing her husband who, to save him, has the courage to summon the infernal gods from the black shadows of the night in a fearful forest, and who in the final agony of death fears for the fate of her sons, and tears herself from a husband she adores. We are dealing with a young lover confronted with the waywardness of a proud and virtuous woman, who finally triumphs by using all the ingenuity of a cunning passion. I was obliged to strive to find some variety of colour, seeking it in the different characters of the two nations of Phrygia and Sparta, by contrasting the roughness and savagery of one with the delicacy and tenderness of the other. I believed that since singing in opera is nothing but a substitute for declamation, I must make Helen's music imitate the native ruggedness of that nation, and I thought that it would not be reprehensible if in order to capture this characteristic in the music, I descended now and then to create a coarse effect. I believed that I must vary my style in the pursuit of truth, according to the subject in hand. The greatest beauties of melody and harmony become defects and imperfections when they are misplaced. I do not expect any more success with my *Paride* than with *Alceste* in achieving the aim of producing among composers of music the desired change, on the contrary, I foresee ever greater obstacles in the way; but I myself shall not desist from making new attempts on the worthy aim, and should I win Your Highness's confidence, I shall be happy to repeat, *Tolle Syparium sufficit mihi unus Plato pro cuncto populo.**

I have the honour to be, with the deepest respect, Your Highness's most humble, devoted, and obedient servant,

Chevalier Christof Gluck.

Preface to Paris and Helen, quoted in Patricia Howard, *Gluck: an Eighteenth-Century Portrait*, 1995

To Jean François de Laharpe, October 1777

It is impossible, sir, for me to do anything but agree with the intelligent observations on my opera that appear in the number of your journal for the fifth of this month; I find in it nothing, absolutely nothing, to contravene.

I have been simple enough to believe, till now, that music, like the

---

* Up with the curtain! One Plato suffices for me, rather than everybody.

other arts, embraces the whole sphere of the passions, and that it cannot please less when it expresses the troubles of a madman and the cry of grief, than when it paints the sighs of love.

> Il n'est point de serpent ni de monstre odieux,
> Qui, par l'art imité, ne puisse plaire aux yeux.*

I have thought that this rule should hold in music equally as in poetry. I have persuaded myself that song, when it thoroughly takes the colour of the feeling it is to express, should be as various and as many-sided as feeling itself; in fine, that the voices, the instruments, the tones, even the pauses, should strive after one end – expression – and the agreement between the words and the song should be such that neither the poem should seem to be made for the music nor the music for the poem.

However, this was not my only error; I thought I had noticed that the French language was less rhythmical than the Italian, and that it had not the same definition in the syllables; I was astonished at the difference between the singers of the two nations, as I found the voices of the one soft and pliable, those of the other stronger and more suited for the drama; and so I had decided that Italian melody could not link itself with French words. Then, when I came to examine the scores of their old operas, I found that in spite of the trills, runs, and other inappropriate devices with which they were overladen, there were yet so many genuine beauties in them that I was prompted to believe that the French had within themselves all that was required to do good work.

These were my ideas before I had read your observations. Now, however, you have lightened my darkness; I am wholly astonished that in a few hours you have made more observations on my art than I myself in a practical experience of forty years. You prove to me that it is sufficient to be a well-read man, in order to speak on everything. Now I am convinced that the Italian is the most excellent, the true music; that the melody, if it is to please, must be regular and periodic, and that even in a moment of confusion, where we have to do with the vocal utterances of several persons swayed by varying passions, the composer must still maintain this regularity of melody.

I agree with you that of all my compositions *Orfeo* alone is

---

* There is no serpent or odious matter, that under the guise of art cannot please the eye.

supportable; and I sincerely beg the forgiveness of the gods of taste for having deafened the hearers of my other operas; the number of their performances and the applause the public has been good enough to bestow on them do not prevent my seeing how pitiable they are. I am so convinced of it that I wish to re-write them; and as I see that you are passionate for tender music, I will put in the mouth of the furious Achilles a song so tender and so sweet, that all the spectators will be moved to tears.

As for *Armide*, I will be very careful to leave the poem as it is; for, as you very perspicaciously observe, 'the operas of Quinault, although full of beauties, are yet not well adapted for music; they are fine poems but bad operas'. So that if they are written to bad poems, which, according to your view, will make fine operas, I beg you to introduce me to a poet who will put *Armide* in order, and give two airs to each scene. We will between us settle the quantity and measure of the verse, and when the syllables are complete I will take the rest on my own shoulders. I, for my part, will go over the music again, and con-scientiously strike out, according to reason, all the loud instruments, especially the kettle-drums and trumpets; I will take care that nothing shall be heard in my orchestra but oboes, flutes, French horns, and muted violins. And there will be no more question whence the text of the airs was taken; this can no longer matter, since we have already taken up our position.

Then will the part of Armide no longer be a monotonous and fatiguing shriek; she will no longer be a Medea, a sorceress, but an enchantress; I will make her, when in despair, sing an aria so regular, so periodic, and at the same time so tender, that the *petite maîtresse* most afflicted with the vapours will be able to listen to it without the least damage to her nerves.

If some wicked person should say to me, 'Sir, be careful that Armide mad does not express herself like Armide amorous,' I will reply: 'Sir, I do not wish to frighten the ear of M. de La Harpe; I do not wish to contravene nature; I wish to embellish it; instead of making Armide cry out, I want her to enchant you.' If he insists, and shows me that Sophocles, in the finest of his tragedies, dared to show to the Athenians Oedipus with his bloody eyes, and that the recitative or the kind of *arioso* by which the eloquent plaints of the unfortunate king were rendered must have expressed the deepest sorrow, I will retort that M. de La Harpe does not wish to hear the cry of a man in suffering. Have I not well grasped, sir, the meaning of the doctrine laid down in your observations? I have done some of my friends the pleasure of letting them read your remarks.

'We must be grateful,' said one of them as he handed them back to me; 'M. de La Harpe has given you excellent advice; it is his confession of faith in music; do thou likewise. Get all his works in poetry and literature, and search out in them everything that pleases you through your friendship for him. Many people maintain that criticism does nothing more than upset the artist; and to prove it, they say, the poets have at no time had more judges than now, and yet were never more mediocre than at present. But get the journalists here together in council, and if you ask them, they will tell you that nothing is so useful to the State as a journal. One might object to you, that, as a musician, you had no right to speak about poetry; but is it not equally astounding to see a poet, a man of letters, who wants to have despotic opinions on music?'

That is what my friend told me; his reasons seemed to me very well founded. But, in spite of my regard for you, I feel, Monsieur, after due reflection, that I cannot possibly become involved, without incurring the fate of the expositor who, in the presence of Hannibal, gave a long discourse on the art of war.

Collected Correspondence and Papers of Christoph Willibald Gluck, ed. H. Muller von Asow and E. H. Muller von Asow, tr. S. Thomson, 1962

'Don't try to sell a libretto that breaks the rules'
CARLO GOLDONI

All my hopes were founded on my *Amalasunta*. I decided to take it to Milan, thinking that the impresarios of the famous Theater would pay me well for it, would commission me to write more, and that in a short while I should have obtained credit and made my fortune. It happened to be the Carnival season [when I arrived there], and the Theater was presenting Metastasio's *Demofoonte*, and the principal part in the Drama was being played by the celebrated [castrato] Caffariello, whom I had met in Venice. The Director and composer of the Ballets was Signor Gaetan Grossa-Testa. I knew this excellent man and his kind Spouse, Signora Maria; so that, through these three acquaintances and the merits of my Drama, I hoped the Impresarios would accept it, and pay me handsomely for it. Therefore, having chosen a Friday, when there are no performances at the Theater, I paid a visit to that expert Ballerina and found there, besides her Husband, Caffariello and some others of her acquaintance, among them the Milanese Nobleman Count Prata, a great connoisseur of the Theater and amateur of music and theatrical poetry. When I made my wish known to them, they all offered to lend me their support; but they wisely suggested that, before exposing the Drama to the judgment of the impresarios, it would be well to expose it to that of my friends. Since there was nothing I wished for more eagerly than to read my Composition, I pulled it out of my pocket, and begged them to give me their attention. These listeners were neither erudite nor learned; but, being schooled by practice, and finding that my Drama did not accord with the rules, they began to grow weary. Some yawned, others whispered among themselves, and one Castrato, who played the smallest role in *Demofoonte*, took a sheet of music and began singing in an undertone. Afire with enthusiasm and anger, I now declaimed louder to oblige them to listen more attentively, but this only made some of them laugh and others grow impatient, and it vexed the Lady of the house, who urged them, in vain, to be silent. At last, with the kindest and most civil apologies, she begged me to save the rest for another occasion. I thanked her for her courtesy, but being piqued, especially with the Castratos, made ready to leave at once. Count Prata kindly requested me to accompany him to another room, and obliged me to read him the rest. I did so the more willingly, in that I hoped his approval might render me the justice I had been denied by the rudeness of the others. He listened to the whole Work patiently; and this, approximately, is what he said to me when I had finished:

'Your Work, if it were written differently, might make a good Tragedy; but the *Dramma per musica*, in itself an imperfect [type of] Composition, has been subjected by custom to certain rules – contrary, it is true, to those of Aristotle, Horace, and all who have treated of Poetics, but necessary if it is to serve the Music, the Actors, and the Composers. The profound Apostolo Zeno, the mellifluous, elegant, most learned Metastasio have conformed to those rules, and what might seem a fault in a regular Tragedy becomes a thing of beauty in a *Dramma per musica*. Read the two above-mentioned Authors attentively, and you will gain some notion as to the nature of the

Drama we are discussing, and you will mark its rules. I will indicate some of the main ones, whose absence disgusted the Castratos who were listening to you. The leading male soprano, the leading lady, and the tenor, who are the principal Actors of the Drama, must each sing five arias: one *pathetic*, one *virtuosic*, one *speech-like*, one of *mixed character*, and one *brilliant*. The second male and second female must each have four, and the last male three, and a seventh character the same number, should the Work require him; for (by-the-bye) there cannot be more than six or seven characters in it, and you have nine in your Drama. The seconds are always demanding that they, too, be given *pathetic arias*, but the firsts will not hear of it, and if the Scene itself is pathetic, their aria can only be, at the very most, *of mixed character*. The principal Actors' fifteen arias must be so distributed that no two of the *same color* shall follow upon each other's heels, and the other Actors' arias serve to provide the *chiaroscuro* [i.e., the contrast]. You make a character sing and then remain onstage, and this is against the *rules*. On the other hand, you allow a principal Actor to exit without singing an aria, and this again is against the *rules*. You have only three *Scene changes* in your Drama, whereas six or seven are required. The third Act of your Drama is the best in the Work, but this too is against the *rules* . . .'

I could contain myself no longer; I rose to my feet with unintentional vehemence, apologized, thanked him for his friendly admonishments, and concluded by saying that, as I was horrified by the *rules* of the Drama, I was quite determined never to write one again. In taking my leave of the Nobleman I begged him, as a friend of the House, to have me shown out so that I should not need to re-enter the parlor. This he did. I returned to my hotel, ordered a fire, and with unabated bitterness burnt my *Amalasunta* piecemeal.

Memoirs of 1732, quoted in Taruskin and Weiss, *Music in the Western World*

'The main task is to find a plot that suits music'
CHRISTOPH MARTIN WIELAND

Mr Burney, whose musical tour through France, Italy and Germany once made such an impact, rightly wondered that though he travelled throughout all the German provinces, he nowhere came upon a

German lyric theatre. He recognized that the explanation does not reside in a lack of ability or inclination in our nation. In fact, we Germans love music just as much as all the other peoples of the world. It has long been a part of public and private life here. There is scarcely a German province that has not brought forth virtuosos on all manner of musical instruments for at least one hundred years. And the famous names of Kayser, Telemann, Handel, Hasse, Graun, Bach, Gluck, Naumann, Haydn, Mozart and others form a list of our century's composers that we can compare (to say the least) with the greatest contemporaries of which Italy is proud. It is true that recently we have for the most part neglected the foremost and liveliest type of music, the song. But one can easily see from experience that the musical nature here is not to blame, and that with encouragement and exposure, we may in a few years have as many singers of the highest standard as in Italy. Well-managed schools under the direction of skilled masters will work wonders, and how easily could the dukes and rulers of the German states, if they so desired, divert misused funds into new and better foundations for the encouragement of patriotic composers whose genius is already flowering. With this small expenditure, and having cleared Germany of what remains of its old barbarism, a good singing tradition – a sure sign of a passionate and moral people – can be created here among us. [...]

It is then neither the lack of talent in Germany, nor the tuneless nature of the German language that stands in the way of the desire to see a German odeon, a temple to the German muses. It is a different prejudice that works against the lyric theatre, namely the almost universal opinion that the so-called *opera seria* must be a festive work in which all the fine arts compete for the attention of the eyes and ears of the astonished and pampered viewer. In other words (at the risk of using those of Algarotti), 'in the Opera, all the related stimuli of poetry, music, speech, dancing and painting must unite in order to fuse the senses, enliven the heart and amaze the soul through the progressive changes'. As long as one associates the word opera with this notion, there will be few rulers rich enough to afford such an expensive production or at least to maintain one, and nobody will resist the idea that the German language lags behind the Italian when it comes to lyric theatre. [...]

Algarotti, who some time ago intended to reform the lyric theatre, has himself undertaken a lifetime's research into opera, and wanted not only to record the most significant of its influences, but also to go far wider than any of his predecessors. [...] It is not in my present project to undertake an assessment of the value of his suggestions, either in terms of influence, or whether they still stand from the point of view of more recent facts. Nevertheless, it would be wrong to take all his suggestions, made from the point of view of the Italian opera of his time, and use them for all composers and singers without exception. It would be unjust to suppose that, having assessed the problems, it should not be in the power of the composer, whatever genius, insight and taste he may have, to follow these alone. [...]

Opera, insofar as it is a dramatic work, has all the qualities of other types of play and, inasmuch as it comes out of the tragedy of ancients, especially Euripides, more fully than any other modern genre, shares the same aims and means. Nevertheless, it differs – if not from Greek tragedy, which was probably a form of opera – but from the other modern forms of drama inasmuch as everything that in these is speech or mime is, in opera, song or instrumental music. In a word, music is precisely the language of opera.

Those people who have a greater innate sense of reason than of feeling and musical taste, have presented exactly this case against opera, namely that being unnatural, it is absurd and incapable of affecting illusion. Had they attended a performance of *Dido abbandonata*, the incontrovertible evidence of their senses would have been that a singing and accompanied heroine can be moving. However, beyond this, a little reflection would show them that their argument has no ground because it works too widely and against them. These critics want to banish opera as unnatural, since no one sings to themselves or to others or reveals their passions, needs and decisions in great arias. But they must for the same reasons throw out not only ancient drama and modern French or English tragedy in rhymed or blank verse, but all other drama. Because it is absurd and unnatural for people to discuss their important, secret affairs aloud with themselves or those they trust, with a hundred listeners sitting close by, while affecting to be alone. All drama presupposes a certain necessary contract of the poet and actor with the audience. The latter concedes that, insofar as there is a certain reality to characters, passions, mores, speech, action and plot, he will not allow the illusion to be disturbed by any other aspect of the representation, neither those necessary to the production, nor those introduced for the pleasure of the audience. In opera, the poet, composer and singers step forward and say, 'Together we want to attempt, as best we can, to present to you an interesting story at a highest possible level of illusion. We are not such fools as to suppose that we can make you believe that Iphigenia, Dido or Alceste have died singing notes to the accompaniment of basses, violins, flutes and oboes. We do not require of you that you should mistake our poetical, musical and dramatic representation for nature. The painter who paints the sacrifice of Iphigenia on canvas and places it in a gold frame, doesn't ask you to believe that his Iphigenia, Agamemnon and Calchas live and breathe. It is enough for him that they appear to you to live and breathe, despite your conviction that they are only painted. The same rule applies to us as to our utilitarian sister arts. If, at certain moments, we bring your imagination to the point of delusion, make your heart flutter, your eyes fill with tears – then we have what we want, and ask no more. Why should you want more?' I think that this is a proposition against which few objections can be raised. [...]

Music is the language of the passions. One expects the subject of an opera to be weighty and for the poet to work in great moral characters, lofty feelings, noble struggles between virtue and passion; and therefore to have plenty of opportunity to delight our spirit with beautiful moral ideals to bring to it noble maxims. Once the subject is political, and the hero is a statesman – like Thermistocles, or even a stoic, like Cato – then the composer, singers and even the audience will find their come-uppance. [...] The greatest possible simplicity of plot is integral and necessary to opera. Action cannot be sung, it must be acted; the more action, therefore, the less singing. A good deal of unexpected action, turmoil, episodic scenes and so on certainly give the play variety and can draw a particular type of audience, who are fond of noise and too flighty to stay with even the important scenes. But the music gains nothing thereby, and the sensitive audience even less. Which are the scenes in which the composer allows his genius truly free flight, in which the music can manifest its entire soul-searching power, in which are all ear and feeling, in which our heart races, glows and melts? Are they not those in which the poet and the composer seek with all their powers to take us from one emotion to another through a series of effects, and do not cease until they have brought us through the same events as the characters themselves? And are they not those in which a few words, often a single word, a sound, a look, a movement of the hand move our heart? And how can such a small cause work such an effect? Surely simply because our souls have been gradually prepared for it, softened and, so to speak, unconsciously undermined? It often requires a long preparation of ideas and feelings to give full weight to the single blow that the poet will deliver to our heart. If the poet or composer has failed to make these preparations, then he must not feel alienated if he sees us left cold at a scene that should have had a great effect. [...]

The view that the subject-matter of opera must be taken from the realm of the wonderful [das Wunderbare] and not from causal reality, since in opera everything is music, seems to me to make little more sense than if one were to want to limit an engraver to wonderful subjects because everything is black or white in his pictures. It is no more wonderful to portray feelings and emotions in a number of similar or contrasting sounds than it is to do the same with a few black marks on a piece of white paper; and nature and truth are no more betrayed in one than the other. The opera, as stated above, sets up a silent contract between the work of art and the listener. The latter knows full well that he is being deceived, but he wants to let himself be deceived. The former does not long to be taken for nature, but it triumphs in producing greater and more beautiful effects than nature itself through its magic. [...]

Still, insofar as the music and song of opera constitute an ideal language, which is far superior to the usual speech of men, it is not to be denied that there is something in its nature, which we cannot help but associate with the idea of wonder. If we wanted to produce an actual, sensual idea of the speech of the gods, it seems to me that it would have to be this musical speech. It seems to follow, therefore, for some intrinsic reason, that we naturally associate the Greek gods and demigods with the lyric theatre as though it were, so to speak, their own sphere. They would, by contrast, be indecent on the tragic and even the Greek stage. In this respect, therefore, mythological subjects, all things being equal, seem more appropriate to opera than historical ones. [...]

For the librettist, the choice of subject-matter lies not only in the Greek gods, heroes and pastoral, but also the age of chivalry and even actual history. However, not every plot drawn from these sources is suitable, rather the choice of the poet must fall to that which is appropriate for musical treatment. I hope to have shown the following: first, that he must discard all those subjects that are better suited to tragedy than opera because of the nature of the plot, or because they are overworked and laden with too many events. Secondly, he must choose characters, emotions and situations that lose none of their veracity by musical embellishment. Thirdly, he should provide a plot as simple and with as few characters as possible, and absolutely avoid all episodes that will detract from the main theme, in order to highlight this. Lastly, he should generally work to present his characters more in terms of feelings and emotions than actions.

Beyond rules that apply to all drama, it seems to me that these are the self-serving principles that the poet has to rely on for the choice and handling of his material, and that listeners can rely on and demand of the poet, because to relinquish them would be to reduce their own pleasure.

'Essay on German Opera and some subjects relevant to it' ['Versuch über das Deutsche Singspiel und einige dahin einschlagende Gegenstände', 1775], tr. Matthew Scott

'How licensed gambling subsidized opera'
JOHN ROSSELLI

Gambling promotion was an entry to the running of opera seasons for the simple reason that as the centre of social life the opera house was usually the place where the upper classes gambled: that was the purpose of the spacious foyers in eighteenth-century Italian opera houses. The old Italian governments sometimes permitted games of chance, sometimes not; but even when faro and roulette were forbidden operagoers were allowed to bet small sums on milder games like backgammon. In the eighteenth century the normal practice was to forbid games of chance everywhere else but to grant a monopoly concession to the impresario of the opera house. This monopoly was abolished at various dates between 1753 and 1788 as 'enlightened' principles spread through the Italian states; but from 1802 the new states of Napoleonic Italy revived it as a means of raising badly needed revenue.

The Opera Industry in Italy from Cimarosa to Verdi, 1984

'A word in the composer's ear'
JOHANN WOLFGANG VON GOETHE

Goethe to Kaiser
Frankfurt am Main, 29th December 1779

I am enclosing, my dear Kaiser, an operetta that I have produced for you *en route*. These are the bare bones that you must transform with light, shadow and colours if they are to please and amaze. I don't want to say anything about the piece itself until you have read it, at which point please write to me at length on whether you want to take it up and how you think of getting to grips with it. Without my pointing it out, you will see that throughout the aim was to stir up a host of emotions within a fast-moving plot and to get this in such a sequence that the composer can show off his mastery both of transitions and of contrasts. More on this once you have written to me of your thoughts. I must just say one thing as a preliminary: I ask you please to give some attention to bringing three distinct types of singing to the work.

First of all, songs which we suppose the singers will have learnt somewhere by heart, so they can bring them off whatever the situation. These can and must have individual, distinct and rounded melodies that attract attention and that everyone easily remembers.

Secondly, arias in which the character expresses the sentiment of the moment and, losing himself in it, sings from the bottom of the heart. These must be simple, true and pure expressions of all emotions, from the gentlest to the weightiest. Melody and accompaniment must be very conscientiously handled.

Thirdly comes the rhythmic dialogue. This lends movement to the whole work, by means of which the composer can both speed things up and slow them down; at one point making it declamatory through broken rhythms, at another letting it move forward at pace in rolling melody. The dialogue must be coherent with the position, direction and movement of the actor, and the composer must watch him closely for fear of complicating his gestures and actions. In my play, you will find that almost all this dialogue has the same meter. If you are lucky enough to alight upon a main theme that suits it, you will do well to bring it out over and over, and only to nuance the individual scenes through various modulations, through major and minor keys, and through the slower and faster pace of the tempo. At the end of my play the singing is unceasing, and you will understand what I am saying, for care must be taken that it doesn't become too colourful. The dialogue must be like a smooth gold ring on to which the arias and songs are mounted like gems. Of course, I am not talking about the prose dialogue, as this must be spoken as I intend, though you can add accompaniment as and where you choose. All in all, you will find that there is plenty of opportunity to deliver a host of musical riches. Should you decide to compose the piece, I must ask you to get it back to me nice and soon, so that it can be produced in good time here, where the interest in Swiss stories has not yet subsided.

I await your forthcoming answer and will save till then all that I have further to say.

Take care. I have spoken of you to your father, send him something of your composition, one must keep such men happy as long as they live.

Goethe

Weimar, 20th January 1780

Dear Kaiser, only on my return to Weimar did I find your letter of 16th December, and since the promised operetta was sent from Frankfurt in the New Year, you must have had it a while, and I await your related thoughts. As you wished, I am sending a second sample, in which I have included the most general notes for the songs in red ink, these are really to be little more than the verses to you. You won't mistake the character of the piece. All the different passions, from sincere emotion to the most extreme anger, are to alternate in an essence that is light-hearted, pleasing and open. Noble figures are dressed as farmers and the nobility of nature shall always persist in such a realistic and appropriate expression. Perhaps even as I write this, you have already thought more about the piece than I can tell you. Still, I remind you once again really to get to know it before you begin to compose, arrange your melodies, accompaniments etc., so that everything works in and as a whole. I advise moderation in the accompaniment; only in moderation is righteousness, and he who understands his job does more with two violins, a viola and bass than the other with the whole orchestra. Make use of the woodwind instruments as of a spice and alone; here the place of the flute, here that of the bassoon, there the oboe. This defines their expression and one knows what one is enjoying, while most modern composers are like the cook who adds everything to his stew, so that fish tastes like meat, the boiled like the grilled. You need no recitative at all according to my plan. If, at any point, you want to slow the action, or moderate the movement, it is up to you to do so either through the tempo or through pauses, in any case, the decision is yours depending on what your ear dictates. I am keen to hear what you think about the piece. Please report back to me from time to time during the work, one good idea produces another.

There's one more thing I must refer to! From the moment that Thomas begins to sing his *quodlibet* [medley], the music is to be without interruption right to the end of the work and it becomes, if you want a musical term, a protracted finale. With any musician other than you, I am sure that I would have many arguments because such varied melodies and expressions follow on from one another, without the necessary mimed scenes to leave space for the long preparations of expositions and transitions. With you, however, I have nothing to fear, thank God. What I most value in your work is just this chastity, the surety of bringing much forth from little and of doing more with one single, changing idea than others would, giving full vent to their wildest passions. In this case, one melody will do you as much service as many, and it makes a very beautiful and simple impression to hear one brought through from minor to major. I am stating the obvious that you know better than me, but it does you good to know that we are apart but of one mind. Give this little piece your undivided attention, and use it to show the wealth of your ability by not putting more into it than is appropriate. Write to me soon.

I had almost forgotten to say the most important thing. The actress under consideration for Bätely's part has a beautiful range and is a practised singer; the two men are tenors, both novices but quick to learn. Thomas should be a bass really, but we haven't one. The mother is a good singer.

G.

Monday, 23rd January 1786

You have richly rewarded me, with your reply, for my long letter – if I may say so, the longest I have written in several years – and moved me to write again. Your remarks reflect your consideration of the subject, your artistic conscientiousness and your good taste. Here is my reply.

I think we may leave the first act as it is until you are through with the rest, in order to review it as a whole. We will want to talk about it further afterwards and you will do the right thing without much discussion.

You are quite right to say of my play that it is so to speak musically composed; in the same sense, one could also say that it is arranged for performance. If you want to stick with the metaphor: the drawing is done, but the shading, inasmuch as it doesn't lie in the drawing, and the colouring, remain for the composer. It is true that he cannot increase the scope, but the height remains up to the third Heaven, as high as you have yourself climbed above the level of melody and melancholy, of waterfalls and nightingales. I have written the piece with you in mind, you understand me and exceed my expectations; my next will be for you if you want it; we will understand each other better, and I am to deal with no one else for this one.

Unfortunately, the other observation is also correct that for a musical drama the piece is too condensed and strained. There is too much work for three characters. I can say little in defence except that I will not do the same again (although I do have another similar plot with three characters that is much richer and better than this). Every invention has something arbitrary. My highest notion of drama is restless action. I conceived of the subject-matter, began and saw too late that it was too overwrought for musical drama. I stopped in the middle and left it for more than half a year. Finally, I finished it and here it is now at last.

It is a bravura piece and we've no actors for it, so let them learn that from it. It is true that singers want to have more physical rest: to run, jump, gesticulate, fight and sing is fine in a finale, but it's too much, I accept, if carried throughout. The next piece is in every way more sedate.

Your reminders about rhythm come at the right time. I want to tell you my end of the story. I know the rules well, and you will find them for the most part obeyed in the pleasing arias and the duets in which the characters agree or little differ in their views and actions. I also know that the Italians never deviate from the flowing rhythm once introduced, and that this is probably why their melodies have such beautiful movements. As a poet, I am simply so tired of perpetual iambs, trochees and dactyls with their poor, staggered meter that I am rid of them willingly and knowingly. Primarily, Gluck's compositions have led me to do this. If I wanted to put a German text in place of the French with his melodies, I would have to break the rhythm that the French is thought to have rendered so fluently. But Gluck had really exchanged long and short syllables because of the ambiguity of the French feet, and thus introduced a different meter from that which he should have followed according to the text. Furthermore, his settings of Klopstock's poems, in which he conjured up a musical rhythm, struck me. I began to break the fluency of the aria when emotion is introduced, or rather, I thought to enhance and emphasize, just as I would if I were reading or reciting. In the same way, in those duets in which there are arguments, differences of opinion, or which are merely transitional, I avoided parallelism or expressly destroyed it. And as on any new path, one doesn't always stop at the right point.

Letters to Kaiser (29 December 1779, 20 January 1780 and 23 January 1786), tr. Matthew Scott

'The worst aspects of drama avoided'
JOHANN CHRISTOPH FRIEDRICH VON SCHILLER

Your present project [*Faust*], which aims to separate and refine two genres is, of course, of the greatest importance. But like me you will be convinced that in order to exclude everything that is foreign to the genre of the artwork, one must be able to decide what the genre requires. And it still fails in this. Because we cannot initially decide on the things that constitute each of the two genres, we are still inclined to mix them up. If there were still rhapsodists and their world, then the epic poet would have no need to distance himself from the tragic poet. And if we had the aid and intense powers of the Greek tragedians, and thereby the privilege of taking our audience through a sequence of seven scenes, then we would not need to make our dramas so excessively wide-reaching. The potential feeling of the viewer and listener must first be sought and pushed to the limit; this capacity is the measure for the poet. And since moral value is so developed in most, such that it is in the greatest demand and yet we like to venture there to our peril, it must be neglected.

If drama is really to be rescued from this worst tendency of the age, as I do not doubt it will be, then one must begin the reform with drama itself, and by ousting the vulgar imitation of nature in art, find light and air. And it seems to me that among other things, this effect would best be achieved through the introduction of symbols to stand in place of the object whenever it does not belong to the poetic world and is therefore not a representation but a mere referent. I have not yet been able to develop fully this concept of the poetic symbol, but it seems to me that there is much to it. If there were certain use of this, it would naturally follow that poetry would purify itself; it would draw its world together more narrowly and fuller of meaning, and within this world would be all the more effective.

I always had a certain feeling about opera, namely that the noblest form of tragic drama should have developed from it and from the choruses of ancient Bacchanals. In opera, one truly forgoes any servile imitation of nature and in this way, though only in the name of indulgence, one can restore the ideal to the theatre. Opera moves the soul to greater sympathy through the power of music and through a freer harmonious stimulation of the senses. Here truly, there is in pathos a freer sense of play because music accompanies it, and the fact that one dwells primarily upon the sense of wonder must necessarily reduce the relative importance of subject-matter.

Letter from Schiller to Goethe (extract) Jena, 29 December, 1797, tr. Matthew Scott

Goethe's reply: 'You would have seen the hope which you had for opera newly fulfilled to a high level in Don Juan, though this piece stands quite alone and any prospect of something similar is gone with Mozart's death.' 30 December 1797.

'Life, chat and cards carry on regardless in the boxes'
SAMUEL SHARP

Naples, Nov. 1765

There are some who contend, that the singers might be very well heard, if the audience was more silent; but it is so much the fashion at

Naples, and, indeed, through all *Italy*, to consider the Opera as a place of rendezvous and visiting, that they do not seem in the least to attend to the musick, but laugh and talk through the whole performance, without any restraint; and, it may be imagined, that an assembly of so many hundreds conversing together so loudly, must entirely cover the voices of the singers.

Notwithstanding the amazing noisiness of the audience, during the whole performance of the Opera, the moment the dances begin, there is a universal silence, which continues so long as the dances continue. Witty people, therefore, never fail to tell me, the *Neapolitans* go to *see*, not to *hear* an Opera. A stranger, who has a little compassion in his breast, feels for the poor singers, who are treated with so much indifference and contempt: He almost wonders that they can submit to so gross an affront; and I find, by their own confession, that however accustomed they be to it, the mortification is always dreadful, and they are eager to declare how happy they are when they sing in a country where more attention is paid to their talents.

The *Neapolitan* quality rarely dine or sup with one another, and many of them hardly ever visit, but at the Opera; on this account they seldom absent themselves, though the Opera be played three nights successively, and it be the same Opera, without any change, during ten or twelve weeks. It is customary for Gentlemen to run about from box to box, betwixt the acts, and even in the midst of the performance; but the Ladies, after they are seated, never quit their box the whole evening. It is the fashion to make appointments for such and such nights. A Lady receives visitors in her box one night, and they remain with her the whole Opera; another night she returns the visit in the same manner. In the intervals of the acts, principally betwixt the first and second, the proprietor of the box regales her company with iced fruits and sweet meats.

Besides the indulgence of a loud conversation, they sometimes form themselves into card parties; but, I believe, this custom does not prevail so much at present, as it did formerly, for I have never seen more than two or three boxes so occupied, in the same night.

Samuel Sharp, *Letters from Italy*, 3rd ed. (London, 1767)

'Opera embraces all theatrical genres'
PIERRE-AUGUSTIN CARON DE BEAUMARCHAIS

I cannot adequately stress the following fact and ask you to reflect on it: the flaw in our grand operas lies in their having too much music in their scores. This is why they drag on. While the actor sings (by which I imply that he sings for the sake of singing), the scene stops, and wherever the scene stops, our interest is abated. But, you will say, 'Surely he has to sing, there being no other idiom?' – Yes, but let me try to forget that fact. The composer's art should derive from this. Let the singer sing his piece for the reasons it is versified – solely as an adornment. Let me work to add charm, not to make it a source of distraction:

'I, who have always cherished music with constancy and faithfulness, often surprise myself by shrugging my shoulder as I listen to the pieces that I love most, and saying softly but testily, 'That's enough music! Why so much repetition? Isn't it slow enough? Instead of telling a lively story, you keep harping on; instead of portraying passion, you stick pointlessly to the words.'

(Beaumarchais, Preface to *Le Barbier de Séville*.)

So what comes of all this? If the poet tries to tighten his style and to concentrate his thought by saving his words, while by contrast the composer delays, draws out the syllables, and drowns them in trills that remove the force and sense, then the one moves right and the other left, and we don't know whom to listen to. Then yawning seizes me and the tedium drives me from the room.

What do we ask of the theatre? That it bring us pleasure. The union of all the charming arts should surely give us one of the liveliest forms of it at the Opéra. Isn't it precisely from their union that the spectacle takes its name? Their displacement and abuse has made it a scene of boredom.

Let us try to restore the pleasure by re-establishing their natural order without depriving this great theatre of any of the advantages that it offers. This is a task worth undertaking. [...] First of all, let us remember that an opera is not a tragedy, nor a comedy, and yet that it participates in both and is able to embrace all genres. I will not therefore take a subject that is absolutely tragic: the tone would become so severe that any festive moments dropping out of the blue would destroy the overall effect. Equally, let us distance ourselves from any purely comic plot, where the passions have no place and in which grand effects are excluded, for musical expression would then be without dignity.

It has seemed to me that, in opera, historical subjects have less success than imaginary ones. Is it therefore necessary to take subjects of pure fantasy – those subjects wherein the marvellous, always appearing impossible, seems to us both absurd and shocking? Experience has shown that any plot resolved by a wave of the wand or by the intervention of the gods leaves us cold, and all mythological subjects suffer somewhat from this. Furthermore, in my operatic system, I cannot skimp on music except as it augments the dramatic interest.

Let us not forget above all that, as the slow progression of the music works against plot development, the dramatic interest must focus entirely on the main sections and these need to be energetic and clear. For if the most eloquent aspect of theatre lies in the action, then it becomes absolutely indispensable in sung drama by virtue of replacing the force of the other aspect that one is all too often constrained to renounce.

I have therefore thought that one needs to take a subject mid-way between the marvellous and the historical. It also occurred to me that over-civilized manners were too methodical to appear theatrical. The manners of the Orient, more irregular and less well known, leave the imagination more freedom and seem to me highly appropriate for our end.

Wherever despotism rules, we imagine truly peremptory manners. There, slavery is close to grandeur, love touches ferocity, the passions of the great are without limits. There one can see united in the same man the most imbecilic ignorance with unlimited power, an undigni-fied and cowardly weakness with the most contemptible arrogance. There I see the abuse of power playing with the lives of men and the modesty of women, revolution marching side by side with atrocious tyranny. The despot causes all to tremble right up until he trembles himself, and frequently the two look each other in the eye. This disorder suits our subject well; it stimulates the imagination of the poet and it excites the mind, which (according to Montaigne) is well disposed to the exotic. These are the manners that are called for in opera; they allow us the full range of tones. The harem also offers all sorts of devices. I can show myself off in lively form: imposing, gay, serious, playful, terrible or light-hearted. Strange customs, especially the oriental, have something of a magical air, something marvellous, something that allows the mind to enter in and enlivens our interest in the action. [...]

Since finishing the play, I have found, in an Arabian tale, certain situations similar to those in *Tarare*. They reminded me that I had previously read this tale in the country. 'Fortunately,' I said to myself, turning the pages once again, 'I have got such a bad memory.' What stayed with me has its value: the rest was no use. [...] But what belongs far less to me is the beautiful music of my friend Salieri. This great composer, the pride of Gluck's school with the style of a grand master, is naturally endowed with an exquisite sense, a just mind, and a dramatic talent with a unique versatility. For my sake, he had the decency to renounce a host of the musical beauties that filled his opera, because they prolonged the action. But the masculinity and energy of colour; the rapidity and honesty of tone will more than make up for his sacrifices. [...] Our discussions, I think, would have formed a very reasonable poetics of opera, for M. Salieri is a born poet and I am something of a musician. One will never get on without this co-incidence. [...]

The real task of our rehearsals then was to simplify the recitative without reducing the harmony, in order to bring it closer to real speech. I will publicly praise the efforts of our singers. Short of having straight speech, the composer could not have done much better. And to use speech would have deprived the production of the reserves of energy that our able composer was determined to provide through the orchestra at every possible opportunity.

Orchestra of our Opéra! Noble player in this system of Gluck, Salieri and me! If you only make noise, you will stifle the words: your real glory lies in the expression of passion. You will know this as well as me. But if I got my composer to agree to split the work in two, so that the music was relieved by the poem, the poem by the music, then the orchestra and singers would need to sign a similar agreement. If the composer's soul entered that of the poet, in a sense, espousing it, then all the contributing arts should listen to and wait for each other rather than impeding and stifling one another. From the union arises pleasure; from their vanity, boredom.

The best orchestra possible, were it to render the finest effects, would destroy our pleasure if it hid the voices. In theatre, there's the old problem of a beautiful face outshone by a set of diamonds: the beauty is hidden, not increased. From this perspective, you can see that we were constantly trying to bring a few remaining beauties to the greatest show on earth: rapid action, a lively and pressing plot, and above all the honour of being listened to.

'To the season-ticket holders of the Opéra, who wish to love opera: a discussion preliminary to *Tarare*', ['*Aux abonnés de l'Opéra qui vondraient aimer l' opéra*', 1787], tr. Matthew Scott

'The Poet and the Composer'
ERNST THEODOR AMADEUS HOFFMANN

[Prologue]

'My dear friend Theodor', said Ottmar, 'Your story* has clearly demonstrated what tribulations you have suffered in the noble cause of music. Each of us tried to tempt you in a different direction. While Lothar wanted to hear only instrumental pieces by you, I insisted on comic operas; and while Cyprian, as he would now admit, expected the impossible by asking you to set librettos that completely lacked form and balance, you preferred serious church music. As things stand at the moment, serious tragic opera would seem to be the highest pinnacle to which a composer can aspire, and I don't understand why you did not attempt that genre and produce something remarkable long ago.'

'But who else', replied Theodor, 'who else is to blame for my negligence but you, Ottmar, together with Cyprian and Lothar? Has any of you been able to agree to write a libretto for me, despite all my begging, pleading, and nagging?'

'What an amazing fellow you are', said Cyprian. 'Have I not spent long enough discussing texts for operas with you, and did you not dismiss the sublimest ideas as utterly impracticable? Did you not end by demanding, rather absurdly, that I should make a formal study of music in order to understand your requirements and be able to satisfy them? Any interest I had in poetry of that kind evaporated when you made it clear – something I would never have believed possible – that

---

* story: *Die Fermate* (*The Cadenza*; or *An Interrupted Cadence* in Alexander Ewing's translation of 1886), told by Theodor in the first person and concerning his experiences with the singers Teresina and Lauretta who inspire him to compose contrasting types of music. [Footnotes for this extract are by David Charlton.]

you stick to conventional forms and are totally unwilling to depart from them, just like the most mechanical composer, kappellmeister, or musical director.'*

'But what', interjected Lothar, 'what is more inexplicable – tell me, why in the world does Theodor, who is a master of words and of poetic expression, not write a libretto himself? Why does he expect us to become musicians and squander our poetic gifts merely in order to create a thing to which *he* then gives life and movement? Doesn't he know his own needs best? Isn't it simply because of the imbecility of most composers, and their one-sided training, that they need the help of others in their work? Isn't perfect unity of text and music possible only when poet and composer are one and the same person?'

'That all sounds remarkably plausible', replied Theodor, 'but it's completely wrong. I maintain that it's impossible for anyone to create a work by himself that is equally outstanding in word and music.'

'But my dear Theodor', continued Lothar, 'you only imagine that to be the case, either out of unwarranted pessimism or out of – well, innate laziness. The idea of having to work your way through the lines of text in order to arrive at the music is so distasteful to you that you refuse to have anything to do with it, whereas I believe that music and word flow from the inspired poet and composer at the *same* instant.'†

'Quite right', cried Cyprian and Ottmar.

'You drive me into a corner', said Theodor. 'Instead of trying to refute your argument, let me relate to you a conversation between two friends, which I wrote down several years ago, about the requirements of opera. The fateful period we have lived through was then just beginning. I thought that my existence as an artist would be endangered, or even destroyed, and a feeling of despair came over me, to which poor physical health may also have contributed. So I created for myself a serapiontic friend‡ who had taken up the sword instead of the quill. He gave me comfort in my anguish, and pitched me right into the

---

* The 'conventional forms' – symmetrical vocal and instrumental forms as developed in the eighteenth century – show that Theodor is no duplicate of the composer Hoffmann.
† Lothar goes much further in speculation here than anywhere else in the discussion. The tendency of what he says accurately foreshadows the nineteenth-century concern with creating truly musico-dramatic librettos. For a sustained study of Richard Wagner's methods in writing both words and music of opera, see Curt von Westernhagen, *The Forging of the 'Ring'*, tr. Arnold and Mary Whittall (Cambridge, 1976), esp. pp. 9ff.
‡ serapiontic friend: one worthy of the friends' rule of 'Serapion the Hermit': 'that they should never torment each other with inferior hack-work'.

bewildering maelstrom of great events and deeds of that momentous time.'

Thereupon Theodor began:

The Poet and the Composer

The enemy was at the gates, guns thundered all around, and grenades sizzled through the air amid showers of sparks. The townsfolk, their faces white with fear, ran into their houses; the deserted streets rang with the sound of horses' hooves, as mounted patrols galloped past and with curses drove the remaining soldiers into their redoubts. But Ludwig sat in his little back room, completely absorbed and lost in the wonderful, brightly coloured world of fantasy that unfolded before him at the piano. He had just completed a symphony, in which he had striven to capture in written notation all the resonances of his innermost soul; the work sought, like Beethoven's compositions of that type, to speak in heavenly language of the glorious wonders of that far, romantic realm in which we swoon away in inexpressible yearning; indeed it sought, like one of those wonders, itself to penetrate our narrow, paltry lives, and with sublime siren voices tempt forth its willing victims. Then his landlady came into the room, upbraiding him and asking how he could simply play the piano through all that anguish and distress, and whether he wanted to get himself shot dead in his garret. Ludwig did not quite follow the woman's drift, until with a sudden crash a shell carried away part of the roof and shattered the window panes. Screaming and wailing the landlady ran down the stairs, while Ludwig seized the dearest thing he now possessed, the score of his symphony, and hurried after her down to the cellar.

Here the entire household was gathered. In a quite untypical fit of largesse the wine-seller who lived downstairs had made available a few dozen bottles of his best wine, and the women, fretting and fussing but as always anxiously concerned with physical sustenance and comfort, filled their sewing-baskets with many tasty morsels from the pantry. They ate, they drank, and their agitation and distress were soon transformed into that agreeable state in which we seek and fancy we find security in neighbourly companionship; that state in which all the petty airs and graces which propriety teaches are subsumed, as it were, into the great round danced to the irresistible beat of fate's iron fist. Their grievous situation, even their apparent mortal danger, was quite forgotten and cheerful talk poured from animated lips. Tenants who scarcely raised their hats when meeting on the stairs sat arm in arm beside each other, revealing their innermost feelings in mutual warmheartedness. The shots were now heard only intermittently, and there was already talk of going up again, as the street appeared to have become safer. One old soldier went further; after vouchsafing a few instructive words about the art of fortification in Ancient Rome and the efficacy of catapults, and also mentioning the renown of Vauban* in more recent times, he roundly asserted that all fears were groundless since the house lay well beyond the line of fire. Whereupon a stray shot smashed the bricks protecting the ventilation holes and flung them into the cellar. No one was injured, however, and when the soldier with full glass in hand leapt onto the table from which the bottles had been dashed by the bricks, and expressed contempt for any further shot, they all recovered their spirits.

This was indeed the last scare. The night passed quietly, and on the following morning they learned that the army had taken up a different position and had voluntarily left the town to the enemy. When they came out of the cellar, enemy troops were already moving through the town, and a public notice promised the inhabitants peace and security of property. Ludwig plunged into the motley crowd eagerly awaiting the new spectacle and pressing towards the enemy commander,[†] who was just riding through the gate amid the joyful sound of trumpets and surrounded by guards in gleaming uniforms.

He could hardly believe his eyes when among the officers he recognised his beloved university friend Ferdinand who, in a simple uniform and carrying his left arm in a sling, came prancing past him on a magnificent dun. 'It was him – it was really and truly him!' Ludwig burst out involuntarily. In vain he tried to follow his friend, who was quickly carried out of sight by his impetuous steed. Deep in thought Ludwig hurried back to his room, but he could make no progress with his work; his head was filled by the appearance of his old friend, with whom he had completely lost touch years before, and all the happy hours of his youth that he had spent with good old

---

* Sébastien Le Prestre de Vauban (1633–1707), French military strategist and engineer, also author, who revolutionised the arts of siege-craft and fortification. His treatise *De l'attaque et de la défense des places* was reprinted as late as 1829.
† Hoffmann recalls the events of 8 May 1813 when he witnessed the withdrawal of the Prussians and Russians from Dresden, the burning of bridges, and the entry of the French headed by Napoleon. This was followed by bombardments.

Ferdinand passed luminously through his mind. At that time Ferdinand had not shown the least propensity towards military life; he lived purely for the muses, and the gifts revealed in several of his works bore witness to his calling as a poet. All the more incomprehensible to Ludwig, therefore, was this transformation of his friend, and he burned with longing to speak to him, without having any idea how he might begin to track him down.

There was now more and more excitement in the town. A large section of enemy troops rode past led by the allied princes, who were allowing themselves a few days' respite there. The greater the congestion at headquarters became, however, the more Ludwig lost hope of ever seeing his friend, until at last, in an out-of-the-way, unfrequented coffee-house where Ludwig usually ate his frugal evening meal, Ferdinand suddenly fell into his arms with a loud cry of heartfelt joy. Ludwig remained silent, for a certain uneasiness soured in him the longed-for moment of reunion. It was like a dream in which one embraces those one loves, only to find them suddenly changed into strangers, so that the most sublime pleasures instantly dissolve into mocking phantoms.

The gentle son of the muses, the poet of numerous romantic lyrics which Ludwig had clothed with melody and harmony, now stood before him in a plumed helmet, a great, rattling sabre at his side, even profaning his voice with the harsh cry of greeting. Ludwig's troubled eyes took in the wounded arm, then moved to the medal on Ferdinand's breast. But then Ferdinand embraced him with his right arm and pressed him warmly to his heart. 'I know', he said, 'what you are thinking, what feelings this sudden meeting must arouse in you! My country needed me, and I could not hesitate to follow the call. It was with joy, with that burning enthusiasm a noble cause kindles in any breast which cowardice has not condemned to slavery, that this hand, previously accustomed only to guiding the gentle quill, took up the sword! My blood has already been shed and only chance, which caused the Prince himself to witness my deed, obtained the decoration for me. But believe me, Ludwig! The strings vibrating in my soul, whose notes so often spoke to you, are still unharmed. In fact, even after the horror of bloody battle, on lonely guard duty, or when my comrades sat around the campfire, I would pour my inspiration into poems which uplifted and strengthened me in my glorious vocation to fight for freedom and honour.' Ludwig felt his heart open up at these words, and when Ferdinand sat down with him in a small side-room and removed his helmet and sword, it was as though his friend had only been teasing him with a ludicrous disguise now cast aside. As the two friends ate the modest meal that had meanwhile been brought for them, and their glasses rang merrily together, they were filled with joy and elation; the bright lights and colours of the old days surrounded them, and all the profound feelings produced by their combined artistic efforts, as though by some powerful magic, came back to them in the warm glow of renewed youth. Ferdinand earnestly enquired what Ludwig had composed since that time, and was very much surprised when Ludwig confessed that he had still not managed to write an opera and have it produced, having not yet found a single libretto whose subject and treatment had been able to inspire him to composition.

'I cannot understand', said Ferdinand, 'why you, with your vivid imagination and more than adequate command of language, have not written a libretto yourself long ago!'

LUDWIG: I am willing to admit that my imagination may well be lively enough to devise several good subjects for an opera; indeed, especially when at night a slight headache produces in me that dreamlike state halfway between sleeping and waking, I not only conceive quite good, genuinely romantic operas, but actually see them performed before me together with my music. So far as the gift of grasping hold of them and writing them down is concerned, however, I am afraid I do not possess it; and really it is hardly right to expect us composers to develop the mechanical skills necessary for success in every artistic medium, and learned only through constant diligence and long practice, that we would need in order to compose our own texts as well. But even if I did acquire the ability to work out a story, and to set it properly and tastefully into poetic and dramatic form, I could still never bring myself to write my own libretto.

FERDINAND: But no one could ever be so much in sympathy with your musical objectives as you yourself.

LUDWIG: That may well be true, but it seems to me that the composer who set himself the task of constructing his own libretto line by line would feel like a painter who had to make a laborious copper engraving of the picture he had conceived in his imagination, before he was allowed to begin painting with living colours.

FERDINAND: You mean that the spark necessary for composition would be smothered and extinguished in the process of versification?

LUDWIG: That's precisely it! And eventually my verse would seem to me just as wretched as the paper cases of the rockets that only yesterday were hissing up into the sky with fiery energy.* But seriously, if success is to be achieved, it seems to me that in no art is it so necessary as in music to embrace the whole work in the first, most intense flash of inspiration, down to the smallest detail of every part. Nowhere is filing and altering more futile and destructive; for I know from experience that the melody conjured up as though by a thunderbolt immediately on first reading the libretto is always the best, and in the composer's mind perhaps the only valid one.† It would be quite impossible for a musician, as soon as he started writing the text, not to occupy himself with the music called for by the situation. He would be completely immersed and carried away by the melodies flooding over him, and would struggle in vain to find the words; and if he succeeded in forcing himself to do so, then no matter how forcefully the waves surged over him the torrent would soon drain away as though into barren sand. In fact, let me put my inner conviction in even plainer terms. At the moment of musical inspiration any word or any phrase would seem to him inadequate, lifeless, pitiful, and he would have to descend from his exalted state in order to be able to beg for the necessities of his existence in the lower region of words.‡ But wouldn't his

---

* Fire and sparks, however (in spite of Ludwig's topical joke), were an abiding Hoffmann metaphor for musical creation: see 'Ombra adorata', p. 90, and Ludwig's 'tongues of fire' speech later in the dialogue.

† This should not be taken to mean that Hoffmann himself never revised his music. We know, in the case of *Undine*, that he made many improvements and re-composed certain items such as Undine's Act 2 aria, 'Wer traut'. See Jürgen Kindermann (ed.), *Undine. Zauberoper in 3 Akten* (E. T. A. Hoffmann, *Ausgewählte musikalische Werke*, i) (Mainz, 1971), i, Vorwort.

‡ This account is by no means far-fetched. We know that various composers have, at times, been impelled to write part of an operatic score without yet having received the precise form of words for the vocal line. In such cases, either the rhythm and metre had been agreed already, or else the librettist added words to the musician's patterns. Evidence exists in the cases of A. E. M. Grétry, W. A. Mozart, and G. Meyerbeer.

wings then soon become useless, like those of a caged eagle, so that he would try in vain to reach for the sun?

FERDINAND: There is certainly something in that. But you probably realise, my friend, that more than convincing me, you are excusing your reluctance to beat a path towards musical creation through all the inevitable scenes, arias, duets, and what have you.

LUDWIG: That may be, but I must bring up an old grievance again: why were you never willing, when the same artistic aspirations bound us so intimately together, to satisfy my fervent plea to write a libretto for me?

FERDINAND: Because I consider it the most thankless task in the world. You will grant me that nobody can be more stubborn in his demands than you composers are. And when you assert that the musician cannot be expected to acquire the skill necessary for the mechanical task of versification, then I retort that the poet may well be hard pressed to pay such strict regard to your requirements, to observe the structure of your trios, quartets, finales, etc., and to make sure he is not every moment trespassing, as happens sadly all too often, against the form that you have fixed (though with what right you only know yourselves). When we have striven with the utmost care to render every dramatic situation in true poetry, and to depict it in the most inspired words and the most well-turned phrases, then it is quite horrifying that you so often ruthlessly strike out our finest lines, abuse our noblest words by twisting and inverting them, in fact by drowning them in music.* And this is to speak only of the fruitless toil of carefully working the libretto out. Many a splendid subject, conceived by us in moments of poetic rapture and proudly placed before you in the expectation of your delighted response, has been rejected out of hand as worthless and unsuitable for musical embellishment. And often this is sheer

---

* Ferdinand returns to this concept near the close of the dialogue. He refers to the fact that composers of vocal music frequently repeat words or phrases in the course of a setting, either for immediate dramatic emphasis or for reasons of musical elaboration. In any case, the passage recalls, by inversion, Diderot's *Le Neveu de Rameau*, where the Nephew calls for a new approach to writing librettos: 'phrases must be short and the meaning self-contained, so that the musician can utilise the whole and each part, omitting one word or repeating it, adding a missing word, turning it in all ways like a polyp, without destroying it'. *Rameau's Nephew*, tr. Tancock, 105.

wilfulness, or something of the sort, for frequently you turn instead to texts that are beneath contempt, and...

LUDWIG: Stop, my dear friend! There are admittedly composers to whom music is as alien as poetry is to many versifiers; they are the ones who have often set texts that really are beneath contempt in every way. True composers, who live and move amid the hallowed splendour of music, have chosen only poetic texts.

FERDINAND: But Mozart...?

LUDWIG: ... chose for his classical operas* only librettos that genuinely suited the music, paradoxical though this may seem to many. But leaving them aside for the moment, I believe that it can be determined very precisely what sort of subject is suitable for opera, so that the poet need never run the risk of making a mistake.

FERDINAND: I confess that I have never considered that, and with my lack of musical knowledge I would not even have known where to start.

LUDWIG: If by musical knowledge you are referring to so-called academic music, then there is no need of that in order to gauge the real needs of composers; without it one can recognise and grasp the essential nature of music to such an extent that in this respect one is a much better musician than the man who by the sweat of his brow works through the whole academic system with its numerous wrong turnings, who glorifies the dead letter as the living god like a self-carved fetish, and who by this idolatry is denied the bliss of higher realms.

FERDINAND: And you believe that the poet can penetrate this essential nature of music without having received that lowlier initiation from the academy?

LUDWIG: I certainly do! Indeed, in that far realm which often envelops us in curious presentiments, from where mysterious voices echo down to us and awaken all the resonances dormant in the burdened breast, which once awake shoot joyfully upwards like tongues of fire, so that we become partakers in the bliss of that paradise – it is there that poets and musicians are closely kindred members of *one* church; for the secret of words and

---

* classical: i.e. which stand as authoritative monuments; not here in contradistinction to 'romantic'.

sounds is one and the same, unveiling to both the ultimate sublimity.

FERDINAND: I hear my dear friend striving to describe the mysterious nature of art in profound utterances, and I do begin to see the gap ceasing to exist that previously seemed to me to separate the poet from the musician.

LUDWIG: Let me try to express what I feel about the essential nature of opera. Briefly, genuine opera seems to me to be only that in which the music springs directly from the poetry as a necessary product of it.

FERDINAND: I must confess that I do not quite see what you mean.

LUDWIG: Is not music the mysterious language of a distant spirit-realm, its wonderful accents resounding in our souls and awakening a higher, intenser awareness? All the emotions vie with each other in dazzling array, and then sink back in an inexpressible longing that fills our breast. This is the indescribable effect of instrumental music. But now music is expected to step right into everyday life, to come to grips with the world of phenomena, adorning words and deeds and dealing with specific emotions and actions. Can one use sublime language to speak of ordinary things? Can music proclaim anything other than the wonders of that region from which it echoes across to us? Let the poet be prepared for daring flights to the distant realm of romanticism, for it is there that he will find the marvellous things that he should bring into our lives. Then, dazzled by their brilliant colours, we willingly believe ourselves as in a blissful dream to be transported from our meagre everyday existence to the flowery avenues of that romantic land, and to comprehend only its language, words sounding forth in music.

FERDINAND: So you are making a case exclusively for romantic opera with its fairies, spirits, miracles, and transformations?

LUDWIG: I certainly consider romantic opera to be the only true sort, for only in the realm of romanticism is music at home. Of course you know that I utterly despise those wretched productions in which absurd spiritless spirits appear and miracle is heaped upon miracle without cause or effect, merely to amuse the gaze of the idle rabble. Only the inspired poet of genius can write a truly romantic opera, for only he can bring before our eyes the wonderful apparitions of the spirit-realm; carried on his wings we soar across the abyss that formerly separated us from it, and soon at home in that strange land we accept the miracles that are seen to take place as natural consequences of the influence of higher natures on our lives. Then we experience all the powerfully stirring sensations that fill us now with horror and fear, now with utter bliss. In short it is the magical power of poetic truth that the poet who describes these miracles must have at his command, for only this can carry us away, whereas a merely whimsical sequence of pointless magical happenings, often inserted as in many such productions just to tease the buffoon in his squire's costume,* will seem farcical and silly and will only leave us cold and unmoved.

So, my friend, in opera the influence of higher natures on us should be seen to take place. Then a romantic dimension reveals itself before our eyes in which language is raised to a higher power, or rather (since it is part of that distant realm of music) takes the form of song. Then even action and situation, carried forward by irresistible sonorities, seize and transport us more potently. In this way, as I have already asserted, the music should spring directly and inevitably from the poetry.

FERDINAND: Now I understand you clearly, and I am reminded of Ariosto and Tasso. But I think it would be a difficult task to construct a musical drama according to your requirements.

LUDWIG: It must be the work of a truly romantic poet of genius. Think of the excellent Gozzi.† In his dramatic fairy-tales he has provided exactly what I demand of a librettist and it is incredible that this rich storehouse of outstanding operatic subjects has not been more exploited before now.

FERDINAND: I do admit that when I read Gozzi several years ago he made the most lively impression on me, although I naturally did not consider him from the standpoint you are adopting.

---

* pointless magical happenings: such as favoured by Kotzebue and many others, especially set by southern composers in the 1790s. Kotzebue's *Der Spiegelritter* (1791), for example, is summarised in Bauman, *North German Opera*, 277. Hoffmann probably had in mind *Das Donauweibchen* (1798), music by Ferdinand Kauer, which was extremely well known and much imitated; or other musical plays featuring knights and comic subsidiary characters who are the butt of jokes perpetrated by fairies or spirits.
† Carlo Gozzi (1720–1806), author of the ten celebrated dramatic fairy-tales (*fiabe*), 1761–65; but also twenty other plays, including sentimental and tragicomic works.

LUDWIG: One of his finest tales is indisputably *Il corvo*.*

Millo, King of Frattombrosa, knows no other pleasure than hunting. In the forest he catches sight of a magnificent raven and transfixes it with an arrow. The raven plunges to earth on to a tombstone of whitest marble lying beneath the tree, and bespatters the marble with its blood as it stiffens and dies. Then the whole forest begins to tremble, and from a grotto a terrible monster advances and bellows a curse at poor Millo: 'Find a wife as white as this tombstone's marble, as red as this raven's blood and as black as this raven's feathers, or you will die a raving madman.' All attempts to find such a woman are in vain, so the king's brother, Jennaro, who loves him most dearly, resolves not to rest until he has found the beautiful girl who will save his brother from incurable insanity. He traverses land and sea and finally, after receiving guidance from an old man experienced in necromancy, he sees Armilla, the daughter of the powerful sorcerer Norand. Her skin is as white as the tombstone's marble, her hair as red as the raven's blood, and her eyebrows as black as the raven's feathers.† He contrives to abduct her, and after surviving a storm they soon land near Frattombrosa.

Hardly has he stepped ashore when a splendid stallion and a falcon of the rarest quality fall by chance into his hands, and he is overjoyed, not only to be able to save his brother, but also to be able to delight him with gifts he will value so highly. Jennaro is about to rest in the tent that has been pitched under a tree, when two doves land in the branches and begin to speak: 'Unfortunate are you, O Jennaro, that you were born! The falcon will peck out your brother's eyes; if you do not present it to him, or if you reveal what you know, then you will be turned to stone. If your brother mounts the stallion, it will kill him instantly; if you do not give it to him, or if you reveal what you know, then you will be turned to stone. If Millo marries Armilla, a monster will tear him to pieces in the night; if you do not

---

* *Il corvo* (*The Raven*): dramatic fairy-tale, originally produced in Milan, 1761. The story originated in a much older collection by Giambattista Basile.
† In the *A M Z* version of this text Armilla's lips, not hair, were red, and her hair was black, like her eyebrows. 'Norand' was the orthodox Germanic rendering of Gozzi's original 'Norando'.

deliver Armilla to him, or if you reveal what you know, then you will be turned to stone.'

Norand appears and confirms what the doves have said, laying down the punishment for Armilla's abduction. As soon as Millo sees Armilla he is cured of the madness that had possessed him. The horse and the falcon are brought in and the king is overjoyed by his brother's love in gratifying his greatest passions with such splendid gifts. Jennaro hands the falcon to him, but just as Millo takes it Jennaro cuts off its head and his brother's eyes are saved. Similarly, just as Millo places his foot in the stirrup in order to mount the stallion Jennaro draws his sword and with a single stroke cuts off both of the horse's forelegs so that it crashes to the ground. Millo now feels convinced that insane love is driving his brother to act in this way, and Armilla verifies this supposition, since Jennaro's surreptitious sighs and tears and his eccentric behaviour have long since made her suspect that he loves her. She assures the king of her deepest affection, which had already formed during the journey, when Jennaro spoke of his beloved brother in the most animated and moving terms. In order to avoid any mistrust she now begs the king to hasten their union, and this duly takes place. Jennaro expects his brother's destruction at any moment; he is in despair to see himself so misunderstood, and yet a terrible fate awaits him if the least word of his dreadful secret escapes his lips. So he decides to save his brother, whatever the cost may be, and during the night he makes his way to the king's bedroom along a subterranean passage. A horrible, fire-breathing dragon appears; Jennaro attacks it, but his blows are ineffectual. The monster gets closer to the bedroom, so in utter desperation he seizes his sword in both hands, but the dreadful blow intended for the monster smashes the door. Millo comes out of the bedroom, and since the monster has disappeared he sees his brother as a hypocrite driven to fratricide in a fury of jealous love. Jennaro cannot explain himself; the guard is summoned and he is disarmed and dragged off to prison. He is found guilty of the crime and must pay with his life on the scaffold.

Just before his execution he asks to speak to his dearly beloved brother. Millo grants him an audience, and Jennaro in the most moving terms reminds him of the ardent love that has united them since their birth; but when he asks whether Millo really considers him capable of murdering his brother, Millo asks for proof of his innocence. In a torment of agony Jennaro now reveals the terrible prophecies of the doves and the necromancer Norand; but when he has finished speaking, to Millo's speechless horror he is transformed into a marble statue. Millo now recognises Jennaro's brotherly love and, tortured by heart-rending reproach, he resolves never to leave the statue of his beloved brother, but to die at its feet in remorse and despair. Then Norand appears. 'In the eternal ordinances of fate', he announces, 'the raven's death, your curse and Armilla's abduction were already prescribed. Only one deed can restore your brother to life, but that deed is a terrible one. If Armilla dies by this dagger beside the statue then the cold marble, bespattered by her blood, will quicken into life. If you have the courage to kill Armilla, then do it! Mourn and complain, as I do!'

He vanishes. Armilla wrings from the unfortunate Millo the secret of Norand's fearful words. Millo leaves her in despair. Overcome with horror and dread, and no longer valuing her own life, Armilla stabs herself with the dagger thrown down by Norand. As soon as her blood splashes the statue Jennaro is restored to life. Millo returns and finds his brother alive again but his beloved wife lying dead. In despair he is about to kill himself with the same dagger that Armilla had used, when the gloomy vault is suddenly transformed into a bright and spacious chamber. Norand appears; the great, mysterious prophecy has been fulfilled; all sorrow is at an end; Armilla, touched by Norand, comes back to life and everything ends happily.

FERDINAND: I remember the extraordinary play exactly now, and I can still recall the profound impression it made on me. You are right; the miraculous element seems entirely in place here, and has such poetic truth that one willingly accepts it. Millo's action in killing the raven knocks, as it were, at the bronze portal of the shadowy spirit-realm, so that it swings open with a clang and the spirits emerge into the world and enmesh men in the mysterious fate that governs their own movements.

LUDWIG: Precisely, and consider the irresistible situations that the author was able to fashion from this conflict with the spirit-world. Jennaro's heroic self-sacrifice and Armilla's noble deed contain a greatness of which our moralising playwrights, grubbing among the trivialities of everyday life as in the sweepings thrown into the dust-cart from a stately hall, have no conception. How splendidly the comic rôles of the masks are also woven in.*

FERDINAND: I agree! Only in a truly romantic work can the comic be so smoothly blended with the tragic that they combine into a single overall effect and seize the listener's spirit in a strange and magical way.

LUDWIG: Even our opera-manufacturers have darkly perceived this. It is doubtless for this reason that their so-called heroic-comic operas[†] came about; in these the heroic is often really comic, but the comic is heroic only to the extent that it disregards with true heroism all the dictates of taste, propriety and manners.

FERDINAND: According to your definition of a libretto then, we certainly have very few true operas.

LUDWIG: Precisely! Most so-called operas are merely inane plays with singing added, and the total lack of dramatic force, imputed now to the libretto, now to the music, is entirely attributable to the dead weight of successive scenes with no inner poetic relationship or poetic truth that might kindle the music into life. Often the composer has unconsciously worked entirely on his own, and the wretched libretto trots along beside him quite independently of the music. In such a case the music can be very good in some ways; that is, without necessarily seizing the listener with the magical power of its inner meaning, it can still provide a certain pleasure, like a brilliant play of iridescence. But then the opera is merely a concert given in a theatre with costumes and scenery.

---

* masks: Gozzi's dramatic fairy-tales all employed the 'masks', the improvising actors of the traditional *commedia dell'arte all'improvviso*; their parts were not so much written out by Gozzi as left in outline. When the plays were adapted or translated (into German first by Friedrich Werthes, 1777–79) the masked rôles naturally posed various problems.
† heroic-comic operas: Hoffmann alludes to the mixed genre-descriptions of Italian opera, and probably a work that he well knew: Paer's *Sargino, a dramma eroicomico*. (See *Kreisleriana*, p. 82, for mention of its duet, 'Dolce dell'anima'.) The 'heroic' aspect of the opera refers to the action surrounding the Battle of Bouvines in 1214, and the 'comic' aspect refers to the sentimental education of the eponymous hero.

FERDINAND: If you therefore only recognise operas that are romantic in the fullest sense, what do you think of musical tragedies, and of comic operas in modern costume? Must you completely reject them?

LUDWIG: Not at all! In the majority of older tragic operas, such as are sadly no longer written and set to music, it is again the true heroism of action and the inner strength of character and situation which so powerfully seize the spectator. The dark, mysterious forces governing gods and men pass visibly before his eyes, and he listens as the eternal, immutable decrees of providence to which even the gods are subject are proclaimed in strange and ominous tones. Strictly speaking, these purely tragic subjects exclude fantastical elements, but in dealings with the gods, who rouse men to a higher existence and to godly deeds, a higher language must also be spoken using the enchanting accents of music. Incidentally, were the ancient tragedies not musically declaimed, and did that not clearly express the need for a loftier means of expression than ordinary speech can provide?

Our musical tragedies have in a quite distinct way inspired the composer of genius to write in a lofty, one might almost say sacred style; it is as though men, with profound dedication, borne on sounds emanating from the golden harps of cherubim and seraphim, were making a pilgrimage into the realm of light where they learn the secret of their own existence. I would like to point out nothing less, Ferdinand, than that church music and tragic opera form an intimate kinship, from which the older composers fashioned their own glorious style* which more recent ones do not remotely understand, not even Spontini, for all his exuberant abundance.† I need hardly mention the magnificent Gluck, who stands forth like a demigod; but in

---

* style: used in a particular sense by Hoffmann, akin to 'authentic, personal musical language'. Here he is thinking of composers of the High Baroque like Alessandro Scarlatti and Johann Adolf Hasse. See 'Old and New Church Music', p. 366.
† Gaspare Spontini (1774–1851): the Italian composer most recently celebrated for his Paris operas *La vestale* (1807) and *Fernand Cortez* (1809). Hoffmann's initial unfavourable analysis of his music appears in 'Letters on Music in Berlin', p. 392. Subsequently, he came to believe that Spontini – who was appointed as royal composer to the Berlin court in 1820 – might become the Romantic successor to Gluck.

order to realise how even inferior talents embraced that truly great, tragic style, think of the chorus of Priests of the Night in Piccinni's *Didon*.*

FERDINAND: Now you make me feel just as I used to in our meetings in the good old days. When you speak so enthusiastically about your art, you lift me up to see things that I previously had no inkling of, and you can believe me when I say that at this moment I feel as though I understand a great deal about music. Indeed, I do not think a good line of poetry could awaken in my heart without issuing forth in music and song.

LUDWIG: Isn't that the librettist's real inspiration? I maintain that he must inwardly compose everything in musical terms just as well as the musician, and it is merely a conscious awareness of specific melodies and specific notes from the accompanying instruments, in a word a secure mastery of the inner realm of sounds, which distinguishes the latter from the former. But I still owe you an explanation of my views about opera buffa.

FERDINAND: You will surely not value it very highly, at least in modern costume?

LUDWIG: For my part, my dear Ferdinand, I confess not only that I like it best in contemporary costume, but also that only in that style, preserving as it does the character and feeling with which those mercurial, excitable Italians endowed it, does it seem to me genuinely to exist. Here a sense of the fantastic, arising partly from the eccentric folly of individual characters and partly from the bizarre fluctuation of fortune, boldly invades everyday life and turns everything topsy-turvy. We must concede that yes, it is the fellow next door in his familiar light-brown Sunday suit with gold-covered buttons, but what on earth can have got into the man to make him behave so absurdly? Or imagine a respectable family gathering including a love-sick daughter, together with a few students who serenade her eyes and play the guitar below her window; then Puck appears among them in a mood of roguish mischief

---

* Niccolò Piccinni, *Didon, tragédie lyrique* (1783), Act 3 sc. 10: general ensemble in E flat with the Priests of Pluto, 'Appaisez-vous, mânes terribles' ['Be satisfied, ye awful deities'].

and everything disintegrates into wild imaginings and all manner of outlandish capers and eccentric contortions. A special star has risen and everywhere chance sets up its coils in which the most respectable of people get entrapped if they stick out their noses even just a whit.

This incursion of eccentricity into everyday life and the contradictions arising from it contain, in my opinion, the essence of true opera buffa. And this perception of the fantastic, previously remote but now encroaching upon reality, is precisely what makes the acting of Italian comedians so inimitable. They understand the poet's allusions and by their performance clothe the skeleton, which is all he is able to provide, with flesh and colour.*

FERDINAND: I think I understand you exactly. In opera buffa then, the fantastic actually takes the place of the romantic which you lay down as an indispensable requirement of opera. And the art of the librettist should consist in making the characters appear not only fully rounded and poetically true but lifted straight from everyday life and so individual that one instantly says to oneself: Look! That's my neighbour whom I talk to every day! That's the student who goes to lectures every morning and sighs terribly below his cousin's window! And so on. But then the adventures that they get up to, as though seized by some strange paroxysm, or that befall them, should give us the curious feeling that a mad demon is abroad, irresistibly drawing us into the circle of its amusing drolleries.

LUDWIG: You express my most heartfelt conviction, and I need hardly point out how, following my principle, music is readily fitted to opera buffa, and how here too a particular style emerges of its own accord, stirring the listener's heart in its own way.

FERDINAND: But can music be expected to express comedy in all its nuances?

LUDWIG: I am absolutely convinced it can, and artists of genius have proved it a hundred times. Music can convey, for example,

---

* Allusion to the improvising actors mentioned in the note on p. 185, whose rôles were traditionally Pantalone, the Doctor, Arlecchino, Brighella, Truffaldino, Pulcinella, Tartaglia, the Captain, and Smeraldina.

an impression of the most delicious irony, such as that pervading Mozart's splendid opera *Così fan tutte*.

FERDINAND: The thought now strikes me that, according to your principle, the despised libretto of that opera* is in fact truly operatic.

LUDWIG: And that's precisely what I meant when I said earlier that Mozart had chosen for his classical operas only librettos that exactly suited opera, although *Le nozze di Figaro* is more a play with songs than a true opera. The shameful attempt to translate sentimental plays into opera can only fail, and our orphanages, oculists,† and suchlike are certainly destined for early oblivion. Thus nothing could be more wretched, or more opposed to true opera, than that whole series of Singspiels which Dittersdorf produced,‡ whereas I very much defend operas like *Das Sonntagskind* and *Die Schwestern von Prag*.§ One could call them genuinely German opera buffas.

FERDINAND: Those operas, as long as they were well performed, have at least never failed to give me real enjoyment, and I have certainly taken to heart what the poet tells the public in Tieck's *Der gestiefelte Kater*: If they are to find pleasure in it, they must set aside all the education they may have had and in effect

---

* 'This libretto was denounced throughout the nineteenth century as being intolerably stupid, if not positively disgusting, and various attempts were made in Germany and elsewhere to "improve" it.' Edward J. Dent, *Mozart's Operas. A Critical Study* (2nd edn, London, 1947), 190. Objections to it dating from 1791 and 1808 are recorded in Otto Erich Deutsch, *Mozart. A Documentary Biography* (Stanford, 1965), 365, 394, 508. Yet it was issued in two editions before 1800 and six more before *c*. 1830: A. Hyatt King, *Mozart in Retrospect* (London, 1955), 11, 260.

† sentimental plays: Ludwig's term *weinerliches Schauspiel* is the equivalent of *comédie larmoyante*, or sentimental bourgeois domestic plays originating in the 1760s. 'Orphanages' refer to Joseph Weigl's Singspiel of the same name (*Das Waisenhaus*, 1808); 'oculists' refers to Adalbert Gyrowetz's Singspiel of the same name (*Der Augenarzt*, 1811). Both were reviewed by Hoffmann.

‡ Carl Ditters von Dittersdorf (1739–99), composer of some thirty-nine Italian and German operas, chiefly comedies, between 1771 and his death. Hoffmann here objects to works of immense popularity like *Doctor und Apotheker* (1786), *Das rote Käppchen* (1788), *Hieronymus Knicker* (1789), and *Das Gespenst mit der Trommel* (1794). See Bauman, *North German Opera*, 300–10.

§ *Das Neusonntagskind* [*recte*] (1793); *Die Schwestern von Prag* (1794): Singspiels by Wenzel Müller (1767–1835), Viennese-based composer of some 250 musical theatre works. The first-named was conducted by Hoffmann in 1813 and 1814.

become children again and be able to experience childlike amusement and delight.*

LUDWIG: I'm afraid that those words, like so many others of that sort, fell on hard and sterile ground, in which they could not lodge and take root. But the *vox populi*, which in matters of the theatre is usually a veritable *vox dei*, drowns out the occasional sighs vented by hyper-refined natures over the dreadful perversions and absurdities that these in their view footling affairs contain; and there are instances where some of them, despite all their airs and graces, have even burst out into horrible laughter, as though caught up by the madness that possesses the people, and yet have asserted that they could not explain their own laughter at all.

FERDINAND: Wouldn't Tieck be a poet who, if he felt like it, could offer the composer romantic librettos tailored exactly to the requirements you have laid down?

LUDWIG: Quite assuredly, since he is a genuinely romantic poet. I remember in fact having a text of his in my possession; it was truly romantic in conception, but overloaded in subject-matter and too lengthy. If I am not mistaken it was called *Das Ungeheuer und der bezauberte Wald.*†

FERDINAND: You yourself bring me to a difficulty that you composers place upon the librettist. I refer to the incredible brevity that you expect of us. All our efforts to conceive and present in exactly the right words this or that situation, or the

---

* Ludwig Tieck (1773–1853), leading Romantic writer whose work much influenced Hoffmann. The latter returns here to a central position of the Romantics, and a key idea in *Kreisleriana*. In the Epilogue to *Der gestiefelte Kater* (*Puss-in-Boots*, 1797) the Author comes on stage to explain his purpose, only to be greeted by coarsely ironic responses of the (acting) audience. This play remains a supreme example of experimental writing (not staged until 1844), and by mentioning it even obliquely, Hoffmann reminds us how ambitious his standards for opera were, and he will certainly have had Tieck's Prologue in mind:
    MÜLLER: I do hope they're not going to bring childish foolery on to the stage.
    SCHLOSSER: Is it an opera then?
See the translation by Gerald Gillespie (Edinburgh, 1974), 37.
† *Das Ungeheuer und der verzauberte Wald* [*recte*] occupies 117 pages in *Ludwig Tiecks Schriften* (Berlin, 1829, reprinted 1966), xi. Described as 'a musical fairy-tale in four acts', it was intended as a libretto when written in 1768 (published 1800), but was itself a revision of the fairy play *Das Reh* (*The Deer*, 1790), which was influenced by Shakespeare and by Gozzi. See Edwin H. Zeydel, *Ludwig Tieck, the German Romanticist* (2nd edn, Hildesheim and New York, 1971), 24–5. Its cast includes a King, Queen, Ministers, a Fairy, a Monster, Prophets, ghosts, etc.

outbreak of this or that passion, are in vain; everything must be dealt with in a few lines, which must also be capable of being ruthlessly twisted and turned according to your pleasure.

LUDWIG: I would say that the librettist, like the scene-painter, must make a proper drawing but should then dash off the whole painting in a few powerful strokes; the music then places the whole work in a proper light and suitable perspective, so that everything stands out vividly and the separate, apparently arbitrary brush-strokes blend into boldly striking forms.

FERDINAND: So we are supposed to provide only a sketch rather than a libretto?

LUDWIG: Not at all. It surely goes without saying that with regard to overall layout and economy, the librettist must remain faithful to the dramatic rules dictated by the nature of the subject; but he really must be especially careful so to arrange the scenes that the subject-matter clearly unfolds before the spectator's eyes. Almost without understanding one word, the spectator must be able to form an idea of the plot from what he sees taking place. No dramatic medium needs this clarity to a greater degree than opera. Besides the fact that even with the clearest singing the words are always harder to understand than elsewhere, the music all too easily transports the listener to distant regions and can be kept under control only by being continually directed to the point at which the dramatic effect is concentrated. As for the words, the composer likes them best when they powerfully and concisely express the passions and situations to be portrayed. No special frills are necessary, and especially no similes.*

FERDINAND: But what about the rich imagery of Metastasio?†

LUDWIG: Yes, he had the most curious belief that the composer's inspiration should always proceed from some poetic image, particularly in an aria. Hence we have his continually recurring opening stanzas: 'Come una tortorella', 'Come spuma in tempesta', and indeed we frequently hear, at least in the

---

* This demand is echoed in actuality in C. M. von Weber's letter to the English librettist of his *Oberon* (1826): 'The composer looks more for the expressions of feelings than the figurative; the former he may repeat and develop in all their gradations, but verses like 'Like the spot the tulip weareth / Deep within its dewy urn ...' must be said only *once*.' John Warrack, *Carl Maria von Weber* (2nd edn, Cambridge, 1976), 331.
† Pietro Metastasio (1698–1782), the leading Baroque opera librettist.

accompaniment, the cooing of doves, the raging sea, and so on.*

FERDINAND: So are we not only to refrain from poetic devices but also to forgo all further elaboration of interesting situations? When, for example, the young hero goes into battle and bids farewell to his grey-haired father, the old king whose realm is being shaken to its foundations by a conquering tyrant, or when a terrible misfortune separates the ardent youth from his beloved, are they to say nothing but 'Goodbye'?

LUDWIG: The former could certainly speak briefly of his determination and faith in his just cause; and the latter could also tell his beloved that life without her will be but a slow death. But for the composer who expects inspiration not from words but from action and situation, even a simple 'Goodbye' will enable him to depict in powerful strokes the mental state of the young hero or the parting lover. To remain with your example, what a countless variety of heart-rending inflections the Italians have employed when singing the little word *addio*! How many thousand upon thousand nuances musical expression is capable of! And that is precisely the wonderful mystery of music, that only when our clumsy words dry up does it release its inexhaustible stream of expressive resources!

FERDINAND: In that case the librettist should strive for the utmost simplicity of language, and it would be sufficient merely to indicate the situation with nobility and force.

LUDWIG: Indeed, for as I say, it is the subject-matter, plot, and situation, rather than fine words, which inspire the composer. Not only so-called poetic imagery, but any sort of reflection, is a positive mortification for the musician.

FERDINAND: But surely you realise that I can't help feeling how difficult it is to write a good opera according to your requirements. This simplicity of language especially...

LUDWIG: ... may certainly be difficult for you poets, who so much enjoy painting with words, yes. But just as the operas of

---

* These opening lines are not in fact present in the works of Metastasio or even of his predecessor Apostolo Zeno (1668–1750). This does not of course invalidate the point, which is that Baroque arias were reflective elaborations of an emotion, during which the action ceased.

Metastasio, in my view, clearly show how texts must *not* be written, there are many Italian librettos that can be held up as perfect models of what a proper text should be. What could be more simple than stanzas like this well-known one.*

Almen se non poss'io	If I must therefore part
Seguir l'amato bene,	From him my well-beloved
Affetti del cor mio,	The feelings of my heart
Seguite lo per me!	Remain at least instead!

How these few simple words contain an evocation of the spirit seized by love and pain, which the composer can respond to. He can then depict the mental state suggested using the full forces of his musical eloquence. In fact the particular situation in which those words are to be sung will so fire his imagination that he will give the music a highly distinctive character. For this very reason you will find that the most poetic composers often set to music even inferior lines with great success. In such cases it is the genuinely operatic, romantic subject-matter which provides their inspiration. I would suggest Mozart's *Die Zauberflöte* to you as an example.

Ferdinand was just about to reply, when outside the windows in the street the call to arms was sounded. He seemed thunderstruck. With a deep sigh Ludwig pressed his friend's hand to his breast. 'Oh Ferdinand, my dearly beloved friend!' he cried. 'What is to become of art in our harsh and turbulent times? Will it not perish, like a delicate plant that turns its drooping head in vain towards the dark storm-clouds behind which the sun has vanished? Oh Ferdinand, where are the golden days of our youth? Every nobler impulse is engulfed by the seething torrent ravaging our landscape in its headlong course; bloody corpses stare forth from its black waves,† and in the tide of horror

---

* With unintended irony, Hoffmann selected the first quatrain sung by Servilia in Act 2 sc. 5 of Metastasio's libretto *La clemenza di Tito* (1734). It is not found in Mazzolà's version of the text for Mozart, which Hoffmann knew. The reason why he quoted it is probably that he remembered it from Zingarelli's opera *Giulietta e Romeo* (1796), Act 1, where it is incorporated into Romeo's scena, 'Prendi, l'acciar ti rendo' (British Museum, Add. MS. 30795, fo. 125v). This opera furnished the imaginative material for 'Ombra adorata' in *Kreisleriana* (I–2). His own setting of this scena dates from 1812.
† At this point Hoffmann's writing recalls his nightmarish prose picture *Die Vision auf dem Schlachtfelde bei Dresden* (*The Vision on the Battlefield of Dresden*): see *Nachlese*, 601–5.

washing over us we lose our footing – we have no handhold – our cry of anguish is lost in the desolate air – victims of implacable fury we sink down helplessly!'

Ludwig fell silent, lost in his thoughts. Ferdinand got up. He took his sabre and helmet and like the god of war in battle array he stood before Ludwig who looked at him in amazement. Then a glow spread across Ferdinand's countenance, his eyes shone with a fiery passion and he spoke in sonorous tones: 'Ludwig, what has become of you? Has the prison air that you must have been breathing here for so long corroded your spirit so deeply that you are now too weak and ill to feel the warming breath of spring, that plays outside among the clouds made golden by the blush of morning? Nature's children* luxuriated in sluggish inactivity; they scorned the finest gifts she offered them and trampled them under foot with wanton stupidness. And so the wrathful mother awoke the juggernaut of war which had long lain asleep in her fragrant flower-garden. Like an armour-plated giant it moved among the degenerate breed; fleeing from its dreadful voice which made the mountains resound, they sought the protection of the mother in whom they had ceased to believe. But with belief there came a new awareness: only strength can guarantee prosperity! Godliness is generated from struggle, as life from death!

'Yes, Ludwig, our time of destiny has come. As though from the eerie gloom of ancient legends that echo down to us like mysterious rumblings of thunder from the distant twilight, we hear again the unmistakable voice of eternal omnipotence; bursting visibly into our lives it awakens in us the faith by which the mystery of our existence is revealed. The dawn is breaking; enraptured voices rise into the fragrant air proclaiming godliness and praising it in song. The golden gates are open, and art and science kindle in a single incandescence all the holy aspirations that unite mankind into a single church. So, my friend, direct your gaze upward, with courage, trust, faith!'

Ferdinand clasped his friend to him. Ludwig took up his filled glass: 'Eternally united in a higher cause through life and death!' 'Eternally united in a higher cause through life and death!' repeated Ferdinand, and in a few minutes his impetuous steed was carrying him into the lines that moved towards the enemy, rejoicing in their wild urge for battle.

---

* Cf. the words on mankind and Mother Nature quoted from *Die Automate* on p. 74.

[Epilogue]

The friends felt profoundly moved. Each of them thought of the time when the burden of a hostile fate had lain upon them and all their appetite for life had seemed to wither away and be irrevocably lost. How brightly then the first rays from the star of hope broke through the dark clouds, becoming ever more brilliant and breath-taking as it rose, quickening and nurturing new life. How their hearts had leapt and rejoiced in the joyful struggle. How their courage and faith had been crowned by the sublimest victory!

'As a matter of fact', said Lothar, 'each of us has probably spoken to his inner self in the same way as the serapiontic Ferdinand. And fortunately for us, the ominous storm that thundered about our heads, instead of destroying us, has merely strengthened and invigorated us like a powerful sulphur-bath. It seems that only now, among you, with the storm completely past, do I feel my full health returning, together with a new desire to apply myself seriously again to art and science. That is what Theodor is doing, I know, and very diligently too. Once again he is devoting himself totally to earlier music, although he has by no means neglected poetry. For this reason I believe he will soon surprise us with a first-rate opera, whose libretto and music will be entirely his. Everything that he has so sophistically argued concerning the impossibility of devising and composing an opera oneself may sound quite plausible, but it has not convinced me.' [...]

'The Poet and the Composer', 1813, tr. Martyn Clarke, ed. David Charlton, 1989

'Lacing opera with lots of laudanum'
THOMAS DE QUINCEY

I seldom drank laudanum at that time, more than once in three weeks: this was usually on a Tuesday or a Saturday night; my reason for which was this. In those days Grassini sang at the Opera: and her voice was delightful to me beyond all that I had ever heard. I know not what may be the state of the Opera-house now, having never been within its walls for seven or eight years, but at that time it was by much the most pleasant place of public resort in London for passing an evening. Five shillings admitted one to the gallery, which was subject to far less annoyance than the pit of the theatres: the orchestra was distinguished by its sweet and melodious grandeur from all English orchestras, the composition of which, I confess, is not acceptable to my ear, from the predominance of the clangorous instruments, and the absolute tyranny of the violin. The choruses were divine to hear: and when Grassini appeared in some interlude, as she often did, and poured forth her passionate soul as Andromache, at the tomb of Hector, &c. I question whether any Turk, of all that ever entered the paradise of opium-eaters, can have had half the pleasure I had. But, indeed, I honour the Barbarians too much by supposing them capable of any pleasures approaching to the intellectual ones of an Englishman. For music is an intellectual or a sensual pleasure, according to the temperament of him who hears it.

Confessions of an English Opium-Eater, 1822

'Bridling, slightly, at the operatic convention'
WILLIAM HAZLITT

On the Opera

The Opera is a fine thing: the only question is, whether it is not too fine. It is the most fascinating, and at the same time the most tantalising of all places. It is not the *too little*, but the *too much*, that offends us. Every object is there collected, and displayed in ostentatious profusion, that can strike the senses or dazzle the imagination; music, dancing, painting, poetry, architecture, the blaze of beauty, 'the glass of fashion, and the mould of form'; and yet we are not satisfied – because the multitude and variety of objects distracts the attention, and by flattering us with a vain shew of the highest gratification of every faculty and wish, leaves us at last in a state of listlessness, disappointment, and *ennui*. The powers of the mind are exhausted, without being invigorated; our expectations are excited, not satisfied; and we are at some loss to distinguish an excess of irritation from the height of enjoyment. To sit at the Opera for a whole evening, is like undergoing the process of animal magnetism for the same length of time. It is an illusion and a mockery, where the mind is made 'the fool of the senses,' and cheated of itself; where pleasure after pleasure courts us, as in a fairy palace; where the Graces and the Muses, weaving a gay, fantastic round with one another, still turn from our pursuit; where art, like an enchantress with a thousand faces, still allures our giddy admiration, shifts her mask, and again eludes us. The Opera, in short, proceeds upon a false estimate of taste and morals; it supposes that the capacity for enjoyment may be multiplied with the objects calculated to afford it. It is a species of intellectual prostitution; for we can no more receive pleasure from all our faculties at once than we can be in love with a number of mistresses at the same time. Though we have different senses, we have but one heart; and if we attempt to force it into the service of them all at once, it must grow restive or torpid, hardened or enervated. The spectator may say to the sister-arts of Painting, Poetry, and Music, as they advance to him in a *Pas-de-Trois* at the Opera, 'How happy could I be with either, were t'other dear charmer away;' but while 'they all tease him together,' the heart gives a satisfactory answer to none of them; – is ashamed of its want of resources to supply the repeated calls upon its sensibility, seeks relief from the importunity of endless excitement in fastidious apathy or affected levity; and in the midst of luxury, pomp, vanity, indolence, and dissipation, feels only the hollow, aching void within, the irksome craving of unsatisfied desire, because more pleasures are placed within its reach than it is capable of enjoying, and the interference of one object with another ends in a double disappointment. [...]

What makes the difference between an opera of Mozart's, and the singing of a thrush confined in a wooden cage at the corner of the street? The one is nature, and the other is art: the one is paid for, and the other is not. Madame Fodor sings the air of *Vedrai Carino* in *Don Giovanni* so divinely, because she was hired to sing it; she sings it to please the audience, not herself, and does not always like to be *encored* in it; but the thrush that awakes us at daybreak with its song, does not sing because it is paid to sing, or to please others, or to be admired or criticised. It sings because it is happy: it pours the thrilling sounds from its throat, to relieve the overflowings of its own heart – the liquid notes come from, and go to the heart, dropping balm into it, as the gushing spring revives the traveller's parched and fainting lips. That stream of joy comes pure and fresh to the longing sense, free from art and affectation; the same that rises over vernal groves, mingled with the breath of morning, and the perfumes of the wild hyacinth, that waits for no audience, that wants no rehearsing, and still —

'Hymns its good God, and carols sweet of love.'

This is the great difference between nature and art, that the one *is* what the other *seems to be*, and gives all the pleasure it expresses, because it feels it itself. [...]

The Opera is the most artificial of all things. It is not only art, but ostentatious, unambiguous, exclusive art. It does not subsist as an imitation of nature, but in contempt of it; and instead of seconding, its object is to pervert and sophisticate all our natural impressions of things. When the Opera first made its appearance in this country, there were strong prejudices entertained against it, and it was ridiculed as a species of the *mock-heroic*. The prejudices have worn out with time, and the ridicule has ceased; but the grounds for both remain the same in the nature of the thing itself. At the theatre, we see and hear what has been said, thought, and done by various people elsewhere; at the Opera, we see and hear what was never said, thought, or done any where but at the Opera. Not only is all communication with nature cut off, but every appeal to the imagination is sheathed and softened in the melting medium of Siren sounds. The ear is cloyed and glutted with warbled ecstacies or agonies; while every avenue to terror or pity is carefully stopped up and guarded by song and recitative. Music is not made the vehicle of poetry, but poetry of music: the very meaning of the words is lost or refined away in the effeminacy of a foreign language. A grand serious Opera is a tragedy wrapped up in soothing airs, to suit the tender feelings of the nurselings of fortune — where tortured victims swoon on beds of roses, and the pangs of despair sink in tremulous accents into downy repose. Just so much of human misery is given as is proper to lull those who are exempted from it into a deeper sense of their own security: just enough of the picture of human life is shewn to relieve their languor, without disturbing their indifference; it is calculated not to excite their sympathy, but 'with some sweet, oblivious antidote,' to pamper their sleek and sordid apathy. In a word, the whole business of the Opera is to stifle emotion in its birth, and to intercept every feeling in its progress to the heart.

The Yellow Dwarf, 23 May 1818

'A blend of ostensible action with inner feeling'
GEORG WILHELM FRIEDRICH HEGEL

'Independent Music'

While we could compare melody to plastic sculpture, being completely finished and dependent only on itself, in singing we recognized the comparison with painting, which goes into greater detail. Since specific characterization is replete with connotations that the human voice cannot describe entirely accurately, instrumental accompaniment is introduced as the composition itself develops a more complex vitality.

Secondly, as well as both the melody that accompanies a libretto and the characterizing expression of the words, we have to propose the liberation from an implicit content, beyond the musical notes, produced in the form of specific ideas. Subjective inwardness constitutes the principle of music. However, the innermost part of the concrete self is subjective experience itself, defined by no fixed content and therefore not bound to move this way or that, but at ease with itself in unconstrained freedom. For subjectivity likewise to come into its own in the experience of music, it must free itself from any given text and from itself alone draw the content, the progress and form of expression, the unity and development of the work, the exposition of a main theme, the intermittent introduction and growth of others, and so forth. And to do so, it must limit itself to the purely musical medium, since the meaning of the whole is not expressed in words. This is the case in the sphere that I have earlier described as 'independent music'. In terms of what it aims to express, accompanied music has something outside itself, which therefore relates to that which is not music, but belongs to a foreign art: poetry. If music wants to stay pure, however, then it must distance itself from this foreign element and then, in its new position of freedom, completely forswear the reference of words. This is the point that we now have to consider more closely.

We already begin to see this act of liberation in the realm of accompanied music. For although the poetic word did indeed suppress the music and made it subservient, music also floated in blessed peace over the exact specificity of the words or tore itself free from the meaning of the articulated ideas, in order to sway between joy and sorrow as it chose. Again we also find the same phenomenon in the audience and general public, especially in reference to dramatic music. Opera, namely, has several ingredients: on the one hand, landscape or some other setting, the progress of the plot, events, processions, costumes etc., and on the other, passion and its expression. Therefore, the content is two-sided: the ostensible action and the inner feeling. Now whatever the plot concerns as such, and although it holds all the individual parts together, its progress nevertheless has comparatively little to do with music and is developed largely in recitative. The listener easily frees himself from this aspect of the content, he accords the statements and repetitions of the recitative little attention, and dwells merely upon that which is musical and melodious. This is especially the case with the Italians, most of whose new operas have after all such an original style that, instead of listening to the musical twaddle or the other trivialities, one rather talks or otherwise amuses oneself, only attending again with real pleasure to the individual overtures, which are then appreciated purely musically. Here the composer and the public are therefore on the brink of freeing themselves from the verbal content to enjoy and produce music itself as an independent art.

Lecatures on Aesthetics [*Vorlesungen über die Ästhetik*, 1835], tr. Matthew Scott

'Weber's revolt against melody drove me out'
FRANZ GRILLPARZER

What I had already criticized on the appearance of *Der Freischütz* appears to be confirmed all the more. Weber is certainly a poetic mind, but no musician. There is no trace in the melody, not merely of pleasantness, but of melody altogether. (However, I call melody an organically connected phrase, whose individual elements necessitate one another musically.) Separate thoughts are drawn together straight from the text and without internal musical order. No inventiveness, simply treatment without originality; a complete lack of structure and colour; the light Romantic content weighed down and overblown so that one must feel uneasy and anxious; no lighter moment interspersed, the whole maintained in a gloomy and dreary tone. In this composer I see a musical Adolf Müllner. Both appeared on the stage in splendour when, beginning only in their late adulthood, they raised the meagre poetry of their early life with some powerful subject-matter, and let off a crashing firework display (*Guilt, Freischütz*). Both are men of sharp understanding, with widespread talents; both have an excessive sense of their own worth, and of its value to their productions; both are theorists and therefore not artists; both are susceptible to criticism. Criticism was the end of Weber as much as Müllner. As he sinks in public opinion, he will do anything to pull himself up, and this, like Müllner, without actually becoming conscious of the basis of the criticism. It is God's will that I do wrong, and He forgives when I do so.

Yesterday I was once again at *Euryanthe*. This music is horrible. This revolt against melody, this rape of beauty would have been punished by the state in the Golden Age of Greece. Such music should be policed; it would make us inhuman if it could only find a way to a general audience. The first time I heard the opera, I got through the worst bits by not paying attention. Yesterday the wish to do the composer no harm left me, and I listened. At the start it was quite passable: the overture is in part less eccentric and my tolerance was not wholly undermined, but by degrees the inner horror rose up and finally became a bodily revulsion. Had I not left the theatre after the second act, someone would have to have carried me out in the middle of the third. Only fools could like this opera, or imbeciles or theorists, or street-robbers and assassins.

Diary Extracts, 1823, tr. Matthew Scott

'Opera fans and their rooted obsessions'
JOHN EBERS

An Italian gentleman at Paris, the firmest item of whose creed was, that none but Italians could possibly sing well, refused to admit that Sontag (whom he had never heard) could be at all equal to the singers of Italy. With great difficulty he was induced to hear her. After listening five minutes, he rose to depart. 'But do stay,' said his friend, 'you will be convinced presently.' 'I know it,' said the Italian, 'and therefore I go.'

It was reported, I know not with what correctness, that, during her residence at Berlin, a young man of rank there was so desperately enamoured of her, as to resort to the romantic expedient of hiring himself, in disguise, as a servant in the family, to have the pleasure of constantly seeing her, nor was the truth suspected by the object of his adorations, or any one else, until the gentleman's own relations discovered him, and removed him from the vicinity of the attraction.

Seven Years of the King's Theatre, 1828

'Twin poles of Tragedy – imagination and ecstasy'
FRIEDRICH WILHELM NIETZSCHE

The Greeks, who simultaneously declare and conceal the mystery of their view of the world in their gods, established as the double source of their art two deities, Apollo and Dionysos. In the realm of art these names represent stylistic opposites which exist side by side and in almost perpetual conflict with one another, and which only once, at the moment when the Hellenic 'Will' blossomed, appeared fused together in the work of art that is Attic tragedy. For there are two states in which human beings attain to the feeling of delight in existence, namely in *dream* and in *intoxication*. Every human being is fully an artist when creating the worlds of dream, and the lovely semblance of dream is the father of all the arts of image-making, including, as we shall see, an important half of poetry. We dream with pleasure as we understand the *figure* directly; all forms speak to us; nothing is indifferent or unnecessary. Yet even while this dream-reality is most alive, we nevertheless retain a pervasive sense that it is *semblance*; only when this ceases to be the case do the pathological effects set in whereby dream no longer enlivens and the healing natural energy of its states ceases. Within that boundary, however, it is not just the pleasant and friendly images in us which we seek out with that complete sense of comprehension; things which are grave, sad, gloomy, and dark are contemplated with just as much pleasure, always provided that here too the veil of semblance is in fluttering movement and does not completely cover up the basic forms of the real. Thus, whereas in dream the individual human being plays with the real, the art of the image-maker (in the wider sense) is a *playing with dream*. As a block of marble the statue is something very real, but the reality of the statue *as a dream figure* is the living person of the god. [...]

We shall have gained much for the science of aesthetics when we have come to realize, not just through logical insight but also with the certainty of something directly apprehended (*Anschauung*), that the continuous evolution of art is bound up with the duality of the *Apolline* and the *Dionysiac* in much the same way as reproduction depends on there being two sexes which co-exist in a state of perpetual conflict interrupted only occasionally by periods of reconciliation. We have borrowed these names from the Greeks who reveal the profound mysteries of their view of art to those with insight, not in concepts, admittedly, but through the penetratingly vivid figures of their gods. Their two deities of art, Apollo and Dionysos, provide the starting-point for our recognition that there exists in the world of the Greeks an enormous opposition, both in origin and goals, between the Apolline art of the image-maker or sculptor (*Bildner*) and the imageless art of music, which is that of Dionysos. These two very different drives (*Triebe*) exist side by side, mostly in open conflict, stimulating and provoking (*reizen*) one another to give birth to ever-new, more vigorous offspring in whom they perpetuate the conflict inherent in the opposition between them, an opposition only apparently bridged by the common term 'art' – until eventually, by a metaphysical miracle of the Hellenic 'Will', they appear paired and, in this pairing, finally engender a work of art which is Dionysiac and Apolline in equal measure: Attic tragedy.

In order to gain a closer understanding of these two drives, let us think of them in the first place as the separate art-worlds of *dream* and *intoxication* (*Rausch*). Between these two physiological phenomena an opposition can be observed which corresponds to that between the Apolline and the Dionysiac. As Lucretius envisages it, it was in dream that the magnificent figures of the gods first appeared before the souls of men; in dream the great image-maker saw the delightfully proportioned bodies of super-human beings; and the Hellenic poet, if asked about the secrets of poetic procreation, would likewise have reminded us of dream and would have given an account much like that given by Hans Sachs in the *Meistersinger*:

My friend, it is the poet's task
To mark his dreams, their meaning ask.
Trust me, the truest phantom man doth know
Hath meaning only dreams may show:
The arts of verse and poetry
Tell nought but dreaming's prophecy.

Every human being is fully an artist when creating the worlds of dream, and the lovely semblance of dream is the precondition of all the arts of image-making, including, as we shall see, an important half of poetry. We take pleasure in dreaming, understanding its figures without mediation; all forms speak to us; nothing is indifferent or unnecessary. Yet even while this dream-reality is most alive, we nevertheless retain a pervasive sense that it is *semblance*; at least this is my experience, and I could adduce a good deal of evidence and the statements of poets to attest to the frequency, indeed normality, of my experience. Philosophical natures even have a presentiment that hidden beneath the reality in which we live and have our being there also lies a second, quite different reality; in other words, this reality too is a semblance. Indeed Schopenhauer actually states that the mark of a person's capacity for philosophy is the gift for feeling occasionally as if people and all things were mere phantoms or dream-images. A person with artistic sensibility relates to the reality of dream in the same way as a philosopher relates to the reality of existence: he attends to it closely and with pleasure, using these images to interpret life, and practising for life with the help of these events. Not that it is only the pleasant and friendly images which give him this feeling of complete intelligibility; he also sees passing before him things which are grave, gloomy, sad, dark, sudden blocks, teasings of chance, anxious expectations, in short the entire 'Divine Comedy' of life, including the Inferno, but not like some mere shadow-play – for he, too, lives in these scenes and shares in the suffering – and yet never without that fleeting sense of its character as semblance. Perhaps others will recall, as I do, shouting out, sometimes successfully, words of encouragement in the midst of the perils and terrors of a dream: 'It is a dream! I will dream on!' I have even heard of people who were capable of continuing the causality of one and the same dream through three and more successive nights. All of these facts are clear evidence that our innermost being, the deep ground (*Untergrund*) common to all our lives, experiences the state of dreaming with profound pleasure (*Lust*) and joyous necessity.

The Greeks also expressed the joyous necessity of a dream-experience in their Apollo: as the god of all image-making energies, Apollo is also the god of prophecy. According to the etymological root of his name, he is 'the luminous one' (*der Scheinende*), the god of light; as such, he also governs the lovely semblance produced by the inner world of fantasy. The higher truth, the perfection of these dream-states in contrast to the only partially intelligible reality of the daylight world, together with the profound consciousness of the helping and healing powers of nature in sleep and dream, is simultaneously the symbolic analogue of the ability to prophesy and indeed of all the arts through which life is made possible and worth living. But the image of Apollo must also contain that delicate line which the dream-image may not overstep if its effect is not to become pathological, so that, in the worst case, the semblance would deceive us as if it were crude reality; his image (*Bild*) must include that measured limitation (*maßvolle Begrenzung*), that freedom from wilder impulses, that wise calm of the image-making god. In accordance with his origin, his eye must be 'sun-like'; even when its gaze is angry and shows displeasure, it exhibits the consecrated quality of lovely semblance. Thus, in an eccentric sense, one could apply to Apollo what Schopenhauer says about human beings trapped in the veil of maya:

Just as the boatman sits in his small boat, trusting his frail craft in a stormy sea that is boundless in every direction, rising and falling with the howling, mountainous waves, so in the midst of a world full of suffering and misery the individual man calmly sits, supported by and trusting in the *principium individuationis* [...] (*World as Will and Representation*, 1, p. 416)

Indeed one could say that Apollo is the most sublime expression of imperturbable trust in this principle and of the calm sitting-there of the person trapped within it; one might even describe Apollo as the magnificent divine image (*Götterbild*) of the *principium individuationis*, whose gestures and gaze speak to us of all the intense pleasure, wisdom and beauty of 'semblance'.

A. W. Schlegel [...] recommends us to think of the chorus as, in a certain sense, the quintessence and distillation of the crowd of spectators, as the 'ideal spectator'. When set next to the historical evidence that tragedy was originally only a chorus, this suggestion is revealed for what it really is: a crude, unscientific, but brilliant assertion, but one which derives its brilliance from the concentrated manner of its expression alone, from the characteristic Germanic prejudice in favour of anything that is called 'ideal', and from our momentary astonishment. For when we compare the public in the theatre, which we know well, with that chorus, we are simply astonished and we ask ourselves if it would ever be possible to distil from this public something ideal that would be analogous to the tragic chorus. In the privacy of our own thoughts we deny this possibility and we are as much surprised by the boldness of Schlegel's assertion as we are by the utterly different nature of the Greek public. This is because we had always believed that a proper spectator, whoever he might be, always had to remain conscious of the fact that what he saw before him was a work of art and not empirical reality, whereas the tragic chorus of the Greeks is required to see in the figures on stage real, physically present, living beings. The chorus of the Oceanides really believes that it sees before it the Titan Prometheus, and takes itself to be as real as the god on the stage. [...]

But the historical evidence explicitly speaks against Schlegel here: the chorus as such, without a stage, which is to say the primitive form of tragedy, is not compatible with that chorus of ideal spectators. What kind of artistic genre would be one derived from the concept of the spectator, one where the true form of the genre would have to be regarded as the 'spectator as such'? The spectator without a spectacle is a nonsense. [...]

In his famous preface to the *Bride of Messina* Schiller betrayed an infinitely more valuable insight into the significance of the chorus when he considered it to be a living wall which tragedy draws about itself in order to shut itself off in purity from the real world and to preserve its ideal ground and its poetic freedom.

This is Schiller's main weapon in his fight against the common concept of the natural, against the illusion commonly demanded of dramatic poetry. He argued that, although in the theatre the day itself was only artificial, the architecture symbolic, and metrical speech had an ideal character, on the whole error still prevailed; it was not enough merely to tolerate as poetic freedom something which was, after all, the essence of all poetry. The introduction of the chorus was the decisive step by which war was declared openly and honestly on all naturalism in art. It seems to me that this way of looking at things is precisely what our (in its own opinion) superior age dismisses with the slogan 'pseudo-idealism'. I fear that, with our current veneration for the natural and the real, we have arrived at the opposite pole to all idealism, and have landed in the region of the waxworks. They too contain a kind of art, as do certain of today's popular novels; but let nobody torment us with the claim that, thanks to this art, the 'pseudo-idealism' of Schiller and Goethe has been overcome.

It is admittedly an 'ideal' ground on which, as Schiller rightly saw, the Greek chorus of satyrs, the chorus of the original tragedy, is wont to walk, a ground raised high above the real path along which mortals wander. For this chorus the Greeks built the hovering platform of a fictitious *state of nature* on to which they placed fictitious *creatures of nature*. Tragedy grew up on this foundation, and for this very reason, of course, was relieved from the very outset of any need to copy reality with painful exactness. Yet it is not a world which mere caprice and fantasy have conjured up between heaven and earth; rather it is a world which was just as real and credible to the believing Greek as Olympus and its inhabitants. As a member of the Dionysiac chorus, the satyr lives in a religiously acknowledged reality sanctioned by myth and cult. The fact that tragedy begins with the satyr, and that the Dionysiac wisdom of tragedy speaks out of him, is something which now surprises us just as much as the fact that tragedy originated in the chorus. Perhaps it will serve as a starting-point for thinking about this if I now assert that the satyr, the fictitious creature of nature, bears the same relation to the cultured human being as Dionysiac music bears to civilization. Of the latter Richard Wagner has said that it is absorbed, elevated, and extinguished (*aufgehoben*) by music, just as lamplight is superseded by the light of day. I believe that, when faced with the chorus of satyrs, cultured Greeks felt themselves absorbed, elevated, and extinguished in exactly the same way. This is the first effect of Dionysiac tragedy: state and society, indeed all divisions between one human being and another, give way to an overwhelming feeling of unity which leads men back to the heart of nature. The metaphysical solace which, I wish to suggest, we derive from every true tragedy, the solace that in the ground of things, and despite all changing appearances, life is indestructibly mighty and pleasurable, this solace appears with palpable clarity in the chorus of satyrs, a chorus of natural beings whose life goes on ineradicably behind and beyond all civilization, as it were, and who remain eternally the same despite all the changes of generations and in the history of nations.

[...]

The *chorus* of Greek tragedy, the symbol of the entire mass of those affected by Dionysiac excitement, is fully explained by our understanding of the matter. Because we are accustomed to the position of the chorus, particularly the operatic chorus, on the modern stage, we were completely unable to understand how the tragic chorus of the Greeks was supposedly older, more original, indeed more important than the 'action' proper – although this is clearly what the historical evidence says; equally, we could not see how the high importance and originality traditionally attributed to the chorus was to be reconciled with the fact that it was said to be composed of lowly, serving creatures, indeed, initially, only of goat-like satyrs; the placing of the orchestra before the stage remained a constant puzzle to us; now, however, we have come to realize that the stage and the action were originally and fundamentally thought of as nothing other than a *vision*, that the only 'reality' is precisely that of the chorus, which creates the vision from within itself and speaks of this vision with all the symbolism of dance, tone, and word. This chorus sees in its vision its lord and master Dionysos, and is therefore eternally the *serving* chorus; it sees how the god suffers and is glorified, and thus does not itself *act*. Despite its entirely subservient position in relation to the god, however, the chorus is nevertheless the highest, which is to say Dionysiac, expression of *nature*, and therefore speaks in its enthusiasm, as does nature herself, oracular and wise words; the chorus which *shares in suffering* is also the *wise* chorus which proclaims the truth from the heart of the world. This gives rise to that fantastical and seemingly distasteful figure of the wise and enthusiastic satyr who is at the same time 'the foolish man' in contrast to his god; a copy of nature and its strongest impulses, indeed a symbol of them, and at the same time the proclaimer of her wisdom and art; musician, poet, dancer, seer of spirits, all in one person. [...]

Those who invented the recitative, [...] and their age, believed indeed
that the *stilo rappresentativo* had solved the secret of ancient music
and that this alone explained the enormous effect of Orpheus,
Amphion, and indeed of Greek tragedy. The new style was held to be
the rediscovery of the most effective kind of music, that of Ancient
Greece; indeed, given the general and wholly popular belief that the
Homeric world was the *world in its original state*, people at that time
could give themselves over to the dream that they had descended once
more to the paradisiac beginnings of humankind when music, too,
must necessarily have possessed that incomparable purity, power, and
innocence of which the poets spoke so touchingly in their Arcadian
tales. Here we can see down to the very heart of that truly modern
genre, opera: a form of art is forced into existence here by a powerful
need, but a need of a non-aesthetic kind: the longing for the idyll, the
belief that at the very beginning of time mankind was both artistic and
good. Recitative was thought to be the rediscovered language of those
original humans, and opera to be the rediscovered land of that idyllic
or heroic good being who follows a natural artistic drive in all his
actions; who, whenever he speaks, at least sings a little; and who
promptly bursts into full song at the slightest stirring of emotion. It no
longer matters to us that the Humanists of the period used this newly
created image of the paradisiac artist to oppose the church's old view
of mankind as being inherently corrupt and lost, so that opera must be
understood as the opposing dogma of the good human being (which
also meant, however, that they had simultaneously discovered a
source of solace against the pessimism which, given the terrifying
uncertainty of all the conditions of their existence, affected serious
minds at the time most powerfully). We only need to recognize that
the true magic, and thus also the genesis, of this new form of art,
lay in satisfying an entirely un-aesthetic need, in the optimistic
glorification of mankind as such, in the view that primal man was
both good and artistic by nature – an operatic principle which
gradually transformed itself into the threatening and terrible *demand*
which we, faced by the socialist movements of the present, can no
longer ignore. 'Man in his original goodness' demands his rights; what
a paradisiac prospect!

Next to this I shall now place another, equally clear confirmation
of my view that opera is built on the same principles as our
Alexandrian culture. Opera is born of theoretical man, of the layman

as critic, not of the artist – one of the most astonishing facts in the history of all the arts. Genuinely un-artistic listeners demanded that they should be able, above all, to understand the words, so that a rebirth of music could only be expected through the discovery of some form of singing in which the words of the text governed the counterpoint as a master governs his servant. For, just as the spirit was so much nobler than the body, the word was supposedly nobler than the accompanying system of harmony. When opera was just beginning the connection between music, image, and word was discussed on the basis of the crudely unmusical opinions of these laymen; and it was in the circles of aristocratic laypeople in Florence, and among the poets and singers whom they patronized, that the first experiments based on this aesthetic were made. A man with no artistic capability generates for himself a form of art precisely by being the un-artistic man *per se*. Because he has no inkling of the Dionysiac depths of music, he tranforms for himself the enjoyment of music into the reason-governed rhetoric of passion in sound and word in the *stilo rappresentativo*, and into the sensuous pleasure afforded by the arts of singing; because he is incapable of seeing a vision, he presses the theatrical technician and stage-decorator into his service; because he cannot grasp the true essence of the artist, he conjures up before his mind's eye 'original man, the artist' in accordance with the demands of his own taste, i.e. a man who sings when he is passionate and who speaks in verse. He dreams himself into a far-off time when passion sufficed to create song and poetry – as if the affects had ever been capable of creating anything artistic. The precondition of opera is an erroneous belief about the artistic process, or more precisely the idyllic belief that every man of feeling is actually an artist. In line with this belief, opera is the expression in art of the lay mentality which dictates its laws with the cheerful optimism of theoretical man.

If we wanted to unite conceptually the two sets of ideas which were described above as having contributed to the genesis of the opera, we would have to speak of the *idyllic tendency of opera*, and Schiller's explanation and vocabulary would be all we required in order to do so. Schiller states that nature and the ideal are either objects of mourning, when the former is represented as lost and the latter as unattained; or both are objects of joy, when they are imagined as real. The first condition produces the elegy in the narrower sense, the second the idyll in the widest sense. At this point we must immediately draw attention to a characteristic shared by both of the ideas which contributed to the genesis of opera, namely that in opera the ideal is not felt to be unattained and nature is not felt to be lost. According to this sentiment, there was once a time at the beginning of time when man lay in the bosom of nature and, in this natural state, had achieved the ideal of humanity in a unity of paradisiac goodness and artistry; we are all supposedly descended from this perfect original human being, indeed we are all still its faithful likeness; it was just that we needed to cast off certain things, voluntarily rid ourselves of excessive learning and excessive cultural opulence, in order to recognize ourselves in the image of that original being. The educated man of the Renaissance allowed himself to be accompanied back to an idyllic reality, to just such a consonance of nature and the ideal, by his operatic imitation of Greek tragedy; he used this tragedy, as Dante used Virgil, to be led to the gates of Paradise. From this point onwards he made his own way, proceeding from an imitation of the Greeks' highest form of art to the 'bringing back of all things', to a re-creation of the original artistic world of mankind. What confident good nature these reckless ventures in the very womb of theoretical culture displayed! One can only explain this as the result of a comforting faith that 'man *per se*' is the eternally virtuous operatic hero, the eternally singing or flute-playing shepherd who, if ever he were truly to lose himself for a time, was always bound to re-discover eventually that this was indeed his true nature; it can only be explained as the fruit of the optimism which arises during this period, like some sweetly seductive column of perfume, from the depths of the Socratic view of the world.

Thus what the features of opera express is not at all the elegiac pain caused by eternal loss but rather the cheerfulness of eternal re-discovery, comfortable delight in an idyllic reality which one can at least imagine to be real at any time; admittedly one does perhaps guess occasionally that this supposed reality is nothing but a fantastic, ridiculous dalliance which is bound to elicit the exclamation, 'Away with the phantom!' from anyone capable of measuring it against the fearful gravity of nature as it truly is, or of comparing it with the actual, original scenes from the beginnings of mankind. Nevertheless it would be an illusion to believe that one could simply shoo away the flirtatious creature that is opera with a loud shout, as if it were a ghost. Anyone who wants to destroy opera must take up arms against that Alexandrian cheerfulness which expresses its favourite idea so naively in opera, an idea which indeed finds its true artistic form in opera. But what can art itself expect from a form of art which does not originate in the aesthetic sphere, but rather has stolen into the territory of art from a semi-moral sphere, and which can only occasionally disguise the fact of its hybrid origins? From which juices does this parasitic creature called opera nourish itself, if not from those of true art? Are we not driven to assume that its idyllic seductions, its Alexandrian arts of flattery, will cause the supreme and truly serious task of art to degenerate into an empty, amusing distraction – that task being to free the eye from gazing into the horrors of the night and, with the healing balm of semblance, save the subject from the vain exertions of the will? What will become of the eternal truths of the Dionysiac and the Apolline where there is such a mixture of styles as I have shown to lie at the heart of the *stilo rappresentativo*? – where music is regarded as the servant and the libretto as master, where music is compared to the body and the words to the soul? – where the highest that is aimed for will be periphrastic tone-painting at best, just as it once was in the new Attic dithyramb? – where music is deprived of its true dignity, which consists in being a Dionysiac mirror of the world, so that all that remains to music, as the slave of the world of appearances, is to imitate the forms of the world of appearances and to excite external pleasure in the play of line and proportion. On close scrutiny, this fateful influence of opera on music can be seen to be virtually identical with the entire development of modern music; the optimism lurking in the genesis of opera and at the heart of the culture it represents has succeeded in divesting music with frightening speed of its Dionysiac purpose in the world and in imposing on it the character of a pleasurable play with form. The only thing to which this change could perhaps be compared is the metamorphosis of Aeschylean man into the blithe spirit of the Alexandrian world.

The Birth of Tragedy, 1872, tr. Ronald Speirs

'The essential completeness of *Parsifal*'
VIRGINIA WOOLF

The commonplace remark that music is in its infancy is best borne out by the ambiguous state of musical criticism. It has few traditions behind it, and the art itself is so much alive that it fairly suffocates those who try to deal with it. A critic of writing is hardly to be taken by surprise, for he can compare almost every literary form with some earlier form and can measure the achievement by some familiar standard. But who in music has tried to do what Strauss is doing, or Debussy? Before we have made up our minds as to the nature of the operatic form we have to value very different and very emphatic examples of it. This lack of tradition and of current standards is of course the freest and happiest state that a critic can wish for; it offers some one the chance of doing now for music what Aristotle did 2,000 years ago for poetry. The fact, however, that so little has yet been done to lay bare the principles of the art accounts for the indecision which marks our attempts to judge new music. As for the old, we take it for granted, or concentrate our minds upon the *prima donna*'s cold. It is criticism of a single hour, in a particular day, and tomorrow the mark has faded. [...]

Ecclesiastical music is too rigidly severe and too final in its spirit to penetrate as the music of *Parsifal* penetrates. [...] The Grail seems to burn through all superincumbrances; the music is intimate in a sense that none other is; one is fired with emotion and yet possessed with tranquillity at the same time, for the words are continued by the music so that we hardly notice the transition. It may be that these exalted emotions, which belong to the essence of our being, and are rarely expressed, are those that are best translated by music; so that a satisfaction, or whatever one may call that sense of answer which the finest art supplies to its own question, is constantly conveyed here. Like Shakespeare, Wagner seems to have attained in the end to such a mastery of technique that he could float and soar in regions where in the beginning he could scarcely breathe; the stubborn matter of his art dissolves in his fingers, and he shapes it as he chooses. When the opera is over, it is surely the completeness of the vast work that remains with us. The earlier operas have always their awkward moments, when the illusion breaks; but *Parsifal* seems poured out in a smooth stream at white heat; its shape is solid and entire.

'Impressions at Bayreuth', *The Times*, 21 August 1909

'How not to drown the dialogue that serves the plot'
RICHARD STRAUSS

In classical opera there are two methods of managing the dialogue which serves to develop the plot: pure prose or the so-called *rectitativo secco* with cembalo accompaniment. Only Beethoven and Marschner effectively used an emotional melodrama in important passages. In Mozart's German operas the plot proper is almost exclusively expressed in spoken prose followed without transition by vocal music in the form of songs, ensembles in somewhat freer forms, the great finales elaborated into somewhat longer symphonic compositions, and the arias preceded by an orchestral recitative (*recitativo accompagnato*) all of which are inclined to slow down the action. Apart from Gluck's operas and Nicolai's *Merry Wives*, *The Magic Flute* alone contains a recitative passage of greater length which really serves to develop the action: the great scene between Tamino and the priest: a scene which constitutes the zenith of Mozart's dramatic work. In his Italian operas Mozart adopted the *recitativo secco* from the *opera buffa*, with the considerable improvement in *Così fan tutte* of allowing the orchestra to play the accompaniment at times when the dialogue contains lyrical passages.

These brief remarks should suffice to remind experts with what care our great masters treated the dialogue on which the action on the whole depends. But it is striking that none of our classical composers made use of the subtle nuances which may result from the development from ordinary prose via melodrama, *recitativo secco*, and *recitativo accompagnato* to the unimpeded flow of the melody of a song.

Perhaps it was inevitable that the peculiar subject matter taken completely from real life and embracing the whole gamut from the sober prose of everyday life through the various shades of dialogue to sentimental song, should induce me, who had in my previous works taken much care to render the dialogue natural, to adopt the style realized in *Intermezzo*.

I have always paid the greatest possible attention to natural diction and speed of dialogue, with increasing success from opera to opera. While in my first opera *Guntram* the distinction, so carefully observed by Richard Wagner, between passages which are merely recited and those which are purely lyrical, was almost completely neglected, the dialogue in *Salome* and *Elektra* was largely rescued from being drowned by the symphonic orchestra. But it is unfortunately still very much handicapped by instrumental polyphony unless extremely careful observation of my dynamic markings gives the orchestra that pellucidity which I took for granted when composing the operas, and which I know from perfect performances to be capable of achievement.

But since it is indeed rare that we can count on such ideal performances on the stage, I found myself more and more compelled to secure from the start the balance between singer and orchestra to such an extent that even in less perfect performances the action above all should, at least in broad outline, be plain and easily intelligible, lest the opera be disfigured or open to misrepresentation. The scores of *Die Frau ohne Schatten* and *Ariadne* are the fruits of these endeavors.

In the former I attempted, especially in the part of the nurse, to inject new life into the style and pace of the old *recitativo secco* by means of an orchestral accompaniment using mainly solo instruments and filling in the background with light strokes. Unfortunately, this attempt did not succeed in making the dialogue, which is of the utmost importance particularly in these scenes, absolutely clear.

The fault may lie either in a lack of talent on my part, as a result of which even this tenuous and diaphanous orchestra appears still too polyphonic, and the scoring so erratic as to impede the spoken word on the stage, or it may be due to the imperfect diction on the part of the majority of our operatic singers, or again to the unfortunately often guttural tone of German singers, or to the excessive forcing of sound on our big stages.

There can be no doubt that orchestral polyphony, no matter how subdued its tones or how softly it is played, spells death to the spoken word on the stage, and the devil himself is to blame that we Germans imbibe counterpoint with our mothers' milk, to keep us from being too successful on the operatic stage.

Not even our greatest dramatic master succeeded in creating 'ideal recitatives' except in *Lohengrin* and *Rheingold*, so that no listener will ever be able to enjoy the poetry of the text, no matter how subdued the orchestral playing, in the great polyphonous symphonies of the second act of *Tristan* and the third act of *Siegfried*.

Anybody who knows my later operatic scores well, will have to admit that, provided the singer pronounces the words clearly and the dynamic markings in the score are strictly observed, the words of the text must be clearly understood by the listener, except in a few passages where these words may permissibly be drowned by the orchestra as it plays with increasing intensity for the purpose of pointing a necessary climax. No praise pleases me more than when after I have conducted *Elektra* somebody says to me: 'Tonight I understood every word': if this is not the case you may safely assume that the orchestral score was not played in the manner exactly prescribed by me.

On this occasion I should like to draw attention to the peculiar nature of the dynamic marking I use in my scores. I am no longer content with prescribing *pp*, *p*, *f*, *ff*, for the whole orchestra, but give a large variety of dynamic markings for individual groups and even individual instruments, the exact observance of which, although it is the main requirement for the correct performance of my orchestral scores, presupposes indeed the existence of a type of orchestral discipline which is somewhat rare today, but is absolutely necessary for a performance of my scores in accordance with my intentions. Special attention should be paid to the accurate execution of *fp* and of every *expressivo* calling for a frequently all but unnoticeable preponderance of one part over its neighbors. Only thus can finely articulated polyphony be clearly represented. If one particular part predominates, important subsidiary strands may be destroyed.

No rendering of the orchestral part, however brilliant and noisy, given by one of the many concert-hall conductors who have unfortunately nowadays taken to conducting opera can silence the just complaints against aural feasts at the expense of the intelligibility of plot and libretto.

It was out of this necessity that the score of *Ariadne* was born. The orchestra has not been relegated to the role of accompanist and yet, in spite of the expressive force of the 'chamber orchestra,' the sounds and words uttered by the singers are bound to be intelligible in any performance, no matter how heartless the officiating conductor may be.

It was in the first act of *Ariadne* that I first used with full assurance, in the alternation between ordinary prose, *recitativo secco*, and *recitativo accompagnato*, the vocal style which I have now, in *Intermezzo*, carried to its logical conclusion. But in none of my other works is the dialogue of greater importance than in this bourgeois comedy, which offers few chances to development of the so-called *cantilena*. The symphonic element has been so carefully and repeatedly revised and polished that in many instances it is merely hinted at and cannot, even when dynamic markings are carelessly observed, prevent the natural conversational tone, derived and copied from everyday life, from being not only heard but also clearly understood. This applies to the context as well as to each individual word; the lyrical element, the description of the spiritual experiences of the *dramatis personae* is developed mainly in the comparatively long orchestral interludes. Not until the final scenes of the first and second acts is the singer really given a chance of extended *cantilena*.

Wherever the dialogue contains lyrical elements in the other scenes, the singers as well as the conductor should carefully distinguish between *cantilena* and *recitativo*, and the listener must be able to follow the natural flow of the conversation without interruption and must be able to follow clearly all the subtle variations in the development of the characters as portrayed in the opera; if he fails to do so, the performance will have the effect of intolerable tedium since the listener, inadequately understanding the text, will not be able to comprehend the plot in all its details, nor will the musically trained ear find sufficient compensation in symphonic orgies.

The singer in particular should remember that only a properly formed consonant will penetrate even the most brutal of orchestras, whereas the strongest note of the human voice, even when singing the best vowel 'ah', will be drowned without difficulty by an orchestra of eighty or a hundred players playing no louder than *mezzo forte*. The singer has only one weapon against a polyphonic and indiscreet orchestra: the consonant. I have myself seen it happen, especially in Wagner's music dramas, e.g. in Wotan's Narration and in the Erda scene of *Siegfried*, the singers with great voices but poor diction were left to flounder impotently in the waves of orchestral sound, whereas singers with considerably weaker voices but decisive pronunciation of consonants, could carry the poet's words victoriously and without the slightest difficulty against the maelstrom of the symphonic orchestra.

I would, on the other hand, ask the conductor when rehearsing

Intermezzo to pay the greatest attention to the gradual transition from the spoken word to the sung and half-spoken word, to all the subtle turns in the conversation where prose hesitates between *recitativo secco* and the style of the *recitativo accompagnato*, to reach its climax at last in the so-called *bel canto* in which absolute clarity could at times be sacrificed to beauty of intonation. The chief precept for the practical execution of the *Intermezzo* dialogue is that all passages of pure dialogue – in so far as they do not change for short periods of time into lyrical outpourings of emotions – in other words, all passages resembling *recitativo secco*, should be presented *mezza voce* throughout. Practical experience teaches us that with full volume the precision of pronunciation and especially the formation of consonants suffer considerably. This is illustrated by the fact [...] that during orchestral rehearsals even in an empty theater, which is acoustically unfavorable, every word of the singers singing *mezza voce* can usually be understood, whereas barely half the words are understood when they sing with full voice during the performance [...]

By turning its back upon the popular love-and-murder interest of the usual operatic libretto, and by taking its subject matter perhaps too exclusively from real life, this new work blazes a path for musical and dramatic composition which others after me may perhaps negotiate with more talent and better fortune. I am fully aware of the fact that in breaking new ground unthought-of difficulties will stand in the way of the correct realization of my intentions. May this preface assist and guide the worthy and generous interpreters of my art, the excellent singers and hard-working conductors, in the solution of these problems.

Preface to *Intermezzo*, 1924

'Wagner's *Tristan* crowns 2000 years of theatre'
RICHARD STRAUSS

On this last piece of headed paper from the dear Vienna Opera, now probably quite doomed to decline, I want to declare to you, along with best wishes for the New Year, that I've now read your excellent History of Theatre with the greatest pleasure and liveliest interest nearly to the end.

Concerning your thoughts about the relationship between Schiller and Goethe (one of your best chapters!) and your particularly perceptive admission that Iphigenia is the work you regard as having given world theatre *'its final spiritual form, never since attained'*, I must ask, as a musician and dramatic composer, to voice a small criticism. That 'spiritual form' is not merely attained but even surpassed – *thanks to music* – in *Tristan*.

It is notable that you describe works like Tasso, which are wholly taken up with *'inner questions'* and which *'for the sake of their inner wealth deliberately forgo the theatrical effectiveness of public staging'*, as theatre's most recent high point.

You quite rightly call the few, very simple actions in Tasso just *'symbols of the inner life of the characters'*.

If Goethe's great works, in order to confront the highest human questions in the theatre 'with the hand of genius', often *'assumed forms seemingly opposed to theatre itself'*, it remained for the universal genius Richard Wagner to combine the ultimate theatrical power of Schiller's incomparable dramatic architecture (this his great riposte to Shakespeare's dramatic novels, as Wagner calls them) with Goethe's inner mental questions in *Tristan*, where Romanticism is not, as you suggest, enjoying a 'glittering resurrection', but where the end of all Romanticism is signalled, where, at one flashpoint, all 19th-century longing is caught up and, in the 'dialogue between day and night' and in Isolde's Liebestod, *finally laid to rest*.

Tristan is the final outcome of Schiller and Goethe and the highest fulfilment of 2,000 years of theatrical development. And this because of the *discovery of the modern orchestra*. Fully described in 'Opera and Drama'! The modern orchestra, created by Haydn, Weber, Berlioz and Wagner, has become the only instrument capable of realising, in symbols intelligible only to instinctive feeling, the *Incommensurable* of which old Goethe speaks (unattainable by the intellect alone); only music can dare to enter the 'World of the Mothers' without fear and horror. It is right that you treat actual opera, inasmuch as it is just a feast for the ear, as being secondary, but musico-dramatic manifestations stretching from Gluck's *Iphigenia* through Mozart's *Don Juan* (trapdoor scene), *Die Zauberflöte* with the Isis chorus, the psychological stratagems of *Così fan Tutte* and through *Freischütz*, *Euryanthe*, and from *Tannhäuser* to the *Ring of the Nibelung*, are, because of the orchestra, the ultimate fulfilment, with their emotional content and inner spirituality, of that which even the greatest verbal poet, aided by the greatest actor and the most complicated theatre machinery, is never in a position to realize completely.

I'm thinking of the psychological counterpoint in *Tristan*'s Act III, of Tristan's vision of Isolde approaching, of the 'Kingdom of World Night', the 'endless divine oblivion', of the opening of *Götterdämmerung*, the purification of the dying Siegfried in his last call to Brünnhilde, the scenes between Erda and Wotan, many parts of Kundry in Act II; indeed, as the final extreme in complete mental realization of the theatre, one could even name the third Leonore overture, in which the idea of the *Fidelio* drama achieves the purest imaginary performance, just as in the overture to *Lohengrin* all the mystery plays of the Middle Ages, summed up in a symphonic complex, are visible only to the mental eye of the listener (Tristan's: 'Do I *hear* the light?'), or as *Parsifal* can be claimed to be the highest crowning point of Jesuit theatre, with sections like the overture to Act III, the 16 bars of the radiant Grail, being the purest, most serene realization of the Christian idea, far beyond any preaching. –

Only with the discovery and ultimate differentiation of the modern orchestra has world theatre risen to its highest perfection. What the most beautiful verses of the greatest poet in pages of *description* can at best merely suggest to the reader's or listener's fantasy, music can with *one* chord express as *emotion itself*; the feeling of love, or longing, of repentance, of readiness for death – the first 2 bars of the overture to *Tristan* say more to the listener than the most beautiful poem in words.

Without such an assessment of the effect of music and its exercise in drama, your excellent book lacks the proper ending. Perhaps you will provide it in the next edition. –

Also the event of Bayreuth, the theatrical achievements of 1876 and 1882 under the personal direction of the 'great actor', and the re-awakening of *Tristan*, *Die Meistersinger*, *Tannhäuser*, *Lohengrin*, in Cosima's productions of genius, deserve to be placed above the achievements of a Georg in Meiningen, or a Possart, or Max Reinhardt's special services to Shakespeare. Also the latest *Parsifal*s, which I personally had the honour of conducting in Bayreuth, can confidently be designated as theatrical high points, as regards perfect playing, stage performance and purity of style, praise which to the best of my knowledge could not be lavished to this extent on any productions of Schiller, whether in Meiningen or with Reinhardt, whose most glittering periods I personally experienced. Near perfection was chiefly reached in Reinhardt's *Robbers* and *Kabale und Liebe*, not in the verse dramas. –

Without being immodest, may I conclude by also describing – naturally at a suitable remove – my life's work in conjunction with Hofmannsthal – as perhaps the most recent manifestations of world theatre developing into the realm of music.

Unthinking critics have called *Salome* and *Elektra* 'symphonies with voice accompaniment'. That these 'symphonies' activate the core of the dramatic content, that only a symphony orchestra (rather than one just for accompanying singers, as mostly in opera houses) could *develop* a fully exhaustive treatment, just as in my dramatic biography, *Intermezzo*, really only the 'symphonic interludes' inform us about what is happening within the characters, exactly as in the famous scene between Siegfried and Mime, before the latter is killed; a perfect example of what can be achieved on the stage only with the help of musical themes – all of this will perhaps only be fully grasped by those who come after us. Also perhaps Hofmannsthal in the ending of *Ariadne* drew Renaissance theatre and *commedia dell'arte* to a final conclusion. But only my so finely differentiated orchestra with its subtle 'nerve-counterpoint', if this bold expression is permitted, could, in the last scene of *Salome*, in Clytemnestra's anxiety states, in the recognition scene between Elektra and Orestes, in Act II of *Helena*, in the Empress's dream (Act II of *Frau ohne Schatten*), have ventured into areas granted only to music to unlock.

Only along this path, even if past high points of a thousand-year cultural development like *Tristan* and *Meistersinger* can probably never be attained again, is a modest new territory perhaps to be won.

Now goodbye and sincere greetings from your most devoted admirer

Dr Richard Strauss

Letter to Joseph Gregor, 8 January 1935, tr. Meredith Oakes

Dear friend Gregor

I've now gone through the second half of *Friedenstag* again as well. I don't think I shall ever be able to find music for it. These are not real people: the commander and his wife, everything is stilted. I don't believe that in the Thirty Years' War any captain in the field would ever have said one word about '*the splendid thought* of war'. That is a kind of 'poetry' which absolutely fails in the theatre. Probably our friend feels this as well! Also the whole scene from the entrance of the Holsteiner onwards is flawed in construction. The dialogue of the two commanders is completely undramatic: this is the way two school pupils might discuss the subject: The Thirty Years' War. Forgive me for saying so openly what I think; but I would consider a kindly veiling of the truth to be an insult, and it wouldn't get us anywhere.

Could you not try first to translate the whole thing back into natural prose in a manner in which people of this time and in this situation, who hadn't read Schiller's *Wallenstein*, might have thought and spoken.

I've now gained a certain perspective on your otherwise so valuable work. In its present form, it is not suitable *for me*.

Please make the effort to rework the whole thing once more in *heightened prose*, but as spoken by *natural* people – no theatrical figures from the Thirty Years' War. *And then* we'll have to thoroughly plough through the whole of it again, *and then* we'll have to send it to our friend for merciless criticism and the most fundamental revision with the request for active (critical and productive) collaboration, unless you want to do this straight away, before you come here to me.

Please also write him my brutal thoughts, of which you in no way need to be ashamed. – [...]

With best wishes your ever (perhaps too) honestly devoted

Dr Richard Strauss

Letter to Joseph Gregor, 6 October 1935, tr. Meredith Oakes

'Headhunting for a hero the composer can stand'
RICHARD STRAUSS AND STEFAN ZWEIG

Richard Strauss to Stefan Zweig, 1 May 1935

I finished reading Byron's *Sardanapal*. Poetically the main figure is superb but entirely undemonic. The end is beautiful, but, unfortunately, already adapted by Richard Wagner for his *Ring*. Can it be used a second time? I am waiting for your further news. [...]

Dr Richard Strauss

Stefan Zweig to Richard Strauss, 3 May 1935

This is only an interim letter. I shall write to you in more detail
tomorrow about my long conference with Joseph Gregor about
Semiramis, which have [sic] led to a basic dramatic outline. As for
myself, I cannot quite overcome my fear that Semiramis will arouse
negative feelings in the audience. In the drama, and even more so in
music, the listener is moved by a character expressing pure feelings,
not by a hating, violent, demonic figure; even Electra would be
intolerable as a musical figure if (in the scene with her sister and when
recognizing Orestes) her bitterness did not find that beautiful lyrical
and feminine solution. I discussed with Gregor a similar break in the
domineering, destructive, demonic temperament of Semiramis; I will
explain our suggestion for a solution in my detailed letter tomorrow. I
am wondering whether the predominating force of Semiramis does
not reside in her superhuman rather than her human nature – well, I'll
talk about this tomorrow.

Another plan in which we see an opportunity for a colorful opera
would be the world of Mexico – in very distant similarity to Gerhart
Hauptmann's *Der weisse Heiland*. You may be familiar with the
legend, according to which before Cortez, that is before the brutal
conquerors, another European, a legendary figure, arrived in Mexico.
He was revered there as a saint, but finally cruelly murdered by the
priests. It would be thrilling to revive the lost wonder world of the
Aztecs with their dances, festivals, war expeditions, and songs, and
to juxtapose the cruel, barbarian sacrifices with the lyrical figure of
that stranger who will be slaughtered (in connection with female
episodes); and as a finale, in revenge, the invasion of the Spaniards,
the lightning destruction of this barbarian-aristocratic world. Perhaps
you know Eduard Stucken's novel *Die weissen Götter*, in which that
orgiastic atmosphere is described. This theme would provide the
basis for a spectacular opera (quite different from Gasparo Spontini's
dry opera *Fernand Cortes*) and at the same time show the religious
ethical conflict between the pure (in a high sense Christian) stranger
and those demonic-fascinating civilizations. I note this plan in the
margin, as it were; perhaps you feel inclined to read Hauptmann's
(dramatically weak) *Der weisse Heiland* or Stucken's outstanding *Die
weissen Götter* – they make stimulating reading. I could imagine
that you would find the strange, pungent scent of that world even

more attractive than that of *Semiramis*. Tomorrow you will hear from me about my as yet only summarized structure for *Semiramis*, which, of course, would have to be raised far beyond the Calderon plot. Meanwhile just hasty greetings, tomorrow my full letter. Respectfully,

Stefan Zweig

Richard Strauss to Stefan Zweig, 5 May 1935

Thank you so much for your Mexican letter, which I received this morning. I will be glad to read Stucken and Hauptmann. Perhaps you are not aware how passionate an anti-Christ I am, and that the red Savior will be as obnoxious to me as the white one will probably be uninteresting. In *Salome* I tried to compose the good Jochanaan more or less as a clown; a preacher in the desert, especially one who feeds on grasshoppers, seems infinitely comical to me. Only because I have already caricatured the five Jews and also poked fun at Father Herodes did I feel that I had to follow the law of contrast and write a pedantic-Philistine motif for four horns to characterize Jochanaan.

No – such a passive prophet battling the ol' high priests, and at the end the awful Cortez: I don't think that's my dish. And the good Aztecs are not in my backyard either. If I have to choose, I'd rather take that monster Semiramis, who has at least some air of grandeur as a general and ruler. I do not always need to compose the Sweet Viennese Girl. Perhaps that Assyrian woman could be assigned some features of your Maria Stuart in that Semiramis is invincible as long as she dominates men in every respect until the moment that she succumbs to a Bothwell. Or is such 'slave love' incompatible with the idea of Semiramis?

For the time being, then, I'll stick to my request in my letter yesterday: Celestine or Semiramis. Sincerely,

Dr Richard Strauss

A Confidential Matter: The Letters of Richard Strauss and Stefan Zweig, 1931–1935, tr. Max Knight

'The fatal curse of the Vienna Opera contract'
HENRY-LOUIS DE LA GRANGE

At that time, all the energies of the court theatre authorities were directed towards the building of a new opera-house, close to the Kärntnerthortheater, but situated on the Ring itself. Work began on the foundations in 1861, the first stone was laid two years later, and construction proceeded in accordance with the designs of two Viennese architects, Eduard van der Nüll and August Siccard von Siccardsburg. Their project, presented in strictest anonymity, along with thirty-four others, to a selection committee, had been chosen purely on merit. Construction went on for seven years and cost six million gulden (Charles Garnier's Opéra in Paris took eleven years, from 1863 to 1874). Long before it was completed, alarming rumours began circulating in Vienna that the building was beginning to sink into the ground, and that there were structural weaknesses in the design. The architects' names became bywords in the city and everyone began to expect the worst. Van der Nüll, who had always had depressive tendencies, was so much affected by this campaign of disparagement that he eventually committed suicide a year before the opening. And two months later Siccardsburg also died, probably from the shock caused by the death of his friend and collaborator. These tragic happenings provide yet another instance of the Viennese propensity to believe the worst, for once the building was finished it was found, apart from some minor imperfections inevitable in a project of this scale, to fulfil its functions successfully. The auditorium proved to have one of the best acoustics in Europe, even though it took several months to discover the optimal level for the orchestra pit.

Gustav Mahler, 1995

'Why *Wozzeck* cannot be a model'
ALBAN BERG

It is now ten years since I started to compose *Wozzeck*; already so much has been written about it that I can hardly say anything without plagiarizing my critics. I should like, however, to correct an error that arose in 1925 soon after it was produced and that has spread widely since.

I have [never] entertained the idea of reforming the structure of opera through *Wozzeck*. Neither when I started nor when I completed the work did I consider it a model for further efforts by any other composer. I never assumed or expected that *Wozzeck* should become the basis of a school.

I simply wanted to compose good music; to develop musically the contents of Georg Büchner's immortal drama; to translate his poetic language into music. Other than that, when I decided to write an opera, my only intention, as related to the technique of composition, was to give the theater what belongs to the theater. The music was to be so formed that at each moment it would fulfill its duty of serving the action. Even more, the music should be prepared to furnish whatever the action needed for transformation into reality on the stage. The function of a composer is to solve the problems of an ideal stage director. On the other hand this objective should not prejudice the development of the music as an entity, absolute, and purely musical. No externals should interfere with its individual existence.

That I accomplished these purposes by a use of musical forms more or less ancient (considered by critics as one of the most important of my ostensible reforms of opera) was a natural consequence of my method. It was first necessary to make a selection from Büchner's twenty-five loosely constructed, partly fragmentary scenes for the libretto. Repetitions not lending themselves to musical variation were avoided. Finally, the scenes were brought together, arranged, and grouped in acts. The problem therefore became more musical than literary, and had to be solved by the laws of musical structure rather than by the rules of dramaturgy.

It was impossible to shape the fifteen scenes I selected in different manners so that each would retain its musical coherence and individuality and at the same time follow the customary method of development appropriate to the literary content. No matter how rich structurally, no matter how aptly one might fit the dramatic events, after a number of scenes so composed the music would inevitably create monotony. The effect would become boring with a series of a dozen or more formally composed entr'actes which offered nothing but this type of illustrative music, and boredom, of course, is the last thing one should experience in the theater.

I obeyed the necessity of giving each scene and each accompanying piece of entr'acte music – prelude, postlude, connecting link or interlude – an unmistakable aspect, a rounded off and finished character. It was imperative to use everything essential for the creation of individualizing characteristics on the one hand, and coherence on the other. Hence the much discussed utilization of both old and new musical forms and their application in an absolute music.

The appearance of these forms in opera was to some degree unusual, even new. Nevertheless novelty, pathbreaking, was not my conscious intention. I must reject the claim of being a reformer of the opera through such innovations, although I do not wish to depreciate my work thereby, since others who do not know it so well can do that much better.

What I do consider my particular accomplishment is this. No one in the audience, no matter how aware he may be of the musical forms contained in the framework of the opera, of the precision and logic with which it has been worked out, no one, from the moment the curtain parts until it closes for the last time, pays any attention to the various fugues, inventions, suites, sonata movements, variations, and passacaglias about which so much has been written. No one gives heed to anything but the vast social implications of the work which by far transcend the personal destiny of Wozzeck. This, I believe, is my achievement.

'A Word about *Wozzeck*', 1927, reprinted from *Musical Quarterly*, XXXVIII (1952), tr. Willi Reich

'The frankness of French sexuality is ideal for *Fledermaus*'
MAX REINHARDT

[...] I have seen a number of new plays. I have also been reading a variety of other works of French drama. I found it highly characteristic that virtually all French authors somehow react in a directly autobiographical fashion.

The immediacy with which experience is translated into theater here is rarely found in the German theater. Here, everything flows into everything else. And in every comedy one easily recognizes the original experience of the self. The days glide by in this magical city – rich and ever new. And the dream of love also is dreamed richly and ever new. People here are used to revealing their feelings with a naive matter-of-factness and without any false sense of shame, whereas the chaste Teutons veil them as if they were the most secret emotions. Here is a small example which struck me as psychologically significant a few minutes ago. After the rehearsal I walked home through the Rue Pigalle, which is always crowded at this time of day. There I saw a man taking leave of a woman, embracing and kissing her passionately. This was taking place as if the couple were completely alone. The crowd streamed past indifferently. My gaze lingered on the lovers. The French find all that so natural. For them, the fact that two people in love with one another should kiss is as much a matter of course as eating and drinking.

You see, this little example is very instructive. It explains to me why French theater and French productions are sometimes considered alien or 'risqué' abroad. But this freedom is nothing other than the carefree naivety of a mentality that is deeply rooted in the erotic. It was the uninhibited and yet always graceful affirmation of the right to love that presented itself to me among the milling crowd in the Rue Pigalle. It is lived and experienced naively.

It is for this reason, because his roots are in the same soil, that the French author does not try to clothe his experience in symbols, as the German author does, thereby making it obscure. He builds a comedy, a drama out of the hours of pleasure and sadness experienced by himself or by his friends. Death rarely features. Again and again life and love go on. Love, being in love, flirting – time and again these are the major themes. Often they are treated with profound poetic insight, often with cynical wit, often with burlesque grace. But the tradition of a culture which is in touch with the earth can always be felt.

Just as the French author frequently transmutes autobiographical material into drama, so, too, the idiosyncracies of the French actor are his originality and immediacy. What he too is seeking is not so much transformation as the chance to be himself! The boulevard theaters here are still unique in the inimitable lightness of their dialogue. I am captivated every time by that wonderful elasticity, by the inner rhythm of the tempo. And then that painstakingly polished language, the way it sparkles. In scenes that work up to a climax, the way they time and again let themselves fall gracefully back, gliding into a swift, gentle transition – what a sublime pleasure it is to watch!

Berry, a very strange and most interesting actor, whom I am directing as Eisenstein, has no rival in this! I wanted to meet him in person first. For it is especially in personal contact that I always immediately feel the duality, the potentialities and the limits of an actor. The sensitive mouth, altering its expression ten times in a second, the eyes, veiled one moment, flashing the next, the vital tension that fills Berry, immediately told me that this was an outstanding actor. Berry is already strewing exuberant good humour from his cornucopia at the rehearsals. Similarly, the Prison Governor, who is played by Charpentier, will be a cabinet piece of kind-hearted and good-humoured humanity. Absolutely all of them surprise me with their weightless elegance, the perfect appropriateness of their gestures and the nuances of their speech to the demands of the moment and the situation. I find it an interesting task to preserve this talent of improvisation, which makes the rehearsals so fascinating, for the performance. [...]

Interview with Max Reinhardt by Bertha Zuckerkandl-Szeps [Paris], November 1933, concerning the French theatre and rehearsals for the production of *Die Fledermaus* at the Théâtre Pigalle, Paris, *Neues Wiener Journal*, 12 November 1935

'Method acting with the operatic voice'
KONSTANTIN SERGEIVICH STANISLAVSKY

'No,' interupted Stanislavski, 'you are not giving out anything but sounds. You do not as yet need such large sounds for your feelings. Singing is beautiful only when it is natural and expresses something. But singing made up only of pretty sounds is anti-artistic because it is not sparked by inner feelings. You have a voice, a living organ which better than any instrument can express emotion, and you treat it like a trombone [Stanislavski was speaking here to the basso who sang the role of Sobakin]. This is unnatural and therefore you cannot speak expressively as in real life. The audience, which has come to the theatre and has never heard *The Tsar's Bride*, will have no idea of what it is about because with that kind of singing it is impossible to hear the words or know what they signify.'

Stanislavski on Opera, tr. Elizabeth Reynolds Hapgood, 1975

'Notes on culinary opera versus epic theatre'
BERTOLT BRECHT

Opera – with innovations!

For some time past there has been a move to renovate the opera. Opera is to have its form modernized and its content brought up to date, but without its culinary character being changed. Since it is precisely for its backwardness that the opera-going public adores opera, an influx of new types of listener with new appetites has to be reckoned with; and so it is. The intention is to democratize but not to alter democracy's character, which consists in giving the people new rights, but no chance to appreciate them. Ultimately it is all the same to the waiter whom he serves, so long as he serves the food. Thus the *avant-garde* are demanding or supporting innovations which are supposedly going to lead to a renovation of opera; but nobody demands a fundamental discussion of opera (i.e. of its function), and probably such a discussion would not find much suppport.

The modesty of the *avant-garde*'s demands has economic grounds of whose existence they themselves are only partly aware. Great apparati like the opera, the stage, the press, etc., impose their views as it were incognito. For a long time now they have taken the handiwork (music, writing, criticism, etc.) of intellectuals who share in their profits – that is, of men who are economically committed to the prevailing system but are socially near-proletarian – and processed it to make fodder for their public entertainment machine, judging it by their own standards and guiding it into their own channels; meanwhile the intellectuals themselves have gone on supposing that the whole business is concerned only with the presentation of their work, is a secondary process which has no influence over their work but merely wins influence for it. This muddled thinking which overtakes musicians, writers and critics as soon as they consider their own situation has tremendous consequences to which far too little attention is paid. For by imagining that they have got hold of an apparatus which in fact has got hold of them they are supporting an apparatus which is out of their control, which is no longer (as they believe) a means of furthering output but has become an obstacle to output, and specifically to their own output as soon as it follows a new and original course which the apparatus finds awkward or opposed to its own aims. Their output then becomes a matter of delivering the goods. Values evolve which are based on the fodder principle. And this leads to a general habit of judging works of art by their suitability for the apparatus without ever judging the apparatus by its suitability for the work. People say, this or that is a good work; and they mean (but do not say) good for the apparatus. Yet this apparatus is conditioned by the society of the day and only accepts what can keep it going in that society. We are free to discuss any innovation which doesn't threaten its social function – that of providing an evening's entertainment. We are not free to discuss those which threaten to change its function, possibly by fusing it with the educational system or with the organs of mass communication. Society absorbs via the apparatus whatever it needs in order to reproduce itself. This means that an innovation will pass if it is calculated to rejuvenate existing society, but not if it is going to change it – irrespective whether the form of the society in question is good or bad.

The *avant-garde* don't think of changing the apparatus, because they fancy that they have at their disposal an apparatus which will serve up whatever they freely invent, transforming itself sponta-neously to match their ideas. But they are not in fact free inventors; the apparatus goes on fulfilling its function with or without them; the theatres play every night; the papers come out so many times a day; and they absorb what they need; and all they need is a given amount of stuff.*

You might think that to show up this situation (the creative artist's utter dependence on the apparatus) would be to condemn it. Its concealment is such a disgrace.

And yet to restrict the individual's freedom of invention is in itself a progressive act. The individual becomes increasingly drawn into enormous events that are going to change the world. No longer can he simply 'express himself'. He is brought up short and put into a

---

* The intellectuals, however, are completely dependent on the apparatus, both socially and economically; it is the only channel for the realization of their work. The output of writers, composers and critics comes more and more to resemble raw material. The finished article is produced by the apparatus.

position where he can fulfil more general tasks. The trouble, however, is that at present the apparati do not work for the general good; the means of production do not belong to the producer; and as a result his work amounts to so much merchandise, and is governed by the normal laws of mercantile trade. Art is merchandise, only to be manufactured by the means of production (apparati). An opera can only be written for the opera. (One can't just think up an opera like one of Böcklin's fantastic sea-beasts, then hope to exhibit it publicly after having seized power – let alone try to smuggle it into our dear old zoo. . . .)

Opera

Even if one wanted to start a discussion of the opera as such (i.e. of its function), an opera would have to be written.

Our existing opera is a culinary opera. It was a means of pleasure long before it turned into merchandise. It furthers pleasure even where it requires, or promotes, a certain degree of education, for the education in question is an education of taste. To every object it adopts a hedonistic approach. It 'experiences', and it ranks as an 'experience'.

Why is *Mahagonny* an opera? Because its basic attitude is that of an opera: that is to say, culinary. Does *Mahagonny* adopt a hedonistic approach? It does. Is *Mahagonny* an experience? It is an experience. For . . . *Mahagonny* is a piece of fun.

The opera *Mahagonny* pays conscious tribute to the senselessness of the operatic form. The irrationality of opera lies in the fact that rational elements are employed, solid reality is aimed at, but at the same time it is all washed out by the music. A dying man is real. If at the same time he sings we are translated to the sphere of the irrational. (If the audience sang at the sight of him the case would be different.) The more unreal and unclear the music can make the reality – though there is of course a third, highly complex and in itself quite real element which can have quite real effects but is utterly remote from the reality of which it treats – the more pleasurable the whole process becomes: the pleasure grows in proportion to the degree of unreality.

The term 'opera' – far be it from us to profane it – leads, in *Mahagonny*'s case, to all the rest. The intention was that a certain unreality, irrationality and lack of seriousness should be introduced at the right moment, and so strike with a double meaning.*

The irrationality which makes its appearance in this way only fits the occasion on which it appears.

It is a purely hedonistic approach.

As for the content of this opera, *its content is pleasure*. Fun, in other words, not only as form but as subject-matter. At least, enjoyment was meant to be the object of the inquiry even if the inquiry was intended to be an object of enjoyment. Enjoyment here appears in its current historical role: as merchandise.†

It is undeniable that at present this content must have a provocative effect. In the thirteenth section, for example, where the glutton stuffs himself to death; because hunger is the rule. We never even hinted that others were going hungry while he stuffed, but the effect was provocative all the same. It is not everyone who is in a position to stuff himself full that dies of it, yet many are dying of hunger because this man stuffs himself to death. His pleasure provokes, because it implies so much.

In contexts like these the use of opera as a means of pleasure must have provocative effects today. Though not of course on the handful of opera-goers. Its power to provoke introduces reality once more. *Mahagonny* may not taste particularly agreeable; it may even (thanks to guilty conscience) make a point of not doing so. But it is culinary through and through.

Mahagonny is nothing more or less than an opera.

– with innovations!

Opera had to be brought up to the technical level of the modern theatre. The modern theatre is the epic theatre. The following table shows certain changes of emphasis (not absolute antitheses but mere shifts of accent) as between the dramatic and the epic theatre.

---

* This limited aim did not stop us from introducing an element of instruction, and from basing everything on the gest. The eye which looks for the gest in everything is the moral sense. In other words, a moral tableau. A subjective one, though...

> Jetzt trinken wir noch eins
> Dann gehen wir nicht nach Hause
> Dann trinken wir noch eins
> Dann machen wir mal eine Pause.

– The people who sing this are subjective moralists. They are describing themselves.

† Romanticism is merchandise here too. It appears only as content, not as form.

DRAMATIC THEATRE	EPIC THEATRE
plot	narrative
implicates the spectator in a stage situation	turns the spectator into an observer, but
wears down his capacity for action	arouses his capacity for action
provides him with sensations	forces him to take decisions
experience	picture of the world
the spectator is involved in something	he is made to face something
suggestion	argument
instinctive feelings are preserved	brought to the point of recognition
the spectator is in the thick of it, shares the experience	the spectator stands outside, studies
the human being is taken for granted	the human being is the object of the inquiry
he is unalterable	he is alterable and able to alter
eyes on the finish	eyes on the course
one scene makes another	each scene for itself
growth	montage
linear development	in curves
evolutionary determinism	jumps
man as a fixed point	man as a process
thought determines being	social being determines thought
feeling	reason

When the epic theatre's methods begin to penetrate the opera the first result is a radical *separation of the elements*. The great struggle for supremacy between words, music and production – which always brings up the question 'which is the pretext for what?': is the music the pretext for the events on the stage, or are these the pretext for the music? etc. – can simply be by-passed by radically separating the elements. So long as the expression 'Gesamtkunstwerk' (or 'integrated work of art') means that the integration is a muddle, so long as the arts are supposed to be 'fused' together, the various elements will all be equally degraded, and each will act as a mere 'feed' to the rest. The process of fusion extends to the spectator, who gets thrown into the melting pot too and becomes a passive (suffering) part of the total work of art. Witchcraft of this sort must of course be fought against. Whatever is intended to produce hypnosis, is likely to induce sordid intoxication, or creates fog, has got to be given up.

Words, music and setting must become more independent of one another.

(a) Music

For the music, the change of emphasis proved to be as follows:

DRAMATIC OPERA	EPIC OPERA
The music dishes up	The music communicates
music which heightens the text	music which sets forth the text
music which proclaims the text	music which takes the text for granted
music which illustrates	which takes up a position
music which paints the psychological situation	which gives the attitude

Music plays the chief part in our thesis*

(b) Text

We had to make something straightforward and instructive of our fun, if it was not to be irrational and nothing more. The form employed was that of the moral tableau. The tableau is performed by the characters in the play. The text had to be neither moralizing nor sentimental, but to put morals and sentimentality on view. Equally important was the spoken word and the written word (of the titles). Reading seems to encourage the audience to adopt the most natural attitude towards the work.

(c) Setting

Showing independent works of art as part of a theatrical performance is a new departure. Neher's projections adopt an attitude towards the events on the stage; as when the real glutton sits in front of the glutton whom Neher has drawn. In the same way the stage unreels the events that are fixed on the screen. These projections of [Caspar] Neher's are quite as much an independent component of the opera as are [Kurt] Weill's music and the text. They provide its visual aids.

Of course such innovations also demand a new attitude on the part of the audiences who frequent opera houses.

Effect of the innovations: a threat to opera?

It is true that the audience had certain desires which were easily satisfied by the old opera but are no longer taken into account by the

---

* The large number of craftsmen in the average opera orchestra allows of nothing but associative music (one barrage of sound breeding another); and so the orchestral apparatus needs to be cut down to thirty specialists or less. The singer becomes a reporter, whose private feelings must remain a private affair.

new. What is the audience's attitude during an opera; and is there any chance that it will change?

Bursting out of the underground stations, eager to become as wax in the magicians' hands, grown-up men, their resolution proved in the struggle for existence, rush to the box office. They hand in their hat at the cloakroom, and with it they hand their normal behaviour: the attitudes of 'everyday life'. Once out of the cloakroom they take their seats with the bearing of kings. How can we blame them? You may think a grocer's bearing better than a king's and still find this ridiculous. For the attitude that these people adopt in the opera is unworthy of them. Is there any possibility that they may change it? Can we persuade them to get out their cigars?

Once the content becomes, technically speaking, an independent component, to which text, music and setting 'adopt attitudes'; once illusion is sacrificed to free discussion, and once the spectator, instead of being enabled to have an experience, is forced as it were to cast his vote; then a change has been launched which goes far beyond formal matters and begins for the first time to affect the theatre's social function.

In the old operas all discussion of the content is rigidly excluded. If a member of the audience had happened to see a particular set of circumstances portrayed and had taken up a position *vis-à-vis* them, then the old opera would have lost its battle: the 'spell would have been broken'. Of course there were elements in the old opera which were not purely culinary; one has to distinguish between the period of its development and that of its decline. *The Magic Flute*, *Fidelio*, *Figaro* all included elements that were philosophical, dynamic. And yet the element of philosophy, almost of daring, in these operas was so subordinated to the culinary principle that their *sense* was in effect tottering and was soon absorbed in sensual satisfaction. Once its original 'sense' had died away the opera was by no means left bereft of sense, but had simply acquired another one – a sense *qua* opera. The content had been smothered in the opera. Our Wagnerites are now pleased to remember that the original Wagnerites posited a sense of which they were presumably aware. Those composers who stem from Wagner still insist on posing as philosophers. A philosophy which is of no use to man or beast, and can only be disposed of as a means of sensual satisfaction.

[. . .]

In our present society the old opera cannot be just 'wished away'. Its illusions have an important social function. The drug is irreplaceable; it cannot be done without.

Only in the opera does the human being have a chance to be human. His entire mental capacities have long since been ground down to a timid mistrustfulness, an envy of others, a selfish calculation. The old opera survives not just because it is old, but chiefly because the situation which it is able to meet is still the old one. This is not wholly so. And here lies the hope for the new opera. Today we can begin to ask whether opera hasn't come to such a pass that further innovations, instead of leading to the renovation of this whole form, will bring about its destruction.

Perhaps *Mahagonny* is as culinary as ever – just as culinary as an opera ought to be – but one of its functions is to change society; it brings the culinary principle under discussion, it attacks the society that needs operas of such a sort; it still perches happily on the old bough, perhaps, but at least it has started (out of absent-mindedness or bad conscience) to saw it through. [...] And here you have the effect of the innovations and the song they sing.

Real innovations attack the roots.

'The Modern Theatre is the Epic Theatre' (Notes to the opera *Aufstieg und Fall der Stadt Mahagonny*), rpt in *Brecht on Theatre: 1918–1932*, tr. John Willett

'Poet and composer must be on the same wavelength'
BENJAMIN BRITTEN

Many people think that composers can set any old kind of poetry to music; that any pattern of words may start his imagination working. In many cases that is true. Some of the greatest composers have found inspiration in very poor verse (see Schubert in many places), although not many have gone as far as Darius Milhaud in his 'Machines Agricoles' – which is a setting of a catalogue. But I believe that if the words of a song match the music in subtlety of thought and clarity of expression it results in a greater amount of artistic satisfaction for the listener. This applies equally to the larger forms – oratorio, cantata and opera. In many oratorios, of course, where the words come from the liturgy or the Bible the composer has the greatest possible inspiration for his music; but with a few exceptions, like Metastasio, Dryden, Da Ponte and Boito, few serious poets have provided libretti for these kinds of works. There may be many reasons for this. Opera composers have a reputation for rutheless disregard of poetic values (in some cases rightly) – and all they need is a hack writer to bully, and serious poets won't stand for that. Besides, it takes a great deal of time to learn the operatic formulae – the recitatives, the arias and the ensembles. The bad enunciation of many singers doesn't seem to provide a suitable show place for a poet's finest thoughts. One of the most powerful reasons for a poet's operatic shyness I suspect to be this. To be suitable for music, poetry must be simple, succinct and crystal clear; for many poets this must be a great effort, and the psychological epic poem to be read (or not read) in the quiet of the study is more attractive. I think they are wrong. Opera makes similar demands of conciseness on the composer. He must be able to paint a mood or an atmosphere in a single phrase and must search unceasingly for the apt one. But this is everlastingly fascinating and stimulating, as it must be to the poet. Similarly fascinating to him should be the problem of continuity, or degrees of intensity, development of character and situation. Also, if he is working together with a sympathetic composer, then the timings and inflections of the dialogue can be fixed exactly and for ever – a thing not possible in any other medium.

This 'working together' of the poet and composer mentioned above seems to be one of the secrets of writing a good opera. In the general discussion on the shape of the work – the plot, the division into recitatives, arias, ensembles and so on – the musician will have many ideas that may stimulate and influence the poet. Similarly when the libretto is written and the composer is working on the music, possible alterations may be suggested by the flow of the music, and the libretto altered accordingly. In rehearsals, as the work becomes realised aurally and visually, other changes are often seen to be necessary. The composer and poet should at all stages be working in the closest contact, from the most preliminary stages right up to the first night. It was thus in the case of 'The Rape of Lucretia.'

Foreword to *The Rape of Lucretia*

'Re-establishing the useful clichés of classicism'
IGOR STRAVINSKY

Rather than seek musical forms symbolically expressive of the dramatic content (as in the Daedalian examples of Alban Berg), I chose to cast *The Rake* in the mould of an eighteenth-century 'number' opera, one in which the dramatic progress depends on the succession of separate pieces – recitatives and arias, duets, trios, choruses, instrumental interludes. In the earlier scenes the mould is to some extent pre-Gluck in that it tends to crowd the story into the secco recitatives, reserving the arias for the reflective poetry, but then, as the opera warms up, the story is told, enacted, contained almost entirely in song – as distinguished from so-called speech-song, and Wagnerian continuous melody, which consists, in effect, of orchestral commentary enveloping continuous recitative.

Having chosen a period-piece subject, I decided – naturally, as it seemed to me – to assume the conventions of the period as well. *The Rake's Progress* is a conventional opera, therefore, but with the difference that these particular conventions were adjudged by all respectable (i.e. progressive) circles to be long since dead. My plan of revival did not include updating or modernising, however – which would have been self-contradictory, in any case – and it follows that I had no ambitions as a reformer, at least not in the line of a Gluck, a Wagner or a Berg. In fact, these great progressivists sought to abolish or transform the very clichés I had tried to re-establish, though my restitutions were by no means intended to supersede their now conventionalised reforms (i.e. the leitmotif systems of Wagner and Berg).

Can a composer re-use the past and at the same time move in a forward direction? Regardless of the answer (which is 'yes'), this academic question did not trouble me during the composition, nor will I argue it now, though the supposed backward step of *The Rake* has taken on a radically forward-looking complexion when I have compared it with some more recent progressive operas. Instead, I ask the listener to suspend the question as I did while composing, and, difficult as the request may be, to try to discover the opera's own qualities. For a long time *The Rake* seemed to have been created for no other purpose than journalistic debates concerning: (a) the historical validity of the approach; and (b) the question of pastiche. If the opera contains imitations, however – especially of Mozart, as has been said – I will gladly allow the charge if I may thereby release people from the argument and bring them to the music.

The Rake's Progress is simple to perform musically, but difficult to realise on the stage. I contend, however, that the chief obstacles to a convincing visual conception are no more than the result of an incapacity to accept the work for what it is. True, Tom's machine-baked bread may be hard to swallow, but even *it* will go down, I think (with a lot of butter and more than a few grains of salt) if the stage director has not lost sight of the opera's 'moral fable' proposition by over-playing the realism of 'the Rakewell story'. As Dr Johnson said, 'Opera is an exotic and irrational art.'

It is easy to find faults of this sort in *The Rake*, to be sure, though, alas, it offers nothing quite so foolish as the concealed-identity scene in *Un ballo in maschera*, or the post-stabbing coloratura concert in *Rigoletto*, to name two far greater operas which, like my own, I love beyond the point where criticism can make a difference. Having perfect 20–20 hindsight, like most people, I am now able to see that Shadow is a preacher as well as a Devil; that the Epilogue is much too 'nifty' (as Americans say); that the ostinato accompaniment style could do with an occasional contrast of polyphony, the dramatic opportunity for which might have been found in an extra ensemble or two during which the minor characters might also have been given more development and connection. But though such things matter, they are not fatal. And in any case, I am not concerned with the future of my opera. I ask for it only a measure of present justice.

Paris, 16 August 1964

I chose Wystan Auden as librettist for my opera *The Rake's Progress* because of his special gift for versification; I have never been able to compose music to prose, even poetic prose. That he was a great poet others had assured me – I felt as much, but was too new to English to judge for myself – yet my first requisite was more modest and more specific; after all, successful collaborations between musicians and poets in dramatic works have been rare, and in fact Dryden and Purcell, Hofmannsthal and Strauss, Boito and Verdi (Boito was, rather, a great adapter, but that is almost as valuable), are the only names that come to mind. What I required was a versifier with whom I could collaborate in writing songs, an unusual starting point for an opera, I hardly need to add, as most composers begin with a search for qualities of dramatic construction and dramatic sensation. I had no knowledge of Wystan's dramatic gifts or even whether he was sensible to operatic stagecraft. I simply gave all priority to verse, hoping that we could evolve the theatrical form together and that it would inspire Wystan to dramatic poetry.

I think he *was* inspired, and in any case he inspired me. At the business level of the collaboration he wrote 'words for music', and I wonder whether any poet since the Elizabethans has made a composer such a beautiful gift of them as the 'Lanterloo' dance in our opera. Wystan had a genius for operatic wording. His lines were always the right length for singing and his words the right ones to sustain musical emphasis. A musical speed was generally suggested by the character and succession of the words, but it was only a useful indication, never a limitation. Best of all for a composer, the rhythmic values of the verse could be altered in singing without destroying the verse. At least, Wystan has never complained. At a different level, as soon as we began to work together I discovered that we shared the same views not only about opera, but also on the nature of the Beautiful and the Good. Thus, our opera is indeed, and in the highest sense a collaboration.

Wystan has lived in Austria too long now, and I wish you could convince him to come back. After all, we cannot afford to give our best poet to the Germans.

For a BBC television documentary on Auden. Hollywood, 5 November 1965, from *Themes and Episodes*, 1966

'The stimulus and delight of ambiguities and untidiness'
ROLAND BARTHES

[...] opera remains, for the moment, a spectacle for a distinct social class, first of all because tickets are expensive, and also because the enjoyment of opera requires certain cultural reflexes – of background, *ambiance*, sophistication – which are still class reflexes. And yet opera itself contains many progressive elements: it's a total spectacle, mobilizing many of the senses, many sensual pleasures, including the possibility for the public to enjoy *itself*, in a way, and this all-encompassing, spectacular theatricality has been much sought after by our culture, from ancient theater to rock concerts.

And opera is very well suited to avant-garde interpretations: everything is possible, the stage is a blank canvas, the technical means are there. Finally, the operative performance can divide into two spectacles in a curious but quite enjoyable fashion: I recently saw Gluck's *Orpheus*, and aside from the wonderful music, it really was a silly thing to watch, an unconscious parody of its own genre, but not only did this element of kitsch fail to upset me, it positively entertained me: I enjoyed the double truth of both the spectacle and its parody: laughter (or a smile) which is not destructive – perhaps that is one form of the culture of the future.

The Grain of the Voice: Interviews 1962–1980, 1981, tr. Linda Coverdale, 1985

'Rules and objectives of realistic Music Theatre'
WALTER FELSENSTEIN

The aim of true Music Theatre is to turn music and singing in the theatre into a convincing, true and utterly indispensable mode of human expression.

You may, however, feel such a definition stifling. But let me quote briefly from a lecture I based on this text two years ago. In it I said: 'Scarcely anyone can object to these demands. But can they actually be fulfilled? That stage action set to music be *true*; that singing on the stage be an *indispensable* mode of human expression; and that all who make music in the theatre are concerned in saying something so meaningful, and moving, that they cannot express it in any other way than with music. When, and where, does one meet all this? So seldom that, of the vast majority of people who would undoubtedly be capable of apprehending Music Theatre, only a small fraction have experienced it in its full potentiality, have recognized its uniqueness, and will believe in it despite all disappointments. The majority, while conceding our theoretical intentions, have never seen them carried into practice, are forced to report again and again that the singer-actors have either ignored them or misunderstood them, and have therefore concluded that they are pure Utopia, and abstractions only fit for experts and arty intellectuals to play around with – not really worth talking about. So they have become indifferent to opera or, quite rightly, prefer the delights of opera productions based on less valid theatrical principles, to these experiments that fail.'

Since then several theatres have made these principles their own. In their work they have been making certain discoveries that are already beginning to fall into some kind of shape. The technical journals, brochures, books, in which they are recorded, already form a small body of literature on the subject. Unfortunately the uninitiated reader of these writings might be misled into thinking that the demand that 'music and singing in the theatre should be made into a convincing, true and utterly indispensable mode of human expression' had in many instances been fulfilled. It has not been fulfilled, neither at the Komische Oper [in Berlin] itself nor elsewhere. But attempts and partial successes have proved that it can be fulfilled. And whenever the interpretations of the performers have shown a genuine feeling for it, public reaction has been extraordinarily positive. This has more and more led exponents of the conventional opera technique into attacking and discrediting us. They fear for their popularity. And some musicologists who were, under the old opera convention, allowed to lay claim to *Don Giovanni* and *Otello* as being absolute music, have joined the fray. But the attack is premature. It is directed at known imperfections and faults and misunderstandings in a method of production that is still at a very early stage. Among a hundred attempts there are perhaps five that clearly show the 'humanizing' of the stage singing, and the complete integration of the music with the dramatic action.

To attack something only just formed, still incomplete, hardly as yet recognized, often provokes the defence into using arguments that go beyond actual experience, and cannot yet always be proved. In word and letter these debates are argued out by critics, literary men of the theatre and by authors, only seldom by producers and conductors who are busy at their work, and hardly ever at all by singers, who rarely have any interest in theoretical matters. The consequences are all obvious.

In the various publications of recent years the generally apt formulations mirror one's own experiences very accurately. And many of these discoveries and statements are of definite scientific worth. But they take too little account of the standard of production reached by the day-to-day routine performances. Large numbers of productions regrettably fail to let the piece speak for itself, obscuring it instead with affected pseudo-experiments. But even in productions tackled honestly, the intentions, while they are valid and could be put into practice, are only partially recognizable. Not enough for the public to understand, though enough for the public to misunderstand. And this is a state of emergency. I dare call it that because it *can* be changed. The theoreticians often get into such complicated aesthetic arguments that those who are supposed to make practical use of them can no longer follow them. They don't know enough about the capacity of a singer's understanding and of his aesthetic awareness, and can therefore not influence the singer's working methods. The singer, on his side, has been discouraged by both his training and his career from being master over his own interpretation, and from using his vocal and physical resources to their limits. He therefore feels that the demands that a progressive opera theatre makes on him are excessive, and that he is at the mercy of the producers and conductors. If he is not encouraged to take responsibility for the conception of a role, and to have the confidence to interpret it accordingly, he is useless as a creative performer. However divergent the conceptions of contemporary opera producers may be, there can be no doubt about their unanimity over the central role played by the singer-actor.

Between the traditional and the new in the art of opera production there is war: especially over the function of the music in the play, and the relationship between the acting and the singing. Isolated battles and their repercussions can even be found in our own workshop. As long as the realistic Music Theatre is imperfect, and cannot convince by action alone, theory is bound to take on greater importance. But if the theory is dictated and formulated only by those who never stand on a stage, then the war will take place without an army to fight it. The training of the singer-actor must include a new subject: he must be made aware of his *creative* task; must have his own views on aesthetic matters; must learn to do his share in the task of turning theory into stage practice.

Perhaps the most serious problem is the split in the performer, his difficulty, sometimes his inability, to bring together his characterization and his vocal technique. I do not speak of lesser talents, or of victims of bad voice production, but of artists whose acting and vocal qualities and intelligence would suffice to make them useful members of a Music Theatre. With helpful guidance they have already proved themselves in this or that role: but for each new role that is studied the same problem again arises. If there is the necessary time, an understanding and patient producer experienced in dealing with singers, and a conductor interested in teaching, then the result, with patient work, may finally be a performance that approximately combines the acting and the singing into a homogeneous whole. But that performance is tied exclusively to the actual production into which it has been rehearsed, and is both in conception and method entirely subject to *that* producer and *that* conductor. If these singers then get into the hands of a producer who blithely follows his own interpretations and steamrollers over their difficulties, if the conductor is solely concerned in producing the sound that he hears in his imagination, there will be complete failure, or the result will be forced and impersonal. In both cases the artist who carries the stage action is placed in a position of uncreative dependence. His memory is put under far too great a strain for him to be able to achieve a credible interpretation of his own, and he can therefore only recite his role. Isolated in his own problem, he neglects his relationship with his partner, or he simulates it. The three deadly sins of the theatre have been committed: personal slavery; recitation; lack of proper relationship with the stage partner. And committed not by an amateur, in which case it would be irrelevant, but, absurdly enough, by somebody who has learnt from experience, and knows the significance of these faults. But he is powerless to remedy them. Thus he impedes his stage partner from aptly interpreting the work for himself, he gets into conflict with the producer, and by trying to do justice to the producer's demands, gets into conflict with the conductor. Depending on the size of his role he either detracts from, or actually endangers, the entire production.

This description fits the majority of singers, even at leading opera houses. And these are particularly gifted artists, in whom it was possible to awaken and foster the instinct for poetry from the very beginning of their training in stage singing. And their great need for self-expression has enabled them to subordinate their vocal technique effortlessly to their interpretation.

But whoever accepts literally that singing in the theatre must be a 'convincing, true and utterly indispensable mode of human expression' must demand that the performer should be a *creative phenomenon*, and must reject any interference in his freedom of expression.

Undoubtedly the cardinal interference in his freedom of expression is the functional split in the singer, caused by the mutually interfering duality of music and acting. And yet it is possible for every singer who has musicality, powers of concentration, average imagination, acting talent, and intelligence, and whose voice is healthy and not maltrained, to acquire the technique of combining a fully expressive interpretation with faultless vocal control, even if he has missed acquiring this technique during his training. It is only a question of his application, and of having a suitable and patient teacher at his disposal in the theatre. He must learn intellectually, and through practical exercises in interpretation, to push the purely physical and phonetic functions of the voice to the back of his mind, so that he is quite free to concentrate on the interpretation. The singing then becomes merely a habit that he can forget about. The exercises must run parallel to his ordinary voice exercises, on which he must cut down progressively, to leave himself free to concentrate on that heightened, poetic 'indispensable mode of expression' which would be unthinkable without music. These exercises, which should preferably cover as wide a range of emotions as possible, should have the effect of enabling the singer to adapt his normal vocal technique to the emotional requirements of the role. They should, in contrast to his purely technical exercises, seek to make the singer averse to producing any sound that is not tied to a definite meaning and feeling. As soon as they are successful, these exercises make his voice more beautiful and expressive, and enable him to achieve a larger vocal range, and greater flexibility, than he could ever attain with technical exercises alone.

Once he has gained this basic attitude it will go against the grain for him merely to memorize the music and text, and know nothing of the deeper significance of the stage action. By becoming conscious of what he is singing for, by seeking to understand why a phrase of music has been written in that way and not in another, he discovers the cause or reason for singing, and begins to recognize the composer's intentions. He can no longer be satisfied with knowing only the vocal score, because he feels its relationship to the orchestral score. A knowledge of the entire score therefore becomes indispensable to him.

This process of self-discovery, and the sense of enrichment and new creativity that stems from it, can find no substitute in even the most brilliant expositions by teacher, producer or conductor who can, and should, only augment it, correct it, deepen it. The search for a cause or reason to sing being now a necessity to him, the danger that his singing will degenerate into mere recitation has been finally overcome. The music is recognized as valid for the theatre, and as a part of the performance as a whole, only if there is evident cause and reason for making a musical statement.

The causes and reasons for singing are naturally various. Sometimes it is the immediate, concrete communication to the stage-partner, sometimes it is contemplation, sometimes a monologue addressed to the imagination or the unconscious expression of some powerful emotional experience. In every case it stems from some particular need for expression, and this will have a decided influence on the function of the voice. But as every single expression is connected to something or other, the singer can never cease in his search. He finds the connecting links between his own role and the action of the play, between himself and the other roles. The *creative individual route* of the singer-actor – so essential to a vital Music Theatre – has been embarked upon. On it he knocks against his colleagues, his producer, his conductor, either provoking them, or gaining experience necessary for putting him on the right track. Either way the conflicts are creative conflicts – unlike those of the ordinary singer who does not enjoy this freedom – through which he is forced to get to know the whole work. This is possible only with the most detailed study of the score, which should not take place in private, but in the presence of the whole cast, before rehearsals commence. Though I confess that, while it is obligatory with us at the Komische Oper, it is generally only possible to gather, at this pre-rehearsal stage, the production and musical teams and a few of the leading singers.

In such an analysis of a work we find out that the information and actions contained in it are not sufficient for getting to know the complete character of a role. We find that the actions and characters become fully recognizable and comprehensible only by learning about the situation that existed *before* the start of the play. This situation we must discover largely from references to it in the score, and must partly augment from conjecture. The amount of imagination used is a question of the artistic responsibility and the taste of the performer.

The situation that existed before the play started produces the relationships of the characters from which stems the action. The characters face each other with their different, sometimes directly opposing, interests and intentions, and by pursuing their interests and intentions alter their relationships to each other. And thus they create new dramatic situations. The singer recognizes that these processes are far more variegated and complicated than they appear from a reading of the text and the score. He recognizes that he is, whether singing or not singing, 'in action' on the stage, the whole time he appears. Only now he learns what is meant by stage action.

It is often pointed out that the term stage action must not be simplified and limited to 'Story' or 'Movement' or 'Content' or 'Play' or 'Action'. But in pointing it out one should not give the impression that one has discovered something new. Stage action, in the most comprehensive sense, is always the basic element in theatre, the force that determines all existence on the stage. And this rule must be adopted in the interpretation of opera, so that opera may gain theatrical validity. One must not claim the concept of stage action as something new for the Music Theatre: that could lead only to mis-understanding and confusion. It would be equally wrong to deny the concept as a valid criterion of the Music Theatre merely because it happens to be a valid criterion in the straight theatre.

The acting singer, the musical performer who has reached that degree of independence, can also no longer neglect his relationship to his partner on the stage – that most important prerequisite for enabling one to believe in what is going on on the stage. He will no longer 'sing at' his stage partner, but rather communicate with him by singing. And any self-indulgent vocal technique, through which so many of his colleagues have lost their artistic consciousness, would be below his dignity. He knows that the beauty of sound that comes from his voice is based only on the truth of the communication that he is making as a human being.

[...]

[I]f conductors acknowledge that the training of an ensemble, in which each member has his own artistic responsibility, is their first and highest duty, then they must participate in, and have influence over, rehearsals from the very beginning, and must conduct all per-formances themselves, and not allow substitutes or guest conductors to take over. During the performance the conductor *alone* is that evening's producer, responsible advocate for the validity and compre-hensibility of that evening's conception, and mentor and friend of each of the creative performers. To put into practice the conception of a collective, and to develop it, requires abilities that even today, when the producer's value is rated too highly, are underestimated on both sides of the footlights to an amazing degree. It is the producer who should be the public's spokesman, from the earliest consultations with the Dramaturg or literary adviser of the theatre, with the conductor, with the designer, and during casting. It is not enough for his conception of the work to be interesting; it must stimulate his musicians, designers and cast, so that their work with him goes far beyond mere obedience.

The conception of a work can come out quite clearly and successfully on the opening night if the intentions of the producer have been duly observed. But it can remain clear and convincing only if during the process of rehearsal the performers have been able to make it their own, and can perform it as their own at each rehearsal. And that can be achieved only by a producer who, independent of his age or maturity, gains the confidence of his colleagues, who disregards his personal likes and dislikes, and who manages to allow the production to develop step by step, making its own discoveries, without demanding effects that have not yet been recognized as necessary or possible. He must have practical stage experience, and know a fair amount about the disciplines of singing, acting and dancing, not in order to show the performers how to do their parts, but so that he is enabled to express the incommunicable. He also must seek to prevent the designer's work from separating itself off. The designer must participate in the original conception of the work, so that he is not tempted into designing *décors*, but rather creates a space that not only makes the realization of the conception possible, but actually promotes it. The designer must also give emphasis optically to the stage action, and encourage the audience to participate in it, and to evaluate its processes correctly. [...]

'Towards Music Theatre', *Opera 66*

Putting flesh on ambitious dreams

Opera in action

'A memory of opera and Handel in 1728'
PIERRE-JACQUES FOUGEROUX

The Opera, which was once negligible, has become a spectacle of some importance in the last three years. They have sent for the best voices [and] the most skilled instrumentalists from Italy, and they have added to them the best from Germany. This has made the cost so great that when I left London people were saying that it would break the Opera. They were only six solo voices, three of whom were excellent – the famous Faustina from Venice, Cuzzoni, and Senesino the famous castrato; two other castratos, Balbi [Baldi] and Palmerini [a bass], and Boschi for the bass, who is as good as an Italian can be for that voice, which is very rare with them. I had previously heard the three good voices in Venice, and as [that was] 12 years ago they were even better than at present. Faustina has a charming voice, with quite a big sound though a little rough, [but] her face and her looks are very ordinary. Cuzzoni, although her voice is weaker, has an enchanting sweetness, with divine coloratura, in the manner of the famous Santine of Venice, who no longer appears on the stage. Up to now Italy has had no finer voices than these two women; Senesino is the very best they have ever had, is a good musician, has a good voice and is a reasonably good actor. They are paying Senesino £1600 sterling (equal to 35,000 francs in French money), and £1600 to each of the two actresses, even though the opera plays only two days a week, on Tuesdays and Saturdays, and stops during Lent. It is an enormous amount, and is the way they acquire all the best voices from Italy.

The orchestra consisted of 24 violins led by the Castrucci brothers, two harpsichords (one of which was played by the German Indel [Handel], a great player and great composer), one archlute, three cellos, two double basses, three bassoons and sometimes flutes and trumpets. This orchestra makes a very loud noise. As there is no middle part in the harmony, the 24 violins usually divide only into firsts and seconds, which sounds extremely brilliant and is beautifully played. The two harpsichords [and] the archlute fill in the middle of the harmony. They use only a cello, the two harpsichords and the archlute to accompany the recitatives. The music is good and thoroughly in the Italian style, although there are some tender pieces in the French style. Handel was the composer of the three operas that I saw. The first was Ptolemy King of Egypt, the second Siroe King of Persia, the third Admetus King of Thessaly. These used old Italian librettos for the texts, and the words had been translated into English verse [and printed] alongside the Italian for the benefit of the ladies. As there is nothing spectacular by way of dancing, scenic decoration or stage machinery, and there are no choruses [i.e. movements for independent choral singers] in the performance* nor that crowd of actors who should adorn the stage, one might say that the name of opera is ill-suited to this spectacle: it is more like a fine concert on the stage.

The auditorium is small and in very poor taste; the stage is quite large, with poor scenery.† There is no amphitheatre, only a pit, with large curved benches right down to the orchestra, where the gentlemen and the ladies are crowded uncomfortably together. The boxes are rented for a whole year. At the back of the auditorium is a curved gallery, which is supported by pillars reaching down to the pit, and is raised to the height of our second tier boxes. This is for the ordinary citizens, and yet you still have to pay 5 shillings, which is 5 francs in French money. Seats in the pit cost half a guinea, equivalent to 11 francs 10. The king has two boxes at the side of the stage, and he came twice with the queen. The princesses were opposite, in another box. Everyone applauds when the king arrives, and cheers when they [the royal party] leave: he had only a couple of guards to protect him. The sides of the stage are decorated with columns, which have mirrors fixed along them with brackets and several candles; the pillars supporting the gallery at the back of the auditorium are similarly fitted. Instead of chandeliers there are ugly wooden candlesticks suspended by strings like those used by tightrope walkers. Nothing could look more wretched, yet there are candles everywhere.

As you are not a lover of Italian music, I hardly dare to tell you, sir, that, apart from the recitative, and the graceless way of accompanying it by cutting short the sound of each chord, there are arias with string accompaniment and wonderfully rich harmony which leave nothing to be desired. The overtures to these operas are what you might call sonatas in fugal style, and very fine they are. I heard a 'sleep' number

---

* There is only a trio or a quartet at the end and [there are only] two duets in the whole opera.
† For the scene-changes they use a bell instead of a whistle.

which imitated those you are familiar with in our operas. One of these overtures included hunting-horns, and so did the chorus at the end,* and this was marvellous.

[...]

You will be surprised, sir, at what I am going to say, that among people of quality, gentlemen and ladies, there are few who are keen on music. They do not know what it is to play together, their only pleasure is drinking a great deal and smoking; you know, sir, how the practice of music in France is turning young people away from debauchery, and how it is being more and more taken up by everyone [...]

They also performed [at Lincoln's Inn Fields Theatre] a kind of comic opera, called the Beggars' Opera, because it is about a band of highwaymen with their Captain; there were only two good actors, and a girl called Fenton who was quite pretty. The orchestra is as bad as the other [at Drury Lane]. It is all ballads with worthless music. People were insisting that the librettist had made references to the present government. They drink all the time, they smoke, and the Captain with eight women who keep him company in prison kisses them a great deal. They were going to hang him in the fifth act, but with money he manages to save himself from the gallows. The opera finishes with that. I would bore you if I told you about the country dances at the end.

from 'Voyage d'Angleterre, d'Hollande, et de Flandre', tr. Donald Burrows and Terence Best, 1994

'The great Gluck spied skipping to it'
ÉTIENNE NICOLAS MÉHUL

I came to Paris in 1779, possessing nothing but my sixteen years, my fiddle, and my optimism. I had a letter of introduction to Gluck: this was my treasure. To see Gluck, to hear him, to talk to him – such was my only desire when I came to the capital, and the thought of it made me tremble with joy. I could scarcely breathe as I rang the doorbell. His wife admitted me, but said that M. Gluck was working and she

* The chorus consists of only four voices.

could not disturb him. My disappointment must have shown in my distressed expression, which touched the worthy lady. She asked about the purpose of my visit. The letter of which I was the bearer came from a friend. I grew confident, I spoke warmly of her husband's work and of the happiness I would have in merely seeing the great man, and Mme Gluck yielded entirely. Smiling, she suggested I might see her husband at work, but without speaking to him and without making the slightest noise.

She then led me to the door of the study from which issued the sound of a harpsichord which Gluck was striking with all his might. The door was opened and closed again without the illustrious artist suspecting that an uninitiated was entering the sanctuary. Here was I, behind a screen, which by good luck was pierced here and there so that my eye could feast on the least movement or the slightest grimace of my Orpheus. His head was covered with a black velvet cap in the German fashion. He wore slippers, his hose were carelessly drawn in to his nether garments, and his only other item of dress was a sort of cotton nightshirt with wide sleeves, which barely reached his belt. I thought him magnificent in these clothes. All the pomp of Louis XIV's attire could not have filled me with such wonder as Gluck's informal dress.

Suddenly I saw him leap from his chair, seize the seats and armchairs, position them around the room to form the wings [of a stage], return to his harpsichord to sound a note, and here he was, holding a corner of his nightshirt in each hand, humming an *air de ballet*, curtseying like a young dancer, performing *glissades* around his chair, leaping and prancing, adopting the poses, gestures, and all the dainty attitudes of a nymph from the Opéra. Then he seemed to want to direct the *corps de ballet*, and as he had insufficient space, he attempted to enlarge his stage; to this end he struck the first leaf of the screen, which unfolded suddenly, and I was discovered. After an explanation, and further visits, Gluck honoured me with his protection and his friendship.

'Desnoiresterres, Gluck et Piccinni', in *Le Ménestrel*, 29 May 1836, quoted in and tr. Patricia Howard, in *Gluck, An Eighteenth-Century Portrait*, 1995

'Idomeneo and Entführung – different styles, same agenda'
WOLFGANG AMADÉE MOZART

Munich, 27 December 1780

Mon très cher Père!

I have received the whole text, Schachtner's letter, your note and the pills. In regard to the two scenes which are to be shortened, it was not my suggestion, but one to which I have consented – my reason being that Raaff and dal Prato spoil the recitative by singing it without any spirit or fire, and *so* monotonously. They are the most wretched actors that ever walked on a stage. I had a desperate row the other day with Seeau about the inexpediency, inconvenience and the practical impossibility of omitting anything. However, everything is to be printed as it is, to which he at first refused *absolument* to agree; but in the end, as I scolded him roundly, he gave in. The last rehearsal was splendid. It took place in a spacious room at Court. The Elector was there too. This time we rehearsed with the whole orchestra (I mean, of course, with as many players as can be accommodated in the opera house). After the first act the Elector called out to me quite loudly, Bravo! When I went up to kiss his hand he said: '*This opera will be charming and cannot fail to do you honour*'. As he was not sure whether he could remain much longer, we had to perform the aria with obbligatos for wind-instruments and the thunderstorm at the beginning of Act II, when he again expressed his approval in the kindest manner and said with a laugh: '*Who would believe that such great things could be hidden in so small a head?*' And the next day at the levée too he praised my opera very highly. The next rehearsal will probably be in the theatre. A propos. Becke told me a few days ago that he had written to you after the last rehearsal but one and among other things had mentioned that Raaff's aria in Act II did not suit the rhythm of the words. '*So I am told*,' he said, '*but I know too little Italian to be able to judge. Is it so?*' I replied, 'If you had only asked me first and written about it afterwards! I should like to tell you that whoever said such a thing knows very little Italian.' The aria is very well adapted to the words. You hear the *mare* and the *mare funesto* and the musical passages suit *minacciar*, for they entirely express *minacciar* (threatening). On the whole it is the most superb aria in the opera and has also won universal approval. Is it true that the Emperor is ill? Is it true that the Archbishop is coming to Munich? To return, Raaff is the best and most honest fellow in the world, but so tied to old-fashioned routine that flesh and blood cannot stand it. Consequently, it is very difficult to compose for him, but very easy if you choose to compose commonplace arias, as, for instance, the first one, 'Vedrommi intorno'. When you hear it, you will say that it is good and beautiful – but if I had written it for Zonca, it would have suited the words much better. Raaff is too fond of everything which is cut and dried, and he pays no attention to expression. I have just had a bad time with him over the quartet. The more I think of this quartet, as it will be performed on the stage, the more effective I consider it; and it has pleased all those who have heard it played on the clavier. Raaff alone thinks it will produce no effect whatever. He said to me when we were by ourselves: 'Non c' è da spianar la voce. It gives me no scope.' As if in a quartet the words should not be spoken much more than sung. That kind of thing he does not understand at all. All I said was: 'My very dear friend, if I knew of one single note which ought to be altered in this quartet, I would alter it at once. But so far there is nothing in my opera with which I am so pleased as with this quartet; and when you have once heard it sung as a whole, you will talk very differently. I have taken great pains to serve you well in your two arias; I shall do the same with your third one – and shall hope to succeed. But as far as trios and quartets are concerned, the composer must have a free hand.' Whereupon he said that he was satisfied. [...]

I have had my black suit turned, for it was really very shabby. Now it looks quite presentable. Adieu. My greetings to all my good friends, and particularly to your beautiful and clever pupil. I embrace my sister with all my heart and kiss your hands a thousand times and am ever your most obedient son

Wolfg: Amd: Mozart

Munich, 30 December 1780

Mon très cher Père!

A Happy New Year! Forgive me for not writing much this time, but I am up to the eyes in work. I have not quite finished the third act, and, as there is no extra ballet, but only an appropriate divertissement in the opera, I have the honour of composing the music for that as well; but I am glad of it, for now all the music will be by the same composer. The third act will turn out to be at least as good as the first two – in fact, I believe, infinitely better – and I think that it may be said with truth, *finis coronat opus*. [...] The day before yesterday we had a rehearsal of recitatives at Wendling's and we went through the quartet together. We repeated it six times and now it goes well. The stumbling-block was dal Prato; the fellow is utterly useless. His voice would not be so bad if he did not produce it in his throat and larynx. But he has no intonation, no method, no feeling, but sings – well, like the best of the boys who come to be tested in the hope of getting a place in the chapel choir. Raaff is delighted that he was mistaken about the quartet and no longer doubts its effect.

Munich, 3 January 1781

Mon très cher Père!

My head and my hands are so full of Act III that it would be no wonder if I were to turn into a third act myself. This fact alone has cost me more trouble than a whole opera, for there is hardly a scene in it which is not extremely interesting. The accompaniment to the subterranean voice consists of five instruments only, that is, three trombones and two French horns, which are placed in the same quarter as that from which the voice proceeds. At this point the whole orchestra is silent. The dress rehearsal will take place *for certain* on January 20th and the first performance on the 22nd.* All you will both require and all that you need bring with you is one black dress – and another, for everyday wear – when you are just visiting intimate friends, where there is no standing on ceremony – so that you may save your black one a little; and, if you like, a more elegant dress to wear at the ball and the académie masquée. I shall tell you about the stove next post-day. I shall probably have to send this letter too by the post. I have told the conductor a hundred times always to send for my letters at eleven o'clock. The coach goes at half past eleven. I never dress before half past twelve, as I have to compose. So I can't go out. I can't send him the letter, for he takes it by private arrangement, as they don't like my doing this at the post office. Herr von Robinig is already here and sends greetings to you both. I hear that the two Barisanis are also coming to Munich. Is this true? Thank God that the cut in the Archbishop's finger was of no consequence. Heavens! How frightened I was at first. Cannabich thanks you for your charming

---

* In the end the first performance did not take place until 29 January.

letter, and the whole family send their greetings. He told me that you had written very humorously. You also must have been in good spirits.

No doubt we shall have a good many points to raise in Act III, when it is staged. For example, in Scene 6, after Arbace's aria, I see that Varesco has Idomeneo, Arbace, etc. How can the latter reappear immediately? Fortunately he can stay away altogether. But for safety's sake I have composed a somewhat longer introduction to the High Priest's recitative. After the mourning chorus the king and all his people go away; and in the following scene the directions are, '*Idomeneo in ginocchione nel tempio*'. That is quite impossible. He must come in with his whole suite. A march must be introduced here, and I have therefore composed a very simple one for two violins, viola, cello and two oboes, to be played *a mezza voce*. While it is going on, the King appears and the priests prepare the offerings for the sacrifice. Then the king kneels down and begins the prayer.

In Elettra's recitative, after the subterranean voice has spoken, there ought to be an indication – *Partono*. I forgot to look at the copy which has been made for the printer to see whether there is one and, if so, where it comes. It seems to me very silly that they should hurry away so quickly for no better reason than to allow Madame Elettra to be alone. I have this moment received your five lines of January 1st.

When I opened the letter I happened to hold it in such a way that nothing but a blank sheet met my eyes. At last I found the writing.

I am delighted to have the aria for Raaff, for he was absolutely determined that I should set to music the words he had found. With a man like Raaff I could not possibly have arranged it in any other way than by having Varesco's aria printed and Raaff's sung. Well, I must close, or I shall waste too much time. I thank my sister most warmly for her New Year wishes, which I cordially return. I hope that we shall soon be able to have some fun together. Adieu. I kiss your hands a thousand times and embrace my sister with all my heart and am ever your most obedient son

Wolfg: Amad: Mozart

My greetings to all my good friends – and please do not forget Rüscherl. Young Eck sends her a little kiss – a sugary one, of course.

Vienna, 12 September 1781

Mon très cher Père!

[...] I think I mentioned the other day that Gluck's 'Iphigenie' is to be given in German and his 'Alceste' in Italian. If only one of the two were to be performed, I should not mind, but both – that is very annoying for me. I will tell you why. The translator of 'Iphigenie' into German is an excellent poet, and I would gladly have given him my Munich opera to translate. I would have altered the part of Idomeneo completely and changed it to a bass part for Fischer. In addition I would have made several other alterations and arranged it more in the French style. Mme Bernasconi, Adamberger and Fischer would have been delighted to sing it, but, as they now have two operas to study, and such exhausting ones, I am obliged to excuse them. Besides, a third opera would be too much.

I must now hurry off to Marchall (for I have promised to introduce him to Count Cobenzl), or I shall be too late. Now farewell.

Vienna, 26 September 1781

Mon très cher Père!

Forgive me for having made you pay an extra heavy postage fee the other day. But I happened to have nothing important to tell you and thought that it would afford you pleasure if I gave you some idea of my opera. As the original text began with a monologue,[*] I asked Herr Stephanie to make a little arietta out of it – and then to put in a duet instead of making the two chatter together after Osmin's short song.[†] As we have given the part of Osmin to Herr Fischer, who certainly has an excellent bass voice (in spite of the fact that the Archbishop told me that he sang too low for a bass and that I assured him that he would sing higher next time), we must take advantage of it, particularly as he has the whole Viennese public on his side. But in the original libretto Osmin has only this short song and nothing else to sing, except in the trio and the finale; so he has been given an aria in Act I, and he is to have another in Act II. I have explained to Stephanie the words I require for the aria[‡] – indeed I had finished composing most of the

---

[*] In the original text by C. F. Bretzner.
[†] It is worthy of note that the part of Osmin, which in Bretzner's libretto is negligible, was transformed by Mozart in collaboration with Stephanie into the towering figure in *Die Entführung*. Possibly Mozart was encouraged to do this as he was composing for a magnificent singer.
[‡] 'Solche hergelaufne Laffen' in Act I.

music for it before Stephanie knew anything whatever about it. I am enclosing only the beginning and the end, which is bound to have a good effect. Osmin's rage is rendered comical by the use of the Turkish music. In working out the aria I have (in spite of our Salzburg Midas)* allowed Fischer's beautiful deep notes to glow. The passage 'Drum beim Barte des Propheten' is indeed in the same tempo, but with quick notes; and as Osmin's rage gradually increases, there comes (just when the aria seems to be at an end) the allegro assai, which is in a totally different metre and in a different key; this is bound to be very effective. For just as a man in such a towering rage oversteps all the bounds of order, moderation and propriety and completely forgets himself, so must the music too forget itself. But since passions, whether violent or not, must never be expressed to the point of exciting disgust, and as music, even in the most terrible situations, must never offend the ear, but must please the listener, or in other words must never cease to be *music*, so I have not chosen a key foreign to F (in which the aria is written) but one related to it – not the nearest, D minor, but the more remote A minor. Let me now turn to Belmonte's aria in A major, 'O wie ängstlich, o wie feurig'. Would you like to know how I have expressed it – and even indicated his throbbing heart? By the two violins playing octaves. This is the favourite aria of all those who have heard it, and it is mine also. I wrote it expressly to suit Adamberger's voice. You see the trembling – the faltering – you see how his throbbing breast begins to swell; this I have expressed by a crescendo. You hear the whispering and the sighing – which I have indicated by the first violins with mutes and a flute playing in unison.

The Janissary chorus is, as such, all that can be desired, that is, short, lively and written to please the Viennese. I have sacrificed Constanze's aria a little to the flexible throat of Mlle Cavalieri, 'Trennung war mein banges Los und nun schwimmt mein Aug' in Tränen'. I have tried to express her feelings, as far as an Italian bravura aria will allow it. I have changed the 'Hui' to 'schnell', so it now runs thus – 'Doch wie schnell schwand meine Freude'. I really don't know what our German poets are thinking of. Even if they do not understand the theatre, or at all events operas, yet they should not make their characters talk as if they were addressing a herd of swine. Hui, sow!

* i.e. the Archbishop.

Now for the trio at the close of Act I. Pedrillo has passed off his master as an architect – to give him an opportunity of meeting his Constanze in the garden. Bassa Selim has taken him into his service. Osmin, the steward, knows nothing of this, and being a rude churl and a sworn foe to all strangers, is impertinent and refuses to let them into the garden. It opens quite abruptly – and because the words lend themselves to it, I have made it a fairly respectable piece of real three-part writing. Then the major key begins at once pianissimo – it must go very quickly – and wind up with a great deal of noise, which is always appropriate at the end of an act. The more noise the better, and the shorter the better, so that the audience may not have time to cool down with their applause.

I have sent you only fourteen bars of the overture, which is very short with alternate fortes and pianos, the Turkish music always coming in at the fortes. The overture modulates through different keys; and I doubt whether anyone, even if his previous night has been a sleepless one, could go to sleep over it. Now comes the rub! The first act was finished more than three weeks ago, as was also one aria in Act II and the drunken duet* (*per i signori viennesi*) which consists entirely of *my Turkish tattoo*. But I cannot compose any more, because the whole story is being altered – and, to tell the truth, at my own request. At the beginning of Act III there is a charming quintet or rather finale, but I should prefer to have it at the end of Act II.† In order to make this practicable, great changes must be made, in fact an entirely new plot must be introduced – and Stephanie is up to the eyes in other work. So we must have a little patience. Everyone abuses Stephanie. It may be that in my case he is only very friendly to my face. But after all he is arranging the libretto for me – and, what is more, as I want it – exactly – and, by Heaven, I do not ask anything more of him. Well, how I have been chattering to you about my opera! But I cannot help it. Please send me the march‡ which I mentioned the other day.§ Gilowsky says that Daubrawaick will soon be here. Fräulein von Auernhammer and I are longing to have the two double concertos. I hope we shall not wait as vainly as the Jews for their

---

* The duet between Pedrillo and Osmin, 'Vivat Bacchus, Bacchus lebe'.
† This is the quartet at the end of Act II, 'Ach Belmonte! ach – mein Leben!'
‡ Possibly K. 249, written in 1776 for the wedding of Elizabeth Haffner to F. X. Späth, for which Mozart also composed K. 250 [248b], the Haffner serenade.
§ The letter in which Mozart made this request has unfortunately been lost.

Messiah. Well, adieu. Farewell. I kiss your hands a thousand times and embrace with all my heart my dear sister, whose health, I hope, is improving, and am ever your most obedient son

W. A. Mozart

The Letters of Mozart and his family, tr. Emily Anderson

'How I stood up to the little guy for the sake of his *Figaro*'
MICHAEL KELLY

There was a very excellent company of German singers at the Canatore Theatre; it was more spacious than the Imperial Court Theatre. The first female siger was Madame Lange, wife to the excellent comedian of that name, and sister to Madame Mozart. She was a wonderful favourite, and deservedly so; she had a greater extent of high notes than any other singer I ever heard. The songs which Mozart composed for her in L'Enlèvement du Sérail, show what a compass of voice she had; her execution was most brilliant. Stephen Storace told me it was far beyond that of Bastardini, who was engaged to sing at the Pantheon in London, and who, for each night of her performance, of two songs, received one hundred guineas, an enormous sum at that time; and (comparatively speaking) more than two hundred at the present day.

A number of foreign Princes, among whom were the Duc de Deux Ponts, the Elector of Bavaria, &c., with great retinues, came to visit the Emperor, who, upon this occasion, signified his wish to have two grand serious operas, both the composition of Chevalier Gluck; – 'L'Iphigenia in Tauride,' and 'L'Alceste', produced under the direction of the composer; and gave orders that no expense should be spared to give them every effect.

Gluck was then living at Vienna, where he had retired, crowned with professional honours, and a splendid fortune, courted and caressed by all ranks, and in his seventy-fourth year.

L'Iphigenia was the first opera to be produced, and Gluck was to make his choice of the performers in it. Madame Bernasconi was one of the first serious singers of the day, – to her was appropriated the part of Iphigenia. The celebrated tenor, Ademberger [*sic*], performed the part of Orestes, finely. To me was allotted the character of Pylades, which created no small envy among those performers who thought themselves better entitled to the part than myself, and perhaps they were right; – however, I had it, and also the high gratification of being instructed in the part by the composer himself.

One morning, after I had been singing with him, he said, 'Follow me up stairs, Sir, and I will introduce you to one, whom, all my life, I have made my study, and endeavoured to imitate.' I followed him into his bed-room, and, opposite to the head of the bed, saw a full-length picture of Handel, in a rich frame. 'There, Sir,' said he, 'is the portrait of the inspired master of our art; when I open my eyes in the morning, I look upon him with reverential awe, and acknowledge him as such, and the highest praise is due to your country for having distinguished and cherished his gigantic genius.'

L'Iphigenia was soon put into rehearsal, and a corps de ballet engaged for the incidental dances belonging to the piece. The ballet master was Monsieur De Camp, the uncle of that excellent actress, and accomplished and deserving woman, Mrs Charles Kemble. Gluck superintended the rehearsals, with his powdered wig, and gold-headed cane; the orchestra and choruses were augmented, and all the parts were well filled.

The second opera was Alceste, which was got up with magnificence and splendour, worthy an Imperial Court.

For describing the strongest passions in music, and proving grand dramatic effect, in my opinion, no man ever equalled Gluck – he was a great painter of music; perhaps the expression is far fetched, and may not be allowable, but I speak from my own feelings, and the sensation his descriptive music always produced on me. For example, I never could hear, without tears, the dream of Orestes, in Iphigenia: when in sleep, he prays the gods to give a ray of peace to the parricide Orestes. What can be more expressive of deep and dark despair? – And the fine chorus of the demons who surround his couch, with the ghost of his mother, produced in me a feeling of horror, mixed with delight.

Dr Burney (no mean authority) said, Gluck was the Michael Angelo of living composers, and called him the simplifying musician. Salieri told me that a comic opera of Gluck's being performed at the Elector Palatine's theatre, at Schwetzingen, his Electoral Highness was struck with the music, and inquired who had composed it; on being informed that he was an honest German who loved *old wine*, his Highness immediately ordered him a tun of Hock.

Paesiello's Barbiere di Siviglia, which he composed in Russia, and brought with him to Vienna, was got up; Signor Mandini and I played the part of Count Almaviva alternately; Storace was the Rosina. There were three operas now on the tapis, one by Rigini, another by Salieri (the Grotto of Trophonius), and one by Mozart, by special command of the Emperor. Mozart chose to have Beaumarchais' French comedy, 'Le Mariage de Figaro', made into an Italian opera, which was done with great ability, by Da Ponte. These three pieces were nearly ready for representation at the same time, and each composer claimed the right of producing his opera for the first. The contest raised much discord, and parties were formed. The characters of the three men were all very different. Mozart was as touchy as gunpowder, and swore he would put the score of his opera into the fire if it was not produced first; his claim was backed by a strong party: on the contrary, Rigini was working like a mole in the dark to get precedence.

The third candidate was Maestro di Cappella to the court, a clever shrewd man, possessed of what Bacon called, crooked wisdom; and his claims were backed by three of the principal performers, who formed a cabal not easily put down. Every one of the opera company took part in the contest. I alone was a stickler for Mozart, and naturally enough, for he had a claim on my warmest wishes, from my adoration of his powerful genius, and the debt of gratitude I owed him, for many personal favours.

The mighty contest was put an end to by His Majesty issuing a mandate for Mozart's 'Nozze di Figaro', to be instantly put into rehearsal; and none more than Michael O'Kelly, enjoyed the little great man's triumph over his rivals.

Of all the performers in this opera at that time, but one survives – myself. It was allowed that never was opera stronger cast. I have seen it performed at different periods in other countries, and well too, but no more to compare with its original performance than light is to darkness. All the original performers had the advantage of the instruction of the composer, who transfused into their minds his inspired meaning. I never shall forget his little animated countenance, when lighted up with the glowing rays of genius; – it is as impossible to describe it, as it would be to paint sun-beams.

I called on him one evening; he said to me, 'I have just finished a little duet for my opera, you shall hear it.' He sat down to the piano, and we sang it. I was delighted with it, and the musical world will give me credit for being so, when I mention the duet, sung by Count Almaviva and Susan, 'Crudel perchè finora farmi languire così.' A more delicious morceau never was penned by man, and it has often been a source of pleasure to me to have been the first who heard it, and to have sung it with its greatly gifted composer. I remembered at the first rehearsal of the full band, Mozart was on the stage with his crimson pelisse and gold-laced cocked hat, giving the time of the music to the orchestra. Figaro's song, 'Non più andrai, farfallone amoroso', Bennuci gave, with the greatest animation, and power of voice.

I was standing close to Mozart, who, *sotto voce*, was repeating, Bravo! Bravo! Bennuci; and when Bennuci came to the fine passage, 'Cherubino, alla vittoria, alla gloria militar', which he gave out with Stentorian lungs, the effect was electricity itself, for the whole of the performers on the stage, and those in the orchestra, as if actuated by one feeling of delight, vociferated Bravo! Bravo! Maestro. Viva, viva, grande Mozart. Those in the orchestra I thought would never have ceased applauding, by beating the bows of their violins against the music desks. The little man acknowledged, by repeated obeisances, his thanks for the distinguished mark of enthusiastic applause bestowed upon him.

The same meed of approbation was given to the finale at the end of the first act; that piece of music alone, in my humble opinion, if he had never composed any thing else good, would have stamped him as the greatest master of his art. In the sestetto, in the second act, (which was Mozart's favourite piece of the whole opera,) I had a very conspicuous part, as the Stuttering Judge. All through the piece I was to stutter; but in the sestetto, Mozart requested I would not, for if I did, I should spoil his music. I told him, that although it might appear very presumptuous in a lad like me to differ with him on this point, I did; and was sure, the way in which I intended to introduce the stuttering, would not interfere with the other parts, but produce an effect; besides, it certainly was not in nature, that I should stutter all through the part, and when I came to the sestetto speak plain; and after that piece of music was over, return to stuttering; and, I added, (apologizing at the same time, for my apparent want of deference and respect in placing my opinion in opposition to that of the great Mozart,) that unless I was allowed to perform the part as I wished, I would not perform it at all.

Mozart at last consented that I should have my own way, but doubted the success of the experiment. Crowded houses proved that nothing ever on the stage produced a more powerful effect; the audience were convulsed with laughter, in which Mozart himself joined. The Emperor repeatedly cried out Bravo! and the piece was loudly applauded and encored. When the opera was over, Mozart came on the stage to me, and shaking me by both hands, said, 'Bravo! young man, I feel obliged to you; and acknowledge you to have been in the right, and myself in the wrong.' There was certainly a risk run, but I felt within myself I could give the effect I wished, and the event proved that I was not mistaken.

I have seen the opera in London, and elsewhere, and never saw the judge pourtrayed as a stutterer, and the scene was often totally omitted. I played it as a stupid old man, though at the time I was a beardless stripling. At the end of the opera, I thought the audience would never have done applauding and calling for Mozart; almost every piece was encored, which prolonged it nearly to the length of two operas, and induced the Emperor to issue an order on the second representation, that no piece of music should be encored. Never was any thing more complete, than the triumph of Mozart, and his 'Nozze de Figaro', to which numerous overflowing audiences bore witness. (I was not aware at that time of what I have since found to be the fact, that those who labour under the defect of stuttering while speaking, articulate distinctly in singing. That excellent bass, Sedgwick, was an instance of it; and the beautiful Mrs Inchbald, the authoress, another.)

Reminiscences of Michael Kelly, 1826

'Meeting the happy challenge of Mozart and Da Ponte'
PETER SELLARS

We were allowed three operas from these ideal collaborators. Overconfident after the spectacular success of *Figaro*, they badly misjudged what would be permissible in *Don Giovanni*, that drama of souls in darkness crying out for light, which offended against the artistic and societal behavioral norms of the Viennese Court. They didn't quite pull it off. Censorship moved in, and such performances as were allowed were already compromised. With *Così*, these men were already on the way out, and the inwardness and extreme elaboration of that piece reflects the sense that private necessity has overtaken public address. It was the end. Da Ponte's life meandered off again into a string of silly little adventures which brought him to America. The Viennese Court never again allowed Mozart access to the large forms and forces of which he was master and for which he hungered. His final operatic masterpieces were created for his beloved left-wing city of Prague, and for a little summer theater in the suburbs.

PepsiCo Summerfare programme, 1989

'A paean to the wonders of true castrato stars'
RICHARD MOUNT EDGCUMBE

In the season of 1778 and 1779, arrived Pacchierotti, decidedly, in my opinion, the most perfect singer it ever fell to my lot to hear. I must enter into some detail respecting him.

Pacchierotti's voice was an extensive soprano, full and sweet in the highest degree; his powers of execution were great, but he had far too good taste and too good sense to make a display of them where it would have been misapplied, confining it to one bravura song (aria di agilità) in each opera, conscious that the chief delight of singing, and his own supreme excellence, lay in touching expression, and exquisite pathos. Yet he was so thorough a musician that nothing came amiss to him; every style was to him equally easy, and he could sing, at first sight, all songs of the most opposite characters, not merely with the facility and correctness which a complete knowledge of music must give, but entering at once into the views of the composer, and giving them all the appropriate spirit and expression. Such was his genius in his embellishments and cadences, that their variety was inexhaustible. He could not sing a song twice in exactly the same way; yet never did introduce an ornament that was not judicious, and appropriate to the composition. His shake, then considered an indispensible requisite, without which no one could be esteemed a perfect singer, was the very best that could be heard in every form in which that grace can be executed: whether taken from above or below, between whole or semi-tones, fast or slow, it was always open, equal, and distinct, giving the greatest brilliancy to his cadences, and often introduced into his

passages with the happiest effect* As an actor, with many disadvantages of person, for he was tall and awkward in his figure, and
his features were plain, he was nevertheless forcible and impressive: for
he felt warmly, had excellent judgment, and was an enthusiast in his
profession. His recitative was inimitably fine, so that even those who
did not understand the language could not fail to comprehend, from
his countenance, voice, and action, every sentiment he expressed. As a
concert singer, and particularly in private society, he shone almost
more than on the stage; for he sung with greater spirit in a small circle
of friends, and was more gratified with their applause, than in a public
concert room, or crowded theatre. I was in the habit of so hearing him
most frequently, and having been intimately acquainted with him for
many years, am enabled to speak thus minutely of his performance. On
such occasions he would give way to his fancy, and seem almost
inspired: and I have often seen his auditors, even those the least
musical, moved to tears while he was singing. Possessing a very large
collection of music he could give an infinite variety of songs by every
master of reputation. I have more than once heard him sing a cantata
of Haydn's, called Arianna a Naxos, composed for a single voice with
only a pianoforte accompaniment, and that was played by Haydn
himself: it is needless to say the performance was perfect. To this detail
of his merits and peculiar qualities as a singer, I must add that he was a
worthy, good man, modest and diffident even to a fault; for it was to an
excess that at times checked his exertions, and made him dissatisfied
with himself, when he had given the greatest delight to his hearers. He
was unpresuming in his manners, grateful and attached to all his
numerous friends and patrons.

The first appearance of Pacchierotti in this country was in
Demofoonte (a pasticcio), in which he sung four songs in different
styles, by as many different composers, which shewed his versatile
talents to the greatest advantage, and at once established his
reputation. [. . .]

To speak more minutely of Velluti. This singer is no longer young,
and his voice is in decay. It seems to have had considerable compass,

---

* This, perhaps the most beautiful of graces, is now entirely lost in Italy: not one singer
of that country so much as attempts it. From the English it still is heard, and often in
great perfection.

but has failed (which is extraordinary) in its middle tones, many of which are harsh and grating to the ear. Some of his upper notes are still exquisitely sweet, and he frequently dwells on, swells, and diminishes them with delightful effect. His lower notes too are full and mellow, and he displays considerable art in descending from the one to the other by passages ingeniously contrived to avoid those which he knows to be defective. His manner is florid without extravagance, his embellishments (many of which were new to me) tasteful and neatly executed. His general style is the *grazioso*, with infinite delicacy and a great deal of expression, but never rising to the grand, simple, and dignified *cantabile* of the old school, still less to the least approach towards the *bravura*. He evidently has no other, therefore there is a great want of variety in his performance, as well as a total deficiency of force and spirit. Of the great singers mentioned before, he most resembles Pacchierotti, in one only, and that the lowest of his styles, but cannot be compared to him in excellence even in this. He is also somewhat like him in figure, but far better looking; in his youth he was reckoned remarkably handsome. On the whole, there is much to approve and admire in his performance, and I can readily believe that in his prime he was not unworthy of the reputation he has attained in Italy. Even here, under so many disadvantages, he produced considerable effect, and overcame much of the prejudice raised against him. To the old he brought back some pleasing recollections; others, to whom his voice was new, became reconciled to it, and sensible of his merits, whilst many declared that to the last his tones gave them more pain than pleasure. However, either from curiosity or real admiration, he drew crowded audiences.

'Musical Reminiscences', the *London Review*, April 1835

'What opera has been and what it should be'
THOMAS LOVE PEACOCK

Lord Mount Edgcumbe's Reminiscences extend over a period of sixty years – a term nearly equivalent to one-half of the entire existence of the Italian Opera in England; and in the conclusion of them he thinks that, in every point of view – music, poetry, singers, audience – the

Italian theatre in England has changed for the worse. 'First impressions,' he says, 'are the most lasting.' This is true; and they are also the most agreeable. [...]

The object proposed by the Italian Opera is to present the musical drama in the most perfect possible form. To this end there must be, in the first place, a good drama: an interesting story, intelligibly told in good poetry, and affording ample scope for strong and diversified expression: good music, adapting the sound to the sense, and expressing all the changes and trains of feeling that belong to the ideas and images of the drama: good performers – persons of good figures and features – picturesque in action, and expressive in countenance – with voices of fine tone and great power, having true intonation, scientific execution, and above all, or rather as the crown of all, expression – expression – expression: the one all-pervading and paramount quality, without which dramatic music is but as a tinkling cymbal: elegant and appropriate dresses – beautiful scenery – a chorus, each of whom should seem as if he knew that he had some business of his own in the scene, and not as if he were a mere unit among thirty or forty automata, all going like clock-work by the vibrations of the conductor's pendulum: a full orchestra of accomplished musicians, with a good leader – and especially without a conductor keeping up, in the very centre of observation, a gesticulation and a *tapage* that make him at once the most conspicuous and most noisy personage in the assembly, distracting attention from the sights and sounds that ought exclusively to occupy it – an affliction to the eye, and a most pestilent nuisance to the ear. But, with all this, there should be (as there used to be) an audience regulating its costume and its conduct by the common conventional courtesies of evening society; not with men wearing hats among well-dressed women, and rubbing dirty boots against white petticoats; nor with an influx of late comers, squeezing themselves between the crowded benches, and sitting down in the laps of their precursors, as we have both seen and suffered. We are aware that some advocates for universal liberty think that the morning liberty of the streets should be carried into all evening assemblies; but, looking back to the Athenians, we cannot consider that cleanliness and courtesy are incompatible with the progress of freedom and intelligence.

Now, by following out the principal points which we have enumerated a little in detail, we shall see what we have had, and what we have wanted – what we are likely to have, and what we are likely to continue to want – for the bringing together of the constituent portions of a perfect musical drama. Lord Mount Edgcumbe touches all these points [. . .]:–

The opera in England, for the period of ten years after the departure of Catalani, will afford much less room for observation than any of the preceding, as far as the singers are concerned; for, with one or two exceptions, there were not any of whom I feel inclined to say much, because there is not much to be said in their praise. But so great a change has taken place in the character of the dramas, in the style of the music, and in its performance, that I cannot help enlarging a little on that subject before I proceed farther.

One of the most material alterations is, that the grand distinction between serious and comic operas is nearly at an end, the separation of the singers for their performance entirely so. Not only do the same sing in both, but a new species of drama has arisen, a kind of mongrel between them, called *semi-seria*, which bears the same analogy to the other two that that non-descript the melo-drama does to the legitimate tragedy and comedy of the English stage. The construction of these newly-invented pieces is essentially different from the old. The dialogue, which used to be carried on in recitative, and which in Metastasio's operas is often so beautiful and interesting, is now cut up (and rendered unintelligible if it were worth listening to) into *pezzi concertati*, or long singing conversations, which present a tedious succession of unconnected, ever-changing motivos, having nothing to do with each other, and if a satisfactory air is for a moment introduced, which the ear would like to dwell upon, to hear modulated, varied, and again returned to, it is broken off before it is well understood or sufficiently heard, by a sudden transition into a totally different melody, time, and key, and recurs no more: so that no impression can be made, or recollection of it preserved. Single songs are almost exploded, for which one good reason may be given, that there are few singers capable of singing them. Even a prima donna, who would formerly have complained at having less than three or four airs allotted to her, is now satisfied with one trifling cavatina for a whole opera.

The acknowledged decline of singing in general (which the Italians themselves are obliged to confess) has no doubt, in a great measure, occasioned this change. But another cause has certainly contributed to it, and that is the difference of the voices of the male performers. Sopranos have long ceased to exist, but tenors for a long while filled their place. Now even these have become so scarce, that Italy can produce no more than two or three very good ones. The generality of voices are basses, which, for want of better, are thrust up into the first characters, even in serious operas, where they used only to occupy the last place, to the manifest injury of melody, and total subversion of harmony, in which the lowest part is their peculiar province.

These new first singers are called by the novel appellation of *basso cantante* (which, by the bye, is a kind of apology, and an acknowledgment that they ought not to sing), and take the lead in operas with almost as much propriety as if the double bass were to do so in the orchestra, and play the part of the first fiddle. A bass voice is too unbending, and deficient in sweetness for single songs, and fit only for those of inferior character, or of the buffo style. In duettos, it does not coalesce well with a female voice, on account of the too great distance between them, and in fuller pieces the ear cannot be satisfied without some good intermediate voices to fill up the interval, and complete the harmony. Yet three or four basses now frequently overpower one weak tenor, who generally plays but a subordinate part.

[...]

The business ... of the lyrical dramatist is to present, with the most perfect simplicity, the leading and natural ideas of an impassioned action, divested of all imagery not arising from spontaneous feeling. A heroine in distress must neither demonstrate her misery by an accumulation of evidence, as in an old French tragedy, nor dress it out in a complication of heterogeneous figures, as in a modern English song, in which everything is illustrated by a chaos of images which never met in the organized world: for instance, in a Venetian serenade, in the opera of *Faustus* –

> Lucy dear, Lucy dear, wake to the spring,
> Hark! how the village-bells merrily ring.

Village bells in Venice! and, moreover, peculiar to the spring – a sort of tintinnabulary efflorescence, characteristic of the season, like the cowslip and the cuckoo! [...]

The poetry of the Italian Opera is quite the contrary of all this. It gives, with little or no ornament, the language of passion in its simplest form: a clear and strong outline to be filled up by the music: which is itself the legitimate ornament and illustration of the leading ideas and sentiments of the scene. The essentials of style, in the composition of dramatic poetry for music, are simplicity and severity. It may be said, that the same rhymes and phrases are of constant recurrence; but though they are the same to read, they are not the same to hear. The cor and amor, fedeltà and felicità, of *Desdemona*, are not those of *Medea*. The music paints the difference. There is nothing in any Italian libretto at all resembling the egregious rigmarol of our modern English songs.

[...]

Our old English songs were models of simplicity, but our modern songs are almost all false sentiment, overwhelmed with imagery utterly false to nature, like the night-flowers and solitary-celled monsters quoted above. Mr Moore, with his everlasting 'brilliant and sparkling' metaphors, has contributed to lead the *servum pecus* into this limbo of poetical vanity: but the original cause lies deeper: namely, in a very general diffusion of heartlessness and false pretension. We will not now pursue the investigation – but as we are speaking of English theatrical songs, we will observe, that the introduction, always objectionable, of airs not belonging to the piece, is nevertheless usually managed on the Italian stage with a certain degree of contrivance, and fitted by a new scena into the business of the drama. The same thing is done in English operas, in a manner marvellously clumsy and inartificial. For instance, Henry Bertram, in *Guy Mannering*, loses his way among rocks, expects to be attacked by thieves – resolves to fight manfully – recollects how manfully Nelson fought at Trafalgar, and strikes up – "Twas in Trafalgar bay!' [...]

Lord Mount Edgcumbe quotes a passage from Schlegel's Lectures:–

A few only of the operas of Metastasio still keep possession of the stage, as the change of taste in music demands a different arrangement of the text. Metastasio seldom has chorusses, and his airs are almost always for a single voice: with these the scenes uniformly terminate, and the singer never fails to make his exit with them. In an opera we now require more frequent duos and trios, and a *crashing* finale. In fact, the most difficult problem for the opera poet is the mixing the complicated voices of conflicting passions in one common harmony, without injuring their essence: a problem however which is generally solved by both poet and musical composer in a very arbitrary manner.

and adds –

The consequence of this is that all the new dramas written for Rossini's music are most execrably bad, and contain scarcely one line that can be called poetry, or even one of common sense.

This sweeping condemnation is by no means merited. Some of Rossini's libretti are detestable enough; but there is much good dramatic poetry in some of them, *Tancredi* and *Semiramide* especially. It is true, that in these dramas the Italian poet had only to condense the essence of Voltaire's tragedies, but the task is well executed. The libretto of Donizetti's *Anna Bolena* is an excellent dramatic poem.

It is seldom that we are enabled to judge fairly either of an Italian libretto, or of the music of an opera as a whole. For example, in 1832 Mr Monck Mason professed to bring forward Pacini's *Gli Arabi nelle*

Gallie. He first cut it into halves, and put the second half aside, or into the fire. He then cut away the beginning and substituted that of Rossini's *Zelmira*. He then tacked a strange air, we forget from whence, to the middle, by way of an end, and thus presented to the public both author and composer literally without head or tail. The critics discovered that the drama was nonsense, and that much of the music was stolen; and Pacini and his poet bore the blame which belonged to the manager. This mode of murdering reputations ought to subject the offender to an action for damages. 'I was induced, unfortunately,' says Lord Mount Edgcumbe, 'to go one night to see *Gli Arabi nelle Gallie*, a very poor opera by Pacini.' What he saw was poor enough, but it was not Pacini's opera. In the same season Bellini's *La Straniera*, which has much beautiful melody, and an interesting and intelligible story, founded on the Vicomte d'Arlincourt's *L'Etrangère*, was presented in such a chaotic fashion, that the intentions of both poet and composer remained an unfathomable mystery.

These liberties are taken more or less with the works of all masters, from the greatest to the least. Mozart himself does not escape them. Interpolation indeed he does escape. The audiences of the King's Theatre are justly strict in this one point only, that they will not permit the sewing on of an extraneous purple shred to any of his great and sacred textures. But garbled and mutilated his works are abominably, to fit the Procrustean bed of an inadequate company, or to quadrate with the manager's notions of the bad taste of the public. A striking instance of this is in the invariable performance of *Il Don Giovanni* without its concluding sestetto. Don Juan's first introduction to a modern English audience was in a pantomime (at Drury Lane we believe), which ended with the infernal regions, a shower of fire, and a dance of devils. Mozart's opera has, properly, no such conclusion. Flames arise – a subterranean chorus is heard – Don Juan sinks into the abyss – the ground closes above him – Leporello remains on the stage: a strongly marked modulation leads from the key of D minor into that of G major, with a change from common time andante to triple time allegro assai; and the other characters, ignorant of the catastrophe, rush in to seek their revenge: –

> Ah! dov' è il perfido,
> Dov' è l'indegno? &c.

Leporello explains the adventure, and after a general exclamation, a solemn pause, and an exceedingly sweet larghetto movement, in which the dramatis personæ dispose of themselves, 'Or che tutti, o mio tesoro,' the opera is wound up by a fugue in D major – 'Questo è il fin di chi fa mal': one of the very finest things in dramatic music, and the most appropriate possible termination of the subject; and yet is this most noble composition, this most fitting and genuine conclusion, sacrificed to a dance of devils flashing torches of rosin, for no earthly reason but that so ended the Drury Lane pantomime.

Le Nozze di Figaro and *Il Flauto Magico* both require a better and more numerous company than is ever assembled in this country. If we have in the former an Almaviva, a Figaro, a Contessa and a Susanna, it is the usual extent of our good fortune. We have seldom an endurable Cherubino; Marcellina is generally a nonentity: Barbarina always so; Bartolo, Basilio, and Antonio take their chance, which is seldom good for any of them, and never for all; and Don Curzio is for the most part abrogated.

Il Don Giovanni and *Le Nozze di Figaro* are both specimens of excellently-written libretti, separating most effectively the action and passion from the ratiocination of the originals; but we have seen the latter especially performed in such a manner, that if we had known nothing of it but from the representation, we should have found it incomprehensible; and this sort of experiment on things which we know well should make us cautious of pronouncing summary judgment on things of which we know nothing but from the showing of the King's Theatre.

Il Flauto Magico is a well-written libretto, but the subject is too mystical to be interesting, or even generally intelligible; and this is a great drawback on its theatrical popularity, which has never approached that of the *Giovanni* and *Figaro*, though the music exhausts all the fascinations of both melody and harmony, and may be unhesitatingly cited as the absolute perfection of both. It requires more good singers than either of the others, and it requires them the more imperatively, as it depends more exclusively on the music. It requires seventeen voices besides the chorus. The music which is assigned to the three nymphs and the three genii is almost supernaturally beautiful: for this alone there should be six good voices, and there are, without these, six principal and five secondary parts. We may therefore despair of ever hearing this opera performed as it ought to be.

The works of Italian composers do not require, in any instance that we remember, so many performers. Those of the most modern composer of any name – Bellini – are singularly restricted in their principal parts. He seems to endeavour to defend himself against the caprices and jealousies of the performers by giving them nothing to quarrel about. A prima soprano, a primo tenore, a primo basso, and the ordinary components of a chorus, can perform his *Pirata*. There can be no dispute here about pre-eminence, but the general effect is necessarily meagre. But the progress of self-conceit among singers has made this result inevitable. A prima soprano is now to be found everywhere, and a seconda nowhere; and though many who assume to be first are scarcely fit to be second, they will not be content with what they are fit for, but will be first or nothing. There appears to be this great difference between a German and an Italian company – that the Germans will co-operate to the production of general effect, and the Italians will look to nothing but their own individual display. We have seen, in a German opera, the same person taking a principal part one night, and singing in the chorus the next. We have seen the same with the French; but with the Italians this never occurs. A German author and composer may therefore give fair scope to their subject; but the Italians must sacrifice everything to their company, and all in vain, except for the first production – for to the whims and inefficiency of every new company the unfortunate opera must be refitted and garbled. Bellini's is the true plan for his own reputation. A soprano, a tenor, a bass, and a chorus, there must be in every company, and they can have nothing to quarrel for; but the musical drama must be ruined if this were to become the rule of its construction. And the scheme, after all, is not always successful: for in 1830 the prima donna transposed the middle and end of *Il Pirata*, in order that she might finish it herself instead of the tenor.

'Ma femme, et cinq ou six poupets,' will not make a company in the opinion of any one but Catalani's husband. No one, indeed, who has seen and heard Catalani, or Pasta, or Malibran, or Giulietta Grisi, would willingly dispense with one such prima donna; but the single star should not be worshipped exclusively to the sacrifice of the general effect. She can be but a component, however important, part of it; and if the general effect fails, the star will fall.

[...]

We do not agree in opinion with Lord Mount Edgcumbe that the decline of singing in Italy has conduced to the composition of melodramas and the frequency of pezzi concertati. There has been an increase of excitement in the world of reality, and that of imagination has kept it company. The ordinary stage deserted the legitimate drama for melo-drama before the musical stage did so. The public taste has changed, and the supply of the market has followed the demand. There can be no question that Rossini's music is more spirit-stirring than Paësiello's, and more essentially theatrical: more suited to the theatre by its infinite variety of contrast and combination, and more dependent on the theatre for the development of its perfect effect. We were present at the first performance of an opera of Rossini's in England: *Il Barbiere di Siviglia*, in March, 1818. We saw at once that there was a great revolution in dramatic music. Rossini burst on the stage like a torrent, and swept everything before him except Mozart, who stood, and will stand, alone and unshaken, like the Rock of Ages, because his art is like Shakespeare's, identical with nature, based on principles that cannot change till the constitution of the human race itself be changed, and therefore secure of admiration through all time, as the drapery of the Greek statues has been through all the varieties of fashion.

Whether singing in Italy has declined is another question. Lord Mount Edgcumbe received his first impressions in the days of 'the divine Pacchierotti.' We, who received ours at a later period, cannot sympathize with him in his regret for the musici [castrati]. We are content with such vocal music as the natural voice will allow us; we listen with unmixed pleasure to such a basso as Tamburini. The whole compass of the human voice finds its appropriate distribution in concerted music, otherwise the distribution is wrong, and not the principle of admitting the bass voice. The basso-cantante does not take the lead in the pezzo-concertato, any more than the double bass takes the place of the first fiddle in the orchestra. The one has its proper place in the instrumental, and the other in the vocal distribution. And if much of the dialogue which was formerly carried on in recitative is now carried on in concerted music, it is because it is found more agreeable and more suited to the changes and varieties of passion, and is at the same time readily followed by the majority of the audience, who would now find an old opera consisting of only recitative and single airs, with at most one or two duets, or a duet and a terzetto, a very insipid production. The favourites of a century, or even half a century back, could not be successfully reproduced without ripienimenti.

Lord Mount Edgcumbe's first impressions make him partial to thin and shrill tones. This is evident to us, in his praise of Camporese and Caradori; but with the decline of the musici, a fuller volume of tone in the female voice has been more and more required to satisfy the ear in concert with tenori and bassi. Tosi, the idol of Naples, with her soprano-sfogato voice, was not endured in England in 1832. The perfection of our domestic musical instruments has also contributed to this result. We have lost all relish, and even all toleration, for the tone of the harpsichord, since we have received our first ideas from that of the piano-forte.

A good opera well performed is a great rarity with us. Good operas there are in abundance; but there are seldom either sense or knowledge in the management to select them, or power or good-will in the company to do them justice. The best singers come here for only a portion of the season: they sing morning, noon, and night, at concerts; they have no time to rehearse. The manager has collected stars, but not a company: there is a soprano too much, and a contralto too little – a tenor wanting, and a basso to spare: they patch up a performance as they may – altering, garbling, omitting, interpolating – and the result is, a bad concert instead of a good opera. A good opera is a whole, as much in the music as in the poetry, and cannot be dislocated and disfigured by omissions and interpolations, without destruction to its general effect. [...]

from *The Works of Thomas Love Peacock, Volume Nine: Critical and Other Essays,* 1834

'The comic aspect of a battle over Oberon'
JOHN ROBINSON PLANCHÉ

According to the courteous custom which has prevailed time out of mind in English theatricals, an Easter piece on the subject of 'Oberon' had been rushed out at Drury Lane in anticipation of Weber's opera, and, in addition to this, Bishop was engaged to write an opera to be produced in opposition to it, the libretto by George Soane being founded on the popular story of 'Aladdin, or the Wonderful Lamp.' It was not very favourably received, and the delicious warbling of Miss Stephens could not secure for it more than a lingering existence of a few nights. Tom Cooke, the leader of the orchestra at Drury Lane, one of the cleverest musicians and most amusing of men, met Braham in Bow Street, and asked him how his opera ('Oberon') was going. 'Magnificently!' replied the great tenor, and added, in a fit of what he used to call *enthoosemusy*, 'not to speak it profanely, it will run to the day of judgment!' – 'My dear fellow,' rejoined Cooke, 'that's nothing! Ours has run five nights afterwards!'

The Recollections and Reflections of J. R. Planché, vol. 1, 1872

'The Examiner assesses Rossini and Mozart hits'
LEIGH HUNT

An Opera, entitled *The Barber of Seville* (*Il Barbiere di Siviglia*), from the pen of Signor Rossini, a young living composer [*sic*] at Rome, has been produced here for the first time in this country. High expectations were entertained of it, especially as it had been performed with great success at various theatres in Italy; but we were among those who thought that the author's having taken up an opera to set to music, which had been already composed by so fine a master as Paesiello, was not a piece of ambition in the best taste, or a very promising symptom of excellence. We expected that we should find little genius exhibited, at least on the score of sentiment; and we conceive that we were not disappointed.

The great excellence of the Italian school (which with all our admiration of Mozart appears to us to be much undervalued now-a-days, partly owing to undoubted merit in the German school, and partly to a court fashion for that school) consists in fine melody and expression. They take up one passion after another, and give you the genuine elementary feeling of it, as if they were undergoing and totally occupied with it themselves. Paesiello's compositions are special instances of this power of expression. His melodies are exquisitely graceful, touching, and original; and his recitatives always appear to us so extremely to the purpose as to be superior even to those of that delightful German by nation, and Italian by nature, Mozart.

In neither of these main qualities, will Signor Rossini's Opera, in our opinion, bear any comparison. We should be loth to speak so decidedly, after only one hearing; but what renders an Opera most delightful, and makes one recur to it over and over again and grow fonder on acquaintance, is a succession of beautiful airs; and of these the new *Barbiere di Siviglia* appears to us to be destitute. We do not recollect one. The passages most resembling them struck us as being traceable to Haydn, Mozart, and to Paesiello himself; and the recitative is singularly bald and common-place. You might always know the comment which the fiddle-bow was going to make. An intelligent daily critic notices, we observe, the resemblance to Haydn of *Zitti, zitti, piano, piano*, the most favourite passage in the Opera. On the other hand, the piece is not destitute of merit, or even, considering the author's youth, of great promise, though not on the higher sides of genius. Its good qualities are a sort of sprightly vehemence, and a talent for expressing oddities of character. We have unfortunately lost our copy of the book; but we have a strong recollection of the most striking passages. Some of them fairly beat it into us. They were the more hurried parts in general, the entrance of the *Count* in the disguise of a singing master, the groans of old *Bartolo*, and the scene where *Figaro* and his master have so much difficulty in getting rid of a set of fellows who have a prodigious pertinacity. We never met with a composer who gave us such an harmonious sense of discord, who set to music with such vivacity what is vulgarly called a *row*. The rest of the opera is of a piece with this kind of talent, not good in the graver, more sentimental, and graceful parts; but exceedingly promising in the ardent, vehement, and more obviously comic. The general effect is raw and inconsistent. Sometimes, for instance, there is hardly any accompaniment, sometimes a numerous one; sometimes the stage is all in a bustle, and sometimes unaccountably quiet. One feature is particularly worth notice; which is, that the young author, in a sort of conscious despair of a proper quantity of ideas, dashes his crotchets about, as it were, at random: and, among a number of grotesque effects, gives now and then a fine hit. He resembles, in the latter respect, the ancient painter, who in a fit of impatience at not being able to express foam at the mouth of a hound, dashed his spunge against the animal's jaws and produced the very thing he despaired of.

We have taken it for granted all this while that Signor Rossini is young, as reported. If not, he will hardly become eminent; but if he is, he undoubtedly may be so; provided he is not as noisy and vehement as his music, and does not get his wild head broken some day, for some over-vivacious serenade.

The Examiner, 22 March 1818

Mozart's Opera of *Così fan tutte* has been revived here, and most delightfully. It is one of his best, ranking next to *Figaro* and *Don Giovanni*; it is altogether taken up with those subjects and feelings which Mozart played to in so happy a manner – gallantry, arch humour, gracefulness, laughing enjoyment, voluptuousness, and an occasional pathos which is rather the suspension of pleasure than the sufferance of pain.

This opera too has the advantage of being simpler and more obvious in its incidents, of telling its own story better, than any we have ever witnessed. There are six people in it, two pair of whom are the lovers, who vow eternal constancy (Fodor, Corri, Begrez, and Garcia), the fifth an old gentleman (Naldi) who is always laughing at them for it, and the sixth, a servant girl (Mori) who joins with the men in a plot to try the fidelity of the ladies, which the good old gentleman in the first instance warned them against, and which, we must say, is tried with a vengeance. It may have been wrong in the two ladies, whose lovers have apparently taken leave for the army, to listen to the same lovers in disguise, and to feel the courage of their constancy shaken by besiegings, and melancholy implorings, and supposed takings of poison. They ought doubtless to have spared not one kiss of compassion, whatever their notion was of the attachment of the sufferers. They ought, if not to have kicked them into atoms, at least to have let them suffer on as much as they pleased, and drink poison like *eau de vie*. But unfortunately, they were made of too pitiful stuff; and of course the lovers have to regret their success, and to forgive them upon the ground of the 'natural viciousness' of the sex. *Così fan tutte*, says the play; 'It's the way of them all'; and so we must think the worst of it, and then make the best. O wise we!

This is also perhaps the most completely performed opera on the stage. All the singers are at home, with some exception on the part of Miss Cori, who is a good singer but wants spirit as an actress. The fault of Garcia, an excellent singer, is of another sort: he is over-vivacious, if not in his gestures, in his attitudes; and while standing still, as an

Irishman would say, keeps writhing and bending himself about like an elephant's trunk. He makes also such doleful mouths, when he is pathetic, that he appears to taste the bitterness of his sorrow literally in his mouth. He seems to want a lump of sugar after it.

What an inexhaustible succession of beautiful airs and harmonies is there in Mozart! One combination after another does not start out with a more sparkling facility in the far-famed Kaleidoscope. The first thing you hear in the present opera is the ardent trio, beginning *La mia Dorabella*, in which the lovers praise their mistresses, and insist that the old gentleman shall give proofs of their possible infidelity; then comes, like a gentler note to the same purpose, the other of *E la fede delle femmine*, the sounds of which absolutely talk and gesticulate; then the happy and polite one of *Una bella serenata*, with that gentlemanly willingness of ascent on the line *Ci Sarete, si signor*, like a bow itself; then the triumphant noises of *Bella vita militar*; then the little sobbing farewell, and entreaty to write every day, *Di scrivermi ogni giorno*; the invocation for gentle winds on the voyage, *Soave sia*, with those delicious risings of the voice, like a siren's from the water; the exquisite laughing trio, *E voi ridete*, with its slipppery rhymes, its uncontrollable and increasing breathlessness, and the grave descending notes of the pitying old gentleman in the base; the quiet triumph and lingering enjoyment of *Un aura amorosa*; the nodding and gentle giddiness of *Prendro quel brunettino*; the breathing passion of *Secondate*; the smiling insinuation of *Il core vi dono*. What do we not owe to an art and a master like this, who as it were spoke music as others speak words; and who left his magic imprinted forever in books, for the hand and the voice to call forth, whenever we want solace in trouble, or perfection in enjoyment!

The Examiner, 2 August 1818

This house is the only theatre, now, at which you are sure of hearing something both modern and masterly. There is occasionally something good at the English winter theatres, but the general run of pieces is deplorable, and reminds one of nothing but the stage itself. It is a melancholy round of stage repetitions, as old and dreary as the jog of a mill-horse.

At the Opera, on the other hand, you are almost sure of hearing a work not only masterly, but of the first kind of masterliness in the art of music – some production from the first-rate composers, such as Paesiello, Mozart, Winter, Cimarosa, and Rossini, who, though of various ranks, are as great in their way as the great poets of England or painters of Italy. And it is to be observed that the insurmountable objection to the English winter theatres – their enormous size – does not apply to a large musical house; because singing is naturally of a louder and more distinct utterance than talking; the instrumental accompaniment would fill any place; and if an objection remains as to countenances, an equal variety of distinctness of expression is not demanded of them, nor even wanted, the vocal expression being clear and just, and supplying the feeling to the spectator. We venture to prophesy that at no great distance of time the English winter theatres will either be totally ruined by their size and bad management, or turned into mere places of spectacle; while, on the other hand, the smaller houses will every day grow richer as well as more respectable.

On Tuesday last the Managers, greatly to the credit of their taste and spirit, brought forward another of the masterpieces of Mozart, *Il Flauto Magico* (*The Magic Flute*), better known and long admired in private circles under its German name of the *Zauber Flöte*. We like to mention objections first, as the little boys bite off the hard edges of their tartlets, in order that they may fall unobstructedly on the body of the sweetness within. The opera then, as performed on Tuesday, is justly accused of being a third too long. It was not over, for instance, till nearly 12 o'clock. Now the music is, throughout, excellent; but setting aside other considerations, the most excellent music in the world will not bear a theatrical performance so continued. Its very excellence, unmingled with intervals of other enjoyment as in private society, would tend to overstretch and exhaust attention, just as it strains the faculties to look for hours together at a variety of fine pictures. But when it comes to be considered that this excellent music is divided among a variety of singers, some of them almost inevitably poor and unequal to it, the discrepancy and confusion become perfectly wearisome; and on Tuesday evening for the first time in our lives, and not without some shame, we found ourselves dropping and shutting our eyes in the company of Mozart, not in order to listen with the greater luxury, but to catch a willing unwilling slumber. The remedy of this however is obvious, and we suppose was put in practice on the second night. With regard to the other objections, the new and younger performers whom it was necessary to add to the

Dramatis Personae are to be treated with tenderness; the most promising young singers may reasonably be allowed to be deficient in giving such compositions their proper effect. We have to find fault however with an agreeable singer, M. Begrez, who whether from negligence or from not having his voice in the best order, gave the sprightly and triumphant air of *Regna Amore in ogni loco* feebly and inefficiently. There is surely, on the other hand, no necessity for the extreme vivacity of the two whirling globes in the scene where the Queen of Night comes down from her throne. They emulated her singing and the orchestra with a noise of which none but tin heads could have been capable.

Such are our objections, all of which are removable. Now to the pleasanter task of approbation. And in the first place, we do not participate in the objection made to the nature of the story, which because it is a fairy tale is thought frivolous. Alas, how frivolous are most of the grave realities of life! We own we have a special liking for a fairy tale; and if we are not greatly mistaken, Mozart himself was of our opinion and got his wife to read one to him before he sat down to write that divine overture to *Don Giovanni*. Thus his pleasurable and fanciful mind made a fairy tale even a medium of inspiration. And it has a right to be so. It is full of some of the pleasantest associations of one's life. It has 'eyes of youth'. It is even more; it anticipates for us something of the good, which the human mind, as long as it is worth anything, is so anxious to realize, something of a brighter and more innocent world, in which the good-natured and flowery will is gratified; and the evil spirit, only furnishing a few more anxieties and occupations by the way, is always felt to be the weaker of the two, and sure to be found so at last. But we must take care of our limits. The story of the *Magic Flute* is made up of a mixture of Fairyism and Egyptian mythology. The Queen of Night (Miss Corri), who is a malignant being, has a daughter (Madame Bellocchi) who is withdrawn from her by the Priests of Isis (suspicious persons it must be owned), in order to be saved from her influence. A young Prince (Garcia) falls in love with the daughter from having seen her picture, which is put in his way by her mother, and the latter induces him with false representations to try and rescue her out of their hands. A bird-catcher (Ambrogetti), who is a sort of clown to the piece, is made to accompany him as servant. The Prince accordingly gets admittance into the temple of Isis, and makes the due impression on the heart of the lady, who endeavours to escape with him. They are detected, and by degrees brought to have a different opinion of the Priests, who after subjecting them to a variety of trials with that Freemasonry of theirs which was once so celebrated, unite them in marriage. The piece, which, by the way, has the double title of the *Magic Flute*; *or, The Mysteries of Isis*, receives its first name from a flute given to the Prince, which, upon being played, has the power of averting dangers, and which he makes use of in going through the fiery vaults and other apparent horrors of the said *Mysteries*. *Papageno*, the bird-catcher, is also gifted with a dulcimer, which has the privilege of setting people a-dancing. It is his resort to this charm, when his master and he are about to be seized and made prisoners, that gives rise to the delicious air of *O Cara Armonia*, to which all their assailants suddenly begin treading a delighted measure. We were going to say that the public are intimate with this air, under the name of *Away with Melancholy*; but we should rather say they are on speaking terms with it. The original, with its accompaniments, and with its appendix of another air, is a great deal finer.

And what divine music is there besides? There is, first of all, the finest Overture in the world; then there is bird-like hilarity of *Gente è qui l'uccellatore*; the prophecy about the three youths (*Tre bei Jargon*) who are to descend from heaven on golden wings (the very music comes stepping down, like a ladder from heaven); the magnificent air, *Te guida palma nobile*, which the youths sing when they do descend, and which answers so completely to the character of their mission; all the various and delightful composition, comprising almost every species of emotion, in Scenes 15 and 16 of Act the First; the abundant pomp and solemnity of all the grand melodies and harmonies connected with the Priests and their worship; the placid depth and dignity of *Sarestro's* description of his earthly paradise – *Qui sdegno non s'accende*; and then again, the delicate and tricksome stepping of the return of the Genii, *Gia fan ritorno*, with a quick and dimpled smilingness running throughout it. But the whole opera is one continued and deep river of music, breaking into every possible turn of course and variety of surface, and exhibiting every aspect of the heavens that lie above it. Mozart's genius is here in its most romantic and passionate character, undoubtedly. We can hardly say it is in his best, for nothing can be better than *Figaro*; neither do we conceive it will be so popular as that opera and *Don Giovanni*. It is, we suspect, too poetical to be so – too much referring to indefinable sentiments and sensations out of the pale of common experience; but numberless passages will delight the genuine lovers of music as much perhaps as any in either of those works. It may give a complete idea of what we think of the *Magic Flute* in general, its peculiarities, its chances, &c., when we say, that it is to Mozart's other works what the *Tempest* is to the most popular of Shakespeare's comedies. We are not sure, for our own parts, that we do not admire it more than any of his operas, if we could candidly rid ourselves of a preconceived notion that Mozart's powers were chiefly confined to the gayer part of enjoyment – a misconception to which all men of various genius seem to have been liable, in return for their bestowing gladness.

We ought not to omit that what Madame Bellocchi has to sing (for it is not much, considering she is the heroine) is sung excellently. Miss Corri also gives some passages *in alto* with so much neatness and truth as to produce an *encore*; but we cannot say we are ever moved by this inexorably frigid performer. We were disappointed, upon the whole, in Ambrogetti. His comedy, perhaps, is naturally of as unpastoral a character as can well be imagined. He looks too beef-eating for a bird-catcher. Angrisani's depth of voice is excellently suited to the part of *Sarestro*; and Garcia, since he has clipped his exuberance, continues to be equally full of power, judgment, and taste. The whole piece is got up with great spirit and magnificence; and when shortened (as we conclude it was, on the second night), will have double the effect.

There is a new ballet here, called *Rose d'Amour*, in which M. and Madame Duport appear with less of the French twirling and a good deal more sentiment. The spectators therefore have reason to enjoy themselves a little, and not merely to stare. They find a little heart in the business, as well as a quantity of legs.

The Examiner, 30 May 1819

'What's wrong with Rossini's *Otello*
STENDHAL [HENRI BEYLE]

The theme of serious love is as foreign to Rossini as it is to Walter Scott; and indeed, when one knows nothing of love as a passion except through what one has read in books (*Werther*, perhaps, or the

Nouvelle Héloïse), it is no easy task to paint a successful portrait of jealousy. It is necessary to have loved as implacably as *la Religieuse portugaise*, and with all the unquenchable ardour of which she has left us so vivid an echo in her immortal *Letters*, if one is to have any understanding of the kind of jealousy *which is powerful enough to move an audience in a theatre*. In Shakespeare's tragedy, we are made to feel that Othello *cannot* go on living when once he has killed Desdemona. Even if we imagine that the sombre Iago were to have perished in some hazard of war, at the very same moment as Desdemona herself, and that Othello were thus doomed for ever to believe in Desdemona's guilt – even so, life could have held no more savour in his eyes (if I may indulge a taste for mixed metaphor, *à l'Italienne*); Desdemona dead, why should Othello live?

I trust, dear Reader, that you will agree with me when I affirm that, if the passion of jealousy is to be effectively conveyed through the medium of art, it must first be rooted in a soul possessed of a love as desperate as that of Werther himself – of a love which may be *sanctified* by self-inflicted death. Any love which fails to rise to this degree of intensity has, in my opinion, no right to be jealous; where love is tepid, jealousy is a mere impertinence.

Love which is not passionate, but simply *fancy* or *infatuation*, can contribute nothing to art save an atmosphere of hilarity and general merriment. The kind of jealousy which often accompanies love of this 'secondary' quality may indeed be just as violent as a jealousy with very different origins; yet it cannot touch the artistic sensibility. Its characteristic feature is *vanity*; and jealousy of this category is invariably farcical (like the infatuated dotards in the old comedies) – unless the sufferer happens to be a personage of autocratic rank and power, in which case wounded vanity must be appeased by blood, and usually receives its satisfaction soon enough. But in all the world, there is nothing more abominable, nor more revolting, than blood shed out of vanity; and our minds turn immediately to the calendar of crimes committed by Nero, by Philip II, and by all the other monsters who have worn crowns and sat on thrones.

Before we may be truly stirred by the tragedy of *Othello*, before we may judge him *worthy* to kill Desdemona, one thing is essential: not a shadow of doubt must remain in our mind (or in that of any other spectator who should chance to consider the question) that, should Othello remain alone in the world after the death of his lover, he must necessarily and immediately strike *himself* with the same dagger. Unless I find this conviction firmly rooted in the bottom of my heart, Othello becomes indistinguishable from somebody like King Henry VIII, who, having chopped off the head of one of his wives, in accordance with the most just and lawful sentence delivered by the Courts of the time, feels nothing but intense relief; he would be the moral equivalent of one of our modern 'dandies', who think it the merriest sport to stand by and laugh while some woman who adores them dies of grief.

This *prophetic vision of Othello's death*, which is not only a moral necessity, but the absolute condition upon which our sympathy in the tragedy depends, is entirely absent in Rossini's *Otello*. This Othello is too patently shallow to convince me beyond reasonable doubt that it is not simply vanity which makes him seize the dagger. And once this uncertainty is allowed for an instant to take root, the whole theme, which is perhaps richer in emotional implications than any other conception springing from the fundamental phenomenon of love, is liable to degenerate with appalling rapidity into some insignificant and sordid little trifle borrowed from the *Tales of Bluebeard*.

However, I should imagine that any considerations such as those which I have just been analysing would have appeared supremely ridiculous to the unmentionable literary hack who prepared the Italian *libretto* which Rossini was expected to use; *his* job was to turn out seven or eight neatly-contrived scenes, all vaguely related to Shakespeare's tragedy, and all competently equipped with sufficient plain narrative to make sure that the public understood what was meant to be happening on the stage. Moreover, out of the total of eight scenes, not more than two or three could safely have *rage* as the dominant *motif*, for music does not possess the power to express fury for any length of time without degenerating into unrelieved monotony.

In Shakespeare's version of *Othello*, the first scene shows us Iago, accompanied by Roderigo, the rejected suitor of Desdemona, on his way to rouse the Senator Barbarigo [Brabantio in Shakespeare's text] and to warn him that Othello has abducted his daughter. This situation holds potential material for a chorus.

The second scene shows us Othello himself, who, in an attempt to justify his love in the eyes of his old comrade-in-arms, Iago, is unwise enough to betray the real extent of his passion. Here we have potential material for an *aria* by Othello.

The third scene shows us Othello telling the 'plain, unvarnished tale' of his love before the assembled members of the Senate of Venice, before whom he is summoned to answer a charge of abduction. It was a stroke of genius on the part of the poet to have created a situation where a narrative episode of this character, which is always so delicate to handle and lends itself so easily to absurdity, becomes in point of fact a *dramatic necessity*. Othello is accused of witchcraft; his Moorish origin, the darkness of his skin, the superstitions of the XVIth century – everything conspires to lend an air of plausibility to the accusation which is brought against him by old Barbarigo the Senator, Desdemona's father. In his defence, Othello tells of the simple means which he used to win the heart of his young bride; how he ran through the story of his life from year to year, filled with 'the most disastrous chances' and 'moving accidents'. At last, one of the Senators exclaims: 'I think this tale would win my daughter too'. Desdemona then enters, summoned at her father's insistence; and there, before the whole Assembly, this timid maiden, no longer obedient to the voice of her own father, throws herself into Othello's arms; at which, the aged Senator, in a fit of passion, cries out:

> Look to her Moor, have a quick eye to see:
> She has deceived her father, may do thee.
>
> (I. iii. 293–4)

This, I feel, provides admirable material for a quintet; it is rich in varied emotional elements, including the passions of love, anger and revenge; it follows a marked line of dramatic development; it provides for a chorus of Senators desperately moved by this strange scene which has come to trouble their midnight deliberations – and nothing of all this which the spectator cannot grasp and appreciate *directly*.

Here, then, we have three consecutive scenes, all of which gradually build up a portrait of an Othello obsessed by love, while at the same time they capture our interest in the quality of this love, by telling us in detail how, despite the copper-colour of his skin, he was able to win the heart of Desdemona – information which is more than necessary, for, once we see him as a lover deliberately preferred above all other rivals, his physical disabilities cease to be of any importance. If *such* a man should murder his beloved, it is inconceivable that the cause should be mere vanity; and so this disastrous suspicion is for ever banished from the picture. And what, may we be so bold as to enquire, did our Italian librettist invent as a substitute for the perfection of this scene where Othello, in our very presence, recounts the history of his love? A 'triumphant entry of a victorious general'! – an inspiration so new, so *original*, that, for a whole century and a half, it has furnished the gala-attraction of every single Grand Opera ever committed in France, and made dazzled provincials gape with astonishment and admiration!

This 'triumphal entry' is followed by a recitative and a full-scale *aria*,

Ah! sì, per voi già sento...*

– a positively supreme blunder, whose immediate consequence is to give us, right from the very outset, a picture of an Othello filled with pride and superb disdain for the enemy whom he has vanquished. And let me repeat, that a *proud*-hearted Othello is the very last conception in all the world which should be foisted upon the audience at this particular moment!

Following upon an initial howler of such devastating magnitude, involving the meticulous selection of that particular platitude which is best calculated to make specific nonsense of the whole plot, the less said about the rest of the *libretto*, the better. It would have needed every scrap of genius which Rossini possessed to save the opera, not merely from the banality of the text (for nothing is more normal), but from the *illogicalities of the plot*, which set another, and far thornier problem.

To perform such a miracle, Rossini would have had to master certain specific qualities which, in all probability, he simply does not possess at all. I confess myself obsessed by the overwhelming suspicion that Rossini himself has never known what it means to love someone *to the pitch of absurdity*. Ever since it has become fashionable in High Society to have *Grand Passions*, and owing to the corollary, that it is every man's ambition to behave 'like High Society', I have been finding myself increasingly reluctant to believe in the genuineness of any *Grand Passion*, until it has given proofs of its sincerity and good faith by inducing the victim to make himself ridiculous.

Poor Mozart, for instance, spent the greater part of his life – a life,

* Ah! Yes, for you I already feel...

it is true, which ended before he was six-and-thirty – in perpetual and imminent danger of plunging into this abysmal heresy of ridicule. Even in the *Marriage of Figaro*, which is the most light-hearted of all his operas, he cannot so much as glance at the subject of jealousy without making it sombre and deeply-moving; think, for example, of the *aria*:

> Vedrò, mentr' io sospiro,
> Felice un servo mio!*

or of the duet:

> Crudel perchè finora . . . ?†

In the presence of this kind of music, the audience is instantly and instinctively aware that, if such jealousy should lead to a crime, the fault must be attributed, not simply to *wounded vanity*, but to the delirium of a mind unbalanced, distraught by the most intolerable anguish which the human soul can experience. But Mozart's characters speak a language which is unknown to Rossini, and the whole of *Otello* is barren of the faintest trace of any such *obsession*; instead of deep grief, we are asked to accept mere *fury* – and to make the best of it we can; again and again we are shown the *injured vanity* of a creature who sways the power of life and death over his victim; never once the anguished and piteous misery of a passion betrayed by the object which it worships.

The librettist *should* have given Othello *two* duets with Iago. In the first of these, the 'damn'd inhuman dog' would have sown the first seeds of suspicion in Othello's heart, while Othello would have replied to the perfidious insinuations of his persecutor by exalting Desdemona ever higher in the mystic enthusiasm of his love.

Thus all the 'sound and fury' would have been reserved for the duet in the second act; and even at this point, we should have had two or three passages in which Othello would have reverted to his obsessing adoration. But the librettist was a man far too well-versed in his academic theories to deign to imitate the monstrous imaginings of a 'barbarian' like Shakespeare; instead, he daringly resorted to our dear, familiar friend, the 'unaddressed letter', which provides the standard

---

* I shall see, while I breathe, one of my servants happy!
† Why cruel until now . . . ?

dénouement in Voltairian tragedy – a platitudinous piece of confidence-trickery, which in our own day would scarcely serve to swindle a stock-exchange speculator out of a paltry couple of hundred, but which, for all that, is assumed to be deep enough to deceive men of the calibre of Orosmane, Tancred and Othello! Moreover, some petty consideration of *backstairs patriotism* (which earned him great favour in Venice), induced our worthy poet to revert to the original Italian legend which had provided Shakespeare with the basic plot of his tragedy. However, *all* the pillaged material, whatever its source, is handled with such unspeakable ineptitude, that he completely fails to suggest the faintest nuance of hesitation, or even to hint at the last glowing sparks of love in Othello's breast; and I fancy that, in all the orgy of blunders composing this so-called *libretto* which Rossini was supposed to manage, none is more fantastic than this. The feeblest of novelettes making the crudest of claims to psychological realism would have furnished our highly-respected scribbler (whom I have the unpardonable audacity to criticize!) with the information that the average human heart struggles more than once, experiences more than one fleeting instant of doubt and hesitation, before it agrees to an eternal renunciation of the greatest, the most god-like happiness which exists on earth – the belief in the untarnished perfection of the beloved object. One factor alone contrives to redeem Rossini's *Otello*, and that is *our* reminiscences of Shakespeare's *Othello*! Shakespeare created, in the person of Othello, a character who is as true, as historically *real*, as Julius Caesar or Themistocles. The very name of Othello is as vivid a symbol of impassioned jealousy as the name of Alexander is symbolic of indomitable courage; so much so, indeed, that if some misguided writer were actually to *show* us Alexander fleeing in panic before the onslaught of his enemies, we should still refuse to think of him as a coward; we should merely conclude that the writer did not know his job. Since the music of *Otello* is admirable in every respect bar one (*dramatic expression*), we can easily allow our imagination to supply the one specific virtue which is missing; for this faculty is never so well-disposed to furnish non-existent qualities as when it is over-whelmed by sudden admiration for a set of qualities which *do* exist – a secret which is perfectly familiar to Italian actors, brought up in the tradition of *improvisation*. We are so astounded to hear verse declaimed on the spur of the moment with the speed and facility of normal speech (a feat which, to us, appears quite incredibly difficult), that the resulting 'poetry' unfailingly sounds most impressive while we are actually listening to it; which is not to say that we should not find it quite intolerably flat on the day following, if anyone should have the double impertinence, firstly to write it down at all, and secondly to show it to us!

In *Otello*, we are so electrified by the magnificent musical quality of the songs, so spellbound, so overwhelmed by the incomparable beauty of the theme, that we invent our own *libretto* to match.

In Italy, the performers themselves are usually so completely dominated by the magic which Shakespeare attached to the fatal name of Othello, that, unconsciously as it were, traces of simple and spontaneous emotion – features which are only too often missing from Rossini's music – creep into the interpretation of their recitatives. In Paris, the various performers who have sung the part of Othello have all been actors of too much talent to quote as examples of this primarily *subconscious* phenomenon which results from contact with the great name of Othello; but I may state with conviction that I have never yet heard an insignificant performance of Desdemona's recitatives. There can scarcely be a single music-lover in the whole of Paris who could forget Madame Pasta's entry on the line

Mura infelici ogni dì mi aggiro!*

and the desperate simplicity in the inflection of her voice. Given actors of such outstanding ability, the illusion of beauty is not difficult to catch, nor is it long before we are sincerely convinced that this score, which is indeed almost overpowering in its torrential impetuosity and a masterpiece in the 'grand manner', is also deeply emotional, and carries with it that sense of fatality, that mark of impending disaster, which impelled Virgil to write of Dido, that she had *the pallor of death that was to be*.

If we insist on looking for *love* in Rossini's works, we should be well-advised to turn to his earliest composition, *Demetrio e Polibio* (1809); for by the time of *Otello* (1816), Rossini has forgotten the haunting echoes of *real* love, except, perhaps, in the scoring which surrounds the part of Desdemona, and in particular in the charming duet,

* Every day I wander about these unhappy walls!

Vorrei che il tuo pensiero...;*

for I must repeat (at the risk of sounding not merely boring, but utterly paradoxical) that, in general, the tone of Rossini's *Willow Song* is one of despair rather than of sincere and moving *tenderness*. Ask any lady with some experience in the gentle art of courtship which of the two moods is harder to portray!

Signor Caraffa, who, as a composer, is not in the same class as Rossini, has nevertheless written a *farewell aria*, which is used at the end of the first act of Viganò's ballet, *les Titans*, and which immediately creates an atmosphere of tender sympathy in the highest degree. If only Othello, bidding adieu to Desdemona after some secret meeting fraught with danger and difficulty, had a similar duet somewhere in the first act, the whole audience would be moved to tears; and this instant of tenderness and love would be all the more heart-breaking, since no one in the entire house could fail to be aware of the kind of death which is ultimately reserved for poor Desdemona. As it is, however, Othello's rages seem to betray nothing save congenital bad-temper – and, what is worse still, bad-temper springing from wounded vanity.

Life of Rossini, tr. Richard N. Coe

'Let's be frank about these French talents'
HECTOR BERLIOZ

The other day I went to the Théâtre-Italien – something that doesn't often happen to me; but when all is said, with a new opera, and an opera entitled *Ernani*, with the composer making his Paris début, and Rubini, Tamburini, Santini and Grisi on the bill, a visit to the Salle Favart was clearly in order.

Ye gods! What gilded visions the young composer must have had before his eyes. No doubt he had heard all about the literary feud generated by Hugo's play; echoes of the tumult that engulfed the pit at every performance, the sarcastic laughter of the hostile faction, the furious threats and passionate enthusiasm of the new school's champions, had reached him and set his heart aflame with noble

* I could wish that your thoughts...

emulation. 'I shall make Victor Hugo's play into an opera,' will have been his response. 'I shall find a way of getting it put on at the Théâtre-Italien in Paris. I shall rekindle the great conflict that the French poet provoked not long ago. There will be confrontations, shouting matches, duels for and against me. And, with a company formed of the finest singers in Europe, I cannot fail to have all my intentions brought out and displayed in the best possible light.'

Poor maestro! What a sad awakening. Nothing could have been cooler and more docile than the audience at the fourth performance of *Ernani*: no trace of confrontation, not a whisper of an argument, everyone on the contrary in perfect agreement. On the way out we talked of everything but the opera we had just heard. It might have been the hundredth performance of a long-established work. That is cruel for a composer. But in all honesty, what can one say of this *Ernani*, which is no more Ernani than I am the Pope? Where are the volcanic passions, the fierce vengefulness, the impetuous, consuming love, the pure and noble devotion of Doña Sol, and the other outstanding features that made Victor Hugo's play absurd to some, sublime to others, remarkable to all? The physiognomy of the Italian drama is such that it might just as well be called *Francesco* or *Pietro*. And the music shares this fault. It wants distinctive colour. The cavatinas are tailored to the pattern of every other example of the kind. The ritornellos have the form used by every other maestro of the Italian school: the same modulation appears exactly at the point where custom decrees it should appear. The tunes have sisters and cousins in every corner of the globe. And this fault, which is a very serious one to our way of thinking in any composition, becomes shocking in a subject as extreme as that of *Ernani*.

In fact, to speak our mind fully, *Ernani* cannot be treated by an Italian composer who wishes to succeed with his fellow-countrymen. The music such a drama demands would be hooted off the stage; the maestro who wrote it would be ill-advised to show himself at the keyboard on the day of the first performance: one couldn't answer for his not being assassinated. Besides, if the score of *Ernani* had been written in such a way as to produce, at the Favart, the sort of advance rumours provoked by Victor Hugo's play at the Théâtre-Français, you may be sure the Théâtre-Italien's management wouldn't have touched it. Opera directors have unerring tact. Put a commonplace piece among four works of originality, and instinct will infallibly guide them to choose the commonplace. All in all, one cannot absolutely blame M. Gabussi for not treating his subject in a fresh and poetic manner. He has made an Italian opera that is no worse than many I could mention, and that our dilettanti find very capital.

Rénovateur, 5 December 1834, tr. David Cairns

Until the recent revival – which I could not discuss without poaching on the preserves of my gifted colleague M. Jules Janin – all I knew of Hérold's opera were the scraps extracted from it for the vaudevilles and quadrilles and barrel-organs. At the time of its first performances I was in Italy, giving little thought to what went on at the Opéra-Comique in Paris. I frequented the theatres – not the San Carlo, the Fondo, the Valle, the Pergola or the Scala but the antique theatres of Pompeii, San Germano, Tusculum and Rome, where the evening breeze playing along the deserted tiers sings airs more expressive than Coccia, Schiafogatti, Focolo, or Vaccai himself could hope to achieve. True, the performance and the staging were a not unimportant part of the magic of that nocturnal music. The wind changes nothing in the text which the great composer of the universe has entrusted to it; it is gay or melancholy, violent or playful, as the eternal maestro commands; it howls, weeps, sighs but never embellishes, never defaces its primordial melodies with nauseating appoggiaturas, and adds no cadenzas. As for the scenery, it beggars description: above all at the tragic theatre of Pompeii, where to your right Vesuvius towers up, roaring and brandishing its fearsome plume while a crimson necklace of lava lies majestically on its exhausted breast, and to your left, on the gleaming bay of Naples, 'the moon spreads its silver fan across the sea';* and over all that sublimity of sky and earth and fire and water a deep enchanted silence – no distracting chatter, no idiotic remarks, no irritating applause, no audience at all, at most a solitary spectator.

Oh memories! oh Italy! oh liberty! oh poetry! oh damnation! – I have to apply myself to the Opéra-Comique! But I have read and seen the piece, so the worst is over. *Zampa, or the Marble Fiancée*: I shall probably be stoned for saying what I think of this much-acclaimed work. So be it. Hérold is no more, and though according to the man

* Victor Hugo, 'La captive'.

who reversed the proverb we owe respect to the dead, I consider I owe it to art – living, progressive art – to be truthful. The long and short of it is that I do not like *Zampa*, and here is why. There is – as doesn't often happen at the Opéra-Comique – some real music in it, there are even some fine ensembles; but as a work, as a score which by its subject, whatever anyone may say, lays a barely concealed claim to be the counterpart of Mozart's *Don Juan*, *Zampa* seems to me a poor piece. The one is as true, as dazzling and noble as the other is bogus, vulgar and commonplace.

A comparison between the words will better convey the difference between the two scores. Everyone is familiar with the originality, the pungent directness of the language of Mozart's protagonist. Here is the language of Hérold's, during an orgy:

> A fig for storm and sorrow!
> For when the cup
> Such wine fills up,
> Come, let us drink!
> Who knows? To sink
> May be our fate tomorrow.

Elsewhere, on the point of violating a young maiden, he says, in all seriousness: 'Yield, yield to my laws!', to which his breathless victim replies:

> Dispel these my fears.
> 'Tis not thus, with tears,
> That happiness comes.
> Subscribe to my prayers.

Nowhere else in the world but the Opéra-Comique do you hear lines like that. Well: the music of *Zampa* is not generally speaking much more elevated in idea, much more truthful in expression or more distinguished in form. But whereas we may be sure the author of the words attached no importance whatever to the rhymes he threw at the composer, the composer sweated blood in a vain attempt to rise above his collaborator. The music, at any rate, has exactly the same effect on me as the lines I have quoted would have on a poet. Its style, moreover, has no distinct character. It is neither pure and austere like Méhul's, brilliant and exuberant like Rossini's, nor dreamy, passionate and brusque like Weber's. Neither Italian, French nor

German, Hérold takes something from each of the three schools but has no style of his own. His music is just like those industrial products manufactured in Paris on foreign models and adapted with minor modifications. It is Parisian music. That is why it goes down so well with the Opéra-Comique audience, which in our view represents the middle class of the inhabitants of the capital, and why those artists and music-lovers whose radically different nature and taste and intelligence set them apart from the multitude think so little of it. [...]

Largely, I find the flower of the Parisian style, tricked out with the patent embellishments of Italian orchestration and the chromatic harmonies, bristling with dissonances, which Spohr and Marschner have so abused, to the reproach of the German school. I should add that in employing these chords of wild and fantastic aspect Hérold rarely hits the mark. The weapon is one that he has not learned to use. Almost always it is the handle and not the blade that strikes; and, in contrast to Mozart, Beethoven and Weber, his blows bruise but fail to draw blood.

There is our entire opinion of *Zampa*. If anything can soften its harshness in the eyes of Hérold's admirers, let me say in conclusion that the score fulfils every condition required of an opéra-comique in Paris today, and that its authors have entirely succeeded in their intentions, having won the undisputed approval of that section of the public to which they were appealing.

Journal des Débats, 27 September 1835, tr. David Cairns

'Meyerbeer and Rossini – a question of timeliness'
HEINRICH HEINE

What then is music? This question occupied me for hours last night before falling asleep. Music is only explained by wonder: I would like to say, it is a miracle. It exists between thought and phenomenon, like a twilight medium, it stands between spirit and matter, related to and yet different from both: it is spirit, but spirit governed by time; it is matter, but matter that can manage without space. We do not know what music is. But what constitutes good music, this much we know; and we are even more aware of what bad music is, for we hear so much of it. Music criticism can only be based upon experience, not synthesis; it should classify music according to its similarities and take as its measure the collective impression produced. [...]

Last year at a restaurant in Marseilles, I heard the best music criticism, and the only type that perhaps proves anything. Two commercial travellers were discussing the topic of the day, whether Rossini or Meyerbeer was the greater master. As soon as one spoke up for the supremacy of the Italian, the other interjected but not using dry words, rather he trilled some of the most beautiful melodies from *Robert le Diable*. Hereupon the other knew of no better response than to counter eagerly with passages from the *Barbiere de Siviglia*. And thus it continued throughout the meal. Instead of a bawling exchange of irrelevant phrases, they gave us rare table music, and at the end I had to admit that when it comes to music, one ought either to avoid dispute or to do so in this realistic manner.

Be sure, dear friend, I will not bore you with the usual comments on opera. But since the discussion is on the French stage, I cannot let this last subject pass unnoticed. Still, you need not fear the usual comparative discussion of Rossini and Meyerbeer from me. I am content to love both, and not to love one at the expense of the other. If I do perhaps sympathize more with the former, it is merely a personal feeling, and in no way an expression of greater value. Perhaps there are imperfections in him that smack of an affinity with my own. [...] For on the waves of Rossini's music, the individual joys and sorrows of man are gently rocked. Love and hatred, tenderness and longing, jealousy and self-pity: each is made the isolated feeling of the individual. A preponderance of melody is therefore characteristic of Rossini, for it is always the direct expression of isolated sentiment. With Meyerbeer, on the other hand, we find the predominance of harmony. In the flow of harmonic measures, the melody is lost, even engulfed, just as the particular feelings of the individual are lost in the collective sentiment of an entire people. And then our soul gladly launches itself into this flowing harmony as it is lost in the sorrows and joys of an entire human race and made party to the greatest social questions. Meyerbeer's music is more social than individual. The grateful present finds its needs and hopes in his music, with its private and public feuds, its struggles with faith and the will; and it celebrates its own agony and ecstasy when it applauds the great master. Rossini's music was better suited to the time of Restoration, after almighty struggles and disappointments, when to the blasé mind of man the sense of one great collective interest had to be forgotten, and the sense of self could again assert its legitimate rights. Rossini would never have had his immense popularity during the Revolution and Empire. Robespierre would have accused him of anti-patriotic melodies, and Napoleon would certainly not have appointed him Bandmaster, which required a communal enthusiasm. [...] The Restoration was really Rossini's time of triumph, and even the stars in heaven that had time off at last, and no longer had to worry about the fate of the people, listened to him with delight. The July Revolution brought forth a great commotion on earth and in heaven. Stars and men, angels and kings, yes, God himself, were roused from their state of peace, had multiple tasks once again and neither the leisure nor the required peace of mind to enjoy the melodies of private sentiment. It was only with the loud choruses of *Robert le Diable* and even *Les Huguenots*, harmonious when groaning, rejoicing and weeping, that their hearts heard, and wept, rejoiced and groaned in spirited accord. This is perhaps the ultimate reason for the unprecedented, colossal success which Meyerbeer's two great operas enjoyed worldwide. [...]

What *Les Huguenots* most especially demonstrates is a balance between enthusiasm and artistic precision, or to put it better, the equal height to which passion and art aspire. The musician and the artist are in close rivalry and if one sounds the warning bell of wildest passion, the other knows to turn these raw sounds into the sweetest penetrating harmony. While the crowd is struck by the inner power of passion in *Les Huguenots*, the educated listener wonders at the mastery evident in the form. This work is a Gothic cathedral, whose spire, reaching for heaven, and colossal cupolas seem to be planted by the hand of a giant. Meanwhile, the innumerable and astonishingly fine festoons, roses and arabesques that are spread over it like a lace veil made from stone, are testament to the tireless patience of a dwarf. A giant in the conception and design of the whole, a dwarf in the exhaustive execution of detail, the architect of *Les Huguenots* is as incomprehensible to us as the masters of the old cathedrals. When I recently stood with a friend before the cathedral at Amiens, he asked, as with cries and compassion he contemplated this monument to the towering, rock-like strength of giants and tireless patient carving of dwarves, how it could be that today we are incapable of bringing forth such a work. I answered him, 'Dear Alphonse, the men of old had conviction. We moderns have only opinions and it takes more than a mere opinion to raise a Gothic cathedral.'

That is that. Meyerbeer is a man of conviction. This is not simply reflected in the social questions of the day, although in this regard his ideas are more firmly grounded than those of other artists are. Meyerbeer, whom the world's princes shower with honours, yet who has for all this so much sense and a heart in his breast that beats with the most sacred interests of mankind, confesses his devotion undeterred for the heroes of the Revolution. [...] Far more than *Robert le Diable*, *Les Huguenots* is a work of conviction, as much in regard to subject-matter as form. As I have already remarked, while the plot takes in the crowd, the silent expert marvels at the unusual progress of the art and the introduction of new forms. According to the most competent judges, all musicians who wish to write for the opera must henceforth first study *Les Huguenots*. Meyerbeer has gone furthest in instrumentation. The handling of the chorus is unprecedented; speaking out as individuals, they have overtaken the entire operatic past. Since *Don Giovanni*, there has certainly been no greater phenomenon in the line of musicology than the fourth act of *Les Huguenots*. On to the horror of the shocking scene of the consecration of the swords, itself the blessing of murderous desire, a further duet is imposed, which surpasses even the initial effect. One would not think this anxious genius capable of this colossal risk, whose success excites our amazement as much as our delight. It occurs to me, and I believe as much, that Meyerbeer did not accomplish this through artistic means, but through natural ones, inasmuch as the famous duet speaks of a series of feelings that have perhaps never before been introduced into opera, not at least with such verisimilitude. But they are, for those Spirits of our age, fiercely sympathetic feelings. [...]

Les Huguenots has been accused of a lack of melody even more than *Robert le Diable*. This prejudice proceeds from an error: 'You cannot see the wood for the trees.' The melody is subordinate to harmony, and so by comparison with the music of Rossini, wherein you find the opposite, Meyerbeer's is characterized as a humane, social music. In fact, it does not lack melodies, only these are not allowed to be distracting, I might even say egotistical, but must serve the whole. They are disciplined whereas with the Italians, they appear isolated, I might say unruly, and they assert their own values rather like their notorious bandits. [. . .] I do not want to contest the value of a certain preponderance of melody, but I must say this much. As a result, in Italy we see a certain indifference towards opera as ensemble, or as a unified artwork, which manifests itself so naively that when no notable piece is being sung, those in the boxes begin to socialize and chatter uninhibited, and do not just merely play cards.

The place of harmony in the works of Meyerbeer is perhaps a necessary consequence of his breadth, of the wealth of thought and vision in his extensive education. Treasures were dispensed upon his education and his mind was fertile. He was introduced to the sciences at an early age and is distinguished from most musicians in this respect, whose ignorance is in any case excusable since they usually lacked the time and means to take on large areas of knowledge beyond their own. The knowledge became a part of his nature and the worldly schooling gave him the highest development. He belonged to the few Germans in whom even France has to recognize a model of urbanity. Such a level of education was perhaps necessary to gather together the material required to create *Les Huguenots*, and to shape it with a firm purpose. It is, however, a question whether or not that which was won in breadth of conception and clarity of vision, was lost in other qualities. In the artist, education destroys that sharp accentuation, that stark colouring, that originality of thought, that directness of feeling, which we so marvel at in those of rough-hewn, uncultured nature.

(Über die Französische Bühne, 'On the French Stage: Intimate Letters to August Lewald', 1837) tr. Matthew Scott

'Trust the French to ruin *Freischütz*'
RICHARD WAGNER

Oh, my dear German fatherland, how can I help adoring you, even if only because it was your soil that produced *Der Freischütz*! Must my heart not go out to a people that loves *Der Freischütz*? That still believes in fairy tales? That still, having reached man's estate, responds with sweet shudders to the mysteries before which it trembled when its heart was young? Delightful dreamers, with your devotion to forests and evening hours, to moon and stars and clocks in village steeples striking seven! Happy the man who understands you, who can share your raptures, who can believe and feel and dream with you! How happy I am to be a German!

These were the thoughts, along with many others defying expression, which recently pierced my heart like a voluptuous dagger. I felt a searing pain, which shot up into my head. Yet it was not blood that flowed, but tears – the most delicious tears. What the occasion was that drove this blissful dagger through my heart I can reveal to nobody in this huge fine city of Paris; here almost everybody is French, and the French are gay and witty people, full of jokes. Their gaiety would certainly increase, their quips and jokes fall even faster, were I to try and tell them what it was that gave me that divinely beneficent wound.

But you, my gifted fellow-countrymen, you will not laugh. You will understand when I tell you that it happened at a passage in *Der Freischütz* – that passage in the first act when the peasant lads seize their girls by the hand and dance with them into the inn, leaving the young hunter bridegroom seated alone at a table outside. There he was, brooding over his misfortunes, while the evening grew darker and the sounds of the dance music faded into the distance. As I watched and listened, my tears began to fall, and my neighbours in the Paris Opéra thought some terrible misfortune had befallen me. As I dried my eyes and polished my glasses, I resolved to write about *Der Freischütz* [...]

In general one might say that the whole cast at the great Paris Opéra dreamed its way through the work. [...] The scenic designers had of course not been sparing with their forests, and so nothing was left for the singers but to provide the dreaming. In addition, they wept a lot, and Samiel even trembled. About Samiel's tremblings I had better speak at once, for it was these that finally overcame my scruples and enabled me to find consolation in laughter.

Samiel was a slim young man of about twenty-five. He wore a handsome Spanish costume, over which he occasionally threw a cloak of black crape. He had a highly expressive face, to which some striking side-whiskers lent even more interest. His general air was alert and cheerful, and in the first act he played the police spy with true Parisian *élan*. Body bent forward and a finger to his lips, he approached Max several times with graceful circumspection as the unhappy young hunter sang his great aria. His purpose, it seemed, was to catch what Max was singing, and that was in truth no simple matter, for even the audience, despite the help of text books, not infrequently seemed uncertain whether he was singing in Italian or French. On one occasion, at the point where Max moved up to the footlights to hurl his despairing question at the fates, Samiel drew so close that he actually heard the word *dieu*, bellowed forth with tremendous force. This word seemed to make a very unpleasant impression on him, for the moment he heard it he fell into a fit of trembling the like of which I have never seen before, even in the French theatre. It is of course well known that in the art of trembling French actors and actresses are unrivalled throughout the world, but what Samiel achieved on this occasion made all previous efforts look like child's play. The stage of the Paris Opéra is, as you may imagine, very broad and deep, so you can appreciate what a huge distance poor Samiel had to cover when, from Max's position at the extreme left of front, he had to make his escape with violently trembling limbs all the way to the extreme right at back. Pursuing his shaky course, he had still, some time later, only reached the middle of the stage, and, in view of the tremendous exertion this manoeuvre had so far cost him, one began to fear that he would never be able to make his distant goal at the back. However, on French stages nothing is ever left to chance. The producer had reckoned at what point in his journey Samiel's powers would give out, and he had arranged with the stage technicians to whisk him away through a trap door. All went according to plan, though only in the nick of time. A flash of lightning over the place where he had been standing completed the effect. We were left with the comforting feeling that the godless man would be given time and treatment in his subterranean dwelling to recover from the exhausting effects of all that trembling.

Max elected to emphasise the dreamy side of his character. Though this suited the part as a whole well enough, he tended on occasions to push his dreamy forgetfulness too far. Frequently he forgot the key in which Weber in his wisdom had directed the orchestra to play and, lost in his dreams, sang in a somewhat lower one, with an effect that was strange, certainly, but not very pleasing. In his aria he strayed about in sad confusion between the forests and the meadows. One might say that he overdid the dreamy confusion as well as the mood of flatness that assailed him.

His friend Kaspar, on the other hand, seemed both cheerful and carefree, although there was something very odd about his appearance: his good-humoured behaviour was in striking contrast with the lugubrious expression on his face, and nothing could have been more melancholy than his manner of walking. The singer playing Kaspar has hitherto shown his laudable public spirit by singing in the chorus – this notwithstanding that he is unusually tall. However, moved by a proper concern for appearances, he has always done his utmost to bring his towering limbs into a seemly relationship with the more modest proportions of his colleagues. Since nothing could be done to his head end without considerable inconvenience to himself, he chose the alternative remedy of reducing his body to an acceptable length by bending his legs both downwards and outwards at the knee. Such self-sacrifice has always – or nearly always – enabled the chorus to maintain an excellent ensemble, and on this occasion his unselfish behaviour proved equally advantageous for the part of the blackly villainous Kaspar. In conjunction with the lugubrious expression on his face, it provided an effective counterbalance for the actor's own inborn air of *bonhomie*. At least, this was how it appeared to the French. However funny they found Kaspar's facial expression and his walk, they were convinced that this was how it was meant to be: the singer, they felt, was simply doing his best to comply faithfully with the demands of his role. But towards the end of the opera even they began to realise that Kaspar was in league with the devil. How in fact could they have doubted it after witnessing the strange death – or rather burial – of the godless fellow? After Kaspar is struck down by that incomprehensible bullet – incomprehensible to the French, that is, owing to its lack of logic – he is, as you will remember, visited once more by Samiel. As villains usually do, he curses both God and the world. But he so far forgets himself as to honour Samiel himself with a curse, and on this occasion the latter was so incensed that he straight away carried the impudent fellow off beneath the stage instead of leaving his corpse lying there. This proved a great embarrassment to the chorus, who still had some words to say to Kaspar, and it also disconcerted the prince who, as we all know, had formed the intention of throwing the corpse into the Wolf's Glen. However, both prince and chorus solved the difficulty with true French presence of mind by carrying on as if nothing unusual had happened, taking their revenge following Kaspar's premature departure by reviling him in his absence.

The prince and his court, incidentally, were seen to be richly deserving of respect. All were dressed in oriental costume, and one got the impression that the prince's rule extended over an empire of truly vast dimensions. He himself, together with some of his nobles, wore Turkish dress, suggesting that he must be the sultan or at least a pasha of Egypt. [...] It was salutary to see the ruler of all the Mussulmans so magnanimously engaged in Christian negotiations with a hermit. It was a lesson to all Christian nations that Moslems and Jews should also be treated as normal human beings.

However, let us now put these production details aside. If I were to spell out all the things which turned my patriotic dismay into helpless laughter, I should have a large but also very exhausting task on my hands. Let me therefore now confine my remarks simply to the interpretation of our *Freischütz* in Paris in terms of the production as a whole.

Quite apart from my misgivings over the disproportionate length of the specially composed recitatives, I had felt some initial fears that M. Berlioz might be tempted, where opportunity offered, to yield to the impetuosity of his own inspiration and thus to give his recitatives too much independence. But – much to my regret, I am amazed to find myself saying – M. Berlioz renounced all personal ambition and did his utmost to make his work as unobtrusive as possible [...]: these recitatives robbed Weber's romantic opera of its freshness and integrity, but offered nothing in their place. They were to a large extent responsible for the audience's despair, for they opened the gates to that most terrible of all torments – utter boredom.

The way in which they were sung also helped to emphasise the reprehensible nature of these recitatives. All the singers seemed to imagine that they were singing *Norma* or *Moses* and treated us to portamentos, tremolos and other such noble devices.

These became most painfully evident in the scenes between the two girls, Agathe and Ännchen. Agathe obviously saw herself throughout as Donizetti's *Favorita* – the wronged innocent – and so she wept a great deal, maintained a look of set gloom and was prone to sudden paroxysms of fear. She had been given a Bohemian peasant costume to wear, all velvet and lace. It was at least in character, whereas Ännchen was clad in a coquettish evening gown. This lady seemed dimly to realise that she was supposed to be a skittish creature, but skittishness is as foreign to French women as coquetry is to ours. The silliest of

Ännchens to be seen on our German stages will, when she sings about handsome boys, take the two corners of her apron in her hands and trip towards Agathe. She will nod her head at appropriate moments and drop her eyes when it is called for. But our Paris Ännchen could do none of these things. She elected to stay rooted to one spot and to flirt with the 'Lions' in their boxes, thereby imagining that she was doing all that was necessary to depict a German girl. The Parisians did not seem to find this in any way remarkable – and nor did I.

But the scene in which the Paris Opéra's disastrous ban on spoken dialogue wreaked the most havoc was the Wolf's Glen. All the words which Weber directed to be spoken in his melodrama by Kaspar and Max had of course to be sung, and this stretched things out to unbearable lengths. It was this factor that most of all incensed the French. They considered this 'devil's kitchen', as they called it, an incomprehensibly stupid affair anyway, and to see so much time spent on it tried their patience beyond endurance. Maybe if they had been given something intriguing to look at – a chain of imps and sylphides instead of boring skulls, a luscious ballerina flashing her skirts and legs instead of an indolent owl stretching its wings, or a bevy of liberal-minded nuns attempting to seduce the phlcgmatic young hunter – if any of these things had happened, then the Paris audience would at least have known where they were. But none of them did, and even Kaspar, who should have been mainly occupied with the task of casting his bullets, seemed to be bothered by the extraordinary lack of happenings. I was in no better state myself. Becoming increasingly aware of the audience's restlessness around me, I found myself silently praying to all the saints in heaven that the stage manager might at least feel the urge to produce something from his box of tricks.

Thus it was that both Kaspar and I, after the first bullet had been cast, responded with undisguised delight to the sound of a sudden unexpected rustling in one of the bushes. But whatever had caused it vanished with the speed of lightning, leaving nothing unfortunately but a very unpleasant smell behind. However, this served to raise our hopes initially, though with the second bullet they remained unfulfilled. Expectantly Kaspar called up the third bullet, and I waited with him, agog. Again nothing happened. We were ashamed by Samiel's inactivity and hung our heads. But only for a moment, for the fourth bullet had to be cast. This time we were gratified to see, beside a couple of bats flying above the circle, a number of will-o'-the-wisps dancing in the air. Unfortunately they got too close to the melancholy Max, who was obviously put out by them. Still, we could now await the casting of the fifth bullet with the most sanguine expectations: if the ghostly wild chase was to be shown, it was now or never. And sure enough, it came. On a mountain, six feet above the heads of the two hunters, we saw four naked boys, bathed in a mysterious light. They were carrying bows and arrows, and for this reason were generally taken to be cupids. They made a few gestures in cancan style and then hurried off into the wings. Much the same thing was then done by a lion, a bear and a wolf, as well as by four more boys who, naked and armed with bows and arrows, likewise followed in the wild hunters' wake.

Alarming as these apparitions had been, both Kaspar and myself would have liked them to continue after the sixth bullet. But at this point the producer prudently opted for a respite – no doubt in order to allow the ladies in their boxes to recover a little from their fright. When, after the casting of the seventh bullet, I saw what transpired, I understood the reason for this pause in the proceedings. Without it the intended spine-chilling effect could never have been achieved. On the bridge across the waterfall three men appeared, dressed in striking black cloaks. Three more appeared in the foreground on the very spot where Max was standing. He must, I suppose, have taken them for undertakers. At any rate, they made such a ghastly impression on him that he immediately fell down full length at their feet. The horrors of the Wolf's Glen were at an end.

I see I have once more relapsed into a catalogue of details. In order to block up this tempting path once and for all, I shall resolve to say not a word more about the production of *Der Freischütz* in Paris, but instead to concentrate my attention upon the public and its reaction to our national work.

Most Parisians tend to think of productions at the Paris Opéra as being above reproach, which is not surprising, since they know of no other establishment where they might see an opera better performed. Thus they were bound to feel that this production of *Der Freischütz* was good all through – certainly better than anything they could have seen in a German theatre. Instead of attributing those aspects of *Der Freischütz* which they found boring and silly to the shortcomings of the performance – this would never have entered their heads – they simply concluded that what the Germans took to be a masterpiece was, so far as they were concerned, just a piece of clumsy hack-work. And this opinion was confirmed by their recollection of *Robin des Bois*, that adaptation of *Der Freischütz* which [...] had been a tremendous success. Since the work on which it was based had failed to match its success, everybody not unnaturally formed the opinion that the adaptation was incomparably the better work. Certainly in *Robin des Bois* the effect of Weber's music had not been spoiled by M. Berlioz's terribly long recitatives, and it had had the additional advantage that the author had contrived to introduce *logic* into the dramatic action.

This logic is a very remarkable thing. Not only have the French constructed their language according to the strictest rules of logic, but they also demand that everything said in it should be logical too. I have met Frenchmen who found a lot of pleasure even in this production of *Der Freischütz*, but every one of them complained that the work lacks logic. I have never in my whole life felt constrained to examine *Der Freischütz* for its logical content, and I therefore asked these Frenchmen to explain exactly what they meant by it. Thus I learned that logical French brains were particularly vexed by the *number* of magic bullets. Why, they asked, were there seven? Was such luxury really necessary? Would not three have done? Three is a number that can always be controlled and managed. How is it possible in one short act to put seven whole bullets to really practical use? One would need at least five complete acts to solve this problem properly, and even then one would be faced with the difficulty of finding a use for more than one bullet in a single act. They were prepared to admit that handling magic bullets is no laughing matter; but in that case was it not a defiance of all reason that two young hunters should shoot off six of them with such glaring irresponsibility, particularly when they knew, as they must have done, that the seventh bullet held an unpleasant surprise in store?

In the same way the catastrophe at the end was mercilessly criticised. 'How is it possible', I was asked, 'that a shot fired at a dove should appear to kill a bride and actually kill a good-for-nothing hunter at one and the same time? Granted, a shot can miss a dove and hit a human being – such unfortunate accidents do happen. But that a bride and all around her should imagine for a full five minutes that *she* had been hit as well – that is really going beyond the bounds of credibility. And in any case, this shot is dramatically so unconvincing. How much more logical it would be if the young hunter, in despair at having missed his mark, were to try to put the seventh magic bullet through his own head! The bride rushes in and tries to wrest the pistol from him. In the struggle it goes off, missing the hunter (thanks to the bride's intervention) and laying low his godless comrade, who happens to be standing in the direct line of fire. Now that would be *logical*!'

I clutched my reeling head. Such obvious truths had never once entered my thoughts: I had always taken *Der Freischütz* in all its illogical entirety exactly as it was. Does that not show what remarkable people the French are? They see *Der Freischütz* once only, and immediately they can demonstrate that for twenty-five years we Germans have been labouring under a monstrous delusion regarding its logicality. What fools we must be, to have always believed without question that a shot fired at an eagle at seven o'clock in the evening could cause the portrait of a great-grandfather to fall from the wall in a hunting lodge half a mile away!

Logic is the Frenchman's consuming passion, and consequently it informs all their judgments. However conflicting the newspaper reports, none of them neglected in this case to base their opinions on the most logical premises, even if this must often have proved difficult. One paper maintained, for instance, that the marksman was wearing grey, whereas another thought his costume was unmistakably green. But it was M. Berlioz in the *Journal des Débats* who contrived things best. In his article on *Der Freischütz* he did not neglect to say nice things about both Weber and his masterpiece, and his words were all the more telling in that he was equally nice about the production. Nobody objected to that of course, for we all knew that the writer had himself been responsible for the musical *mise en scène*, and he was consequently under an obligation to compliment the singers for the trouble they had gone to in studying so disagreeable an opera under his care. But M. Berlioz's true modesty was revealed by the fact that in his article he said not a single word about his recitatives. Thus everyone was touched when, in an ensuing issue of the journal, M. Berlioz's colleague, Jules Janin, graciously took the trouble of reviewing the *Freischütz* production himself and found occasion to praise only one thing about it: the recitatives of his friend, M. Berlioz. There was nobody who did not feel that this division of labour between the two colleagues was completely in line with the principles of Parisian logic.

Der Freischütz has really succeeded only in driving the French and Germans farther apart again. [. . .]

from *Wagner Writes from Paris*, tr. Robert L. Jacobs and Geoffrey Skelton

'Exploiting Jenny Lind fever in the USA'
PHINEAS TAYLOR BARNUM

I may as well state, that although I relied prominently upon Jenny Lind's reputation as a great musical *artiste*, I also took largely into my estimate of her success with all classes of the American public, her character for extraordinary benevolence and generosity. Without this peculiarity in her disposition, I never would have dared make the engagement which I did, as I felt sure that there were multitudes of individuals in America who would be prompted to attend her concerts by this feeling alone.

Thousands of persons covered the shipping and piers, and other thousands had congregated on the wharf at Canal Street, to see her. The wildest enthusiasm prevailed as the steamer approached the dock. A bower of green trees, decorated with beautiful flags, was discovered on the wharf, together with two triumphal arches, on one of which was inscribed 'Welcome, Jenny Lind!' The second was surmounted by the American eagle, and bore the inscription, 'Welcome to America!' These decorations were not produced by magic, and I do not know that I can reasonably find fault with those who suspected I had a hand in their erection. My private carriage was in waiting, and Jenny Lind was escorted to it by Captain West. The rest of the musical party entered the carriage, and, mounting the box at the driver's side, I directed him to the Irving House. I took that seat as a legitimate advertisement, and my presence on the outside of the carriage aided those who filled the windows and sidewalks along the whole route, in coming to the conclusion that Jenny Lind had arrived.

Struggles and Triumphs of P. T. Barnum told by himself, 1882

'Fascination with Wagner in Liszt's Weimar'
GEORGE ELIOT

The Weimar theatre opens about the middle of September. A very pretty theatre it is, and all its appointments show that the Grand Duke does not grudge expense for the sake of keeping up its traditional reputation. The opera here, as every one knows, has two special attractions: it is superintended by Liszt; and Wagner's operas, in many places consigned to the *Index Expurgatorius* of managers, are a standing part of the Weimar *répertoire*. Most London concert-goers, for whom Liszt has 'blazed the comet of a season', think of him as certainly the archimagus of pianists, but as otherwise a man of no particular significance; as merely an erratic, flighty, artistic genius, who has swept through Europe, the Napoleon of the *salon*, carrying devastation into the hearts of countesses. A single morning's interview with him is enough to show the falsity of this conception. In him Nature has not sacrificed the man to the artist; rather, as the blossom of the acacia is a glorious ornament to the tree, but we see it fall without regret because the tree itself is grand and beautiful, so if Liszt the pianist were unknown to you, or even did not exist, Liszt the man would win your admiration and love. See him for a few hours and you will be charmed by the originality of his conversation and the brilliancy of his wit; know him for weeks or months, and you will discern in him a man of various thought, of serious purpose, and of a moral nature which, in its mingled strength and gentleness, has the benignest influence on those about him.

[...]

It seems to be understood that we may write the more freely of our personal admiration for musical and dramatic artists, because their fame does not live after them, except for a few short years in the eulogies of their superannuated contemporaries [...] the memory of the *prima donna* scarcely outlives the flowers that are flung at her feet on her farewell night, and even the fame of a Garrick or a Siddons is simply a cold acquiescence in the verdict of the past. It is possible, however, that Liszt will turn out to be something more than one of those coruscating meteors, who come, are seen, and are extinguished in darkness; he is now devoting himself principally to composition, and may perhaps produce something perennial, though the opponents of the Wagner sect, of which Liszt is the great apostle, will not believe that any good can come out of Nazareth.

Liszt, indeed, has devoted himself with the enthusiasm of earnest conviction to the propaganda of Wagnerism: he has not only used his personal influence to get Wagner's operas put on the stage, but he has also founded a musical newspaper (*Neue Zeitschrift für Musik*), which is the organ of the Romantic School in music, and derives its chief value from the contributions of his pen. Much cheap ridicule has been spent on the 'music of the future'; a ridicule excused, perhaps, by the more than ordinary share Herr Wagner seems to have of a quality which is common to almost all innovators and heretics, and which their converts baptize as profound conviction, while the adherents of the old faith brand it as arrogance. It might be well, however, if the ridicule were arrested by the consideration that there never was an innovating movement which had not some negative value as a criticism of the prescriptive, if not any positive value as a lasting creation. The attempt at an innovation reveals a want that has not hitherto been met, and if the productions of the innovator are exaggerated symbols of the want, rather than symmetrical creations which have within them the conditions, of permanence – like an Owenite parallelogram, an early poem of Wordsworth's, or an early picture of Overbeck's – still they are protests which it is wiser to accept as strictures than to hiss down as absurdities. Without pretending to be a musical critic, one may be allowed to give an opinion as a person with an ear and a mind susceptible to the direct and indirect influences of music. In this character I may say that, though unable to recognize Herr Wagner's compositions as the ideal of the opera, and though, with a few slight exceptions, not deeply affected by his music on a first hearing, it is difficult to me to understand how any one who finds deficiencies in the opera as it has existed hitherto, can give fair attention to Wagner's theory, and his exemplification of it in his operas, without admitting that he has pointed out the direction in which the lyric drama must develop itself, if it is to be developed at all. Moreover, the musician who writes librettos for himself, which can be read with interest as dramatic poems, must be a man of no ordinary mind and accomplishments, and such a man, even when he errs, errs with ingenuity, so that his mistakes are worth studying.

Wagner would make the opera a perfect musical drama, in which feelings and situations spring out of *character*, as in the highest order of tragedy, and in which no dramatic probability or poetic beauty is sacrificed to musical effect. The drama must not be a mere pretext for the music; but music, drama, and spectacle must be blended, like the coloured rays in the sunbeam, so as to produce one undivided impression. The controversy between him and his critics is the old controversy between Gluck and Piccini [*sic*], between the declamatory and melodic schools of music, with the same difference in comprehensiveness as between the disputes of La Motte and the Daciers about the value of the classics, and the disputes of the classical and romantic schools of literature in our own day. In its first period the opera aimed simply at the expression of feeling through melody; the second period, which has its culmination in the joint productions of Meyerbeer and Scribe, added the search for effective situations and a heightening of dramatic movement, which has led more and more to the predominance of the declamatory style and the subordination of melody. But in Meyerbeer's operas the grand object is to produce a climax of spectacle, situation, and orchestral effects; there is no attempt at the evolution of these from the true workings of human character and human passions; on the contrary, the characters seem to be a second thought, and with a few exceptions, such as Alice and Marcel, are vague and uninteresting. Every opera-goer has remarked that *Robert* is a mere nose of wax; or has laughed at the pathos with which the fiend Bertram invites his son to go to the bottomless pit with him, instead of settling into respectability above ground; or has felt that *Jean, the Prophet*, is a feeble sketch, completely lost in the blaze of spectacle. Yet what a progress is there in the libretto of these operas compared with the libretto of *Der Freischütz*, which, nevertheless, was thought so good in its day that Goethe said Weber ought to divide the merit of success with Kind. Even Weber's enchanting music cannot overcome the sense of absurdity when, in a drinking party of two, one of whom is sunk in melancholy, a man gets up and bursts into a rolling song which seems the very topmost wave in the high tide of bacchanalian lyrism; or when Caspar climbs a tree apparently for no other reason than because the *dénouement* requires him to be shot.

Now, says Wagner, this ascent from the warbling puppets of the early opera to the dramatic effects of Meyerbeer, only serves to bring more clearly into view the unattained summit of the true musical drama. An opera must be no mosaic of melodies stuck together with no other method than is supplied by accidental contrast, no mere succession of ill-prepared crises, but an organic whole, which grows up like a palm, its earliest portion containing the germ and prevision of all the rest. He will write no *part* to suit a *primo tenore*, and interpolate no *cantata* to show off the powers of a *prima donna assoluta*; those who sing his operas must be content with the degree of prominence which falls to them in strict consonance with true dramatic development and ordonnance. Such, so far as I understand it, is Wagner's theory of the opera – surely a theory worth entertaining, and one which he has admirably exemplifed so far as the libretto of his operas is concerned.

But it is difficult to see why this theory should entail the exclusion of melody to the degree at which he has arrived in *Lohengrin*, unless we accept one of two suppositions: either that Wagner is deficient in melodic inspiration, or that his inspiration has been overridden by his system, which opposition has pushed to exaggeration. Certainly his *Fliegender Holländer* – a transition work, in which, as Liszt says, he only seeks to escape from the idols to which he has hitherto sacrificed, and has not yet reached the point of making war against them – is a charming opera; and *Tannhäuser* too is still the music of men and women, as well of Wagnerites, but *Lohengrin* to us ordinary mortals seemed something like the whistling of the wind through the keyholes of a cathedral, which has a dreamy charm for a little while, but by and bye you long for the sound even of a street organ to rush in and break the monotony. It may be safely said, that whatever the music of the future may be, it will not be a music which is in contradiction with a permanent element in human nature – the need for a frequent alternation of sensations or emotions; and this need is *not* satisfied in *Lohengrin*.

As to melody – who knows? It is just possible that melody, as we conceive it, is only a transitory phase of music, and that the musicians of the future may read the airs of Mozart and Beethoven and Rossini as scholars read the *Stabreim* and assonance of early poetry. We are but in 'the morning of the times', and must learn to think of ourselves as tadpoles unprescient of the future frog. Still the tadpole is limited to tadpole pleasures; and so, in our state of development, we are swayed by melody. When, a little while after hearing *Lohengrin*, we happened to come on a party of musicians who were playing exquisitely a quartette of Beethoven's, it was like returning to the pregnant speech of men after a sojourn among glums and gowries.

This is a purely individual impression, produced even in spite of favourable prepossessions derived from hearing the *Fliegender Holländer* and *Tannhäuser*, and only accidentally in agreement with the judgment of anti-Wagner critics, who are certainly in the majority at present. Still, those who are familiar with the history of music during the last forty or fifty years, should be aware that the reception of new music by the majority of musical critics, is not at all a criterion of its ultimate success. A man of high standing, both as a composer and executant, told a friend of mine, that when a symphony of Beethoven's was first played at the Philharmonic, there was a general titter among the musicians in the orchestra, of whom he was one, at the idea of sitting seriously to execute such music! And as a proof that professed musicians are sometimes equally unfortunate in their predictions about music which begins by winning the ear of the public, he candidly avowed that when Rossini's music was first fascinating the world of opera-goers, he had joined in pronouncing it a mere passing fashion, that tickled only by its novelty. Not indeed that the contempt of musicians and the lash of critics is a pledge of future triumph: St Paul five times received forty stripes save one, but so did many a malefactor; and unsuccessful composers before they take consolation from the pooh-poohing or 'damnation' of good music, must remember how much bad music has had the same fate, from the time when Jean Jacques [Rousseau]' [s] oratorio set the teeth of all hearers on edge.

If it were admissible for a person entirely without technical quali-fications for judgment, to give an opinion on Wagner as a musician, I should say that his musical inspiration is not sufficiently predominant over his thinking and poetical power, for him to have the highest creative genius in music. So far as music is an art, one would think that the same rule applied to musicians as to other artists. Now, the greatest painters and sculptors have surely not been those who have been inspired through their intellect, who have first thought and then chosen a plastic symbol for their thought; rather, the symbol rushes in on their imagination before their slower reflection has seized any abstract idea embodied in it. Nay, perhaps the artist himself *never* seizes that idea, but his picture or his statue stands there an immortal symbol nevertheless. So the highest degree of musical inspiration must overmaster all other conceptions in the mind of the musical genius; and music will be great and ultimately triumphant over men's ears and souls in proportion as it is less a studied than an involuntary symbol. Of course in composing an oratorio or an opera, there is a prior conception of a theme; but while the composer in whom other mental elements outweigh his musical power will be preoccupied with the idea, the *meaning* he has to convey, the composer who is pre-eminently a musical genius, on the slightest hint of a passion or an action, will have all other modes of conception merged in the creation of music, which is for him the supreme language, the highest order of representation. All this may be wrong, and so may be my conjecture that Wagner is a composer of the reflective kind. We often enough mistake our own negations for a negation out of ourselves, as purblind people are apt to think the sun gives but a feeble light.

Certainly Wagner has admirably fulfilled his own requisition of organic unity in the opera. In his operas there is a gradual unfolding and elaboration of that fundamental contrast of emotions, that collision of forces, which is the germ of the tragedy; just as the leaf of the plant is successively elaborated into branching stem and compact bud and radiant corolla. The artifice, however, of making certain contrasted strains of melody run like coloured threads through the woof of an opera, and also the other dramatic device of using a particular melody or musical phrase as a sort of Ahnung or prog-nostication of the approach or action of a particular character, are not altogether peculiar to Wagner, though he lays especial stress on them as his own. No one can forget the recurring hymn of Marcel in the *Huguenots*, or the strain of the Anabaptists in the *Prophète*, which is continually contrasted with the joyous song or dance of the rustics. Wagner, however, has carried out these devices much more com-pletely, and, in the *Fliegender Holländer* and *Tannhäuser*, with very impressive effect. With all my inability at present to enjoy his music as I have enjoyed that of Mozart, or Beethoven, or Mendelssohn, these two operas left in me a real desire to hear them again.

'Liszt, Wagner and Weimar', *Fraser's Magazine* lii (July 1855)

'The first Bayreuth *Ring*, and adoring Wagnerites'
PYOTR ILYICH TCHAIKOVSKY

At this present time Wagner's theatre, built on a fairly high hill outside the town, attracts the attentions only of the foreigners who have gathered here. In my first article on *Der Ring des Nibelungen*, I have already set out the history of the construction of this huge building, forty-eight metres high and accommodating with ease about two thousand spectators. It was built to the plan of the architect, Brückwald, and, it must be confessed, attracts the observer's attentions not through the grace of its outlines but solely through its colossal dimensions. It is more a huge booth, hurriedly built, as it were, for some industrial exhibition, than a building intended to accommodate a mass of people who have come from all the ends of the earth in search of artistic delights. In that harmonious combination of all the arts for which Wagner strives, architecture has been allotted too modest a place. Not being an expert on architecture, I shall nevertheless allow myself to observe that it should have been possible, while satisfying the practical demands of Wagner's project, to give some attention also to making its facilities artistically satisfying; in no way, I think, could the innovations thought up by Wagner have forced the architect, Brückwald, to sacrifice the beauty of the building for what was judged merely advisable or convenient.

The seating plan is designed in imitation of an ancient amphitheatre; the rows, one behind the other, constantly grow in breadth up to their highest point, above which is placed the gallery for the royal family. There are no boxes. Above the royal gallery are to be found yet more seats which are free to the inhabitants of Bayreuth who have rendered voluntary service to this great undertaking. The orchestra, as I have already said, is hidden; it is housed in a recess between the stage and the amphitheatre. The stage apparatus is under the control of the court theatre's stage manager, Brandt, from Darmstadt, a well-known expert in his field. Decor is by the Brückner brothers from Coburg, after designs by the Viennese artist, Hoffmann. The excellent gas-fuelled lighting was made by the Frankfurt firm of Staudt. Costumes are by the Berlin designer Doepler, who in Germany is considered a genius in this field.

Bayreuth's other top-grade wonder is Wagner's house, built in 1874. It stands in a developing garden, is square in shape, and its facade is adorned with the following inscription: *Hier, wo mein Wähnen Frieden fand – WAHNFRIED Sei dieses Haus von mir benannt.**

* Here where my mad dreams were resolved, Mad-dreams-resolution may this house be named.

Above this inscription a fresco executed by the Dresden artist, Krausse, stands out. It depicts Wotan as the wanderer (as in *Siegfried*) with his two ravens, as though recounting his secret history to the two neighbouring figures. One of these is *Greek Tragedy*, the other is *Music*, and beneath the latter, striving towards her, is depicted the young *Siegfried*, who embodies the art of the future.

The house was built by the architect to the specifications of Richard Wagner himself.* In the basement is the servants' accommodation, kitchen and stoves. Above are the reception rooms, the dining room and the high-ceilinged hall which is lit from above. The upper story contains the living rooms. Wagner's study is appointed – as, moreover, is all the rest of the house – with uncommon luxury. In front of the house there is a statue of King Ludwig of Bavaria.

I arrived in Bayreuth on 12 August on the eve of the first performance of part one of the tetralogy. The town presented an uncommonly lively spectacle. Both the natives and the foreigners, who had flooded in literally from all the ends of the earth, hurried off to the railway station to be present at the reception of the Emperor Wilhelm. I had to observe this reception from the window of a neighbouring house. There flashed past before my eyes several brilliant uniforms, then a procession of musicians from Wagner's theatre with their conductor, Hans Richter, at their head, then the tall, well-proportioned figure of the Abbé Liszt with his splendid, characteristic, grey-haired head which has so often fascinated me in his ubiquitous portraits – then, sitting in a very ornate carriage, a sprightly little old man with an aquiline nose and thin, supercilious lips – the characteristic trait of the initiator of this whole cosmopolitan artistic festival, Richard Wagner. What an overwhelming surge of pride at the triumph about to begin at last, despite all obstacles, must have been experienced by this little man who had attained, through the strength of his will and talent, the embodiment of his audacious ideals!

I set out to wander through this tiny town. Every street is overflowing with a bustling throng searching for something, with an expression of agitation on the faces of those who are visiting Bayreuth. After half an hour this mark of preoccupation on all faces has

---

* The original architect was Neumann, though the contractor who did the effective final designs was Carl Wölfel, Wagner having launched the whole process himself with some sketches.

explained itself to me very simply, and doubtless has appeared on my own physiognomy. All these people hurriedly scurrying about the streets of the town are preoccupied with satisfying the strongest of all needs of everyone living on this earth, the need which even the thirst for artistic enjoyment cannot suppress: they are searching for food. This tiny town has packed itself together and given shelter to all who had arrived, but it cannot feed them. Thus on the very first day of my arrival I discovered through experience what the struggle for a piece of bread could be. There are few hotels in Bayreuth; the majority of those who had come have been accommodated in private quarters. The tables d'hôte to be had in hotels can in no way cater for all those who are hungry. Each morsel of bread, each glass of beer is acquired by force, at the cost of incredible efforts, stratagems, and the most iron patience. And when you have got a place at the table d'hôte, your wait will not be short before there is placed before you, in a not absolutely ruined condition, the dish you wanted. Complete and utter chaos reigns at the table. Everybody shouts at once. The weary waiters give not the slightest attention to your legitimate demands. Getting this or that dish is a matter of pure chance. At the theatre there is a huge booth-like restaurant promising a good meal at two o'clock for all who want it, but to get there and get something in this maelstrom of hungry humanity is a matter of the most lofty heroism and unbridled boldness. I have elaborated so long on this circumstance deliberately in order to reveal to my readers what is by far the most outstanding characteristic of Bayreuth's company of music lovers. During the whole period of the first cycle of performances of Wagner's tetralogy *food* was the prime concern of all, significantly pushing into the background interest in art. There was much more talk of beefsteaks, cutlets, and roast potatoes than of Wagner's music.

I have already said that representatives of all civilized nationalities have congregated in Bayreuth. In fact, on the very day of my arrival I chanced to see a whole mass of famous representatives of the musical world of Europe and America. However, I must confess to having made a slip. The heavyweights among musical authorities, the first-rank celebrities, were conspicuous by their complete absence. Verdi, Gounod, Thomas, Brahms, Anton Rubinstein, Raff, Joachim, Bülow have not come to Bayreuth. Of very famed virtuosi (not counting Liszt, who is to be found with Wagner through their very close family relationship and friendship of many years), I can point only to our

Nikolay Rubinstein. Apart from him, of Russian musicians I have seen here Messrs Cui, Laroche, Famintsïn, and also, of professors from our conservatory, Mr Klindworth who, as is known, has made the piano transcription of all four operas that make up Wagner's tetralogy, and Mrs Valzek, the singing teacher well known to Moscow.

The performance of *Rheingold* took place, as advertised, on Sunday, 13 August at 7 p.m. It lasted two and a half hours without a break. The following three operas, *Die Walküre*, *Siegfried* and *Götterdämmerung*, ran with half-hour intervals and took from four to ten o'clock. Because of the indisposition of the singer, Betz, *Siegfried* was given on Wednesday instead of Tuesday, and in consequence the first cycle took five days instead of four.

Starting from three o'clock the motley crowd of professionals and music lovers who had come to Bayreuth began moving in the direction of the theatre which, as I said earlier, is a considerable distance from the town. This amounted to almost the most painful moment of the day, even for those few who had managed to eat. The road has no protection from the burning sun and, moreover, goes uphill. While waiting for the performance to begin the crowd seeks shade or tries to get glasses of beer in one of the two restaurants. Here old friendships are renewed and new ones made; on all sides can be heard laments about unsatisfied hunger, and there are conversations about the impending performance, or about yesterday's. Precisely on four o'clock a loud fanfare rings out. The whole crowd heads for the theatre. Within five minutes everybody is already in their place. Again a fanfare is heard, the talk and noise ceases, the gas lamps illuminating the auditorium suddenly go out, the entire theatre is submerged in a deep gloom, the beautiful sounds of the prelude are heard from the orchestra seated in the recess, the curtains part, and the performance begins. Each act lasts an hour and a half. Then follows the first interval, rather excruciating because when you come out of the theatre it is very difficult to find a place in the shade: the sun is still high in the sky. The second interval, by contrast, constitutes one of the best moments of the day. The sun has already sunk to the horizon; an evening freshness begins to be felt in the air, the wooded hills around and the pretty town in the distance present a restful sight. At ten o'clock the performance ends, and there begins the most dogged struggle for survival – that is, for a supper place in the theatre's restaurant. Those who have lost out rush to the town, but their disillusionment there is even more frightful. In the hotels all places have been taken. Praise be to God if you find a piece of cold meat and a bottle of wine or beer!

In Bayreuth I saw one woman, the wife of one of the most highly placed persons in Russia, who throughout her whole stay in Bayreuth did not eat once. Coffee was her only nourishment.

*

By now the reader, who has perhaps found that I have talked too much about Bayreuth and its lifestyle, is waiting for me finally to turn to the most important topic, that is, to an assessment of the artistic merits of Wagner's creation and to an account of the musical delights that I have experienced here. If that is so, then I must make my excuses to the reader, and promise him a detailed analysis of *Der Ring des Nibelungen* only in the rather distant future. Having during last winter gained only a rather superficial acquaintance with this weighty work I, in my simplicity, thought that hearing it through once in the present production would suffice for me to master and understand it thoroughly. I was profoundly wrong. Wagner's tetralogy is a composition so colossal in its vast dimensions, stylistically so complex, so finely and deeply thought and worked out, that getting to know it well requires much time and, most of all, several hearings. It is recognized that only after many hearings will the virtues and failings of a work you have studied reveal themselves. Very frequently what you did not give sufficient attention to the first time will, at the second performance, suddenly strike home and unexpectedly enthral you. On the other hand some episode, which at first seduced you and which you found most successful, pales before newly revealed beauties. But that is not enough: having, through repeated performances, become sufficiently acquainted with a new piece of music, you must live with your spontaneous impressions for a while, devote yourself to a study of the score, set what is printed against what you have heard, and then attempt to formulate well-founded and secure judgments. At some time I shall try to do all this, but meanwhile I shall give my readers merely some general observations both regarding the music itself and its stage presentation.

First I must say that everyone who believes in art as a civilizing force, every admirer of artistic merit regardless of its utilitarian objectives, must experience a feeling of exceedingly great pleasure in

Bayreuth at the spectacle of this huge artistic undertaking which has reached a triumphant conclusion and has taken on, because of its scale and the strength of the interest it has aroused, the significance of an historical epoch. At the sight of the huge building founded upon the demand for artistic pleasures inherent in mankind at all stages of our development, at the sight of the crowd of people from every stratum of society who have congregated in this little corner of Europe solely in the name of an art equally dear to all, at the sight of this whole unprecedented musical-dramatic festival, how laughable and pitiable seemed those preachers of tendentious art, who in their blindness hold our century to be marked by true art's complete collapse. The Bayreuth festival is a lesson to those inveterate persecutors of art who relate to it with arrogant disdain, finding that it is not fitting for civilized people to occupy themselves with anything other than that which brings immediate, practical *benefit*. In the sense of promoting the material prosperity of mankind the Bayreuth festival has, of course, no significance; but in the sense of searching for artistic ideals it is destined to have, at all events, colossal historical significance. Whether Wagner is right to have taken service to his ideal to the last extreme, or whether he has upset too radically the balance within those artistic conditions which can guarantee the stability of the artistic work, whether art will go from Wagner's point of departure still further along that way, or whether *Der Ring des Nibelungen* must mark the point from which a reaction will begin – whatever the case, in Bayreuth something has been accomplished which our grand-children and great-grandchildren will remember well.

The following are the principles Wagner uncompromisingly holds on to in the music of the *Nibelungen*. Because opera is nothing except drama accompanied by music, because the dramatic personae in drama must *speak*, not *sing*, Wagner banishes irrevocably from opera all closed musical forms – that is, he banishes the aria, ensembles and even choruses, which are employed by him episodically and very sparsely only in the last part of the tetralogy. He banishes from opera the whole *conventional* element which, only because routine has shut our eyes to it, has not struck us as offensive and false. Because in real life people do not, in passing bursts of passionate emotion, sing songs, there cannot be an *aria*; because two persons do not talk to each other simultaneously but listen to each other, there cannot be a *duet*; because a crowd likewise does not utter one and the same words simultaneously, there cannot be a *chorus*, and so on. Wagner, perhaps too readily forgetting that real-life *truth* and artistic *truth* are two completely different truths, strives, in a word, to be rational. In order to reconcile these demands of truth with the demands of music, Wagner has accepted only *recitative*. All his music – and it is music profoundly conceived, always interesting, at times superb and fascinating, at times a bit dry and incomprehensible, on the technical side amazingly rich, and unprecedentedly beautiful in its scoring – is entrusted to the orchestra. The characters sing for the most part only totally colourless melodic lines that fit with the symphony being played by the unseen orchestra. There are scarcely any departures from this system in *Der Ring des Nibelungen*, and if there are, then for sufficiently fundamental reasons. Thus, for instance, Siegfried in Act 1 of the third part sings two songs, and thanks to the fact that in real life a smith, when forging a sword, may sing a song, the audience gets not one but nearly two fully rounded, outstanding numbers. Each character is furnished with a special brief motif belonging only to him which is heard each time he appears on stage or when he is being talked about. The incessant recurrence of these motifs forces Wagner, in order to avoid monotony, to present them each time in a new form in which he reveals the astonishing richness of his harmonic and polyphonic technique. Yet this richness is too abundant; incessantly straining your attention, the latter finally becomes wearied, and at the end of the opera, especially in *Götterdämmerung*, fatigue reaches a stage where the music ceases to be for you an harmonic combination of sounds: it becomes a sort of wearying roar.

Ought art to strive for this? If I, by profession a musician, experienced a feeling of spiritual and physical weariness close to total exhaustion, then what must be the weariness of the dilettante listener? True, the latter is much more occupied with the marvels happening on stage than by the orchestra sweating itself to death in its recess and by the singers straining themselves to breaking point; but, you see, it surely should be assumed that Wagner composed his music to be attended to, and not to bypass our ears like something secondary, second rate. In general, nothing can stop you having to reflect that what *Der Ring des Nibelungen* gives birth to as a spectacle is musically immoral. The professional musician seeks the musical beauties in this work; he finds them in excess rather than in a proper proportion: it is a musical cornucopia which very quickly gives birth to a sense of surfeit. However that may be, the *professional musician* judges *the music* on *musical* impressions. The dilettante feasts his eyes upon the decor, the conflagrations, the transformation scenes, the appearances of dragons and serpents, the Rhinemaidens swimming, and so on. Being quite unable (as my extreme convictions would have it) to gain musical enjoyment from this tempest of sounds, yet at the same time feeling an inner pleasure at the superlative staging, he mixes the latter with his musical impressions and tries to convince himself and others that he has fully grasped what is fascinating in Wagner's music. I met one Russian merchant who assured me he recognized in music nothing but Wagner. 'But do you know all the rest?' I asked him. It emerged that my amiable compatriot had absolutely no understanding of music in general – but on the other hand, you see, he has the good fortune of being personally acquainted with the celebrated maestro, attends his receptions, is graciously received by the composer's wife and, being uncommonly proud of this acquaintance, considers it his duty to contradict everything that Wagner himself does not recognize. Unfortunately there are many such Wagnerites, and this phenomenon is extremely depressing. Of course Wagner has a huge number of enthusiastic and completely sincere supporters, among them real musicians, but they arrive at intelligent enthusiasm through study, and if anything can serve as moral support to Wagner in his strivings towards his ideal, then it is precisely the passionate devotion of these people. It would be curious simply to know whether he can distinguish these from the swarm of false Wagnerites, and especially those Wagnerites who are as ignorant as they are intolerant regarding views that do not coincide with their own.

I repeat, I had occasion in Bayreuth to meet many excellent experts boundlessly devoted to Wagner's music, and whose sincerity I have no cause to doubt. Rather I am prepared to admit that I am to blame for not having yet grown to a full understanding of this music and that, having devoted myself to a careful study of it, I too shall at some time side with the wide circle of true connoisseurs. To speak with complete honesty: at the present time *Der Ring des Nibelungen* makes on me an overwhelming impression not so much for its musical beauties, which perhaps have been scattered with an excessively liberal hand, as by its length, its massive dimensions.

This gigantic opera also demands gigantic talents for its performance. You have to be a titan to sing such a part as that of Wotan or Siegfried, and because there was nowhere from which to get such vocal titans, no one, with the possible exception of the Viennese singer *Materna* in the role of Brünnhilde, was equal to his task. However, that applied to the roles of the gods and the giants. The parts of the lesser beings, not requiring such striking power, the roles of the Rhinemaidens, in general pretty much all the second-rank parts were performed outstandingly: Mime was particularly good, both as singer and actor. The orchestra was beyond all praise, and when you consider the unimaginable complexity and difficulty of the scoring, you could not but be astonished at the perfection of their playing. The male chorus, which appeared at times in the last opera, was so outstanding that, despite its small numbers, it drowned the orchestra. The staging, with a very few minor exceptions, was splendid.

And so, in conclusion, I will say what in the end I bore away from hearing *Der Ring des Nibelungen*. I bore away indistinct memories of many striking beauties, especially symphonic ones, which is very strange because least of all did Wagner contemplate writing an opera in a symphonic manner; I bore away a reverential surprise at the huge talent of the composer and at his unprecedentedly rich technique; I bore away a doubt about the validity of the Wagnerian view of opera; I bore away a great weariness but, along with this, I also bore away a desire to continue studying this, the most complex music ever written.

Let us grant that *Der Ring des Nibelungen* seems boring in places; let us grant that much of it is, on first acquaintance, unclear and incomprehensible; let us grant that Wagner's harmony at times is confused and *recherché*; let us grant that Wagner's theory is mistaken; let us grant that it contains no small dose of aimless quixotism; let us grant that this huge work is condemned to lie in eternal sleep in the deserted theatre at Bayreuth, leaving behind the fabled memory of a gigantic labour that had briefly focused upon itself the attention of the whole world – all the same, *Der Ring des Nibelungen* constitutes one of the most significant phenomena in the history of art. However you relate to Wagner's titanic work, no one can deny the magnitude of the task he has carried through, and the strength of spirit that roused him to pursue his work to the end and bring to performance one of the grandest artistic plans ever conceived in the head of man.

After the last chord of the final scene of the final opera Wagner was called out by the audience. He emerged and made a short speech which concluded with the words: 'You have just seen what we can do. Now it is up to you: if you wish it, we shall have art.' I leave the reader to make what sense he will of these words. I will say only that these words produced bewilderment among the audience. For a few moments it remained silent. Then cheers began, but these were incomparably less enthusiastic than those which had preceded Wagner's appearance. I think this must have been exactly how members of the Paris parliament reacted when Louis XIV uttered his famous words: '*L'état, c'est moi!*' At first, in silence, they were struck dumb by the magnitude of the task he had laid upon himself – but then, remembering that he was the king, they cried: '*Vive le roi!*'

Russian Gazette, Russkiye vedemosti (/), 26 and 30 August 1876, tr. David Brown

'Table talk about Richard Wagner'
WYSTAN HUGH AUDEN

The second act of *Parsifal* is really wonderful, except for the Flower Maidens' scene. Non-Wagnerians prefer it, but I don't like the plot of *Die Meistersinger* – partly the exaltation of art, partly other things. The only ones I like all through are *Die Walküre*, *Götterdämmerung* and *Tristan*. In the *Ring* my order is *Walküre*, *Götterdämmerung* ... that wonderful oath on the spear. The duet between Brünnhilde and Waltraute. There's one phrase that, when you consider the billowy soprano, is really quite funny: '*Das ist kein Mann.*' One thing I don't like about *Parsifal* is the emphasis on virginity. Of course, celibacy may be desirable, but that isn't saying that if you aren't celibate you are excluded. The whole idea of the Grail, the sacred object, is essentially heretical. Everyone should have an opportunity. All that Good Friday performance in *Parsifal* is terrible. I don't mind the church coming into art. The church bells ring like mad in Italian opera. But in *Parsifal*, it's taken so seriously. That business of no applause is bad. The way Wagner thought he was writing something simple and popular when he started *Tristan* is amazing.

You know, *Tristan* should really be done by two 'lizzies'. They eat each other up, try to replace the world. Isolde is the English Mistress, Tristan the Hockey Mistress.

Don Giovanni is a certain type of male homosexual. Neither extreme, Tristan or Don Giovanni, is compatible with heterosexual love.

The Table Talk of W. H. Auden

'A lesson in librettist's diplomacy'
GIUSEPPE VERDI AND ARRIGO BOITO

Verdi to Franco Faccio

Genoa, 27 March 1884

Dear Faccio,

Two words to thank you for the kindness you showed towards the person I recommended to you. Two other words about a matter that concerns me personally.

Il pungolo* quotes these lines from *Il piccolo* in Naples: 'Concerning *Jago*, Boito said that he treated the subject almost against his will; but that when it was finished he regretted not having been able to compose it himself.'† ... Admittedly those words, spoken at a banquet, are of no great importance; but unfortunately they are subject to comment. It might be said, for example, that I forced him to treat the subject. This by itself would not be so bad; in any case, you know how things went.

The trouble is that when Boito *regrets* not being able to compose the opera himself, it must be supposed, of course, that he could not hope to see it composed by me the way he would like it. I perfectly agree with this, I completely agree; and therefore I address myself to you, Boito's oldest, most steadfast friend, so that upon his return to Milan you may tell him in person, not in writing, that – without the shadow of resentment, without any deep-seated anger – I return his manuscript to him intact. Furthermore, since the libretto is my property, I offer it to him as a gift, for whenever he intends to compose it. If he accepts this I will be happy – happy in the hope of having furthered and served the art we all love.

Forgive the trouble I am causing you, but this is a matter that must be handled discreetly. There is no one better suited to take care of this than you.

Take care of your health, and believe me

Yours

G. Verdi

* A Naples newspaper with Rome and Milan editions.
† The banquet followed the Naples première of *Mefistofele*. According to Boito, many years later, 'Asked about the libretto of *Otello*, I expressed very different feelings from those that were coarsely interpreted by *Il piccolo*.'

Boito to Verdi

Milan, Saturday [26 April 1884]

Dear Maestro,

I ran over to Turin to see the medieval castle, which is wonderful, and arrived in Milan yesterday. For many reasons I am glad I made this trip. In Turin I saw my brother and several good friends, among them Giacosa, who was my guide, and Faccio, who was rehearsing his Cantata, which (especially in the beginning and the cadenza) made the great impression on me that I had expected. But the main reason my trip turned out to be even more fortunate than I had hoped – the unpredictably favourable reason – lay in the confidences Faccio revealed to me concerning a letter you had written to him. Had I not gone to Turin, who knows for how many months I might not have known what you wanted me to know from my friend's own lips.

With all my heart, thank you, my Maestro, thank you, but it seems really too much to have to answer you seriously that I do not accept – that I do not accept your great, your noble offer. These journalists must be of quite a different sort from honest people; I don't say all of them, but most. Here is one who manages to misunderstand my words in such a bestial manner as to produce a sentence that is precisely the opposite of my feelings, and he prints this sentence, and other journalists repeat it, and thus the work of foolish, indiscreet people creates, at my expense, a foolish and indiscreet situation between you and me, a situation from which I find myself set free only today. And if I find myself set free from this unreal situation, Maestro, the credit is yours. For that more than for the offer itself I thank you fervently, because through this my heart finds the occasion to open itself to you with complete confidence.

I read this tasteless report in the *Roma*, a Neapolitan newspaper I had with me while travelling to Genoa. I cannot tell you how indignant and disturbed I was. Throughout the trip I thought how I might remedy the journalist's silly talk. My first impulse was to write to the editor of the *Roma* myself; then I hesitated to write about you without your consent, and I decided to ask you for it. In order to get it, I dropped in at the Palazzo Doria in Genoa the very morning of my arrival; I resolved to do this because I also had the excuse of bringing you Morelli's photograph. When Signora Giuseppina suddenly entered the room, I didn't have the nerve to bore your wife with talk that concerned such a silly thing, and couldn't have done so without showing my annoyance. A few days went by, and I calmed down; I began to think that the *Roma* was a paper known only in the Neapolitan provinces and that no other paper would have published this blunder; I thought that corrections and the writing of letters to papers were almost always vain, and always fruitless. I soon regained my composure, strong though I was in my feelings. I thought the public would have read the report in the *Roma* with indifference, and since this was the case, I hoped that you would never have seen it. But human foolishness has long legs. *Il piccolo* in Naples reproduced the report (I only learned of this in Turin the day before yesterday), and so did *Il pungolo*. This surprises me, because Fortis knows me too well to have believed what he printed; and as soon as I see him I shall ask him in confidence whether he read the galleys of his paper that day, and he will tell me no. The Italian public has little faith in the papers, however, and this enables me not to worry about the public's impression. But I cannot help worrying about the effect this report might have had on you, Maestro. This letter is getting long; forgive me, but now that I have started I must tell you everything. This is the origin of the misunderstanding. (Blessed are you who have such glory and authority that you can decline dinners. I cannot afford this luxury, since I would be accused of being presumptuous and nothing else.) At the supper which some colleagues offered me after the *Mefistofele* in Naples, a polite journalist, a cultivated and courteous man, Signor Martino Caffiero, made this observation to me point-blank: '*Otello* would have been a subject for you, too.' (This proves that a well-mannered man is capable of saying words that embarrass the one who listens to them.) I answered by denying this, adding that I had never thought of *Otello* for myself. But realizing then that by persisting in this negative answer, without any explanation, I was leaving myself open to the interpretation that I had brought little love to the work that Verdi was to compose, I explained my answer. I said that I had never thought about it, because I felt too passionately about Shakespeare's masterwork in its *tragic* form to be able to express it in *operatic* form (and this is partly true). I added that I had never thought it possible to transform Shakespeare's tragedy into a good libretto until I did this work for you, Maestro, and with you (and this is true), and that only now, after much retouching, was I satisfied that the work I had undertaken with great trepidation possessed, in the end, the eminently lyrical qualities and forms which lend themselves perfectly to composition and which are suited in every way to the demands of opera. I spoke these words with the emphasis of profound conviction, and Signor Caffiero, who understood them correctly, did not publish them, because he is not one of those who publish conversations that take place at the dinner table. Somebody else, to whom, obviously, I had not addressed my remarks, and who understood them in the most distorted manner, published them in the *Roma* after his own fashion, perhaps without any malicious intent, but with a twisting of the sense and with the attribution to me of a desire that offends me and is precisely the opposite of my great desire – which is to have you set to music a libretto that I have written solely for the joy of seeing you take up your pen once more *per causa mia*, for the glory of being your collaborator, for the ambition of hearing my name coupled with yours, and ours with Shakespeare's, and because this theme and my libretto have been transferred to you by the sacred right of conquest. Only you can compose *Otello*. The entire world of opera you have given us affirms this truth; if I have been able to perceive the Shakespearean tragedy's enormous capability of being set to music (which I did not feel at first), and if in fact I have been able to prove this with my libretto, it is because I placed myself within the sphere of Verdian art. It is so because, in writing those verses, I felt what you would feel when illustrating them with that other language – a thousand times more intimate and mighty – sound. And if I have done this it is because I wanted to take the opportunity in the prime of my life, at an age when [one's] faith no longer wavers, to take the opportunity to show you, better than by praises thrown in your direction, how much I love and am moved by the art that you have given us.

You must now answer me whether you thought the report by the editor of the *Roma*, [as] reported by *Il piccolo* and *Il pungolo*, was true. I hope not. Yet the report existed, and because you read it you felt the same need I felt, to untie a tangled knot, to resolve a delicate question, and you have resolved it in the most exquisitely suitable manner that was possible. You addressed yourself confidentially to my most trusted friend so that in speaking to me he could question my intentions, and had he detected even a germ of truth in the journalist's report, you would have been ready to give *Otello* to me so that I might set it to music.

For a moment you doubted me, like the wise man who recognizes the weakness of Adam in men, but this doubt within you changed into a kind and generous offer. What you cannot suspect, Maestro, is the irony which this offer seemed to possess for me, without your being at fault. Look: for the past seven or eight years, perhaps, I have been working on *Nerone* (put the *perhaps* where you want it, attached to the word *years* or to the word *working*), and I live in that nightmare. On the days I don't work, I pass the hours like a lazybones; on the days I do work, [I work] like an ox. Thus life goes on and I continue to carry on, slowly asphyxiated by an ideal that is too high for me. Unfortunately I have studied my historical period (that is, the period of my subject) too well, and I am terribly attached to it. No other subject on earth, not even Shakespeare's *Othello*, could distract me from my theme; it corresponds in every way to my artistic temperament and to my concept of the theatre. I may or may not finish *Nerone*, but I will certainly never give it up for another work. If I do not have the strength to finish it, I won't complain, but will spend my life neither sad nor happy, with that dream in mind.

Now you may judge if, with this obstinacy, I could accept your offer. But for Heaven's sake don't abandon *Otello*, don't abandon it. It is predestined for you. You must set it to music; you had already begun work on it, and I was already quite encouraged, and was hoping to see it finished on some not-too-distant day.

You are healthier than I, stronger than I. We engaged in a test of strength, and my arm bent under yours. Your life is tranquil and serene – take up your pen again and write me soon: 'Dear Boito, do me the favour of changing these lines,' etc., etc., and I will change them right away, with joy. I'll know how to work for you, I, who cannot work for myself, because you live the real and true life of art, while I live in the world of hallucinations. But I must end. Many regards to Signora Giuseppina.

An affectionate handshake.

Your
Arrigo Boito

Verdi's Otello *and* Simon Boccanegra *in Letters and Documents*, ed. and tr. Hans Busch

'Tenor whips six policemen'
LEO SLEZAK

I forcibly obtained entrance for Frieda and myself and made for the office, where I wanted to see the sheriff's officers. They tried to stop me, so I got wild, grabbed one hulking policeman after another – six all told – shoved them aside none too gently, wrenched the door open and strode into the office. The sheriff's officers were amazed to find that a single man could break their sixfold police cordon and after a lengthy argument, they listened to what I had to say. I explained that since the whole show had petered out I had to catch the next boat for Europe in order to fulfil an engagement in Russia, that the costumes were my personal property and that I could not possibly be held responsible for the fraudulent conduct of my directors. My determined attitude and vigorous procedure must have impressed them – at any rate, they let me have my dress baskets. The policemen, in whom my scant respect for authority and short shrift for its representatives appeared to have evoked some admiration, helped me to load my stuff on to a truck and just as I was leaving, the biggest of the bunch clapped me on the shoulder, saying: 'You'd make a very good policeman!' I drove to the hotel and we packed our things the same night. The hotel manager – a Viennese – had reserved seats for us in the Chicago express and early the next morning, without having been to bed at all, we drove to the station. Newsboys with the morning papers were calling, 'Giant Czech tenor whips six policemen!'

from *Song of Motley*, 1938

'Lilli Lehmann and immoral coloratura'
EDUARD HANSLICK

Lilli Lehmann is unique, if only in regard to a repertoire which ranges from lyric to dramatic parts, from the Queen of the Night to Fidelio, from Zerlina to Donna Anna.* After having witnessed her great

* Henry Pleasants provided the following note: It ranged more widely than that – from Offenbach and Suppé to all three Brünnhildes. During her guest engagement at the Vienna Court Opera in the season of 1884–1885 (the engagement discussed in this

success as the Queen in *The Huguenots*, a purely coloratura part, it was with almost reproachful admiration that we watched her begin her second engagement as Isolde. Her far from heroic voice is no match for the merciless surf of the Wagnerian orchestra. Such parts demand not only passionate expression and dramatic talent but also uncommon vocal strength. In her own interest, and in that of music lovers generally, I would like to see her safeguarded against such unnatural exertions, to warn her, *nota bene*, against voice-killing roles but not against dramatic parts as such. That so imaginative an artist, and one rejoicing in such potentialities as an actress, should feel impelled to break the bounds of purely virtuoso parts and move on to genuinely dramatic assignments is hardly surprising. On the contrary: just as Miss Lehmann's coloratura roles derived their peculiar charm from their rare dramatic inspiration, so do her eminently dramatic roles benefit from the attributes of the former coloratura singer.

The now conventional division of female parts into coloratura and dramatic categories is of comparatively recent origin. Mozart, Beethoven, and even Weber were not aware of this arbitrary division. Their principal soprano parts demanded dramatic energy and, at the same time, a voice more or less well versed in florid singing. Rossini, Bellini, Donizetti, and often even Verdi wrote for artists schooled in virtuosity and yet also capable of dramatic characterization. No one regrets the disappearance of purely bravura parts, but there is every reason to regret the opposite extreme sanctioned by the newest school, according to which genuine technique is not a requisite for dramatic singers. As late as the thirties, the best German representatives of Donna Anna, Agathe, Euryanthe, and Fidelio were singers well versed in coloratura and not above singing such roles as Norma.

An excellent Norma is the rarest thing in Germany today. And what else could one expect? Our coloraturas haven't the voices, and they

---

review), Lilli Lehmann (1848–1929) sang Isolde, Leonore (*Fidelio*), Donna Anna (*Don Giovanni*), Konstanze (*Die Entführung aus dem Serail*), and Norma. In the last opera her sister Marie was the Adalgisa. Since Marie did not like to sing the lower voice in cadenzas, the sisters changed voices, so to speak, every time a cadenza came along. She made her American debut in the following season as Carmen at the Metropolitan, on November 25, 1885, and sang the *Die Walküre* Brünnhilde five days later. It is pertinent to note – at a time when young singers are being charged with impatience – that Lilli Lehmann made her debut as the First Boy in *The Magic Flute* on October 20, 1865, a month before her seventeenth birthday, and pinch-hit as Pamina a few days later.

can't act: our 'dramatic' singers have no vocal technique. For this reason alone it was a source of artistic gratification that Lilli Lehmann sang Norma as well as Donna Anna and Fidelio. She reacquainted us with the effects which a voice schooled in virtuosity can achieve when combined with dramatic and passionate expression. Some of the critics made a show of annoyance about the reappearance of an opera which we had not heard for years. I can only say that I am sorry for anyone whom the 'dramatic' tendencies of contemporary music have robbed of the capacity to appreciate the simple, beautiful line of these naturally motivated melodies. *Norma* suffers from monotonous stretches, meager accompaniments, and trivial devices. But are there no trivialities in even the best German operas? The difference is only in color. German trivialities are commonly camouflaged as 'drama' or 'scholarship.' Bellini was naïve, even in his trivialities. He was one of the last of the naïve masters. His limited vocabulary was often inadequate for the scope of his emotions, but the emotions were genuine and flowed straight from the heart. With a God-given, if severely restricted, talent he gave to *Norma* and the somewhat weaker *La Sonnambula* the best that was in him. There are excellent things side by side with poor and outmoded stuff. But who since Bellini has written a melody with the sweet long breath of '*Casta diva*,' or a song more expressive in its ultimate simplicity than that of the final duet, '*Qual cor tradisti*,' or a soulful melody so plastically effective as the '*Padre, tu piangi*' in the last finale? One of the best pieces of music Wagner ever wrote, the second finale in *Tannhäuser*, points unmistakably to the final scene of *Norma* as its model in the effective climax, '*Ich fleh' für ihn*' ('I Pray for Him').

In his youth, Wagner had a high opinion of *Norma*. The *Bayreuther Blätter*, in a recent example of imprudent piety, reproduced an old article in which he endorsed the validity of coloratura singing. The editors attempted in a postscript to reconcile these early enthusiasms with his later doctrines – in vain! The Wagner of the *Ring* regarded every vocal ornament as a crime. The coloratura in *Norma* is no crime; it is rather an obsolete fashion. In all of Germany in Mozart's time, and in at least all of Italy in Bellini's, floridity was considered natural and dramatically permissible in leading soprano parts. It was a generally acknowledged fashion, and it was essential that one know how to wear it in good taste. Sensuous beauty and vocal charm dominated the opera in those days, just as the specifically dramatic dominates now. The ultimate consequences of this 'purely dramatic' style – angular declamation, monodic dialogue, endless abuse of deceptive cadence, and the sovereignty of the unbridled orchestra – do all these constitute the irrefutable, sole, and eternal truth? It is a fashion, just as the former preponderance of floridity was a fashion. It will become obsolete sooner or later, and all the more certainly because it is musically unnatural.

Whatever there was of musical unaffectedness in the young Wagner has been destroyed by the Wagnerites. I confess – not without trepidation – that I once found much pleasure in the flowery extravagances of *L'Elisir d'Amore* and *Don Pasquale*, the fine wit of the ornate passages of *Le Domino Noir* or *Fra Diavolo*. I was not then aware of the iniquity of coloratura singing or the perversity of those who enjoy it. The latest issue of the Wagnerite organ, *Parsifal*, has opened my eyes. In a special article on 'The Immorality of Coloratura Singing,' one Bruno Schrader pronounces this cruel verdict (of immorality) and proposes that the indictment be extended to the representatives and adherents of coloratura singing. Even more significant than the verdict is the justification. Why is coloratura singing immoral? Answer: because of the 'damage it has done and continues to do to the popularization and further development of Wagner's works of art.' Cimarosa and Mozart, Rossini and Auber are immoral when they offer coloratura singing because they damage Wagner's work. He who enjoys it is equally guilty. Should there exist a monster so immoral as to consider the vocal style of *The Barber of Seville* or *L'Elisir d'Amore* more musical than that of Alberich or Mime, it should obviously be sentenced to starve in the bowels of Siegfried's dragon.

Our vocal virtuosos, according to Schrader, should not be referred to as coloratura singers or even as artists. 'Away with that rubbish!' he concludes. 'The time for feasting our ears is past. It will not be long before the heavenly strength of Wagner's creations will have purged the temples and thrown the money-changers out.'

It is certainly laudable of myself and some of my peace-loving colleagues that we have resolved not to touch upon the question of Wagner without special provocation. Whole libraries have been written about his works, pro and con. It would be best, I think, to observe silence on this exhausted topic for a few years. Only posterity will be in a position to review the subject without bias. But the best of intentions are frustrated by such manifestations as the above. We consider it our journalistic duty to keep the musical world informed of the latest philosophic discoveries of the Wagnerites and of the refined classical language which they employ to popularize them.

Let us return to more pleasant things: to the singing of Lilli Lehmann. Her Norma was characterized in the slow cantilenas by the most beautiful portamento and the securest and finest intonation and swelling of the high notes, in the florid passages by a pure and fluent coloratura. The latter was never a coquettish intrusion; it remained noble, serious, subordinate to the situation. One may conceive of a thunder of passion more imposing, of lightning flashes of jealousy and anger more incendiary – this reservation is applicable to all the climactic moments of Lilli Lehmann's dramatic roles and is probably attributable to vocal limitations rather than to want of temperament, although the latter cannot be entirely denied.

How decisive an actor's or singer's personal appearance may be in determining the final sum of his effectiveness – much more than talent, technique, and schooling – can be observed in Lilli Lehmann in a twofold sense. Nature denied her penetrating strength and sumptuousness of voice, and thus deprived her of the strongest, most immediate means of passionate communication, but it endowed her with a personality predestined not only for the stage but particularly for tragic and noble roles. The tall, slender figure need only appear, lifting the nobly featured head with the darkly arched eyes, and one believes in her at once as Donna Anna, Norma, and Fidelio. There are, moreover, her matchless carriage and her exemplary costumes. Inspired dramatic characteristics develop naturally from the situation; they never appear contrived or imposed from the outside. She does not commit the fault of acting too much or singing too loudly.

In Lilli Lehmann, refined artistic schooling outweighs strong immediacy of feeling. Her creations do not represent the improvisations of a great natural force; they are rather products of a superior mind which finds its way to the core of every interpretive problem and discloses the inner treasure in unblemished perfection.

Vienna's Golden Years of Music, 1850–1900, tr. Henry Pleasants, 1950

'Ants and white kid at Covent Garden'
MAX BEERBOHM

I am quite indifferent to serious music, and I should not suffer from any sense of loss if all the scores of all the operas that have ever been written, and all the persons who might be able to reconstruct them from memory, were to perish in a sudden holocaust to-morrow. And yet I like going to Covent Garden. In June and July it is not the least pleasant mode of whiling away the half-hour between dinner and supper. With its cool vestibules and colonnades and *foyers*, Covent Garden, despite its humble site and comparatively mean proportions, is an ideal place for a cigarette. Merely to wander behind the Grand Tier and read the illustrious names printed on the doors of the boxes – printed in mere black and white, just as my name will be printed on the label of this wretched book – is an experience to thrill hearts that are far less snobbishly impressionable than my heart is. I seem to breathe, at every step I take in that circuit, the tart ozone of distinction. The sultriness of no night in summer can rob me of the exhilaration which fills my being in that most high and rarefied and buoyant atmosphere. I seem to tread the circuit with very light feet. Soon I am of a mood for the auditorium. As I pass down one of the narrow stairways leading to that sea of sleek heads and jewelled or feathered *coiffures*, the stalls, a stout gentleman unconsciously obstructs my path. As he makes way for me, I recognize in him, from an old drawing in *Punch*, an hereditary legislator, who was once in one of Mr Gladstone's Cabinets. *En passant*, I tread upon his foot, that I may have the honour of apologising to him. He bows courteously. I am happy. On the vast cavernous stage, behind low-burning footlights, some opera or other is proceeding. The fiddlers are fiddling in a quiet monotone, not loud enough to drown the chatter in the stalls and boxes. All around me the people are chattering to one another like so many smart apes. Snatches of discussion here, and of flirtation there, are wafted past me, gaily, ceaselessly. I see the flash of eager gestures in white kid; I see white shoulders, white gardenias, rouge under lurid œiliads, the quivering of *aigrettes*, the light on high collars highly-polished, and the sheen of innumerable diamonds, and the rhythmic sway of a thousand-and-one fans. Row upon row, the little dull-red boxes, receptacles of bravery and beauty, are sparkling,

also, with ceaseless animation. To me they are like an exquisite
panorama of Punch-and-Judy shows. Every lady, I think, should bring
her lap-dog and set it on the ledge of her box, to consummate the
illusion. Just above me, to my right, stretches an omnibus-box.
Olympian! It is empty, save for one of whom nothing can be seen but
a large *lorgnon* upheld by a pair of small, fat, tight-gloved hands.
Who is it? A great man, doubtless. Great; else he were not hidden. A
virtuoso, too; else he were less rapt. Perhaps an Ambassador; for his
cuffs are cut in a foreign mode. Yes, I am sure those are the cuffs of an
old diplomat, and that their wearer has sat, just so, hidden behind the
curtain, in all the opera-houses of Europe – the Ring Theatre, the
Théâtre de la Monnaie, the Hof Opern-Haus, La Scala, and the rest.
So will he yet be sitting next year, here or in some other city.

And the music, the incidental music, is being played all this while. I
do not think it is Wagner's. Wagner is usually rather obtrusive and apt
to forget his place. He forgets the deference due to the stalls and
boxes, forcing their occupants to shout at the tops of their voices if
they would be heard, and has a vulgar trick of playing to the
Amphitheatre and its dowdy freight of listeners. But he has done
undeniably good work in humbling the singers. Thanks to him, the
audience no longer spends its evening in prostration before a *prima
donna*. Bouquets do not hurtle through the air, and the poor singers,
with their diamonds, and their diet, and their rivalries, and their
roulades, are not the cynosure they were in the 'seventies. Yet, there
they still are, those tiny, inadequate puppets on that mammoth-stage,
mere dots like the human figures on one of Turner's widest canvases;
here he still is, this fat little man in trunk hose, with yellow hair
down his back, strutting, storming, spurning, suppliant, passionate,
aspiring, desperate – all for the sake of a little lady in white, with her
hands clasped across her breast and her face upturned to the property
stars. These little marionettes with big voices, making so gigantic a
pother about something or other, have keen pathos in my sight – types
of our poor estate, of our vanity, or pompous endeavouring, our
insignificance, on the world's stage. See! The wee tenor is going to kill
himself with a dagger. No! The wee soprano prevents him. Tiny,
intelligent, full of purpose, performing with all their might tasks for
which I see no reason, they seem to me – these two – like a pair of ants
on a pathway:

Hi motus animorum atque hæc certamina tanta
Pulveris exigui jactu compressa quiescunt.

Hark! They are in the midst of a stormy duet. I vow the little creatures fascinate me! Here comes a whole army of ants in attitudes of surprise. The wee tenor beats his breast, the wee soprano dashes down a cup of wine. I would not throw dust on them for all the world! But some one, less kind than I, rolls down a great curtain, and the ants are hidden. The audience stops talking for a few moments of rather languid applause. Men in the stalls stand up and stare around, sidle their way through the crush in Fops' alley, and seek the Tiers. The Ambassador in the omnibus-box has dropped his *lorgnon* and is quite invisible now. And I reflect that, after all, the ants were rather absurd, and that, really, the house is rather hot, and that, on the whole, I will not stay for the last act.

More, 1899

'Touring the "English *Ring*" round the suburbs'
THOMAS BEECHAM

First opera company (1902)

It was about the beginning of my third year in London that one day I heard of a new opera company which was about to go on tour in the suburbs, with a cast of artists nearly all well known to me. I resolved to try my luck with the management, and with a full score under my arm marched down to its offices, where I found a score of other persons in waiting. Hours went by and I was beginning to think I should never obtain even a glimpse of authority, when suddenly the attention of us all was drawn to signs of what was unmistakably some sort of a scene going on in the inner room, accompanied by a very ineffective improvisation on a piano conspicuously out of tune. Presently the door was flung open and a portly choleric individual appeared and called out: 'Is there anyone here who can play the piano?' Several of those present at once answered in the affirmative. 'But do any of you know *Faust* without the music?' continued the apparition, and to this there was no reply. It dawned upon me that here might be an opportunity of penetrating the stronghold; so I meekly raised my voice and said: 'I think I know the opera.'

'What part of it?' sternly demanded my questioner.

'Any part of it.' Gazing at me incredulously, he said, 'Come in,' and in I went.

It appeared that a singer who had been sent there with a recommendation for the part of Marguerite had neglected to bring a copy of the piece with her, and this oversight had kindled the official wrath. I played through those portions which were required for the trial, and was about to take my leave, when the now partly pacified impresario said, 'Wait a bit. I want a word with you – besides, there may be others out there who have forgotten their music'; and so it proved to be. After the singers had left he enquired: 'Why did you come here?'

'I have an opera with me which I hoped you might hear with a view to performance,' said I.

'Good God, what an idea!' said he. His astonishment seemed so profound that I hardly knew how to continue the conversation, and was thinking of a fresh opening, when he went on, 'How many of the pieces I am giving do you know?' – handing me at the same time a prospectus of his season. I looked at it, informed him that I was familiar with all of them, and he asked me if I had ever conducted. I told him exactly what I had done, and he suggested that I try my hand at opera. Naturally I jumped at the idea, still nourishing the hope that it might lead to the production of one of my works. As it was now about lunch-time, he invited me to come back in the afternoon and talk it over, and when I returned I found him quite alone. He explained that he had given orders that no one should be admitted as he wanted to have a little private singing, declaring himself to be the possessor of the finest tenor voice in England. I was made to sit at the piano and accompany him for the rest of the day in long extracts from operas that contained his favourite roles, and every time there was a brief pause he asked for my opinion as to his performance. Naturally I allowed my enthusiasm to grow with each effort, and the result was that before I left I had been offered and had accepted the post of one of the two conductors of the new company, with instructions to start at once on the rehearsals which were taking place at the 'Old Vic'.

The tour lasted about two months; we visited such outlying places as Clapham, Brixton, and Stratford, and I enjoyed myself hugely, conducting in addition to *Carmen* and *Pagliacci* that trilogy of popular Saturday-nighters dubbed facetiously 'The English Ring' –

The Bohemian Girl, Maritana, and *The Lily of Killarney.* But all the fun and excitement I extracted from the experience (that inveterate old joker, G. H. Snazelle, who was playing Devilshoof, succeeded in setting fire to the stage as a farewell gesture on the last night) could not blind my soberer perceptions to the truth that if there was one especial way in which opera should not be given, then here it was in all its rounded perfection. Some of the singers, of course, were excellent, and I have never heard Marie Duma's rendering of Leonora in *Il Trovatore* bettered anywhere in the world for tone quality, phrasing and insight into the true character of the role. But of attempt, even the slightest, at production there was none, and both scenery and dresses were atrocious. Some of the principals brought their own costumes along, but the detached spectacle of one or two brilliantly clad figures only threw into more dismal relief the larger mass of squalor in the background. The chorus, which was composed mainly of veterans of both the sexes, was accurate but toneless, and the orchestra quite the most incompetent I have known anywhere. I could not help comparing the wretched conditions under which great works of art were being presented to the public with the care, preparation and even luxury bestowed upon any of the half-dozen musical comedies or farces then running in the West End. Sometimes I would feel a touch of astonishment that we had an audience at all for the motley kind of entertainment we were offering, and at others an uncomfortable twinge of conscience, as if I were an accomplice in some rather discreditable racket, which among a community more critical and knowledgeable would have provoked an instant breach of the peace.

The inferiority of the orchestral performance would be an impossibility today in England, so incontestably higher is the general level of playing. But at that time, outside the few great orchestras such as the Covent Garden Opera, the Queen's Hall or the Hallé of Manchester, where at least the technical accomplishment was first rate, the average player was hardly equipped to tackle any music except that of a simple and straightforward kind. The musical culture of the country had for generations been almost entirely choral, and the instrumental side had been relegated to an obscure background from which it was only just beginning to emerge. Sir Edward Elgar has told us how during the earlier days of his career he once conducted a country town orchestra and overheard an elderly fiddler, who was timidly attempting a rather high passage, murmur to his desk colleague, 'You know, this is the first time I have been up here.' But already there were signs of a new and different spirit abroad which during the next few years was to yield gratifying results, chiefly owing to the wisdom of the colleges of music in creating student orchestras where young instrumentalists could be familiarized at an early age with a substantial portion of the classical repertoire. Gradually the old and slightly tatterdemalion world of orchestral playing was rejuvenated by the invasion of a new type of player, who had not only a better knowledge of his instrument but a wider fund of general instruction.

None the less, I have always considered that this rather uninviting initiation into professional life was of the greatest service to me. To be pitchforked into such a chaotic welter and be forced to make something tangible and workable out of it is incomparably more useful to the young conductor than to take command of a highly trained body of experts, accustomed through long routine to fulfil their respective tasks with ease and celerity. Indeed, the youthful or comparatively youthful musician should not be allowed, except on some rare occasion, to conduct an orchestra of the front rank at all; and if he does I am not sure which of the two parties to the transaction suffers the more from it. It is almost impossible that he can teach it anything, and it is more than likely that its accustomed discipline will speedily relax under a leadership that has neither experience nor authority. Further, the unhappy young man will have to decide between the alternatives of assuming an air of omniscience as comical as a child preaching in a cathedral pulpit, or an abnegation of any effort at real direction; either of which will be equally acceptable to that collection of humorists who make up the personnel of nearly every first-class orchestra of the world. For there is no other company of human beings engaged in a communal task that can match it for instant and accurate valuation of competence or incompetence, be it in a conductor, singer, pianist or any other executant whose craft has been daily under its argus eye year in and year out. Be it in the opera house or the concert room, I would in nineteen cases out of twenty abide by the verdict or accept the opinion of a great orchestra far more confidently than I would that of either the Press or the public.

[...]

But returning to my first encounter with opera, the most valuable lesson I learned was, that while all the music which sounded right and effective in the theatre had a character or quality possessed by none other, it failed to make anything like the same appeal when heard outside it. To apply the term 'dramatic' and to be content with such a definition would be inadequate and misleading. The symphonic work of Beethoven more than that of any other composer is essentially dramatic, and if anyone be doubtful on the point, he need only listen to it after a course of Mendelssohn, Schumann, or Dvořák, all of whom wrote quite good symphonies in their way. Yet Beethoven's theatre music is not one quarter as vital and telling as that of Mozart. The Fifth and Sixth Symphonies (particularly the latter) of Tchaikovsky have a distinctly dramatic quality, but of all the Russian composers he is the least successful in opera. What is this intangible element in the music itself which must be half the battle already won for any piece that has to dominate the stage? And how many works do we not know which are admirably constructed and have both capital stories and excellent music, but which fail to hold the public attention really interested and absorbed? It is not easy to answer this question; but it may be a highly developed inner visual sense in the consciousness of supremely gifted writers for the theatre like Mozart, Verdi, Wagner, and Puccini, that sees as in an ever-present mirror the progress of the drama running through every phrase, word, and action, and simultaneously evolves the right sort of music to go along with it. But whatever is its nature, there is no doubt about its existence, and the realization of it was to me at the time important enough to send me back to a reperusal of the operatic efforts of my countrymen, who so far had failed to produce a single work that could hold its own with even the dozens of second-rate pieces turned out by the composers of France or Italy.

It could not be owing to any inherent incapacity for the theatre in our people, who during a period of several hundred years had been giving to the world one of the few great schools of drama known to civilization; but it might conceivably be traced to the predilection among our musicians themselves for those foreign masters like Bach, Beethoven, Mendelssohn, and Brahms, who are a complete antithesis to all that has to do with the essential spirit of it. As I have already indicated, German influence was everywhere omnipotent, while at the same time it was overlooked that the Germans were not really a theatrically gifted people. Their dramatic literature could not compare with that of several other great European nations, and even in the field of opera their composers, outside Weber and Wagner, had produced very little of genuine originality. It therefore seemed to me that until our musicians realized all this more clearly, turned their backs on their Teutonic models, generated a more wholesome respect for the composers of other countries, and (more important than all else) began like the Russians to cultivate a style and idiom of their own, they had better return to the safer and easier task of writing oratorios and cantatas for the thousands of choral societies up and down the kingdom, just as their forefathers had been peacefully and ineffectively doing for the past two hundred years.

A Mingled Chime, 1944

'A singing Czech on bouncing cheques'
LEO SLEZAK

'We won't sing unless we get our salaries first!' shouted several excited Italians, while both the directors were endeavouring to persuade them to carry on until business improved – which it was bound to do before long. In the end, they all got a little on account, and being good-natured souls at heart – as most stage folk are – they agreed to go on. Things gradually improved, the unrest died down, and we started out on tour for the South, to Texas. Every time I got my cheque, I sent it to my bank in New York. The cheques were all drawn on a bank in Keokuk, Missouri. While we were at Dallas, Texas, I had a wire saying that the last three cheques had been dishonoured and, like an enraged lioness robbed of her young, I flew to the director, Mr Buller and, gasping for breath, showed him the telegram.

'I'm very sorry – I know those cheques are phoney!' he coolly informed me.

'But how can you do this sort of thing?' I asked.

'Well, what can I do? If I told you that they were phoney before-hand, you wouldn't sing.'

Song of Motley, 1938

'Three vital pillars of great French opera'
CLAUDE DEBUSSY

I should like to attempt to trace not a portrait of M. Massenet, but rather something of the attitude of mind he was trying to convey through his music. Apart from anything else, the idiosyncrasies of a man's life and the anecdotes surrounding him have to be posthumous before they are of any interest.

It is at once obvious that music was never for Massenet that 'universal voice' which it was for Bach and Beethoven; rather did he make it a pleasing speciality.

If one consults a list of his works, already quite long, you will find an overriding preoccupation underlying all of them. Rather ominously, one could say it was destiny, *la marche*. It has caused him to rework, in his latest opera *Grisélidis*, something of the story of *Eve*, one of his earliest compositions. Can we not conclude that there must be some mysterious guiding hand of fate behind it all? Does it not explain Massenet's insatiable desire to find in music the necessary documents for a complete history of the feminine soul? For they are all there – those females who haunt us in our dreams! Manon, in her billowing petticoats, has a smile that seems reborn on the lips of a modern Sappho – a smile to bring men to tears. And the Navarraise's dagger and the ruthless Charlotte's pistol are brought together.

On the other hand, it is well-known how his music is vibrant with fleeting sensations, little bursts of feeling and embraces that we wish would last forever. The harmonies are like arms, the melodies like the napes of necks. We gaze into the ladies' eyes, dying to know their thoughts ... The philosophical, and those in their right minds, inform us that there are none. But we don't have to believe them: M. Massenet proves that there are (at least melodically). With such preoccupations, he is bound to occupy a position in contemporary art for which, at the very least, he is secretly envied. And that is something which should not be scorned.

Fortune, who is feminine, owed it to M. Massenet both to treat him well and, sometimes, to let him down. So far she has done just that. All this success has meant that for a time it was considered a good thing to copy the idiosyncrasies of Massenet. But then all of a sudden those who had so quietly cribbed from him began to treat him with disdain.

He has been reproached for having too much sympathy for Mascagni and not enough adoration for Wagner. This criticism is as wrongheaded as it is unacceptable. Massenet bravely continues to court the affection of his lady admirers, as he has always done. I must confess that I do not see why it is any better to give pleasure to cosmopolitan old Wagnerian ladies than to those perfumed young ladies, even though they don't play the piano very well. In the end, Massenet is bound to be right ... He can be reprimanded only for not having been faithful to the true Manon . . . There he found the framework that best suited his flirtatious habits, but perhaps he shouldn't have brought them into the opera. One does not 'flirt' at the opera: one screams incomprehensible words at the top of one's voice. If one becomes betrothed, then it is with the trombones as witnesses. All the subtle shades of sentiment are bound to be lost in the noise; Massenet realized he could better express his genius in pastel tints and whispered melodies, in works composed of lightness itself. And that doesn't rule out all artistic depth; it merely demands subtle depth. There will always be those who like their music to be held out at arm's length, while the trumpets bray. Why uselessly augment their number and so encourage this annoying taste for neo-Wagnerian music to develop? This kind of music would do better to return to its country of origin.

Massenet, because of his unique gifts and facility, has been able to do much to counteract this deplorable movement. 'It isn't always a good thing to howl along with the wolves' is a piece of advice that could well have been given him by one of his less discreet lady admirers.

To conclude these hasty notes one might add that not everyone can be a Shakespeare, but it does no harm to try to be a Marivaux.

La Revue blanche, 1 December 1901, tr. Richard Langham Smith

Many people with no vested interest in the matter – that is to say, not musicians – ask themselves why the Opéra persists in performing *Faust*. There are several reasons why, the best of which is that Gounod's art represents a moment in the French sensibility. Whether one likes it or not, these facts cannot be forgotten.

With regard to *Faust*, many eminent musical writers have reproached Gounod for having misrepresented Goethe's ideas. But these same people never bother to notice that Wagner also perhaps falsified the character of Tannhäuser, who in the original legend was nothing like the repentant little fellow Wagner made of him. His staff, burned in memory of Venus, would never have blossomed again. Gounod is perhaps to be forgiven because he is French, but Tannhäuser and Wagner are both German, so for them there is no excuse.

We are fond of so many things in France that music concerns us but little. There are, however, some fine people who show all the signs of being musicians, listening to music every day. But they never write music themselves; they merely encourage others. That is how a school is usually created. Do not speak of Gounod to such people, for they will only heap scorn upon you, drawing support from their present gods (who have the delightful advantage of being interchangeable). Gounod was never part of any school. It is something like that popular attitude held by the masses: when they are encouraged to raise their aesthetic sights, they merely reply by going back to what they are accustomed to. And that is not always in the best of taste, either. It wavers fearlessly between *Père la Victoire* and *Die Walküre*. The people who so curiously make up the elite take off their hats to the famous, the accepted, and they encourage others to do the same. But nothing comes of it all, for these would-be educators soon run out of breath, and the masses will not allow their hearts to be won over: art continues to have a will of its own, and the Opéra persists in putting on *Faust*.

One should, however, take sides on the issue and admit that art is absolutely useless to the masses. But neither is it useful as a means of expression for an elite – often more stupid than the aforesaid masses. It is the power of beauty itself, which makes its voice heard when it must, with an inevitable and secret force. The masses can no more be ordered to love beauty than they can be persuaded to walk around on their hands. And in passing we should remember that Berlioz really did win the approval of the masses without anyone having prepared the way.

If Gounod's influence is questionable, Wagner's is only too apparent. He, however, influenced only the specialists, which leads one to conclude that there must have been something lacking. It must be confessed that there is nothing more deplorable than that neo-Wagnerian school in which French genius is obscured by a lot of imitation Wotans in long boots and Tristans in velvet jerkins.

Even if Gounod didn't tread the harmonious paths we would have liked him to, he must nonetheless be praised for having known how to avoid the imperious spirit of Wagner, whose utterly Germanic nature never lived up to his ideal of a fusion of the arts – an ideal that has now become scarcely more than a fashionable stock in trade among the literary.

For all his weaknesses, Gounod was a necessity. He was, what is more, cultivated: he understood Palestrina and collaborated with Bach, and he was not blinded by a respect for tradition to the extent of glorifying Gluck – another unfortunate foreign influence of ours. Rather did he recommend that young people listen to Mozart – something that is proof of his great impartiality, for Mozart never inspired him. His attitude toward Mendelssohn was somewhat clearer, for it is to him that he owed the idea of piling up melodies one on top of the other, a useful trick when one is not feeling in the best of form. (Mendelssohn's is perhaps a more direct influence than Schumann's.) Also, Gounod took no notice of Bizet, and that's a good thing too. Unfortunately, Bizet died too soon, and although he bequeathed to us one masterpiece, the fate of French music was still left undecided. And here she is still! A beautiful widow who, having nobody strong enough to show her the way, allows herself to fall into the arms of foreigners who murder her. It cannot be denied that in art certain alliances are necessary, but they must be approached with some care: to choose those who make the most noise is not necessarily to follow the greatest. More often than not, these alliances are purposely used to conceal a need for rejuvenation when success is on the wane. But like marriages of convenience, they can only do harm. Let us welcome imported art into France, but let us not be deceived, falling into ecstasies about what are no more than penny whistles. And let us not think that our attitude will necessarily be reciprocated, for on the contrary, our friendship often provokes foreigners to be severe and impolite – something that is hardly funny. In concluding these brief notes, which have brought together a few ideas about Gounod (even if they are sometimes contradictory), let us take the opportunity of paying homage to his name, without any trace of dogmatic closed-mindedness. Let us note that there are many reasons why certain men deserve to be remembered; they don't even have to be very considerable reasons, and, in any case, to have stirred a great number of one's contemporaries is one means. Nobody could deny that Gounod employed this means abundantly.

Musica, July 1906, tr. Richard Langham Smith

Rameau was fifty years old when he began to write for the Opéra, and was ignored almost all his life. Thanks to the efforts of French scholarship, he is better known today than he was among his contemporaries, at least by reputation, although for many people he is still merely the composer of the celebrated Rigaudon from *Dardanus*, and not much more. He was tall and thin in appearance, in character at the same time both enthusiastic and complex. He hated the world. At that time, when refined manners were all that mattered, if one wasn't connected with the court, one was considered a mere nobody.

Musicians and singers at the Opéra feared and detested him, and he was always resentful of them for having forced him to suppress certain passages in his works that they could not, or would not, sing properly. His almost exclusive love of music enabled him to ignore all these troubles, inflicted on him by the elegant but indifferent times.

He was a born philosopher, although that didn't make him indifferent to fame, but it was the beauty of his works he cared about most of all. One day, toward the end of his life, someone asked him whether he found the sound of applause more pleasing to his ears than the sound of his music. He paused for a few moments in thought, and then said, 'I like my own music even better.'

The need to understand – so rare among artists – was innate in Rameau. Was it not to satisfy that need that he wrote his *Traité de l'harmonie*, where he claimed to rediscover the 'laws of reason,' and desired that the order and clarity of geometry should reign in music? One can read in the preface to that same treatise that 'music is a science bound by certain rules,' but that these rules must be based on a general principle that can never be known unless we enlist the aid of mathematics.

To the end, he never for a moment doubted the truth of the old Pythagorean theory that music should be reduced to a combination of numbers: it is the 'arithmetic of sound' just as optics is the 'geometry of light.' He put it all down in words, and traced the paths along which modern harmony was going to progress, including his own. He was perhaps wrong to write down all these theories before composing his operas, for it gave his contemporaries the chance to conclude that there was a complete absence of anything emotional in the music.

His career had hardly ended when a new fashion overtook him – at first the triumph of Lully, then later the domination of Gluck, who reigned for so long over French music that it has still not fully recovered.

For a long time, and for no apparent reason, Rameau remained almost completely forgotten. His charm, his finely wrought forms – all these were replaced by a way of writing music concerned only with the dramatic effect. The discovery of harmonic 'moments' to caress the ear was to give way to massive, easily understood but academic harmonies. Because of this, music split in two, ending up with Richard Wagner, another tyrannical genius.

Rameau's major contribution to music was that he knew how to find 'sensibility' within the harmony itself; and that he succeeded in capturing effects of color and certain nuances that, before his time, musicians had not clearly understood.

Like Nature herself, Art changes: she moves in curved lines but always ends up exactly at the point where she began. Rameau, whatever one may think, is definitely a key figure in music, and we can follow in his footsteps without fear of sinking into any pitfalls.

That is why he deserves our attention. We should treat him with the respect he deserves as one of our ancestors. He may have been a little disagreeable, but he was a man of truth.

'Jean Philippe Rameau', November 1912, tr. Richard Langham Smith

'Memories of dancing in *La Traviata*'
NINETTE DE VALOIS

Back once more in the Royal Opera House, I learned the geography of this great rabbit warren of a theatre which has persistently come into my life through the years. A vast organization was growing up there; disturbing, in its energy, a few angry inhabitants. One night a large rat – rudely shaken by the general onslaught on his favourite haunts – decided to distrupt the performance: he dramatically rushed across the gallery, leaping over outstretched feet in his conception of a rodent Grand National; dexterously a zealous fireman caught him, for nothing could daunt the zeal of the Covent Garden firemen on their night and day vigil of retrieving six years' [wartime] neglect of the underground haunts of the Royal Opera House: darkened haunts that also hold the echo of the voices of Melba and Caruso, and unforgettable visions of Karsavina and Nyjinska...

Along the lengthy corridor upstairs, behind the rows of padlocked wooden doors, there rest the huge wardrobes of clothes that bear the indelible stamp of my old friends the Brothers Comelli. Incredible now appear the richness, the wealth of detail and the elaborate trimmings in these clothes of an opulent past. How immaculate is the tailoring of the men's coats, and how perfect the finish of the finely-boned bodices of Edwardian divas! When daylight first lights up these carefully guarded treasures the perfume of moth balls is strong in its attack; yet it becomes immediately faint – to die with swift relief upon the air of the present.

I am in the wardrobe when the doors of *La Traviata* are unlocked; I seek out my own costume of nearly forty years ago: I finger the delicately made chiffon roses trailing on the wide satin skirt; as I finger them I hear the Brothers Comelli tell me again how to wear my gipsy headdress. Suddenly Monsieur Ambroisine is showing me my dance, and I feel myself dealing the fortune-telling cards – carefully laying them out on the boards of the Opera House stage, as I did on the night of my twenty-first birthday.

At the moment of this theatre's re-opening, one or two familiar faces are still there to greet me as I return to this place destined to be my final theatrical goal; Mr Jackson, the stage-door keeper, a friend of mine since the summer of 1919, and Mr Ballard the chief machinist, who could peer into the depths of the stage and tell you what every rolled-up cloth would prove to be – if he unrolled it. All the mysterious regulations of the L.C.C. were tucked away in his head: he was consumed with the sacred flame of safety first, for his artists, his bridges, his traps and his flying appliances. The 'No' that Mr Ballard said in 1919 rang with the same finality in 1946.

Come Dance With Me, 1957

'The Wagner legacy fifty years on'
MANUEL DE FALLA

I do not think that in any other great artistic work success and error alternate as clearly as in Wagner's, nor that any has been as unfairly attacked, or as unconditionally revered as his. Neither his contemporaries nor the following generation were able to, or wanted to, free themselves from passion when judging Wagner's overwhelming work. No happy medium existed: they either denied the high, the very high, virtues, and the lesson enshrined in that music, or, shutting their ears to the voice of reason, they claimed that the very mistakes that obscure and even sometimes destroy the qualities, were virtues. The case was still worse when the fanatic Wagnerian was a professional composer; incapable of reproducing what only genius can achieve, he clutched at the hope of becoming the master of the treasure he perceived shining through the many shadows, by copying what was false or wrong and therefore within the reach of anybody of normal intelligence. As to those who were not musicians, I have myself met more than one who was demonstrably shocked at the slightest criticism of his idol.

Now, after half a century, we look at Wagner in a very different way: his works live an independent life, and, although full of the force of the master, they do not have that prophetic sense he aspired to give them. In fact, for us they are quite the opposite. We consider them to be eminently representative of the period in which they were written, the music as well as the text. This was precisely Wagner's great failure: he wanted to lay the seeds of the music drama of the future, and from the harvest only his own music remains, and then that part better suited for the concert platform than for the stage. (An exception is that part of his dramatic production where the lyricism and atmosphere more or less conceal those structures of the past he intended to replace.)

I do not intend to write from a human, rather from a musical point of view, the former being fatally subject to fashions, feelings and tastes. All that had to be said about Wagner's aesthetic principles, about his exacerbated romanticism, about his philosophic ideas, and so on, has already been said. Therefore, if this essay contains something which appears to be along these lines, it will be for strictly musical reasons.

Although Wagner strongly yearned for a transcendental ideal, as we all know, he only followed this inclination when it did not upset his egotism. A consequence of this was the mixture of strength and weakness shown by his life and by his works. We do not have to deal with his life, except for the facts concerning his art. To be fair, whenever I listen to Wagner's music, I try not to think of him. I could never abide his arrogant vanity nor his proudly immature determination to embody his characters; he believed himself to be Siegfried, Tristan and Walther, even Lohengrin and Parsifal. That was typical of his time. Wagner, like so many others of his stature, was a gigantic character in that gigantic carnival better known as the nineteenth century, to which only the European War put an end (and thus inaugurated the great asylum our own century is proving to be).

Some of the influences exerted by Wagner's art on the music of his time are still active. This is one of the main points I shall deal with; in his music we are obliged to point out not only the qualities, but also the fundamental errors previously mentioned, trying to restrict their influence (still alive half a century after Wagner's death despite intervening reactions). Let it be clear that I am not trying in the least to diminish the achievement of this great composer. When I mention his errors I shall weigh my words scrupulously, aiming at benefiting future artists, never at the expense of my own tendencies or preferences.

Wagner frequently avoided obstacles and whenever blocked followed strange paths leading into some dark jungle. There is only one exception to this rule: it seems that he never permitted himself to sacrifice to the music whatever in the already published poem might have proved an obstacle. This example of honesty is worth pointing out in these times when more serious commitments, publicly contracted, are eluded for the sake of hidden purposes.

But let us return to the music. Perhaps in this particular instance we find the cause of what many have interpreted as Wagner's excessive preference for his literary creations. Whatever the real reason, it is necessary to confess that, although the rule was very laudable, the way in which Wagner solved its inherent problems was not always exemplary. If the hindrance resisted too much, he yielded to an easy but fatal solution. A proof of this is his famous invention of an infinite melody (melodic sequences without tonal limits); this, with all due respect to conscious mistakes, is only one of those brilliant sleights of hand which since the eighteenth century have been attempts to substitute for truth.

The first of his dogmas beyond discussion is that which required the internal union of rhythm and tonality; only by holding to this eternal principle can the musical devices become powerfully stable. Let us not forget that music develops in time and in space. To perceive effectively time and space, it is essential to determine their limits, to establish the initial, central and final points, or the points of departure and suspense, linked by a close internal relation. Sometimes this relation apparently blurs the tonal sense established by its limits; but it is only for a short time and with the intention of underlining that very tonal value, which becomes more intense when it reappears after having been eclipsed. We should not forget either, that it is necessary to be fully convinced of the fundamental truth offered by the natural acoustic scale in order to establish the harmonic – and therefore contrapuntal – basis of the music, as well as to give a tonal structure to a series of melodic periods which, being generated by the same resonances which integrate that scale, have to move at different levels. What I mean is that the intervals forming that column of sounds are the only real possibility for the constitution of the chord, as well as an infallible norm for the tonal-melodic construction of those periods that, limited by cadential movements, compose every musical work. We can affirm, then, that in those natural principles, fully dependent on rhythm, the whole of music is contained. These forces, measured movements and acoustic resonance, generate all the other elements of art: modal scales, disposition and development of the vocal or instrumental parts, etc. And the very word of the text, which shares the origin of melody, must obey those principles in order to acquire a musical value. But we shall not be able to use these essentials of music efficaciously if we do not constantly watch over the degree of potency determined by the close approach or the withdrawal of their initial point, and if we do not determine the limits of future periods leading to a final point or to a point of voluntary suspense.

And that was what Wagner, who accurately adhered to the laws in the imperishable part of his output, deliberately tried many times to elude, shielding his musical heterodoxy behind the reasoning his philosophical dilettantism inspired in him. In those moments, he abandoned his steady, vigorous pace and entered the dark jungle, creating a constant instability that at the beginning is only a disturbance, whereas at the end it imperceptibly deflects our attention.

This tendency found an easy development in an excess of chromaticism and in an inexorable sequence of enharmonic modulations; the whole of the obvious effects of this was called pantonal music, a pompous notion that matches well with other, more fundamental errors of that century, the results of which are still active.

For myself, I rather like to be told things clearly; that is why, having to choose, I decidedly prefer the chronologically new atonality to that of pantonality. For what happens here happens with every bad example: as it is very easy to imitate, it is followed even by those who reject what the composer's personality stands for.

The essential truth I have affirmed could of course be refuted; it is well known that almost every aberration can be rationalized and defended. It is a human frailty to accept evident errors for fear of being despised by the powerful people who propagate them. Musically it is unnecessary to say that chromaticism and pantonality, like every other artistic device, consciously used can not only be legitimate, but also excellent, provided their use is not the result of too easy a system, but of the reasoned choice of expressive means. Wagner himself proves this in *Tristan*, where the chromaticism (frequently tonal, anyway) finds its appropriate function as a spontaneous expressive force.

At the beginning of this essay, I said that Wagner's work, unique in music and the other arts generally, shows us where right and wrong can occur, thus stimulating us to seek truth and avoid error. For example, the subservience of his music to certain alien purposes compels us to be fundamentally concerned with the defence of music's rights. His pretentious vanity in wishing to eliminate everything inessential; his tonal and melodic restlessness lead us to observe a more serene and strict discipline, whereas the lack of personality of the instruments in the orchestra – admirable in other respects – drives us to isolate and enhance the timbres. His irksome verbosity and his exasperating dramatic realism urge us to strive after conciseness and after a simple, though intense, musical expression. His passivity towards certain nullifyingly overwhelming influences of his time, impels us to take precautions against those of our own epoch.

Where the positive effects of his music are concerned, they are so great and clear, that to state them may seem superfluous to those familiar with the master's work (and these pages are principally meant for them). The marriage of singing and of lyric declamation with the expressive value of word and concept, are among the most outstanding achievements of his art, and as for the craftsmanship, I do not think there has been any more perfect. With the development of the leit-motifs, he reached admirable heights, in spite of their excessive use; a subtle example of his skill to transform a motive is the orchestral beginning of Siegfried's monologue in the wood. This aspect of Wagner's art has value as a rich collection of examples of the techniques of variation.

To Wagner's effort we owe much of music's progress in liberating itself from dead formulae. In many cases his reforms were positive, and even of permanent value, but they were not the only possibilities, as many held who were not musicians. Wagner's art was great, even in its mistakes, and splendid when it abode by the eternal principles: who does not remember the overture to *The Mastersingers*?

Much was said with regret about the influence of Wagner's conscious nationalism on many composers of other races, sometimes opposing his own. This is evident, but I have always thought that Wagner's example, if followed in its positive aspects, not only is not pernicious, but provides a vigorous incentive for all to try to reflect in their own work the characteristic genius of their own nation and of their race.

In *Parsifal*, that eucharist-like play, Wagner's aspiration towards the pure ideal reaches its fulfilment, after appearing unmistakably in many of the poems he later set to music. And let us not forget an appealing facet of his nature; he never sacrificed his art to easy profit; he was never mean. It is true that he incessantly hunted for money, but as a means to achieve his noble artistic aims or his less noble human aims, never to amass it.

I also wish to mention his stubborn firmness, a true example for us, with which he strove for the fulfilment of his purposes, as well as the zeal with which he constantly strove for high standards in music theatre.

Nobody could equal Wagner in endowing the dramatic action with a most propitious musical atmosphere. In this sense he was more than an extraordinary artist: he was a prophet. This quality becomes most apparent when his ardour arouses our highest aspirations. This is the merit of some pages of *Lohengrin* and many of *Parsifal*, that clear testament of faith, of Christian redemption, that Wagner, nearing the end of his life and yielding to a pure impulse of his unruly consciousness, set in opposition to past misdeeds. That act of faith shows itself not only in the deep emotion called forth by the music for the sacred scenes, but also in the way the religious texts of the poem are imbued with love and reverence; the whole frequently inspired by the Catholic liturgy itself. That is doubtless why for me *Parsifal* is one of the most sublime works of art ever achieved in spite of the conscious tonal disintegration that frequently affects the music.

In these pages I have tried to pay tribute to the art and genius of Wagner on the fiftieth anniversary of his death. Something, or much, in my words may have gone against my purpose, yet I think, with Quevedo, that it is not enough to feel what one says; one also has to say what one feels.

Note on Tonality

I believe it can be defined as follows: Melodic form (a series of consecutive sounds, joint or not) that, based on an acoustic scale, forms a musical concept. To this initial form or tonality subsequent ones which constitute every musical work must submit by means of modulations, that is, transposition of the initial tonality one or more degrees higher or lower.

'Notes on Richard Wagner on the fiftieth anniversay of his death', *Cruz y raya*, Madrid, September 1933

'Trouble in *Turandot* at the Met'
CECIL BEATON

New York: January 1961

The first night of *Turandot* was electrifying. Never has there been a more charged atmosphere at the Met. The standing ovation for Stokowski's appearance on crutches was thrilling and throughout the performance the audience applauded enthusiastically at every opportunity.

My evening, however, was ruined by one chorus-woman coming on in Act I in the costume I had designed for her to wear in Act III. It was a particularly unfortunate accident as the hundreds of dresses in Act I were specifically designed to be dark blue and other drab colours in order to create the necessary sinister atmosphere. Suddenly this 'trespasser' appeared in an orange skirt, meant for an entirely different scene later on. All eyes were drawn to her. I was dumbfounded and could only hope that she would somehow fade into the background. But no, she was always in the forefront of the stage. When the chorus lay on the floor, the orange bottom was the biggest and most prominent. Then when she went to the side of the stage and stood in an arc-light, my rage exploded. I darted up the length of the aisle gathering more fury with speed. I rushed backstage and pushed my way through the crowds round the back of the set until I came to the wings where the orange could be seen in full glow. Here the chorus-master helped me to signal the woman off-stage, although even when the guards indicated with their halberds that she must come off-stage, she moved further forward in the light. Eventually she was pulled backwards. Whereupon, in silent fury, I tore at her skirt. I went on pulling at it in an ever-growing frenzy, but it would not give way. I was beside myself in a manner that surprised me. At last I heard a rending screech of a tear. I pulled downwards in spite of 'Mr Beaton!!' coming from the startled chorus-master. At last the lady was standing in her BVDs with an orange skirt in tatters on the floor around her. Then I rushed back to my stall. But to enjoy no peace. I almost had a heart attack. I sat with my face in my hands completely exhausted.

In the first interval, just as I was about to escort Suzy Parker to have a drink in the Opera Club, I was approached by John Gutman and Bob Herman. 'Do you want the show to go on? Unless you make a public apology to the female chorus, there will be a strike. The Union will close the show!' I was frogmarched backstage. I felt what it was like to be handcuffed and taken off in the Black Maria. I was hurried to the dressing-room in which forty angry, half-naked women were changing. A little 'Minnie Mouse' was sitting mopping tears with Kleenex papers rolled into a ball. She wore Chinese make-up and a dressing-gown.

'I've come to apologize for what I did. I didn't know I was capable of behaving so badly. It was inexcusable and I can only say in my defence that we've been working so hard for three months to get the blues just right and to see this orange figure was just too much. But I should never have lost control and I'm extremely sorry. Please shake hands to show you have forgiven me.' The little woman never spoke a word – shook my hand and dabbed away another tear.

Then an angry woman from the chorus said: 'And, another thing, these sandals are all coming apart.' The day was won – Gutman took control of her. We fitted out Minnie Mouse in blue for the last act and, terrified, I returned to the appalled Suzy. For one hour I was alternately overcome by remorse and laughter.

The orange woman had ruined my first night. But despite this I gradually realized what a success the evening had been for me as well as for all concerned. The after-party at Nin Ryan's was unique in that it needed no build-up – all the guests arrived in a state of elation. Noël Coward was adulatory and made a very funny remark about [Franco] Corelli who is known in Italy as the man of the golden legs. 'Well, I wish he'd shown us his fleece.' Adlai Stevenson said, on hearing of my backstage exploits: 'I've known people get worked up about a word or a phrase. I did not know that colour could be of such importance!'

Rudolf Bing became human, all shyness disappeared. He roared with laughter about the orange skirt: 'I can't imagine this calm collected Britisher, this photographer of the Royal Family...'

Self Portrait with Friends, 1979

'The various rewards of working at the words'
CARL NIELSEN

A person's lack of musical qualifications will be proportionate to the insistency of his demand for a clear text, and the wholly unmusical, of course, would rather the music were somewhere hot. But the last generation's exaggerated demand for clarity of diction has resulted in textual exaggerations and has been highly detrimental to music in general and singing in particular. The libretto of an opera should be clearly audible in every passage which either develops the action or contributes to an understanding of the situation. But it is of little importance, and may even be disillusioning, to hear the words too clearly in a cantilena or lyrical-melodic passage. In ensembles – trios, quartets, quintets, etc. – the text is generally of minor importance so long as the situation has been explained. To the performers, however, the words of such items are a splendid stimulus, bringing life to the surface of the whole, as from within. When Schiller lamented the fact that literary artists are denied the facility of having more than one character speak at a time, he doubtless envied music its conflicting rhythms and stresses, like currents and ripples in water.

Living Music, 1953, tr. Reginal Spink

'Wieland Wagner's staging and lighting revolution'
CLAUDE LUST

... Having presented Siegfried with a cup containing a potion destined to make him lose all memory of Brünnhilde, Gutrune stands for a brief moment facing him as his desire is immediately inflamed, then retires on Hagen's order. Wieland Wagner places Siegfried facing the spectator, but distinctly stage left; while he drinks, the cup masks his face. Hagen takes this opportunity to position Gutrune facing Siegfried (with her back to the audience) before retiring to the rear to 'direct' the scene, invisible to Siegfried. The latter, suddenly discovering Gutrune's beauty, marks the violence of the emotion that seizes him with an almost frenetic reaction of his whole body, while still remaining practically motionless. This reaction takes all its force from the slowness and legato of his earlier gesture with the cup. Then, having asked Gunther the name of his sister (without changing position, of course), he takes her face in his hands with infinite tenderness. It is just at this moment that Hagen, with a very cold gesture of his finger, orders his half-sister to leave. Gutrune goes out stage right, that is to say – crossing almost the whole platform. She makes her entire exit with her back to the audience, her body remaining slewed in the direction of Siegfried who follows her. On Hagen's gesture, she makes a first, quite rapid but very gliding movement of retreat. Her back and head bend very far backwards obliquely undulating towards the exit. Her arms are very slightly away from her body. Her hands stretch a little towards Siegfried, but with the elbows already retreating and her hips very far forward, still being offered and as if refusing to follow the rest of her body. Her whole attitude, extraordinarily erotic, amounts to a sort of tearing apart due to the brusqueness of the separation. The movement immediately slows down, and the character stops for a very brief instant, hesitant, then again recoils fairly swiftly in the same manner, but less marked and without really stopping. Arriving at the edge of the platform, she turns round to face her exit and disappear into the shadow. But one more time, when she is already on the stairs leading down from the platform, and away from the lit surface, she quickly turns her head, which alone is visible in the shadow, to look briefly at Siegfried; then, in an instant, completely disappears.

The exceptional expressiveness of this stage action is due essentially to its continuous dynamic variation relative to a physical attitude that is almost unchanging. This dynamic variation makes all the more impact on the spectator because Siegfried, fascinated, follows Gutrune without moving in just the same way. A continuous and regular gait on the part of the female character would have given an impression of movement in the spatial sense, that is to say, in the dramatic rapport created between the characters, but it would have confirmed for the spectator an impression of interior immobility in the character. This physical statement is very important for Wieland Wagner: any regular, repeated or continuous movement, on an opera stage, creates an impression of immobility. Awareness of this principle enables him to succeed at last in making a chorus walk on stage without that semblance of a halted military march that is systematically offered us by producers attached to tradition.

For example, in his last production of *Tannhäuser* at Bayreuth in 1964, he brought an unheard-of suppleness to the entrance of the Guests in the Wartburg during the second act, by bringing in the chorus at intervals of calculated irregularity, in little groups whose gait continually changes, progressively slowing down and stopping in front of Elisabeth and the Landgrave, then moving on to their places. It is the arrangement of different groups on the set that creates the musical crescendo. He arrives at another absolutely astonishing solution for the chorus of Pilgrims in the first and third acts: the gait of each chorus member is rhythmic, but systematically out of phase in relation to each of the others. Further, he uses this stasis in continuous movement in a very refined manner to create a variety of attitudes of very particular expressive value which would be impossible except in relation to immobility, or to a very differentiated play of dynamics. The most extraordinary examples of this were seen in his *Lulu* and *Salome*.

In the *Ring*, this technique permits an impressive interpretation of the first scene in *Rhinegold*. In the glaucous darkness of the stage tableau, the character of Alberich appears centre stage plunged in waves of light; his body is continuously subject to abrupt movements which unceasingly unbalance the character's position. The little movements with which he attempts to hold himself upright are immediately neutralized by other jerks which unbalance him again, bringing him back to his initial position. The suppleness of the Rhinemaidens' undulations, and the speed of their turns – created by the illusion induced with the lighting – reinforce by contrast this impression of instability. Of course, this is not a matter of realistically showing a man's clumsiness in water, but of expressing a feeling of inadequacy in relation to nature – nature being represented in the idea of water, which symbolizes the feminine principle of love as the primary cosmogonic element – the uneasiness within the world experienced by Alberich. This in itself helps us understand the sequence of events in this scene, that is to say the theft of the gold and the curse upon love, and, as a result, the overall meaning of the *Ring*. There is often a tendency to read this scene with the blinkers of Christianity and to equate it with some sort of representation of original sin. This idea has simply no meaning for Wagner. But in this specific case, it is necessary to stress that Alberich does not enter the Rhine for the gold, but to seek love. His curse is merely the consequence of the pitiless sarcasm with which he is rejected by the Rhinemaidens. This sense of collision with the world is also what leads Tristan to curse the love potion. For Wagner, Alberich is a fundamentally tragic figure.

Let us add, in regard to the bodily expression of the actors, that the results Wieland Wagner was able to arrive at in this respect would not have been possible without forming a fixed and homogeneous company, even though this company was never officially constituted.

It is also necessary to stress the contribution of costume to the whole expressiveness of the acting. This element is habitually neglected in opera: costume generally remains purely anecdotal and decorative. Here again, producers are unaware of the extent to which they are fettering the physical work of their singers. The costumes realized by Wieland Wagner are part of the characterization, both by the way they enhance the actor's physical attitude and by the realization of the concept of the character he is performing in dress terms, these two aspects being indissolubly linked. Of course it is by no means a matter of systematically moulding the physique 'regardless' – Wagnerian singers would in any case not always benefit from this – but of modelling it as a function of the play of attitudes selected for the character. That is to say, the choice and treatment of the materials are at least as important as design or colour. It is absolutely essential for the credibility of a production of the *Ring* that the mythic figures should not assume the appearance of dressed-up, 'disguised' persons. Wieland Wagner had all the characters' costumes cut out of leather, while diversifying to the extreme the texture of this material. Leather becomes a 'skin' laid over the skin of the actor and forming a 'substitute' for it. The characters' bodies thus become rigid or supple, smooth or scored, without this sculptural aspect working against the perception of movement. In a certain way, the costume directs the actor, putting him literally in the 'skin of the character'.

Gutrune's costume, for example, one of the most incredible, reveals the phenomenon we have described in the first act of *Twilight of the Gods* by increasing the erotic magnetism emanating from the character. Very fine black leather, decorated with lines of light grey in relief over the bust and on the sleeves, clings to the actress's body from her breasts to her knees in a very smooth line, then flares towards the base; the gait of her thighs, along with all her movements, becomes perceptible in every tremor. It is partly thanks to this costume that Wieland Wagner achieves a proper consistency for the character who, because of the smallness of her role, is generally ignored. Gutrune is the erotic linchpin of *Twilight of the Gods*; only if the production registers this clearly can the dramatic relationships as a whole be perfectly plain. Relieved of all anecdotal function, and thanks to the unified nature of the material used, the costumes connect the characters to one another (either in their direct confrontations, or in links the audience gradually comes to understand) according to their nature and their mythic role, and no longer just to suit the narrative requirements of the plot.

Siegfried in *Twilight of the Gods* wears his costume from the previous opera. Green leather, subtly streaked and creased, and directly recalling the colour and texture of the forest suggested by the design in the second act of *Siegfried*, leaves the character's legs, arms and upper chest bare. The total liberty of movement and attitude thus allowed sets him straight away at odds, on entering the hall of the Gibichungs, with the rigidity of Gunther and Hagen, who are thickly cuirassed from neck to toe.

The definitive meaning and full expressive value of what the actors do ... can only emerge within the entire composition of the stage tableau. Clearly Wieland Wagner's idea of physical expression must imply a new concept of stage design. In a literal imitation of a palace room, whatever the style, the three characters posed as we have described them at the opening of the first act of *Twilight of the Gods* would seem outrageous caricatures, quite ridiculous. And indeed, any attempt to keep to the actual locations in the story would bring the characters into completely different decors, scene by scene, so that the spectator would not visually perceive the dramatic coherence which, through the thematic unity of leitmotifs, he is experiencing so keenly as a listener. Wieland Wagner therefore realizes each design using as his starting point the attitude of the characters who 'inhabit' it, but each character is just a constituent element in bringing into concrete existence the whole emotional world; at the same time, the very structure of each successive design further develops the attitude of the characters who are 'experiencing' it. All the representative elements in the different scenes have their shape sculpted in accordance with one formal concept resulting from one working of the material; their colour, too, varies only within one scale. These elements are not a figurative representation, or even an evocation, of the place of the action. They express the idea the characters have of the place of the action. It is therefore necessary to stress that these scenic elements have no representational value of their own, and that this value is seen only as a function of the attitude of the characters. In the first act of *Twilight of the Gods*, for example, three squat menhirs, split down the centre, stand symmetrically at the back of the stage behind the platform: a huge transverse beam joins them into one mass. The lighting lends this its dark green colour while emphasizing the extraordinary relief within the pitted but smooth surface.

In conjunction with the initial positioning of the characters, the massiveness of scenic shapes, their weightiness and archaic atmosphere perfectly convey to the spectator the feeling of dominating power that motivates these rulers, and the nature of the oppression they exercise over their subjects. At the same time, the striking richness of the material emphasizes the greed of the two male characters so conspicuously crouched forward. When Siegfried enters, he will be coming not just into the Hall of the Gibichungs, but into the stronghold of a world founded on the power of wealth.

However, the links established between characters and their decor, between their mythic universe and the particularities of their being that are thus revealed to us, do not only derive from the semantic exchange set up between the attitudes of the actors and the plastic qualities of the representative elements in the decor. Nor are plastic considerations on their own enough to determine the cosmogonic composition of the various decors as they follow each other. The organization of dramatic space is what will make possible this simultaneous and successive interplay of relationships. First, the delineation of the dramatic space must necessarily be independent of the form and disposition of the representative scenic elements. In other words, if the dramatic space is merely the void left around planted objects, forms charged with signifying, these will, whatever they look like, inevitably take on for the spectator the value of representing a circumstantial place, a place in which the characters live. That is to say: the way we see the dramatic world, and consequently the characters, will no longer have at all the mythic aspect proper to the work. Further, the decors are going to have to follow each other in one scenic space for all acts in all four days, if we are to discover in each of them a (particular) 'phase' of the evolution of one world.

Thus, rather than trying to establish coherence between successive decors, in fact the producer is going to have to realize one decor which changes. Furthermore this changing of the decor will not occur only at changes of act or location. The decor must be capable of perpetual change, because (and this is essential) within an act dramatic progress, such as the arrival of new characters or the development of conflict between protagonists, can lead the characters to perceive where they are in a different way, causing the decor to change in aspect. Finally, it is upon the quality of the space itself that the credibility of the heroes of the *Ring* depends, because it is this which determines their dimension.

The circular or, rather, elliptical platform, raised and sloping down from the back of the stage, bathed in perpetually evolving diffuse light, with which Wieland Wagner circumscribed the whole action of the *Ring*, so impressed the audience that it was immediately used to identify the whole of Wieland Wagner's work, as if it were a very ingenious and apt formula – but one not connected with his personal imagination. In addition, the formula seemed very practical and inevitably became a recipe. You no longer had to think in order to stage the *Ring*; all you had to do was put a cyclorama around a disc-shaped stage and light the magic lanterns.

Of course no one wanted to stumble into the exaggerations and follies of the New Bayreuth. The actors would still have to move about, and the lighting would have to be brighter and more lively. Counting on the spectators' amazement before the twirling lights to mask Richard Wagner's legendary prolixity, producers yet again absolved themselves from trying to understand the meaning and basis of the procedure they were employing. Unfortunately the lighting schemes they devised in this style exposed nothing but their own incoherence. [...]

In elaborating this solution, Wieland Wagner had been trying to show the spectator a new objective reality, which presupposed a new conception of dramatic space and consequently of all dramatic logic. First of all, the platform occupies only a limited area of the stage of the Festspielhaus, and only *it* is lit. Its elevation makes the spectator forget the normal floor of the stage and thus it emerges out of shadow. Besides, it is always empty. All the representative elements of the decor are behind and their placing is independent; they too emerge from the shadow thanks to lighting which is specially for them. Thus the decor never constitutes the enclosure of the playing space, and the dramatic space is no longer a sort of 'ersatz' cube imposed on the producer by the theatre, but is created by light. The proscenium opening is nothing more, for the spectator, than a centring or border, like that established on the screen by cinematic projection. In concentrating all the dramatic action on a space at once limited and indefinitely extended by shadow, Wieland Wagner extraordinarily enlarges the proportions not only of the characters but also of the acts they accomplish; the same goes for the decorative elements, whose limits are never seen.

It is necessary to insist upon the fact that the latter are positioned outside the actors' field of action. Their placing, where they stand on the ground, is imperceptible to the spectator. The mythic place does not present itself as a surrounding to the characters; these no longer live in a world of objects. Their presence is no longer limited within a geographical framework, and their appearance thus becomes the exact image of their mythic role since it is not circumscribed by an anecdotal frame. But it must be noted that the dramatic space is no longer in any way conditioned by the form, the surfaces or the volume of the elements of the decor – as it would be if they were distributed on the performing space. The acting area is no longer defined by objects. It is created solely out of the play of light on darkness. It works freely once the representative elements have been fixed, and can be infinitely modified. Here it is the composition of the dramatic space that defines the face of the decor, as well as giving its meaning and value to the attitudes of the characters.

It is appropriate to discuss the manner in which Wieland Wagner realized his lighting, for there too he has been imitated without being understood. If he was the first to grasp how fully to exploit the prodigious expressive resources of lighting in the lyric theatre, it was because he gave it a precise dramatic role, and didn't content himself with tickling the spectator with effects as glittering as they were gratuitous. Let us say at once that he never considered himself as having to 'support' his grandfather's music, persuaded as he was that it was perfectly well able to take care of itself. In other words, his lighting schemes, contrary to what has so often been claimed, were never in direct correlation with the music as such; they were always conceived as a function of the dramatic situation viewed as a whole.

Forming a theatrically evocative space with light leads to the idea of light as being no longer just a means of rendering the stage event visible, but as the aspect under which the event is seen. In other words, it is the light itself which must be seen. Criticizing Wieland Wagner for the 'parsimony' of his lighting, as if it were just another instance of his obstinacy, was plainly absurd – almost as grotesque as if an art lover were to reproach Rembrandt or Georges Latour, for example, for not providing a clear enough view of the characters or objects in a painting. In a space conceived in this way, everything on the stage has no other possible appearance but that given it by the lighting. It exists only as its lit value. Equally, if one wishes to give light its proper value, lighting must necessarily be conceived as starting from darkness, not from brightness; it is brightness which must appear as an effect. Finally, and above all, playing with shadow, the producer is no longer creating an abstract notion of space in the void left by the hollowness of forms or by the edge of darkness, he is giving it a consistency whose density he can vary. He is 'charging' it.

Thus, in realizing his lighting schemes, Wieland Wagner sets out not to project light on to his stage tableau, but to re-create this tableau in colours. And he does not use the electric projector as a light source, but as an instrument capable of causing a certain expanse of unified colour to float in space. White light is systematically avoided. Further, this unified colour is never used raw, just as its extent is never able to be pinpointed – except to obtain a particular effect. Each dose of colour is adjusted by the superposition of another one. Thus light is to be composed according to painterly principles. Yet its expressive role in the stage tableau will be exactly the opposite of the one it has in paintings. The painter – let us take the case of a painting representing characters in a landscape – distributes characters, on a flat and reduced surface, in relation to the landscape, in order to re-create, by the distribution of shapes and the play of proportions, the impression of space and notably of depth, in order to make us see the bodies in the landscape.

The composition of relationships on canvas aims to make us 'sense' the real dimensions of the space represented. So the painter is trying to diversify to the maximum the light qualities of every element in his picture, particularly the way light plays upon each character and upon the landscape so that we sense the distance separating the figures from the decor and the figures from each other. The general light of the picture results from the juxtaposition on the flat surface of an infinity of localized gradations of light. The producer, on the other hand, distributes his characters in three-dimensional space in such a way as to create the impression that they exist 'in relation' to the decor. The actual distance between actors and decor, and between one actor and another, must be sensed as a fully tangible rapport. Instead of separating the different spatial plans, differentiating each element of the representation one from the other, the light will link them in a homogeneous atmosphere. And the quality of this light will no longer be governed by the localization of the objects in the representation. It no longer defines the spacial significance of the position of the characters, it simply expresses the sense of encounter which this positioning is making evident. Thus Wieland Wagner seeks to compose a unique light for his stage tableau, starting with the totality of colours projected on to the different representative elements, and evolving as a parallel expressive force in the development of the dramatic relationships.

What made Wieland Wagner's lighting schemes so exceptional was that their perfect homogeneity of light in space derived from an extraordinarily refined mixing of colours. Let us emphasize that their quality should in no way be attributed to the technology of the procedures, but solely to the intelligence with which these are used. The lighting equipment is simple enough in itself; most effects are obtained by fitting normal lamps with coloured filters, frosted glass or glass painted with forms in opaque paint, or, for mobile projection, of film likewise painted turning in a loop in front of the light, and finally there are lenses whose chosen focus gives what is being projected the desired dimensions, and whose working enables its form to be more or less blurred. All the magic of the lighting comes from the fact that no projection is ever used to its maximum intensity. The light sources used are multiplied and scattered over the ramp and the lighting towers – as few as possible in the auditorium itself – so as to superimpose on the stage surfaces forms and areas of low-intensity colour. Thus the surfaces are never brightly coloured, they never collect all the light. The diffusion of the light rays through space is rendered perceptible; their multiplication and their scattering fill up the air, and their inter-references make it iridescent. Wieland Wagner still further softens the impression of forms and expanses of colour on the platform by lighting it almost invariably with pools of light (frosted glass plate and lens as well as colour filter in front of the lamp). This also considerably thins out the aureoles of the spotlights. To obtain an effect of luminosity, he does not seek to increase the general power of the lighting; he adds livelier and more strongly contrasted tones which when mixed are capable of creating a burst of light or a scintillation. The power of each lamp depends on the choice of filter and only reaches a certain degree with relatively dark filters to make the colour vibrate.

In the last scene of *Siegfried*, for example, we see a dark blue light, very deep and very intense, progressively taking over from the flamboyant, mobile light which invaded the stage as the curtains opened, and which gradually fades. By the opening of Siegfried's song 'Selige Öde auf wonniger Höh', unified blue has taken possession of the space, also on the cyclorama, which here replaces every element of constructed decor, but on which the projected light is contained in an immense central parabola whose base coincides with the floor of the platform. Meanwhile on the latter, the colour is exceptionally laid very smoothly, emphasizing its bareness. Then, during the orchestral crescendo, while the tone on the cyclorama takes on a slightly differ-ent nuance, a clear yellow, projected in pools, appears progressively on the platform superimposed on the blue. Its intensity increases up to the opening of Brünnhilde's song 'Heil dir Sonne! – Heil dir Licht!'

while still remaining relatively weak. The lighting remains like this to the end of the act. Thus the light for this final scene remains entirely diffused; it is the freshness, the limpidity of the floating of this yellow over this blue, as well as the contrast between the two tones, which creates the impression of luminosity and of brilliance.

Thus conceived, the lighting never crushes or flattens the actor against the surfaces; he 'picks up' the light and becomes absolutely omnipresent in the space. And it is the lights which model his attitude, giving his corporal expression its definitive value...

Wieland Wagner et la Survie du Théâtre Lyrique, La Cité Editeur, Editions l'Age d'Homme S. A., Lausanne 1969, tr. Meredith Oakes

'How I became a Bolshoi non-person'
GALINA VISHNEVSKAYA

In 1976, when I was already living abroad but was still a Soviet citizen and officially a member of the Bolshoi company, a book about Melik-Pashayev was published in the Soviet Union containing reminiscences of him by singers, composers, and music critics. They all recalled his jewel, *Aïda*, saying it was his best opera at the Bolshoi, and that in recent years it was almost always performed by the same cast, each of whom the great conductor had fostered: Andzhaparidze as Radames, Arkhipova as Amneris, Lisitsian as Amonasro, Petrov as Ramfis, and ... others. In all the articles about the opera *Aïda* there was simply no mention of Aïda herself. And in the section entitled 'Opera Productions at the Bolshoi Theater Directed by A. Sh. Melik-Pashayev' the names of my understudies were given – to commemorate all the premieres I sang with him.

In that same year of 1976, 'by imperial order' of the Central Committee, my name was deleted and my photographs removed from the jubilee album issued on the occasion of the 200th anniversary of the Bolshoi. In order to avoid squabbling among the prima donnas, the empty spaces in the book were hastily filled with photographs of young, beginning singers. I imagine they were shocked beyond words, and of course overjoyed, to find themselves featured so prominently. Well then, with all my heart I hope that some day they will occupy a similar place, not only in an album but on the stage.

In their attempt to eradicate all trace of me from the history of the Bolshoi, they went so far as to collect all my photographs from the theater's archives and throw them out. My admirers retrieved them from the trash heap and sent them to me in Paris.

Galina, 1984

'Maria Callas – the legend and the reality'
WALTER LEGGE

Don't let us kid ourselves or allow sudden death at a comparatively early age to distort our judgment of a famous opera singer who had retired early after a short, meteoric career. The name Callas was a household word throughout the civilized world. Thanks to an immediately identifiable voice, her magnetic personality, her many phonograph records and a constant flow of sensational news and gossip-column publicity, her fame was even greater than Caruso's in his heyday. Let us balance this with Tullio Serafin's considered judgment, delivered after more than sixty years work with the best singers of our century: 'In my long lifetime there have been three miracles – Caruso, Ponselle and Ruffo. Apart from these, there have been several wonderful singers.' Though Serafin had been her most important mentor, her fatherly guide and the main architect of Callas' extraordinary career, he did not rank her among his three miracles; she was one of his 'several wonderful singers.' Serafin's words, no doubt unknowingly, echoed Ernest Newman's wise and concise evaluation after her Covent Garden debut: 'She's wonderful, but she is not a Ponselle.'

Even though gallery-girls may lynch me for it, either at Lincoln Center, in the Piazza della Scala or outside Bow Street police station in London, I must try to put into focus the Callas phenomenon as a person and as an artist. My justification is that I knew her for more than twenty-five years and worked closely with her for twelve of them, producing and mid-wifing all her best recordings from preparation to published product.

More than enough has been published about her unhappy childhood, quarreling parents, myopia, avoirdupois and deprivations, but no one has assessed the effects of these disadvantages on her

374

career and character. Callas suffered from a superhuman inferiority complex. This was the driving force behind her relentless, ruthless ambition, her fierce will, her monomaniacal egocentricity and insatiable appetite for celebrity. Self-improvement, in every facet of her life and work, was her obsession. When she was first pointed out to me, a year or two before we met, she was massive, shabbily dressed in a nondescript tweed coat, and her walk had the ungainly lurch of a sailor who, after months on rough seas, was trying to adjust himself to terra firma. At our first meeting I was taken aback by her rather fearsome New York accent, which may have had a booster from G.I.s when she worked as interpreter for the American forces in Athens. Within months Callas was speaking what the English call the King's English until the BBC murdered it. A gifted linguist, she soon learned good Italian and French. When she had slimmed down from over 200 pounds to less than 140, she became one of the best-dressed women in Milan. Her homes in Verona, Milan and Paris paid silent tribute to her taste and love of order. Attached to every garment in her wardrobe in Milan was a list giving the date she had bought it, what it cost, where, when and in whose company she had worn it. Gloves – each pair in a transparent plastic envelope – and handbags were similarly documented, and every object had its place. These were private reflections of the meticulous care she put into her work.

A woman who worked at the Athens conservatory when Callas was a student there gave me a fascinating picture of her: bulky, shabby, serious, her pockets filled with food, which she consumed voraciously throughout the day. She neither had nor made friends. Invariably the first to arrive and the last to leave the building, when she was not having lessons she attended other classes irrespective of musical subject, listening insatiably and silently, absorbing every facet of musical information that might one day be useful to her. De Sabata later said to me, 'If the public could understand as we do how deeply and utterly musical Callas is, they would be stunned.'

I was rather late on the Callas bus. Italy was not officially my territory, but I had found and contracted the then unknown Boris Christoff there in 1947 and spent a lot of time with Karajan at La Scala. My first acquaintance with the Callas voice came from early Cetra 78s recorded in 1949, 'Casta Diva,' 'Qui la voce' and the 'Morte d'Isotta.' At long last, a really exciting Italian soprano! My appetite was further whetted when one of her famous male colleagues described her as 'not your type of singer.' I knew that gambit: it had been tried on me by jealous colleagues of Kathleen Ferrier, Welitsch, Schwarzkopf and many another. At the earliest opportunity, 1951, I went to Rome when I knew she was singing. My wife and I were staying with a singer with whom Callas had recently had a row, so under the discreet pretext of a business engagement I slipped into the Rome Opera and heard her first act of *Norma*. I telephoned my wife to join me at once for something quite exceptional. She declined: she had just heard the first half of a broadcast of arias by one Maria Callas, and neither wild horses nor the promise of supper at Passetto's could drag her from hearing the second half.

At the end of the performance I went to Callas' dressing room and offered her an exclusive contract with English Columbia. She and her husband, Giovanni Battista Meneghini, were delighted. The negotiations, conducted in the friendliest manner over meals in Verona, at Biffi Scala and Giannino's in Milan, seemed interminable: they lasted well over a year. My ally was Dario Soria, who already knew from his Cetra-Soria experience how essential she was to Angel Records, the label we were preparing to launch in the U.S. under his management. She expected tribute at every meeting, and my arms still ache at the recollection of the pots of flowering shrubs and trees that Dario and I lugged to the Verona apartment. Eventually terms were agreed. I signed a copy of the contract for them to keep, asking for her signature on my own copy. Another snag: The Meneghini-Callases explained they had a superstition that prevented them from signing a contract until two weeks after it had been mutually agreed. I was given *parola d'onore* that the signed copy would be mailed in fifteen days.

When three weeks had passed with no signed contract, I sent a member of our Milan staff to Verona. Three visits and three flowering trees later, my young collaborator – who had been hardened to tough operations as an officer parachuted into the Yugoslav civil war – telegraphed:

PAROLA D'ONORE UNKNOWN IN VERONA STOP ONLY POSSIBLE SOLUTION YOU INCREASE TERMS

Dario and I had to follow his advice, and it was not until July 21, 1952, that I could wearily breathe, 'Callas – finalmente mia!' over the signed contract. They had not yet told me she owed Cetra two or three operas under her old contract with them!

Our first recordings together were made in Florence after a series of performances of *Lucia* there with Serafin. The acoustics of the hall our Italian branch had chosen were antimusical and inimical. I decided to make a series of tests of 'Non mi dir' with Callas for two purposes – to get the psychological feel of working with her, sensing how receptive she would be to criticism, and to find placings to give at least a decent sound. It was soon clear that she would take suggestions without a murmur. I had found a fellow-perfectionist as avid to prove and improve herself as any great artist I have ever worked with. Ten years later we were to spend the best part of three hours just repeating the last dozen bars of the *Faust* Jewel Song to get a passable end to it. I have never known anybody to have such a will to repeat. She was always so critical; on one occasion we were recording, and she called over the microphone, 'Walter, is that all right?' I said, 'Maria, it's marvelous, you can go on.' 'I don't want to know if it's marvelous, is it good?'

We delayed publication of this *Lucia* until after *I Puritani*, made a few weeks later: Angel's first Callas recording had to be a revelation, for her sake and for Angel's reputation for quality, which we had yet to establish. Also, *I Puritani* was the first fruit of EMI's contractual collaboration with La Scala – a double coup – though it was recorded in a Milan basilica.

Early in 1952 I had introduced the Meneghini-Callases to Herbert von Karajan one evening when he was conducting at La Scala. Two minutes of mutual courtesies: Karajan couldn't take his eyes off a huge emerald she was wearing. A year later, during the *Lucia* recording in Florence, I called Karajan to say I was catching the first train to Milan with the answer to Antonio Ghiringhelli's plea that he conduct an Italian opera at La Scala. I pocketed a little spool of tape – the last three minutes of *Lucia*, Act II. The maestro listened reluctantly, then telephoned La Scala to send the score of *Lucia* to his hotel. 'I'll stage it myself. Scenery and Scottish costumes raise problems ...' 'No kilts and sporrans for Callas,' I warned him. 'Even Tetrazzini, who was eighteen inches shorter than Callas and a bundle of fun, drew the line at wearing her sporran in its traditional position, because she said it looked rude. It would be all right behind, because the audience could think it was her cushion.'

Karajan took *Lucia* very seriously, even making excursions through the Walter Scott country to know its architecture, iron-work and light. In 1954 Callas, Di Stefano, Panerai and Karajan excited Scala audiences to frenzy. Karajan was so proud of this production that a year later he took it to West Berlin for a few performances. Walter Gieseking went with me to the first. After the second act he said, 'Let's get out of here – I can't stand any more tonic-and-dominant harmony.' The promise of rather better music in the last act and a bottle or more of the best burgundy in Berlin induced the great pianist reluctantly to sit it through. At three in the morning I got back to the hotel, where the concierge told me that Mme Callas and her husband were waiting for me, no matter how late I came home. He let me into their room, where both were sitting up in their beds, woollen undervests visibly projecting above their nightwear (very Italian!), reading Italian illustrateds while they waited for an inquest on the performance. Had she done herself justice? Was her applause louder and longer than anyone else ever had in Berlin? Reassured, they turned on their sides and switched off the lights.

Years later, she flew to London for the dress rehearsal of Sutherland's *Lucia*, insisted we sit with her, had herself photographed with the new prima donna, and then took us off to lunch. Seated, she stated: 'She will have a great success tomorrow and make a big career if she can keep it up. But only we know how much greater I am.'

The supreme Callas recording was her first *Tosca*, after nearly twenty-five years still unique in the history of recorded Italian opera. Callas had opened the 1951–52 La Scala season with *I Vespri Siciliani*, Victor de Sabata conducting. (During the dress rehearsal attended by critics and invited guests, there was a momentary discrepancy in rubato between Callas and the orchestra. De Sabata stopped immediately and shouted, 'Callas – watch me!' Putting on her most seraphic smile, she wagged her forefinger and answered, 'No, Maestro, you watch me – your sight is better than mine.') Nine months later we embarked on *Tosca*. De Sabata and I had been friends since 1946 but never recorded together. In those pre-stereo days, effects of distance were more difficult than now. To achieve Tosca's convincing entry, her three calls of 'Mario!' were done separately – all from the wings, each one nearer the microphones – and spliced together later. The 'Te Deum' took the greater part of two sessions: Tito Gobbi recently reminded me that we had made him sing all his first-act music thirty times, changing the inflections and colors even on individual syllables, before we were satisfied. Callas had arrived in superb voice and, as always in those days, properly prepared. Only for 'E avanti a lui tremava tutta Roma' was she put through de Sabata's grinding mill for half an hour – time well spent. We used miles of tape, and when the recording was finished I warned de Sabata that I needed him for a few days to help select what should go into the finished master tape. He replied, 'My work is finished. We are both artists. I give you this casket of uncut jewels and leave it entirely to you to make a crown worthy of Puccini and my work.'

Callas had that sine qua non for a great career, an immediately recognizable personal timbre. It was a big voice and in her best years had a range of almost three octaves, though the extreme top was sometimes precarious and, as we discovered in trying to record Dalila's 'Mon coeur s'ouvre à ta voix,' the lower register needed more consistent power than she could sustain. The basic quality was luxurious, the technical skill phenomenal. Callas possessed in fact three different voices, all of which she colored for emotional effect at will – high coloratura, ample, brilliant (and when she chose, dark-colored), admirably agile. Even in the most difficult fioriture there were no musical or technical difficulties in this part of the voice which she could not execute with astonishing, unostentatious ease. Her chromatic runs, particularly downwards, were beautifully smooth and staccatos almost unfailingly accurate, even in the trickiest intervals. There is hardly a bar in the whole range of nineteenth-century music for high soprano that seriously tested her powers, though she sometimes went sharp on sustained high notes or took them by force.

The center of the voice was basically dark-hued, her most expressive range, where she could pour out her smoothest legato. Here she had a peculiar and highly personal sound, often as if she were singing into a bottle. This came, I believe, from the extraordinary formation of her upper palate, shaped like a Gothic arch, not the Romanesque arch of the normal mouth. Her rib cage was also unusually long for a woman of her height. This, together with what must have been her well-trained intercostal muscles, gave her unusual ability to sing and shape long phrases in one breath without visible effort. Her chest voice she used mainly for dramatic effects, slipping into it much higher than most singers with similar range when she felt text or situation would gain by it. Unfortunately it was only in quick music, particularly descending scales, that she completely mastered the art of joining the three almost incompatible voices into one unified whole, but until about 1960 she disguised those audible gear changes with cunning skill.

Her legato line was better than any other singer because she knew that a legato must be like a telegraph wire or telephone wire, where you can see the line going through and the consonants are just perched on it like the feet of sparrows. She used the consonants with great effect, but basically the legato line was held so that you could hear that all the time and were not aware of the interruption of the consonants except for their dramatic purpose.

Callas had an absolute contempt for merely beautiful singing. Although she was preoccupied all her career with bel canto, that is, beautiful singing, she was one of the few Italian artists in my memory who quite deliberately produced significant signs of a particular dramatic intensity or meaning on a syllable or even on a single consonant – sometimes over a long phrase to convey dramatic meaning. She herself often said, 'After all, some of the texts we have to sing are not distinctive poetry. I know that to convey the dramatic effect to the audience and to myself I must produce sounds that are not beautiful. I don't mind if they are ugly as long as they are true.'

I am afraid that Callas may harm a generation of singers. Young singers try to imitate not her virtues but some of those things that she did deliberately and could only do because of her intelligence and because she knew the dramatic purpose.

Most admirable of all her qualities, however, were her taste, elegance and deeply musical use of ornamentation in all its forms and complications, the weighting and length of every appoggiatura, the smooth incorporation of the turn in melodic lines, the accuracy and pacing of her trills, the seemingly inevitable timing of her porta-mentos, varying their curve with enchanting grace and meaning. There were innumerable exquisite felicities – minuscule portamentos from one note to its nearest neighbor, or over widespread intervals – and changes of color that were pure magic. In these aspects of bel canto she was supreme mistress of that art.

But ... can you, dear reader, swear that you have never winced at or flinched from some of her high notes, those that were more like pitched screams than musical sounds? Or those she waved at you like Isolde's scarf, so unsteady they could be mistaken for labored trills? They were brave triumphs of will, but remote from the beauty that the term bel canto implies. A couple of years ago, I asked her what she was doing with her time – 'I play and study our records of *Lucia* and *Tosca* and then try to get back to those vocal positions I used then.' She would not or could not accept the fact that after fifty no woman can expect to have the upward range and facility she had at thirty. She was particularly interesting about the pirated recordings made in Mexico in 1951 and 1952. 'Don't listen to them – they're awful! I was singing like a wildcat. Something must have happened to me between these and our *Lucia*, *Puritani* and *Tosca*.' That something was the contract with La Scala, which she had been hoping and striving for in the four years since her debut in Verona, and the luxury and discipline of working under ideal conditions with de Sabata. She knew she had arrived.

Great directors, particularly Visconti and Zeffirelli, like great conductors, invariably got the best out of her. The challenge of a great conductor and/or stage director curiously paralleled her reactions to a less enthusiastic reception than she expected and felt she deserved after a first act. She would pace her dressing room with a hard glint in her eyes and mutter, 'I'll teach those stinkers out there,' or sometimes, 'Don't worry! When I'm furious I'm always at my best.' Then she would sing the rest of the performance with incandescent inner fire and aggressive flamboyance. During several *Sonnambulas* I sat in Ghiringhelli's box watching her move down to the footlights to hurl 'Ah, non giunge' into the very teeth of the gallery. The Scala gallery was a vital factor in Meneghini's operations, especially the seats near the proscenium, which he infiltrated with young fans to throw bouquets to his wife when she took curtain calls. One evening the opponents got there first: fewer floral tributes were mixed in the rain of bunches of small vegetables from the gallery. Callas, trading on her well-known myopia, sniffed each bunch as she picked it up; vegetables she threw into the orchestra pit, while flowers were graciously handed to her colleagues. Not even Strehler could have staged that improvised scene better.

Callas and Meneghini had met in Verona when she made her Italian debut, the launching of her world career. She was twenty-three, he twice her age, a partner in a family brickmaking concern, reputedly fairly rich and a shrewd businessman, a contention I could endorse after negotiating her recording contracts. Their relationship, as I saw it, was staid, his attitude to her one of fatherly solicitude. He never showed himself at rehearsals, but until they separated he attended every recording session without listening to a note of hers. He habitually dozed or fell asleep behind a newspaper.

She ran into a patch of vocal difficulties as early as 1954. During the *Forza* recording the wobble had become so pronounced that I told her if we dared publish the records Angel and EMI would have to give away a seasickness pill with every side, which we could not afford. She took this to heart and worked hard on steadying down the wide pulse in her voice. She had several of her best years ahead of her. When I suggested Rosa Ponselle as the person to give her help, she revealingly snapped back, 'I won't see that woman – she started off with better material than I did.' That was the oft reported evening when Callas, knowing my wife was due in Milan that evening, insisted she have supper with us. Unfounded rumor that I might be looking for a deputy for Callas had magnetized several well-known sopranos, who were buzzing hopefully in and around Biffi Scala, where we habitually ate. Callas walked in as if unconcerned, pecked my wife's cheeks and without sitting down said, 'Show me how you sing top A's and B's and make a diminuendo on them. Walter says mine make him seasick.' When Schwarzkopf demurred, Callas, ignoring the astonished diners, sang with full voice the notes that were giving her trouble, while Schwarzkopf felt her diaphragm, lower jaw, throat and ribs. Waiters froze in their stride, while guests turned to watch and hear the fun. Within minutes Schwarzkopf was singing the same notes while Callas prodded her in the same places to find out how she kept those notes steady. After twenty minutes or so she said, 'I think I've got it. I'll call you in the morning when I've tried it out,' and sat down to supper. She did call next day to say it worked, but the recording shows the cure was not complete.

Her lack of humor and comedy were handicaps she rarely overcame. Hers was the brilliance of the diamond, not of the sun; she could blind without warming. Her *Barbiere* Rosinas with Giulini at La Scala woefully lacked humanity, and in my experience only in the recording of the opera in London with Galliera did comedy brush her with its wings. I rank it among her best.

Among Callas' greatest strengths were her power of projection in the theater and communication with audiences, almost animal instincts that excited a public irrespective of her purely vocal form. Apart from her best singing, the asset I most valued was her skill in the use of words: she charged recitatives with rare intensity. Since her stock in trade onstage so often was murder, suicide, infanticide, poison and hate, she curdled much blood in her time. Her humor was more of the dark variety. One Sunday evening during a Commonwealth conference in London, I had booked her favorite table at the Savoy Grill for dinner. Ushered in by the maître d'hotel, we had to cross the full width of the huge room, every table of which was occupied by black potentates and their entourages. Maria whispered to me, 'Look round discreetly, they think we are the next course.'

Callas was not a particularly lovable character except to her servants and her dressmaker, and of course to the multitudes of admirers who did not know her personally. She could be vengeful, vindictive, malicious in running down people she was jealous of or had taken a dislike to, often without reason. She was ungrateful: for years she refused to work with or even talk to Serafin, who had been her invaluable help and guide since her Italian debut, after he recorded *La Traviata* with Antonietta Stella.

She learned more from Serafin of the qualities that made her what she was than from anybody else. The old man was a great master of that particular sort of repertoire that Callas was to do better than anybody – Rossini, Bellini, Donizetti, Verdi. And nobody else, apart from Toscanini, knew such an enormous amount about singing. After all he had produced – he made – Ponselle.

She was convinced that sooner or later she would quarrel with every friend.

She said to me one day, 'You know when we have our quarrel, it's going to be hell, because you know how to hurt me and I know how to hurt you.' I said to her, 'Maria, there is no need for us to quarrel. Why should we ever quarrel?' She said, 'People of our strength of will and personality always quarrel eventually.'

She quarreled with me because I resigned from EMI, which she claimed I had done solely to ruin her recording career. That did not stop her from begging me, after years of non-communication, to share her Juilliard master classes with her, 'because we are the only two people who know what bel canto is, and you can talk.'

The Callas-Tebaldi feud was wildly overworked in the press but probably useful to agents and impresarios who played one diva off against the other. There were some tetchy exchanges between them in Brazil, but Tebaldi was always a good humored, equable person and Callas played her cards carefully.

With Ghiringhelli's approval I tried to silence the scandalmongers by getting the two ladies to appear together at La Scala alternating as Norma and Adalgisa (both roles were comfortably within their vocal ranges at that time) and/or in *Die Walküre* – Tebaldi as Sieglinde, Callas as Brünnhilde. Callas was eager (except some indecision as to whether she should insist on doing the first *Norma* or trying to overtrump by singing the second), but Tebaldi charmingly explained that she was past singing *seconda donna*. A pity! I should have enjoyed those rehearsals.

Her breach with Meneghini coincided with the decline of her artistic achievements – or caused it. Her life with him had been built on community of interests, mutual respect, Spartan domestic economy, rigorous self-discipline and hard work. The sumptuous party Onassis gave for them after her first London *Medea*, and the luxury of the first Mediterranean cruise on the *Christina* as fellow guests with Sir Winston and Lady Churchill opened new vistas for Callas – and new ambitions. This suddenly appealed to her as the world she had subconsciously craved – the lap of Croesus in the company of celebrities from every walk of life, without a rival in her own field. What bound Callas and Onassis was the mutual admiration of two fiercely ambitious, proud Greeks who had fought their way up from obscurity and deprivation to preeminence.

There were occasional flashes of the 'real' Callas, in the Epidaurus *Medea*, but her career as an important artist lasted hardly thirteen years. Still she fought against declining powers. She lived and danced in Paris and Monte Carlo, where she toyed with the idea of recording, even having her own opera company in a little bandbox theater. She sang at Covent Garden and the Paris Opéra to frenzied audiences and saddened connoisseurs. Concerts with orchestra showed rare flashes of what she had once been. Better to draw a curtain over the last tours, with di Stefano and piano accompaniment.

She was long possessed by the idea of making films, convinced they would widen her public and vastly increase her income. But Onassis was unwilling to finance such an undertaking. Even when she had accepted the fact that she could no longer sing sufficiently well she worked fruitlessly on the idea of using her *Tosca*, *Norma*, and *Lucia* recordings as sound tracks to which she would synchronize her acting. When she finally reached the screen, it was merely as an actress in Pasolini's adaptation of Euripides' *Medea* – a sad but revealing episode in her downward path. I saw an early screening in a cinema not far from La Scala, the theatre she had consistently filled for nearly a decade. The cinema was half-empty, and emptier still at the end of the film.

Her death was sudden, at an age when she ought still to have been singing magnificently. I doubt if she had expected to die so soon, or that she really minded.

'La Divina: Callas Rembered', from Elisabeth Schwarzkopf, *On and Off the Record*, 1982

'Music turns language into "songish" liquid'
WAYNE KOESTENBAUM

I don't care about understanding; I want to be pleased by the Songish Part. I care about an opera's words only because music has garlanded them. I love the words 'Ma il viso mio su lui risplenderà,' from Boito's libretto to Verdi's *Falstaff*, because music has touched them. In the 1957 Angel recording of the opera, soprano Elisabeth Schwarzkopf slides the words 'ma' and 'il' together; I love to hear words lose separateness and become a liquid amalgam. Even in this silent room, the conjunction 'ma' and the pronoun 'il' remain suffused with music, as a pavement retains heat after a scorching day. The words 'Ma il viso mio su lui risplenderà' have lived in a soprano's mouth, and so music glows from the unimposing, plain syllables.

from *The Queen's Throat*, 1993

'*Pelléas* – a play recounted through music'
VIRGIL THOMSON

After all the exasperations and delights of dealing with Berlioz, it was a pleasure to move from the V. and A. over to Covent Garden, where Pierre Boulez was conducting Debussy's *Pelléas et Mélisande*. Here is a work all vaporous, if you like, but nowhere presenting the esthetic obscurities of Berlioz and at no point refusing itself the stage.

For the record, let us set down that the orchestral reading was of a perfection previously not encountered by this reporter, who has heard virtually all of them, including that of André Messager, its first conductor. The textures were everywhere transparent but never misty, the emotions frank, warm, and never dissociated from the stage. It is the special quality of this work that though the orchestra comments constantly, and even individual instruments comment on the progress of the play, the pit never becomes a Greek chorus speaking for the author; it remains an extension of the stage. And in scenes of conflict it speaks for the stronger character, for him who dominates. Even the interludes, added originally to fill up time during changes of set but preserved nowadays for their intrinsic beauty, are extensions of the drama. They are not scenery, not warning of events to come, but quite simply the way some character, the one we are following at that instant, feels.

The composer has in fact so completely identified himself from moment to moment with his characters' sensibilities that he has largely omitted, save possibly in the death scene, any structuring of the music that might support the dramatic structure. Heard in concert the work has continuity but little shape; and even its continuity is constantly broken into by stage emotions so intense that the singers are likely to be left suddenly all alone with the words, unaccompanied. They are alone with the play too, for at all those moments when the orchestra seems to hesitate, the dramatic line, the impetus, is largely a responsibility of the stage.

It is this particular relation between stage and pit that makes *Pelléas* unique. Every other opera in the world, even those with spoken dialogue, is carried forward by musical forms. In classical opera these forms are arranged, in spite of their individual ABA and similar layouts, to move forward as expression, like a cycle of songs. Since Wagner, each act or scene has tended to be an open-ended musical form thematically inspired by the dramatic action but controlled by musico-emotional timings. Even the series of concert forms – sonata, variation, and the like – that underpins Berg's *Wozzeck*, in the end adds up to an open form governed by the needs of expression; and for a certainty that expression is paced at a musical rate of audience absorption rather than at a verbal one, as in a play, or at a visual one, as in a film.

Now *Pelléas* is really an opera, or *drame lyrique*, as Debussy called it. It is a play recounted through music, not a language-play with incidental music. And the timing of that music is under the control of one musician, the conductor. Nevertheless, the music's expressivity does move back and forth from the pit to the stage. And every time the orchestra, by pausing, hands this expressivity to the stage, it becomes necessary that the singers sing their words so urgently and move in a pantomime so convincing that the lack of an instrumental continuity is never felt.

That is why the work requires in its major role not just any singer, but a singing actress. And this leader of the team, whose presence must be felt always, even when she is absent, needs to be surrounded, as in chamber music, by cooperative soloists. The stage director, moreover, should guide them all toward creating a pantomime as tense as the musical score that describes it. Debussy himself, in a 1908 testimonial to the services rendered by Mary Garden in the 1902 premiere, remarked that the role of Mélisande had from the beginning seemed to him virtually impossible to project (*'difficilement réalisable'*) on account of all those 'long silences that one false move can render meaningless.'

Mélisande, so eager to be loved but so skittish about being touched, is rarely shown in the opera as in contact with even her husband. When he is ill she gives him her hand for a moment, only to have him discover she has lost her wedding ring. Later he takes hold of her twice, once by the hair in a jealous fury, again to plead on her deathbed for some fact that might justify his jealousy. Only with Pelléas is she not averse to the laying on of hands; and when standing just below the tower window he winds her hair about him in orgasmic ecstasy, she is probably, though no party to it, aware of what has happened. In any case, from that time on, a magnetic field of force moves them closer and closer till love is declared and the harsh castle gates, by locking them out, precipitate embrace.

The tension of animal magnetism is the basic drama of this opera, its tragedy, and in the long run its theme. For Mélisande, beneath her reticence, is a flame that consumes. That is why she is a star in the play and must be played by a star. The others resist destruction; she resists nothing but physical contact, a resistance that makes it in each case inevitable. And in the emergency that she has brought about, in every emergency indeed, even dying, she lies. She wants to be loved. She will do anything to be loved. Except tell the truth. Or show gratitude. Utterly self-centred and reckless, she wreaks havoc without thinking or recognizing. And the play of her unbridled libido against the fixities of a well-bred French family (Merovingian minor royalty) reveals character in each instance. It turns Golaud, her husband, repeatedly to violence. It lights the fires of passion in his half-brother Pelléas, a young man easily enough inflamed. It brings forward the essential indifference and all the sententiousness of Arkel, their grandfather (according to Pierre Boulez, 'Pelléas grown old'). The other two, Geneviève their mother and Golaud's young son Yniold, horrified by all the violence unleashed, can only view any of it as disaster.

There is somewhere a theory that Mélisande is really Bluebeard's eighth wife. This might explain her having brought along in her flight the golden crown which she has just dropped into a forest pool when Golaud discovers her, 'C'est la couronne qu'il m'a donnée,' she explains. She has clearly been through a traumatic experience which has left her terrified of bodily contact. Whether it is the experience that has turned her psychopathic or whether she just grew up that way we shall never know. But dangerous she is for sure, behind that sweet façade; and never are we to divine what she thinks about. All we shall know are her refusals and her compulsions.

And never does Debussy's orchestra give us her feelings. Her leit-motif is a shifty one, harmonically and rhythmically undecided. The others are all straightforward; and through them the play of passions, fears, joys, and resignations can be expressed. Though her physical presence is a powerful one, we are never allowed to view the story from her point of feeling; she seems to have none. She is the source of everyone else's feelings and consequently of their actions. But she herself sits at the dead center of a storm; everything takes place around her, nothing inside her. Nothing, at least, that we can see or hear.

Now the Covent Garden production, for all its orchestral warmth and musical perfection, gave us little of the Maeterlinck play as I have described it and as Debussy set it into music. It is not that the singers did not work well; they did everything the conductor had asked of them in the coaching rehearsals. They even sang a highly reputable French, though for not one of them was the language native. It was rather that the stage director, Vaclav Kaslik, did not seem to feel the same tensions in the play that Debussy did. His characters moved around the stage like items out of a libretto, who did not need to worry because the music would take care of everything. The fact remains, however, that it does not. There are spots in that opera, many of them, where the poetry is so heightened by a vocal line half sung, half spoken but yet on pitch, and the accompaniment so thinly washed in, or so absent, that only an acting line intensely controlled by a choreographic line naturalistically conceived (and concealed, as was the custom of its time) can sustain the spectacle at the level of its orchestral presence.

The excellent singers will no doubt be able in the recording just now completed to give more character and more conviction by 'acting with the voice,' as they had done occasionally in the seated piano rehearsals. But publicly both stage and staging seem to have got in their way, and certainly some bulky costumes did. The set, a unit structure with changing backdrops and forestage elements added, was the work of Josef Svoboda, the costumes by the third member of a team from Czechoslovakia, Jan Skalicky. Among all these elements I found only the scenery helpful, and that I fancy Debussy might have approved, for its use in outdoor scenes of hanging gauze strips to produce different kinds of hazy weather and different times of day. Quite effectively and often charmingly did these strips, aided by shifting lights and heights and by the imaginative backdrops, produce the dank tarn, house of Usher atmosphere that we know to have been desired by both Maeterlinck and Debussy. The only scenery that squarely failed was that of the final bedchamber, which resists an open stage, since the high small window and shaft of sunlight required by the text, not to speak of Mélisande's hushed fading away and tranquil death, virtually demand enclosure.

Unit sets, whether firmly constructed or assembled out of modules that get regrouped, are ever a disappointment for portraying the difference between indoors and outdoors. And there is nearly always one scene at least in which they fail entirely. The elements that are constantly being reassembled, moreover, are rarely of sufficient intrinsic beauty to permit being looked at for a whole evening. Their lack of visual novelty, by halfway through the show, becomes oppressive. The story advances and the music moves forward, while the scenery just plays a game. I sometimes think the unchanging set, whether built for the purpose or independently monumental like the steps of a library, injures a dramatic spectacle less than the most ingenious selection of movable elements. These can save time at scene changes, though there are other ways of doing that; but nothing can make them suit all parts of a play equally, and nothing can relieve their aggravating monotony.

The conductor, who had hoped for Wieland Wagner to direct the stage, eventually chose the Czech team, though there is little precedent for a well-organized and well-organizing Eastern European mind effectively coming to grips with this seemingly unorganized and ever-so-French triumph of sensibility *over* organization. For *Pelléas* is not only unique as an opera (recitative throughout and a highly emotional, willfully formless accompaniment); it is also an anti-opera. It avoids all the devices that make Verdi and Wagner, Mozart and Monteverdi easy to listen to – sustained song, rhythmic patterns, structural harmony, orchestral emphases, solos, ensemble pieces, built-in climaxes.

Even its naturalistic vocal line is not always so natural regarding the words as one might think. Much of it is closer to psalmody than to speech. Then at times it actually does imitate speech, using small intervals only, as Jean-Jacques Rousseau had recommended for French recitative. At others it employs, as Paul Landormy describes, an evocation of language such as we hear it silently inside ourselves – 'a manner of speech quite strange,' he says, 'but striking, and very hard for singers to achieve, tending as they do to stiffen the vocal line through an overstrict observance of note-values, instead of making it supple, as they should.'

I am afraid the Covent Garden cast, also chosen by Boulez and carefully prepared, sinned in exactly this respect. Being foreigners to French and with little residence in France to loosen their tongues, they gave us the written notes as exactly as any English horn or flute player in the orchestra. They performed indeed as if they were a part of the orchestra rather than as real persons who might be the subjects of the orchestra's comment. Except for the small boy singing Yniold, who really got into his role – the French of it, the music of it, the impersonation of fear – the stage artists in large part simply stood or moved without much meaning, while following in excellent voice the conductor's beat.

I am also afraid that Pierre Boulez, like Toscanini before him, does not really enjoy accompanying star performers. He has chosen before – in the Paris *Wozzeck* of several years back – a cast of just-under-first-class singing actors, exactly as Toscanini was wont to do for his NBC broadcasts. And they have seemed in both cases a bit awed by the honor. Also thoroughly preoccupied with making no mistakes. His casting of the singing voice has long seemed to me less a loving one than that of an executive seeking a sensible secretary. He can love words, I know, especially those of Mallarmé, which have inspired him, and of René Char, whom he has so often set. But the sound of the singing voice, the personality of a singer acting out his role, seem rather to bring out the carefulness in him than to invite the incandescence of joint effort. This he achieves with the orchestra, and it could not be more ravishing to hear. But I do miss, as I so often did with Toscanini, a catering to the stage, a feeling that singing and the acting out of a role could be allowed to give us pleasure without our being held to a one hundred percent concentration on him and his sacred instrumental score.

After all, singers are not oboes or horns. They are voices with personalities, and the opera is a musical exercise that cannot long exist without exploiting voices and personalities. *Pelléas et Mélisande*, in particular, is an opera, or *drame lyrique*, that depends far more than many another on an equality between pit and stage. An intimacy of musical with dramatic communication is its essence, its need, its sine qua non. It is the hardest opera in the world to perform satisfactorily, because it is the model, the dream that all French opera since Gluck has sought to realize, an exact balance of music with dramatic poetry. And wherever this opera has approached equilibration, its needle of balance has become so quivery that many like Toscanini, like Boulez, have seemed to hope that a wholly disciplined rendering would dissolve that nervousness. Which it does, of course, but at the cost of radically unbalancing the spectacle and forcing it to depend not on the vibrancy and miracle of a poetry-and-music duet, as in the best lieder, but on a musical run-through controlled by one man.

And so in Boulez's *Pelléas* we have no opera at all but rather the rehearsal of one, a concert in costume destined to end up as a recording. I will spare its excellent singers publication of their names in this connection. On discs they will surely make a better effect. There a complete subjection to the musical score may seem more suitable than in an opera house. I am sorry about the Covent Garden production, musically so sumptuous, orchestrally so stunningly alive, stage-wise so casual in spite of pretty sets. Musical accuracy is of course always welcome, and far from universal. But for the rest of opera, I have never been convinced that Boulez had much liking for fine voices or for striking personalities. And as for visual investitures, very few musicians have taste in that domain.

A Virgil Thomson Reader, 1981

Acknowledgements

CECIL BEATON, from *Self Portrait with Friends: The Seleced Diaries of Cecil Beaton 1926–74*. Edited by Richard Buckle. Reprinted by permission of The Literary Trustee of the Late Sir Cecil Beaton and Rupert Crew Ltd.

SIR THOMAS BEECHAM, from *A Mingled Chime*. Published by Hutchinson, 1944. Reprinted by permission of Random House Group Ltd.

BERTOLT BRECHT, from *Brecht on Theatre: The Development of an Aesthetic*, translated by John Willett. Reprinted by permission of Methuen Publishing Ltd.

BENJAMIN BRITTEN, from the Foreword to *The Rape of Lucretia*. © The Trustees of the Britten-Pears Foundation. No further reproduction without written permission.

CLAUDE DEBUSSY, from *Monsieur Croche et autres récits* (Debussy on Music). © Editions Gallimard, 1971.

DENIS DIDEROT, from *Rameau's Nephew and D'Alembert's Dream*, translated by L. W. Tancock. Published by Penguin 1966. © L. W. Tancock, 1966.

MANUEL DE FALLA, from *On Music and Musicians*, translated by David Urman and J. M. Thompson. © Hederos de Manuel de Falla 1950, 1972. Reprinted by permission of Marion Boyars Publishers Ltd.

WALTER FELSENSTEIN, from *Opera 66*. © Alan Ross Ltd 1996. Reprinted with permission of Alan Ross.

E. M. FORSTER, from *Where Angels Fear to Tread*. Reprinted by permission of the Provost and Scholars of King's College, Cambridge, and the Society of Authors as the Literary Representatives of the E. M. Forster Estate.

EDUARD HANSLICK, from *Vienna's Golden Years*, translated by Henry Pleasants. © Henry Pleasants III, 1950. Reprinted by kind permission of Virginia Pleasants.

E. T. A. HOFFMAN, from David Chariton, Martyn Clarke, *E. T. A. Hoffman's Musical Writing*; The Poet and the Composer; Music Criticism, 1989. Reprinted by permission of Cambridge University Press and the authors.

WALTER LEGGE, from *On and Off the Record: A Memoir of Walter Legge* by Elisabeth Schwartzkopf. Reprinted by permission of Faber and Faber Limited. Reprinted with the permission of Scribner, a Division of Simon & Schuster. Copyright © 1982 by Musical Adviser Establishment.

ETHAN MORDDEN, from *The Venice Adriana*. Published in London by Quartet Books Limited, 1999. © by Ethan Mordden, 1998. Reprinted with permission of Quartet Books Limited.

MOZART, from *The Letters of Mozart and his Family*. First published by Macmillan, 1985. Reprinted by permission of Macmillan Publishers Limited.

NIETZSCHE, from *Nietzsche: The Birth of Tragedy and Other Writings*, translated by Raymond Geuss and Ronald Speirs. Published by Cambridge University Press, 1999. Reprinted by permission of Cambridge University Press and the authors.

HELMUT PEITSCH, from The Loyal Subject: Heinrich Mann. New English Translation copyright © 1998 by the Continuum Publishing Company, by

Index